TESI GREGORIANA

Serie Teologia

50

D1561332

JOSEPH G. PRIOR

The Historical Critical Method
in Catholic Exegesis

EDITRICE PONTIFICIA UNIVERSITÀ GREGORIANA
Roma 1999

Vidimus et approbamus ad normam Statutorum Universitatis

Romae, ex Pontificia Universitate Gregoriana
die 20 mensis maii anni 1999

R.P. Director GRECH PROSPER, OSA
R.P. Revisor GERALD O'COLLINS, S.J.

ISBN 88-7652-825-3

GREGORIAN UNIVERSITY PRESS
Piazza della Pilotta, 35 - 00187 Rome, Italy

Riproduzione anastatica: 20 giugno 1999
Stab. Tipolit. Ugo Quintily S.p.A. - Roma
Finito di stampare nel mese di Giugno 1999

This dissertation is dedicated

to my parents

Hugh J. and Rosemary G. Prior,

and

Fr. John P. Murray, C.M.

ACKNOWLEDGEMENTS

Many people helped bring this dissertation to a completion, I would specifically like to thank the following:

Anthony Cardinal Bevilacqua, Archbishop of Philadelphia, for assigning me to graduate studies at the Biblicum and the Gregorian University and for his encouragement during these studies. Archbishop John P. Foley for his kindness and hospitality during my studies in Rome.

My parents, Hugh and Rosemary Prior along with my family for their prayers and support during the licentiate and doctoral studies; John and Dottie Prior, Kerri and Kate Crompton, Jeff Prior, Michael and Jeanne Bonner, Michael Bonner, Jr., and Tom and Jean Bartol.

Fr. Prosper Grech, O.S.A, for his direction and guidance during the dissertation. Fr. Gerald O'Collins, S.J., for his suggestions and insights.

Msgr. Charles Elmer, Superior of the Casa S. Maria for his priestly example and friendship; Br. Randal Riede for his steadfast encouragement and friendship; and Sr. Beth Wood for her kindness and assistance.

Fr. John P. Murray for his guidance, mentoring and friendship.

My collegues and friends in Rome especially Frs. Brendan Cahill, Joe Chapel, Jim Checchio, A.J. Costa, Stanislaus Gursky (†1998), Hans Hintermaier, Larry Hostetter, Michael Kesicki, Mike Magee, Hady Mahfouz, Petr Marecek, John O'Driscoll, Jim Oliver, Bob Pesarchick, and Joe Tracy.

My brother priests in the Archdiocese of Philadelphia especially Msgrs. Bill Lynn, John Marine, Tom Mullin, Daniel Murray, Bernard Trinity; Frs. Dennis Carbonaro, Joe Devlin, Phil Ricci, and Joe Watson.

My friends and acquaintances from Philadelphia who have supported me with their prayers and encouragement.

I would also like to acknowledge five libraries used during for research: *The Pontifical Biblical Institute Library, The Pontifical Gregorian University Library, The Randal Riede Library* of the Pontifical North American College and Casa S. Maria, and *The Ryan Memorial Library* of St. Charles Borromeo Seminary, Overbrook — Philadelphia.

INTRODUCTION

The historical-critical method (hereafter HCM) is a collection of procedures and exegetical techniques applied to biblical texts to determine their *literal sense*. This *literal sense* has been described in various ways in the history of biblical interpretation, from the obvious sense, to the author's intention, to the meaning expressed in the words of the inspired author. The basis of this sense is an historical-literary meaning. The roots of the HCM are found in the patristic and medieval exegesis; however, it was not until after the Renaissance that the techniques began to be collated into systematic approaches. From that time to the present, the method has been adapted for different texts, modified by the exegetes utilizing it and developed to meet the demands of scholarly research. Strictly speaking, the HCM did not reach its present form until the development of redaction criticism in the middle of this century. At every stage of this development, questions have arisen concerning its value for exegetical and theological studies. The question asked most recently in the debates among scholars and theologians can be phrased: «What is the place of the HCM in Catholic exegesis?»

Numerous publications have been produced, especially in the last 30 years, regarding the use of the HCM in biblical exegesis by Catholic and Protestant scholars. Some of the studies focus on the principal exegetes in the development of the method. Other studies examine the philosophical underpinnings of the exegetical schools that use the method. The present study does not deal with either of these issues directly. Rather it focuses on the method as accepted and used according to the principles of Catholic biblical interpretation. The goal of this dissertation is describe the place of the HCM in Catholic exegesis by identifying its necessity and limits. These are elaborated most clearly in the recent PBC document *Interpretation of the Bible in the Church*. An historical approach is taken to demonstrate the place of the HCM in Catholic biblical interpretation. Before explaining this approach, however, a brief survey of the method's development is required.

1. Movements Influential in the Development of the HCM

It is difficult to say with precision when the method began to be used[1]. As mentioned above, although procedures and techniques used in the HCM are found in patristic and medieval exegesis, their systemization into a method does not occur until after the Renaissance[2]. Although some scholars speak of different individuals as the originator of the HCM it is more accurate to speak of the method as developing in conjunction with fifteenth century humanism[3].

The general intellectual climate in the fifteenth and sixteenth centuries saw a shift in focus from God to man. The focus on man led to a separation in the study of the physical and metaphysical. Science would study the physical while philosophy or theology would study the metaphysical. Such was the general intellectual atmosphere that fostered the development of the critical approach. Four particular events that aided this process are: the «return to the sources», the invention of the printing press, the development of historical criticism, and the study of cosmology.

The Return to the Sources. One of the characteristics of this period was the desire to study the classical literature of the Greeks and Romans in the original languages. This resurgence of interest in the classics led to the study of ancient languages and to the study of ancient texts[4]. The movement had its impact on biblical studies with an increase of the study of

---

[1] Terminology can pose a difficulty when speaking of the origins of the HCM. In the early stages of scientific biblical criticism several different terms were used to describe the study. Terms such as literary-historical, historical-grammatical, and historical-critical were used to describe critical methodology. The term used today to describe these approaches would be the generic «diachronic method».

[2] For histories of Biblical study for these periods see: R. GRANT – D. TRACY, *Short History of Interpretation*; J.K. RICHES, *A Century of New Testament Study;* J. ROGERSON – C. ROWLAND – B. LINDARS, *The History of Christian Theology;* K. SCHOLDER, *The Birth of Modern Critical Theology;* C. STEINMETZ, *The Bible in the Sixteenth Century;* G. STRECKER, *History of New Testament Literature*

[3] Biblical historians differ as to whom they consider the originator of the method. The suggestions cover a vast time span: L.Valla (d.1457), H. Grotius (d. 1658), B. Spinoza (d. 1677), J. LeClerc (1697), R. Simon (d. 1712), J. Astruc (1753), J. Ernesti (1761), H. Reimarus (d. 1768), J. Semler (d.1791), J. Michaelis (d. 1791) or J. Eichorn (d. 1827).

[4] The resurgence in Greek studies was facilitated by the fall of Constantinople in 1453 and an influx of Greek-speakers to the West.

biblical Greek and Hebrew, and access to the original language texts was opened[5].

The Printing Press. The invention of the printing press greatly increased access to the scriptures. The first book printed on Gutenberg's press was the Bible (@1455). Soon after this Erasmus published his first edition of the NT in Greek. Various editions soon followed. Although textual criticism took some small strides during this period, the major advances did not take place until the nineteenth century[6].

Historical Criticism. Humanism also gave rise to the discipline now called Historical Criticism. The first work in this field was done by L. Valla. His first study was done on the Decree of Gratian. Valla made a literary and philological analysis of the text and concluded that the document could not be dated to the time of Constantine. The document was thus discredited as an historical source. Though the study was not a «biblical study», its principles would eventually be used for biblical stud-

---

[5] The first serious Greek grammar was composed by Robert Grosseteste. Interest in the study of the Greek language increased after publications by Lorenzo Valla. In several works (*On Pleasure, Donation of Constantine, Annotations on the New Testament*) he used philology to raise questions about previous held opinions and notions concerning each work spurring an interest not only in ancient documents but in the languages of origination. Following the invention of the printing press, Erasmus, published the first NT in Greek. This also helped promote original language studies.

Hebrew studies developed later. The first Hebrew grammar composed in the West was published in 1506 by J. REUCHLIN, *De rudiments hebraicis.* Elias Levita was another early grammarian. John Buxtorf the elder was another. For further reading on the history of Hebrew grammars see P. JOUON - T. MURAOKA, *Grammar of Biblical Hebrew,* 12-17; W. GESENIUS – E. KAUTZSCH, *Genesius' Hebrew Grammar,* 17-22 (with bibliography).

[6] The development of the printing press in 1450 and its subsequent first publication — an edition of the Latin Vulgate — led to over 100 editions of the Vulgate in the first 50 years of printing. The first original language edition of the OT was the 1488 Soncino edition of the Hebrew Scriptures. The first NT in Greek was printed in 1514 now referred to as the *Complutensian Polyglot,* but the first publication was not until a year later with an edition by Erasmus. Soon other editions were printed by Erasmus and other publishers. The Erasmus text eventually became the basis for what was termed the *textus receptus* (received text). This text became, in practical terms, the authoritative text and the basis for NT editions for the next 400 years. However there were problems with the text. The text was based on poor manuscript witnesses. The discovery of ancient manuscripts in the libraries and or monasteries of the Near and Middle East led to disputes concerning the value of the *textus receptus.* The disputes lead to the formalization of text critical studies into a scientific methodology. Manuscripts were cataloged along with their variations. Scholars attempted to determine the relationship between the manuscripts and developed rules for determining the best reading.

ies. Texts that were once considered historically sound came under the scrutiny of critical methodology.

Scientific Study of Nature. The study of nature using the scientific principles of observation, evaluation and testing of results led to conclusions that contradict several biblical accounts. For example, the study of astronomy which used newly developed instruments for observation, led to new theories concerning the orbit of the heavenly bodies. The conclusions of Copernicus and Galileo challenged the biblical portrait (e.g. Gen 1, Josh 10).

The implications of these events for biblical studies varied. While the first two events promoted the reading and study of the Scriptures, the second two when applied to the Bible began the demise of biblical authority. This demise can only be understood when one realizes how important the Bible was for that age. Despite the differences in theology that were developing concerning the use of and approach to the Bible, Catholics and the early Protestants considered the Bible authoritative, not only in theological or religious matters, but for any topic represented in the text: history, cosmology, natural science, etc. When scientific and historical data was seen as conflicting with the biblical accounts, the authority of the Bible was weakened. The demise of biblical authority would be further accelerated with the rise of rationalism and deism.

The seventeenth and eighteenth centuries saw the rise of rationalism. In this system of thought reason becomes the sole source of authority calling for previously accepted beliefs and traditions to be questioned. The starting point for the investigation is doubt. According to rationalism, doubt could only be resolved by an individual through the use of reason. In other words, no outside authority could provide a resolution for the doubt. The result on biblical authority was devastating. If humanism undermined biblical authority, rationalism removed it altogether. As rationalism developed into deism, revelation was replaced with a natural religion. The divine character of the biblical text was removed. Biblical studies become secularized. No longer was the Bible considered a sacred book. Rather it was studied as any other piece of literature. When deism was exported from England to France and Germany it developed into the Enlightenment and the trend continued. By this point Catholic involvement in critical studies was nil since the methods were tainted by these philosophical influences[7].

The philosophical influence was most evident in the historical critical studies of the period. The goal of such investigations was to either verify

---

[7] R. Simon (1638-1712) and J. Astruc (1648-1776) were the last Catholics to make a significant contribution to critical biblical studies until the nineteenth century.

or deny the historicity of the persons and events mentioned in the text using philology, textual criticism and eventually elements of source criticism. The use of these critical procedures can be described as tainted because of the philosophical presuppositions attached to them. For example, textual criticism could be used to dismiss passages from the text as inauthentic; philology could be used to identify passages as later additions then dismiss them as historically irrelevant or unreliable; and sources criticism could be used to destroy the integrity of a book and its author. Despite the tainted exegesis, several significant advances took place such as: identifying the composite nature of the Pentateuch, developing rules for textual criticism, the publishing of the first Greek synopsis, and breaking the primacy of the *textus receptus* thus opening the door for better critical editions of the NT.

The nineteenth and twentieth centuries saw the method developing into more specialized disciplines. J. Wellhausen advanced source critical studies in the OT with his formulation of the documentary hypothesis to explain the origins of the Pentateuch. At this time, scholarly attention focused on identifying sources used in the composition of the biblical texts. As a result scholarship concentrated on minute particles of the text to the neglect of larger units. H. Gunkel's dissatisfaction with source critical approaches led him to develop OT form criticism. R. Bultmann, M. Dibelius and K. L. Schmidt did the same in NT studies. At this point a gap developed between historical study and the theological content of a text. Redaction or composition criticism developed in the mid-twentieth century to study the theological implications in the final edition of the individual biblical texts. The scholars and works influential in the development of the method are listed on pages 14 and 15.

2. An Overview of the Dissertation

As mentioned above, the roots of the HCM can be found in the exegetical procedures used in the patristic and medieval periods. Following the Renaissance, the procedures developed into a methodology.

From the seventeenth century to the nineteenth century Catholic involvement in the development of the method was sparse. The first official opening toward critical methodology came in Leo XIII's 1893 *Providentissimus Deus*. This encyclical inaugurated the Catholic use of critical methods. The Catholic use of the HCM has been governed by principles set forth in official ecclesial documents on biblical studies. These documents contain the Church's official response to debates regarding the use of critical methodology in Catholic exegesis and provide an excellent

The Development of the HCM

Some of the influential authors in the development of the method.*

Historical Critical Method in General

Lorenzo Valla (1406-1457), work on the *Donation of Constantine*
Thomas Hobbes (1588-1679), *Leviathan* (1651)
Hugo Grotius (1583-1645), *Notes on the New Testament* (1641).
Baruch Spinoza (1632-1677), *Tractatus Theologico-Politicus* (1676)
John Locke (1632-1704), *The Reasonableness of Christianity as Delivered in the Scriptures* (1695)
Pierre Bayle (1647-1706), *Dictionnaire historique et critique* (1695)
Johann Salamo Semler, (1721-1791), *Treatise on the Free Investigation of the Canon*
J.G. Herder (1744-1803)
G.L. Bauer (1755-1806), *Hermeneutics* 1799
Friedrich Schleiermacher, (1768-1834), *Über die Religion* (1799), *Hermeneutik* (1819)
W.M.L. deWette (1780-1849), *Historico-Critical Introduction to the Bible* (1817)
Leopold von Ranke (1795-1886), *Geschichte der romanischen und germanischenVolker* (1824)
1829ff. Critical commentaries develop e.g: Meyer, H.A.W. *Critical and Exegetical Commentary*
G.W.F. Hegel, (1770-1831), *Philosophy of History*

Historical Criticism of the OT

W. Vatke (1806-1882), *The Religion of Israel* (1835)
H. Ewald (1803-1875), *History of the People of Israel* (1843-55)
S.R. Driver (1846-1914), *Introduction to the Literature of the Old Testament* (1891)
W. Robertson Smith (1846-1894), *The Old Testament in the Jewish Church* (1881), *Lectures of the Religion of the Semites* (1889)
K.H. Graf (1815-1869), *The Historical Books of the Old Testament* (1866)
M.J. Lagrange (1855-1938), *Historical Criticism and the Old Testament* (1905)

Historical Criticism of the NT

J.E. Ernesti (1761)
H.S. Reimarus (1778)
J.D. Michaelis (1717-1791)
J.G. Eichhorn (1752-1827), *Einleitung in das Alte Testament* (1795)
F.C. Baur (1792-1860), *Life of Jesus* (1835)
H.E. Paulus (1761-1851), *Life of Jesus* (1828)
D.F. Strauss (1808-1874), *Life of Jesus* (1835)
E. Renan (1823-1892), 1863, *Life of Jesus* (1863)
J.B. Lightfoot (1828-1889), *Commentaries on Galatians* (1865), *Philippians* (1868), and *Philemon* (1875)
E. Hatch (1835-1889), *The Influence of Greek Ideas on Christianity* (1889)
J.Wellhausen (1844-1918), *Das Evangelium Marci* (1903)
W. Wrede (1859-1906), *Messianic Secret in Mark* (1910)
A.Schweitzer (1875-1965), *Quest for the Historical Jesus* (1910)

Textual Criticism - OT

J. Morinis (1633), LXX as normative
J. Leclerc (1657-1736), *Ars Critica* (1697)

Textual Criticism - NT

Erasmus (1469-1536), His edition of the NT becomes the basis for the textus receptus
J. Mill ,(1707) first extensive set of NT variants
R. Bentley
A. Bengel (1734)
J.J. Wettstein ,1751 Notations for listing NT MSS
J.J. Greisbach, 1774 First reconstructed Greek NT edition
C. Tischendorff, 1859 Discovery of Codex Sinaticus, 1872 Critical Edition of the NT

Figure 1a: The Development of the Historical Critical Method

The Development of the HCM
Some of the influential authors in the development of the method.*

Philology-Grammatical Criticism(OT)

J. Reuchlin (d. 1522), First Hebrew Grammar (1506)
A. Schultens (1733)
W. Schroder (1776)
W. Gesenius (1786-1842), Hebrew Dictionary (1810), Hebrew Grammar (1817)
E. Hatch (1835-1889)-H.A. Redpath (), Concordance of the LXX (1897)

Philology-Grammatical Criticism (NT)

C.F. Burney (1922)
K.C. Torrey (1933)
M. Black (1946)

Literary - Source Criticism - OT

Richard Simon (1638-1712), Histoire critique du Vieux Testament (1678)
Jean Astruc (1684-1766), Conjectures (1753)
J. C. Doderlein (1745-1792) Commentary on Isaiah (1775)
K.H. Graf (1815-1869), The Historical Books of the Old Testament (1866)
B. Duhm (1847-1928), Theology of the Prophets (1875)
J.Wellhausen (1844-1918), Prolegomena to the History of Israel (1883)
A. van Hoonacker (1857-1933), De compositione et de origine Mosaica Hexateuchi (1896-1906, 1946-1st ed.)

Literary-Source Criticism - NT

J.J. Griesbach (1745-1812), Synopsis (1776)
J.G. Eichhorn (1752-1827), Uber die drei ersten Evangelisten (1794)
K. Lachmann (1793-1851), De ordine narrationum in evangeliis (1835)
H. Weisse (1801-1866), Die evangelische Geschichte und philologisch bearbeitet (1838)
H.J. Holtzmann (1832-1910), Die Synoptischen Evangelien Ihr Ursprung und geschichtlicher Charakter (1863)
B.H. Streeter (1874-1937), The Four Gospels: A Study in Origins (1924)

Genre-Form Criticism (OT)

H. Gunkel (1862-1932), Genesis (1901)
H. Gressmann (1877-1927)
A. Alt (1883-1956), The Origins of Israelite Law (1967)

Genre-Form Criticism (NT)

K.L. Schmidt (1891-1919), Der Rahmen der Geschichte Jesu (1919)
M. Dibelius (1883-1947), Die Formgeschichte des Evangeliums (1919)
R. Bultmann (1884-1976), Geschichte der synoptischen Tradition (1921)
V. Taylor (1887-1968), The Formation of the Gospel Tradition (1933)
R.H. Lightfoot (1883-1953), History and Interpretation in the Gospels (1935)
C.H. Dodd (1884-1973), The Parables of the Kingdom (1935)

Tradition Criticism and Redaction Criticism (OT)

I. Engnell (1906-1964), Studies in Divine Kingship in the Ancient Near East (1943)
S. Mowinckel (1884-1965), Prophecy and Tradition (1946)
G. von Rad (1901-1971), Das Formgeschichtliche Problem des Hexateuch (1938)
M. Noth (1902-1968), The Deuteronomistic History (1943,1981)

Redaction Criticism (NT)

G. Bornkamm (1905-1990), Tradition and Interpretation in Matthew (1948,1963)
H. Conzelmann (1915-1989), The Theology of St. Luke (1954)
W. Marxsen ; Der Evangelist Markus (1956)

*The primary sources for these charts are A. Suelzer – J.S. Kselman, «Modern Old Testament Criticism», NJBC, 1113-1129; J.S. Kselman – R.D. Witherup, «Modern New Testament Criticism»; NJBC, 1130-1145. Additional information was gathered from the works listed in footnote 2.

Figure 1b: The Development of the Historical Critical Method

source for evaluating the necessities and limits of the method in different periods of Catholic exegesis. The major documents are: *Providentissimus Deus* (1893), the 1905-1915 Pontifical Biblical Commission (PBC) Decisions, *Spiritus Paraclitus* (1920), *Divino Afflante Spiritu* (1943), *Sancta Mater Ecclesia* (1964), and *Dei Verbum* (1965). The most recent questions regarding the HCM were raised in the 1980's-1990's. The discussions turned into a debate and eventually became referred to as «the crisis in biblical interpretation». The PBC's *Interpretation of the Bible in the Church* (1993) emerged as a response to this crisis.

The argument presented in this dissertation is that the HCM has been and will continue to be an essential and indispensable part of Catholic exegesis albeit a limited one. Special attention is given to *Interpretation of the Bible in the Church* for two reasons. First it is the most recent ecclesial response to the question of exegetical methodology. Second, it provides a clear and in-depth vision of the Catholic interpretive enterprise in which the place of the HCM in Catholic exegesis can be identified. The approach is primarily descriptive and synthetic. After an extensive description of the HCM in Chapter One, the dissertation will identify the necessities and limits of the method in four different periods: the patristic-medieval period; from 1893-1943; from 1943-1965; and from 1965-the present. The primary sources are: for the first period, the literature of the patristic and medieval periods; for the other periods, the ecclesial document mentioned above.

Chapter Two covers the first period, the patristic and medieval period. This chapter identifies the roots of the HCM in the early years of Catholic exegesis. The use of these procedures was governed by the *senses of scripture*, particularly the *literal sense*. The *senses* provided a framework that demarcated the necessity and limits of the critical procedures. Chapter Two contains three sections. The first examines the hermeneutical basis of the HCM, the *literal sense*. The presentation surveys the development of the *literal sense* during this period. The second identifies elements of the HCM that are found in patristic and medieval literature such as the techniques and tools that developed as aids to a critical study of the texts. The third section concludes the chapter identifying the necessity and limits of these critical procedures as understood in this period.

Chapter Three covers the period from 1893 to 1943. The first four sections study the following documents: *Providentissimus Deus*, The PBC Decrees: 1905-1915, *Spiritus Paraclitus*, and *Divino Afflante Spiritu*. The presentation evaluates the documents under the following criteria: the pastoral or scholarly context at the publication of the document and the church's response to the pastoral or scholarly situation, the contents of the document, and the HCM as presented in the document. Documents of lesser significance will be mentioned in summary statements or charts at the appropriate places within the text. The chapter concludes by identifying the necessity and limits of the HCM as well as its relationship to the *literal sense* as understood in the documents of this period.

Chapter Four covers 1943-1965. The first section of this chapter presents the historical background for this period. The second and third sections deal with *Santa Mater Ecclesia* and *Dei Verbum* respectively. The conclusion, in a manner similar to Chapter Three, identifies the necessity and limits of the HCM and its relationship to the *literal sense*.

Chapters Five through Seven cover the period 1965-1998. The period from 1965-1983 has been evaluated in a dissertation by T. Curtin in 1987. His conclusions will introduce the fifth chapter. As mentioned above, this dissertation gives special attention to the document *Interpretation of the Bible in the Church*. The criteria to evaluate the HCM in previous documents (mentioned above under Chapter Three) are applied to *Interpretation of the Bible in the Church*.

Chapter Five considers the scholarly and pastoral situation prior to the publication of the document. The debates regarding the HCM in Catholic biblical studies and the role of the scriptures in the life of the Church continued to be discussed in the years following *Dei Verbum*. The topics discussed ranged from the relationship of scientific exegesis with theological studies to the effectiveness of critical exegesis for pastoral application. Eventually the discussions and debates reached a state of «crisis». This chapter identifies the major concerns and criticisms raised regarding the method, the call for a change in methodology and the responses of those who defended the method.

Chapter Six studies and evaluates *Interpretation of the Bible in the Church*. The chapter contains three sections. The first section considers the introductory statements by John Paul II and Cardinal Ratzinger. The second section presents a summary of the contents of the document and its presentation on the HCM. The third section concludes the chapter evaluating the necessity and limits of the HCM according to *Interpretation of the Bible in the Church*. Included in this evaluation is the relationship of the HCM to the *literal sense* as described in the document.

Chapter Seven considers the continuing discussion on Catholic exegesis particularly the discussions concerning the document's presentation on biblical hermeneutics and the HCM. Recognizing the relatively short period of time since the publication of the document, no attempt is made to evaluate its impact on exegetical studies in the Church.

Chapter Eight contains the general conclusions of the dissertation. It summarizes the place of the HCM in Catholic exegesis as studied in this dissertation. The method has sparked many debates and discussions concerning its place in the Catholic interpretative endeavor. It has consistently been deemed necessary but limited for Catholic exegesis. *Interpretation of the Bible in the Church* describes the framework in which the HCM can be effectively utilized.

CHAPTER I

The Historical Critical Method as Practiced Today

What is the historical-critical method (HCM)? The HCM is a series of critical procedures and techniques applied to a biblical text in order to determine the meaning of the text and to render an interpretation[1]. The method studies both the development of the biblical writings as well as the text in its final form. In other words, the study incorporates both diachronic and synchronic approaches. Diachronic approaches trace the development of the biblical writings «through time». The HCM presumes an importance in understanding the process through which a composition took place. Knowledge of this process will help the exegete understand the imagery, symbols, stories, teachings, etc. as they were understood in their original context. Following the diachronic investigation, a synchronic approach studies the text as a complete and integral unit.

The HCM is a compilation of several different yet complementary methodologies: *introduction*, textual criticism, grammatical criticism-philological analysis, literary criticism, genre criticism, tradition criticism, and redaction criticism. Historical criticism completes the process when either the writing is from an historical genre or a text in a non-historical genre is thought to contain some historical information. All of these criticisms are diachronic except redaction criticism. The criticisms provide a

---

1 Handbooks describing the method include: H. CONZELMANN – A. LINDEMANN, *Interpreting the New Testament*; G.D. FEE, *New Testament Exegesis*; O. KAISER – W.G. KÜMMEL, *Exegetical Method*; S.L. MCKENZIE – S.R. HAYNES, *To Each Its Own Meaning*; R.N. SOULEN, *Handbook of Biblical Criticism*; W.R. TATE, *Biblical Interpretation*; P. YODER, *From Word to Life*.

For a history of the development of the method, see D.A. BLACK – D.S. DOCKERY, «New Testament Criticism and Interpretation»; R.A. HARRISVILLE – W. SUNDBERG, *The Bible in the Modern Culture*; W. E. KRENTZ, *The Historical-Critical Method*; P. YODER, *From Word to Life*, 21-54.

structure for the study of the text. Although the above order is generally followed not all texts will require each criticism, and some of the critical procedures overlap. In other words, one method may build upon the results of another method and many times the approaches complement each other.

The first chapter of this dissertation presents the basic methodological procedures and the rationale that underlies the HCM as it is practiced today. The methodology that will be described below is not from one particular scholar. Footnotes direct the reader to additional reading material such as handbooks on individual critical approaches, applications of the method to biblical texts and histories describing the development of the method[2].

---

[2] A brief clarification regarding terminology is needed. Various terms have been used for similar procedures during the development of the method. Several distinctions are made here, further clarification on terminology will follow.

Higher-lower criticism. The first terms used to describe the methodology were *lower criticism* and *higher criticism*. *Lower criticism* was the term used for textual criticism. *Higher criticism* was the term used for source criticism. The distinction was based on the fact that textual criticism or choosing the correct reading was the first procedure to be done in a study. All other exegetical procedures were labeled *higher criticism*. At that time, the only other critical procedure used was *source criticism*. As a result *higher criticism* became synonymous with *source criticism*. The terms *lower criticism* and *higher criticism* are no longer used by exegetes.

Higher criticism, literary criticism or source criticism. Source criticism developed as a method for studying the composite nature of a literary work. The study concerned itself with identifying the written texts underlying many biblical texts. An innate historical interest was associated with this investigation. The sources sought were considered not only literary sources, as they are today, but historical sources as well. At this point the term *higher criticism* was used (see above). The term *literary criticism* began to be used when the focus of study shifted from a concentration on sources to a study of the integral nature of the text. The term is still used today but can cause some confusion because of the *new literary criticism*. *New literary criticism* bases its evaluation of the biblical text on the methods used in studying secular literature.

Philological Analysis. When one refers to an analysis of the text based on language, one can refer to the analysis as *philological analysis, linguistic analysis, language study, linguistics, semantics,* or *grammatical analysis.* The term *philological analysis - grammatical criticism* is used in this dissertation. Traditionally *philology* described the structure of the text in terms of vocabulary and grammar. Current usage includes the study of language as language and the power of words in communication.

Genre - Form Criticism. The term *genre criticism* is presently used for *form criticism*. This practice, however, is not universal. The older term is still found in many handbooks and commentaries.

1. Introduction

What is an *introduction*?[3] An *introduction* is the technical term used to describe the study of background material for understanding the biblical texts. An *introduction* can be used for biblical studies in general or for specific collections of texts (e.g. Johannine literature, Pauline literature, the Pentateuch, the Gospel of Matthew). Many times an *Introduction* is given at the beginning of a collegiate course in Scripture studies and is usually the first part of a biblical commentary. The term became part of the technical vocabulary of biblical studies in the eighteenth century through the work of J. D. Michaelis.

An *introduction* for the study of Scriptures in general includes such background information such as the history of the ANE and the Greco-Roman world, literary works contemporaneous with the biblical texts, geography of the ANE. The information provided by an *introduction* for an individual book or unit can include these elements: the question of authorship; the date and place of the writing; the intended audience; and any historical, geographic, or comparative literary data relevant to the particular work.

One goal of the HCM is understanding the text in its original historical context. The *introduction* provides much information necessary for this type of understanding as should be evident in the examples listed in the previous paragraph. Furthermore, the traditional hermeneutical basis for the HCM, the *literal sense*, requires the identification of the author's intention. Such an identification requires the information provided in an *introduction*.

2. Textual Criticism

What is textual criticism?[4] Textual criticism is the study of ancient documents for which the original text[5] is no longer in existence with the

---

3 The following are provided as examples of *Introductions*: R.E. BROWN, *An Introduction to the New Testament*; R.F. COLLINS, *Introduction to the New Testament*; O. EISSFELDT, *The Old Testament: An Introduction*; R.H. FULLER, *Critical Introduction to the New Testament*; J.H. HAYES, *An Introduction to Old Testament Study*; W.G. KÜMMEL, *Introduction to the New Testament*; J.A. SOGGIN, *Introduction to the Old Testament*.

See J.A. FITZMYER, *The Gospel According to Luke*, 1-286 for an example of an extensive *Introduction* for an individual biblical book, in this case the *Gospel of Luke*.

4 Handbooks for textual criticism include: K. ALAND, *The Text of the New Testament*; D.R. AP-THOMAS, *Old Testament Criticism*; S.F. BROCK – C.T. FRITSCH – S. JELLICOE, «Studies in the Septuagint»; E. BROTZMAN, *Old Testament Textual Criticism*; K. ELLIOT – I. MOIR, *Manuscripts*; E.J. EPP – G.D. FEE, *New Testament Tex-*

two-fold goal of determining the original reading of specific passages as well as the history of transmission of a particular work. The following description focuses primarily on the first goal.

The texts used as the basis of study are referred to as *witnesses* because they only represent the original text. The *witnesses* are divided into three major groups: ancient biblical texts in their original languages, ancient versions or translations from the original languages and quotations of biblical texts found in extra-biblical sources.

The first group of *witnesses* are the biblical manuscripts in existence today. The OT texts vary in type (fragments, scrolls, codices) and date. The dates span over 1100 years ranging from 250 BC (Qumran Scrolls[6]) to 1009 AD (Leningrad Codex) with a particularly large gap between 135 AD and 930 AD (Aleppo Codex). The NT texts also vary in type and date. The manuscripts are usually characterized by a) the material used to receive the writing, papyrus or parchment; and b) the type of letters used in the text: uncials (upper case letters) or miniscules (lower case letters). The dates of the NT manuscripts range from 100-150 ($\mathfrak{p}^{52}$, a fragment from the Gospel of John) to the great manuscripts of the fourth and fifth

---

tual Criticism; ID., «Textual Criticism»; J. FINEGAN, *Encountering New Testament Manuscripts*; J.H. GREENLEE, *Introduction*; S. JELLICOE, *Septuagint and Modern Study*; R.W. KLEIN, *Textual Criticism of the Old Testament*; P.K. MCCARTER, *Textual Criticism*; E. TOV, *The Text-Critical Use of the Septuagint*; E. TOV, *The Textual Criticism of the Bible*; L. VAGANAY, *Introduction to NT Textual Criticism*; J. WEINGREEN, *Introduction to the Critical Study*; R. WONNEBERGER, *Understanding the BHS*.

For further reading on the development of the method see: D. BARTHELEMY, *Critique textuelle*; E.J. EPP, «The Eclectic Method»; M.H. GOSHEN-GOTTSTEIN, «The Textual Criticism of the Old Testament»; L. VAGANAY, *Introduction to NT Textual Criticism*, 89-171.

[5] The term *original text* needs some clarification. Referring to the complexities of OT textual criticism, E. TOV, «Textual Criticism: Old Testament», 394, refers to the original text or autograph as the «finished literary product which stood at the beginning of the stage of textual transmission». Several factors require caution in using the term *original text* including the following: a) no original biblical text exists today, b) the period of time between the hypothesized writing and the earliest textual witnesses can be lengthy, c) the individual works which comprise the two testaments have gone through different levels of redaction so that the term *original text* can take on a different meaning for each text.

[6] R.E. BROWN – D.W. JOHNSON – K.G. O'CONNELL, «Texts and Versions», 1085, notes that F.M. Cross dates 4QExod^f to 250 BC, 4QSam^b to 200 BC, 4QJer^a to 175 BC.

centuries (*Sinaticus, Vaticanus, Alexandrinus, Bezae, Ephræmi Rescriptus*)[7].

The second group of *witnesses* are the versions. Versions are ancient translations of the biblical works. The primary versions of the OT are the Greek Septuagint (LXX), the Samaritan Pentateuch, the Aramaic Targums, the Syriac Peshitta, and the Latin Vulgate. The primary versions of the NT are the Syriac, Latin, Coptic, Gothic and Armenian. Utilizing the versions in textual criticism requires caution for two reasons. First, the texts are not only translations but also copies of an ancient original version that is no longer in existence. Second, in order to make comparisons a *Vorlage* (a re-translation into the original language) must be constructed for the passages being studied, increasing the chance for error[8]. The LXX which dates to the second or third century BC holds a prominent place among the versions in OT studies.

The third group of witnesses to the biblical texts are biblical citations in ancient extra-biblical literature. These witnesses come from the writings of Philo and Josephus, Rabbinical literature, liturgical texts of the early church and the numerous writings of the Fathers of the Church. The use of quotations from extra-biblical sources in textual criticism present the following difficulties: the extra-biblical texts have their own transmission history that has produced variants and most quotations are not from the original text but from a copy.

Though the witnesses of the original texts are numerous, no two manuscripts are exactly alike. The differences between the textual witnesses are

---

7 For more information on the manuscripts of the Old Testament see E. BROTZMAN, *OT Testament Textual Criticism*, 37-62; F.M. CROSS – S. TALMON, *Qumran*; B.J. ROBERTS, *Text and Versions*; ID., «Textual Transmission»; E. TOV, *Textual Criticism of the Bible*, 21-154. For NT manuscripts see K. ALAND, *The Text of the New Testament*; J.N. BIRDSALL, «The New Testament Text»; R.E. BROWN – D.W. JOHNSON – K.G. O'CONNELL, «Texts and Versions»; J.K. ELLIOT, *A Bibliography*; J. FINEGAN, *Encounter New Testament Manuscripts*; F.G. KENYON, *The Text of the Greek Bible*; B.M. METZGER, *The Text* .

8 D.R. AP-THOMAS, *Old Testament Criticism*, 19-20, refers to six rules for using versions: «a) the *a priori* probability is that the MT is superior to any translation because of its more continuous tradition, b) the possibility must always be borne in mind that the text of the version may have suffered corruption itself, c) a slight variation in rendering may be done merely to a paraphrase and not to indicate a different Hebrew text, d) the rendering of an unusual, or already corrupt, Hebrew word by a word with a quite different meaning may be due to a guess on the part of the translator, and e) a shorter text in the version may be due to accidental or deliberate omission; and a longer text may be due to explanation or comment».

called *variants*[9]. There are four possibilities for variants: variants among the ancient biblical manuscripts, variants among the ancient versions, variations between the ancient biblical manuscripts and the versions and variants among the ancient Jewish and Christian non-biblical literature[10].

The practice of textual criticism involves three principle stages: a) compiling a list of variants, b) determining the best reading, and c) emending the text when necessary (rarely used in NT textual criticism)[11].

Compiling a List of Variants. The first stage of textual criticism is the collection and evaluation of *witnesses*[12]. The two steps involved in this stage are: compiling a list of variants for a particular passage and eliminating variants that can be explained by transcriptional errors — either intentional or unintentional. This process results in a working list of variants that will be the basis of study in the second stage.

Textual criticism begins by listing the variants for a particular passage. Today there are several editions of the Hebrew and Greek Scriptures that include a list of variants in their *apparatus criticus*[13]. Exegetes, for the most part, will take advantage of these editions and their *apparatus*. The

---

[9] As the science of textual criticism developed so too the terminology and language used in the research. The terms *reading, variant, discrepancy*, etc. were at one time used interchangeably. Presently the terminology is more refined. *Reading* refers to any difference that exists for a certain passage. *Variant* is used only when the *reading* is significant for the textual witness. For more on the development of the terminology see: E.J. EPP, «Toward the Clarification of the Term "Textual Variant"»; ID., «Textual Criticism: NT», 412.

[10] J.H. HAYES – C.R. HOLLADAY, *Biblical Exegesis*, 35.

[11] The division of the process into steps or sub-divisions as well as the terminology used in describing the process differs among scholars. For example P.K. MCCARTER, *Textual Criticism*, 62, refers to the steps listed here as *recensio, examinatio* and *emendatio*, while L. VAGANAY, *Introduction to NT Textual Criticism*, 52, uses *verbal-criticism, external criticism*, and *internal criticism*.

[12] For the most part the critic will deal with particular passages. The recovery of a complete text is perhaps beyond the scope of reason. Scholars refer to the original OT manuscripts as the *Ur-manuscripts*.

[13] For the Hebrew OT see *Biblica Hebraica Stuttgartensia* (BHS) which is based on the Leningrad Codex. For the LXX see A.E. BROOKE – N. MCLEAN – H.S.J. THACKERAY, *The Old Testament in Greek*; A. RAHLFS, *Septuaginta. The Old Testament in Greek* is based on the Codex Vaticanus with supplements. Rahlfs is an eclectic edition based primarily on Alexandrinus, Vaticanus, and Sinaticus. For the Greek NT see K. ALAND – B. ALAND, *Novum Testamentum graece*[27] (N-A) and *The Greek New Testament*[4] (GNT) which have the same eclectic texts. The GNT *apparati* are geared for biblical translators while the N-A edition has a much more complete listing of variants. For bibliographic information on additional editions and various editions of the versions see J.A. FITZMYER, *Introductory Bibliography*, 46-55.

compilation of such works are done by specialists in the field of textual criticism. At this point the exegete will examine the list and eliminate any variants that can be explained by transcriptional alterations[14]. Transcriptional alterations are categorized as either unintentional errors or intentional modifications.

Unintentional errors are essentially mistakes made by the copyist through a slip of the eye or a mistake in hearing. The following are some of the examples of unintentional errors: the repetition of letters or words (dittography), the omission of letters or words (haplography), the omission of a group of words with the same ending (homoeoteleuton), the transposition of letters (metathesis), incorrect word or sentence division (especially with the Hebrew text), and «the mistaken juxtaposition of two or more parallel readings in the text itself» (doublets)[15].

Intentional modifications are alterations to the text deliberately introduced by the scribe. There are a number of reasons for such changes. Metzger uses the following as examples: spelling or grammar corrections, harmonizing (making two parallel texts agree), the addition of natural complements and similar adjuncts, clarifying historical and geographical difficulties, conflation of readings, and doctrinal reasons[16].

---

[14] A basic knowledge of the process of reproducing texts in the ancient world may be helpful in understanding the principles used in evaluating the texts. Originally copyists used an *eye-to-hand* method. The copyist would look at a *master copy* of a text, read a line then copy it to a new manuscript. Later, the *ear-to-hand* method developed. A text was recited in a scriptorium with copyists listening. As the copyists listened to the reading, they would write down what they heard producing a new manuscript. In some cases controls to check the accuracy of the copy were in place such as counting the words (as in the Masoretic Text) however the practice was not universal.

The invention and use of the printing press did not eliminate the problems associated with textual reproduction. Both the OT and NT editions that became know as the «textus receptus» were based on limited manuscript evidence but became the standard text for biblical research for several hundred years. In the 1800's with the discovery of more and more manuscripts a break was made with the «textus receptus» and better editions were published. Also see footnote 6 in the *Introduction*.

[15] E. TOV, «Textual Criticism: Old Testament», 409.

[16] B.M. METZGER, *The Text*, 186-206. The list given here (intentional errors) and in the preceding paragraph (unintentional errors) are provided as an example. The types of error could be further refined for work on either the Hebrew text or the Greek text. For examples of transcriptional errors in the biblical text see: D.R. AP-THOMAS, *Old Testament Criticism*, 41-50; E. BROTZMAN, *OT Testament Textual Criticism*, 108-120; K. ELLIOT – I. MOIR, *Manuscripts*, 37-76; J.H. GREENLEE, *Introduction*, 55-61; R.W. KLEIN, *Textual Criticism of the Old Testament*, 74-75; P.K. MCCARTER, *Textual Criticism*, 26-61; E. TOV, *The Textual Criticism of the Bible*, 236-86; L. VAGANAY, *Introduction*, 52-61.

Determining the Best Reading. The first stage of textual criticism resulted in a list of variants that could not be understood as transcriptional errors. The second stage of the study will compare the variants to determine which variant is the best representation of the original reading. The basic principle for this study is Tischendorf's rule — «the reading is to be preferred that best explains the origin of all the other readings in the variation unit»[17]. However, criteria have been developed to aid in the process of evaluating and comparing the variants. The criteria are divided into two groups: external criteria and internal criteria.

External criteria deal with the nature of the manuscripts and the historical factors involved in the transmission process. The criteria include the date of the *witness*, the geographical distribution of the *witnesses* that agree in supporting a variant, and the genealogical relationship of texts and families of *witnesses*[18].

Internal criteria «appeal to the scribal habits, context of passages, and the author's style, language and thought»[19]. The internal criteria are divided into two groups: transcription probabilities and intrinsic factors. Transcriptional probabilities include the following: the more difficult reading is to be preferred, the shorter reading is generally preferred, the reading which is at a verbal dissidence with the others is to be preferred (this concerns parallel passages), and scribal practices are to be considered (for example «replacing an unfamiliar word with a more familiar synonym, altering a less refined grammatical form or less elegant lexical expression in accord with Atticizing preferences, or adding pronouns, conjunctions and expletives to make a smooth text»[20]). Intrinsic factors include the following: the style and vocabulary of the author throughout the book, the immediate context of the passage, and harmony with the author's usage in other texts. When considering the gospels additional factors are considered. These include concord with the Aramaic background of Jesus' teaching, the priority of *Mark*, and the influence of the Christian community upon the formulation and transmission of the passage[21].

---

[17] E.J. EPP, «Textual Criticism: NT», 432.

[18] B.M. METZGER, *The Text*, 209. For other formulation of external criteria see: R.W. KLEIN, *Textual Criticism of the Old Testament*, 74; P.K. MCCARTER, *Textual Criticism*, 71-72; L. VAGANAY, *Introduction*, 62-64; E. TOV, *The Textual Criticism of the Bible*, 301-302.

[19] E.J. EPP, «Textual Criticism: NT», 431.

[20] B.M. METZGER, *The Text*, 210.

[21] B.M. METZGER, *The Text*, 210. For other formulations of internal criteria see: J.H. GREENLEE, *Introduction to New Testament Textual Criticism*, 111-114; R.W.

Although these criteria can be helpful, many exegetes and textual scholars advise against placing too much weight on them. For example, Tov notes that the internal criteria are so «abstractly formulated, they apply only to a small number of instances, and their use is so subjectively determined that evaluation still remains a subjective procedure»[22]. In the end the basic rule mentioned above is the best guide — the best reading is the one that explains the others. NT textual criticism is a two-stage process ending here.[23] OT textual criticism adds the final stage of emendation.

Emending the Text. The final stage in textual criticism involves emendation of the text to provide the best reading. This step is sometimes called *conjectural criticism.* An emendation is a change or alteration to one of the variants of a text as a corrective determined by the exegete. The change is called an emendation because the alteration is made without direct textual evidence as support. In NT studies this procedure is rarely employed due to the large number of *witnesses* available for consideration. In OT studies, however, the procedure is generally accepted and utilized.

As mentioned above, the goal of textual criticism is twofold. The first is to ascertain the original reading of the text. The second is to identify the history of the development of the texts. The two aims are somewhat complementary. As the textual critic attempts to determine the original reading of a passage, he discovers elements of the text's history. At the same time when the exegete studies the transmission history of the text he can get

---

KLEIN, *Textual Criticism of the Old Testament*, 75-83; P.K. MCCARTER, *Textual Criticism*, 72-74; E. TOV, *The Textual Criticism of the Bible*, 298-330; L. VAGANAY, *Introduction to NT Textual Criticism*, 79-86.

22 E. TOV, «Textual Criticism: Old Testament», 410.

23 The various systems of NT textual criticism are sometimes classified according to their use of internal/external criteria. Three of these classifications are the historical-documentary method, the rigorous eclectic method, and the reasoned eclectic method. The historical-documentary method formerly referred to as the historical-genealogical method «attempts to reconstruct the history of the NT by tracing the lines of transmission back through the extant manuscripts to the earliest stage and then selecting the reading that represents the earliest attainable level of the textual tradition». The rigorous eclectic method selects the variant, «that best suits the context of the passage, the author's style and vocabulary, or the authors theology while taking into account also such factors as scribal habits, including their tendency of conforming either to Koine or Attic Greek style, to Semitic forms of expression, to parallel passages, to OT passages or to liturgical forms and usage». The reasoned eclectic method is the most used today and seeks to find a balance between the other two methods. See, E.J. EPP, «Textual Criticism: NT», 430-433.

insights into the original reading of a passage. Textual criticism is such a broad field that many times exegetes will rely on the work of specialists for the history of textual transmission so that they can concentrate their efforts on determining the best reading for a passage under consideration. Textual criticism is the first step in biblical exegesis. Once completed the exegete has a *working text* to study.

3. Grammatical Criticism – Philological Analysis

What is grammatical criticism? Grammatical criticism[24] is a scholarly evaluation of the philological and semantic elements in a passage. After establishing the *working text* through textual criticism the exegete makes a grammatical analysis. The study usually includes translating the text into a modern language[25]. Grammatical criticism consists of three steps: a) evaluating the words of the passage, b) evaluating the grammatical structure, and c) considering idiomatic expressions.

Evaluating the Words. The meaning that a word conveys is described as either lexical or contextual. The lexical meaning of a word is tied to the history of the word. All languages develop meanings for words that are time conditioned. The basic meaning for some words is related to a particular age or period. For example, the English word *mouse* has a meaning today that 16 years ago would never have been associated with it[26]. So much more for the biblical texts that were composed over a period of at least 600 years. In these cases, the way a Hebrew or Greek word is used in a text will be conditioned by time. An exegete will use a lexicon or word dictionary as an aid in evaluating the lexical meaning of a word[27]. This lexical meaning provides a framework for the possible meanings of a word. The exegete could then evaluate the writing to ascertain any nuance

---

[24] Another term used for this type of study is *linguistics*. J.A. FITZMYER, «The Interpretation of the Bible in the Church», 40, suggests using *philology* instead of *linguistics* because of its specialized use today in language studies. See W.R. BODINE, «Linguistics», 327-33, for more information on *linguistics* as the study of language as language in contrast to the study of a specific language.

[25] Such is the case in many scholarly commentaries: i.e. *The Anchor Bible* (Garden City-New York); *Sacra Pagina* (Collegeville); *The Word Bible Commentary* (Waco, TX).

[26] That is «a device used to facilitate "pointing" on a computer screen».

[27] Standard lexicons include: W. BAUER – F.W. GINGRICH – F.W. DANKER, *A Greek-English Lexicon*; W. BAUMGARTNER, *Hebräisches und aramäisches Lexikon*; F. BROWN – S.R. DRIVER – C.A. BRIGGS, *The New Brown-Driver-Briggs-Genesius*; W. GESENIUS, *Hebräisches und aramäisches Handwörterbuch*; H.G. LIDDELL – R. SCOTT, *A Greek-English Lexicon*; J.H. MOULTON, *The Vocabulary of the Greek Testament*; E. VOGT, *Lexicon linguae aramaicae Veteris Testamenti*.

introduced by the author. The lexical meaning may also provide an aid in determining the time of the text's composition. If the meaning of certain words are isolated to a particular time, and this meaning is the only meaning that fits the context of a passage, then it is possible to date that passage to a particular period[28].

While the lexical meaning is important and helpful for determining meaning, the most accurate meaning of a word comes through the context in which it is used. A simple example from the English language is provided as an illustration. The word under consideration is *bat*. The lexical meaning might read: a) a stout solid stick, b) a sharp blow, c) a wooden implement used for hitting the ball in various games, d) to strike or hit as with a bat, e) an order of nocturnal placental flying mammals with forelimbs modified to form wings[29]. Each of these accurately describes a possible meaning for the word *bat*. The precise meaning of the word, in this case, has to be determined by the context in which it is used. If the sentence reads «The *bat* flew over the roof», the reader knows that the author is referring to a winged rodent. If a sentence reads «The boy hit the ball with his new *bat*», the reader knows that the author is referring to a baseball bat. The context provides the particular meaning in these examples.

Two tools that are indispensable for the exegete in this study are concordances and theological dictionaries. The concordance cites the word in its immediate context and lists all the places the word is used in the Bible. Exegetes are able to determine from the list how an individual author used the word and the way the word is used in an entire collection (OT or NT)[30]. Today several computer concordances are available in which the exegete may not only search for a word but can define the type of search: i.e. by tense, by grammatical constructions, by case, number or gender or any combination of these.[31] The theological dictionary, on the other hand, has already made a study of the word as it is used in the Bible. The

---

[28] Qoheleth, for example, has some words and constructions that are considered *late Hebrew*. One example is עניין which occurs 8 times in the Hebrew Bible, all in Qoheleth. The word also appears in later non-biblical Hebrew literature. Even though there are no hard fast rules concerning judgment in these cases, the language can provide indications concerning a relative date.

[29] See «bat», in *Websters New Collegiate Dictionary*.

[30] Standard concordances include: K. ALAND, *Vollständige Konkordanz zum griechischen Neuen Testament*; A. EVEN-SHOSHEN, *New Concordance of the Bible*; E. HATCH – H.A. REDPATH, *Concordance to the LXX*; S. MANDELKERN, *Veteris Testamenti concordantiae hebraicae*; W.F. MOULTON – A.S. GEDEN, *Concordance to the Greek Testament*.

[31] The most widely used computer generated concordance is *Bible Works for Windows*, Hermeneutika, 1996.

meaning of the word is discussed from its roots in extra-biblical literature followed by a presentation of its use in the bible according to section or author[32].

Evaluating the Grammatical Structure. After evaluating the words in a passage, exegetes study the grammatical construction of a passage. The meaning of the words when joined together in phrases, clauses or sentences affects the meaning of the word and unit. The same is true when sentences are joined into paragraphs and paragraphs into even larger subunits. The constructions are governed by the rules of each particular language. Moreover these rules change and develop with time. The rules can provide important information such as identification of the subject and object (either by placement in a sentence, or by morphological rules), and the quality, duration or time of an action[33].

Considering Idiomatic Expressions. The final consideration for grammatical criticism is the sociological/ethnological element of the language. The meaning of the words and phrases can be influenced by the social setting in which they are used or read. Louw uses the example of Acts 14:8-18 where Paul and Barnabas tear their cloaks after being mistaken for gods. In some cultures this was read as a positive sign indicating that Paul and Barnabas were rejoicing at being called gods. However, in the original cultural setting the tearing of the cloak was a sign of utter indignation[34].

4. Literary - Source Criticism

What is literary criticism?[35]. Literary criticism is «the study of literature, especially from the point of view of what in French is called *explication de*

---

[32] Theological dictionaries include: G.J. BOTTERWECK – H. RINGGREN – H.J. FABRY, *Theological Dictionary of the Old Testament*; H. BALZ – G. SCHNEIDER, *Exegetical Dictionary of the New Testament*; G. KITTEL, *Theological Dictionary of the New Testament*.

[33] Examples of Hebrew grammars are: P. JOÜON – T. MURAOKA, *A Grammar of Biblical Hebrew*; E. KAUTZSCH, *Gesenius' Hebrew Grammar*; T.O. LAMBDIN, *Introduction to Biblical Hebrew*; B.K. WALTKE – M. O'CONNOR, *An Introduction to Biblical Hebrew Syntax*. Examples of Greek grammars are: F.W. BLASS – A. DEBRUNNER – W. FUNK, *A Greek Grammar of the New Testament and Other Early Christian Literature*; J. SWETNAM, *An Introduction to the Study of New Testament Greek*; M. ZERWICK, *Biblical Greek*.

[34] J.P. LOUW, «Semantics», 1080.

[35] Handbooks and guides for literary-source criticism include: J. BARTON, *Reading the Old Testament*, 20-29; J.E. BOTHA, «Style in the New Testament»; R.E. CLEMENTS, *A Century of Old Testament Study* 7-30; R.F. COLLINS, *Introduction to*

text: the attempt to read the text in such a way as to bring out its inner co-herence, the techniques of style and composition used by the author, all that makes it a piece of literary art»[36]. Source criticism is included if either the text is a composite text or there are indications that the text *might* be a composite text (in other words one that has incorporated older independent written material).

The methodology originated and developed primarily from the study of the Pentateuch in the OT and the synoptic gospels in the NT. Several factors in these texts suggested to scholars that the works had a composite nature. The factors or indications that sources were used in composing the text include: doublets (two variations of the same story); different terminology for the same or similar concepts (e.g. in the Pentateuch using Yahweh or Elohim for God); stylistic changes within or between passages; contradictions; editorial indications (e.g. epamalepsis or repeating a line before and after an insertion, framing devices)[37]. Originally source criticism focused on these small units and the hypothetical reconstruction of the source documents. Today many scholars focus their studies on how the source is incorporated into the larger work and the reasons for its inclusion or adaptation.

The process of literary criticism involves the following four steps: a) delimiting the text, b) establishing internal coherence of the text, c) identifying literary styles or devices used by the author, and d) investigating sources when the text gives evidence of composite material.

Delimiting the Text. The exegete will divide the text into larger and smaller units. Factors that can indicate a new unit include the following: change of theme, time, or characters in a narrative unit; technical literary devices such as inclusion, chiasm, acrostic patterns; repetition of a certain verse or phrase in several parts of the work; or the switch from narrative to speech or poetry. Many commentators will include an outline of the text at

---

the New Testament 42-55;115-155; N.C. HABEL, *Literary Criticism of the Old Testament.*

For the history of the method, see: O. EISSFELDT, *The Old Testament: An Introduction* 158-218; J.H. HAYES, *An Introduction to Old Testament Study* 155-199. M.E. BOISMARD, «Two-Source Hypothesis»; D.L. DUNGAN, «Two-Gospel Hypothesis»; C.M. TUCKETT, «Synoptic Problem».

[36] J. BARTON, *Reading the Old Testament*, 20.

[37] For a complete list see: for the Pentateuch see R.E. FRIEDMAN, «Torah», 609-622; for the Synoptics see: W.G. KÜMMEL, *Introduction to the New Testament*, 33-62.

the beginning of their work. The outline will indicate the major divisions within the text.

Establishing the Internal Coherence of the Text. The next step will be to demonstrate an *internal coherence* of the text. In other words exegetes or commentators will explain the unifying factors in the work. While delimiting the text they identified sub-units, now they demonstrate the unity that exists among them. Reading the text in light of these over-arching characteristics will help in interpreting the text.

Identifying Literary Styles and Devices. The biblical text is a literary work. Each individual author contributed to the writing process bringing with him certain literary characteristics that mark his style. The characteristics can include certain preferences for particular vocabulary terms and phrases, grammatical constructions and forms of idiosyncratic speech. Variations in style can be distinguished among the different biblical works and sometimes within particular texts. Individual authors also use literary devices in their compositions. Literary devices are such things as irony, comedy, apologetics, etc. The exegete attempts to identify the characteristics of an author's style and any literary devices he is using in his work/s.

Identifying Sources - Source Criticism. The final step in literary criticism is *source criticism*. The exegete seeks to determine whether a particular unit indicates that the author used a written source. The following items may indicate a source: a change in literary style, changes in vocabulary patterns, break in the flow of presentation, change in theological viewpoint, doublets, and inconsistencies in the text[38]. The above list gives *possible* indications of sources. The following set of rules may serve as guidelines for evaluating the material to see if a source is present: the material cannot be explained as orally transmitted; the material forms a text that can reasonably be assumed to have been an independent writing; insertions interrupting the body of the supposed source are clear indications for the use of a source; if the supposed source forms a collection of different traditions originally orally transmitted, a decisive criterion is the proving that there are editorial links or remarks which cannot be assigned to the author of the extant writing; and no *definitive* evidence can be drawn from differences in vocabulary and style[39]. Once a source has been identified the exegete may seek to hypothetically reconstruct the non-existent source. Following this he will attempt to determine how the particular author used the older material in his text.

---

[38] J.H. HAYES – C.R. HOLLADAY, *Biblical Exegesis*, 76-77.
[39] D.A. KOCH, «Source Criticism (NT)», 166.

5. Genre Criticism

What is genre criticism? Genre criticism is the study of the text as a reflection of patterns and conventions used in oral and written communication with the goal of gaining an insight into the social setting in which the genre developed[40]. The study was originally called *form criticism*[41].

The development of the form-critical approach began by H. Gunkel in his work with the OT. Recognizing that the most common practice of communication among the ANE peoples was oral communication, Gunkel developed a methodology that attempted to identify units in the written text that were reflective of an earlier oral form. After he identified the particular form he would seek to determine the *Sitz im Leben* or life setting in which the form developed. Gunkel believed that the *Sitz im Leben* could be identified because speech has a pattern or ritualistic aspect that reflects a particular social context. Thus, the relationship between form/genre and a particular social setting is the basis for a form critical or genre critical approach[42].

All human speech uses conventions — familiar forms or patterns of expression. When we meet someone in the morning, we say «good morning»; when we are going home after an evening out we say «good night» or «good evening». If we are friendly with someone we might say «hi», or in today's language «hey, what's up». At once we realize the convention is not a serious question but a common greeting. A context of friendship and simple conversation is automatically brought to mind. Conventions can also be detected in the written word. The newspaper is the most commonly used example of multiple forms in a written text. The

---

[40] Handbooks or guides for genre criticism include: D.E. AUNE, *The New Testament in Its Literary Environment*; J.L. BAILEY – L.V. BROEK, *Literary Forms in the New Testament*; J.L. BAILEY, «Genre Analysis»; W. BEARDSLEE, *Literary Criticism of the New Testament*; G. LOHFINK, *The Bible: Now I Get It*; R. RENDTORFF, *The Old Testament: An Introduction*; G.M. TUCKER, *Form Criticism of the Old Testament*; R.F. COLLINS, *Introduction to the New Testament*, 156-195; J. BARTON, *Reading the Old Testament*, 30-44.

For a history of the development of the method see: R.E. CLEMENTS, *A Century of Old Testament Study*; J.H. HAYES, *An Introduction to Old Testament Study*; E.V. MCKNIGHT, *What is Form Criticism?*; O. EISSFELDT, *The Old Testament: An Introduction*, 158-218;

[41] The English term is derived from the German *Formgeschichte* a term first used by M. Dibelius in his form-critical study of the synoptic gospels. The methodology, however, was first developed by Gunkel. Using the German terminology, *Formgeschichte* refers to first step mentioned above and *Gattungsgeschichte* refers to the second step.

[42] See footnote 47.

paper contains all different types of writing: headlines, news reports, financial speculations, editorials, sports writing, athletic contest's results, stock market quotes, advertisements, weather reports, comics, etc. Each form elicits from the reader a certain response, usually automatic, that places the reader within a certain framework enabling him to understand the text. For example when reading a news headline we immediately recognize that we are dealing with an item that requires a thoughtful attentive reading. We would *not* read the comic section in the same way for we immediately realize this form of writing is used for entertainment, not for the communication of serious information.

The following steps are used in genre criticism: a) analyzing the structure, b) describing the genre, c) identifying the *Sitz im Leben*, and d) stating the intention of the genre[43].

Analyzing the Structure. The first step of form criticism is an analysis of the form or structure of the text. Many times this step builds upon the work done in literary criticism. The exegete, using the outline provided by literary criticism, will study the individual units looking for an inner structure that might indicate a *form*. A *form* is «the structure or shape of an individual passage or unit, which may be described without regard to the content of the passage»[44]. The form of a text is different than its outline. While the outline is associated with content, the form is associated with structure. Figure 1 will illustrate the difference.

The First Letter of Paul to the Corinthians	
Outline	Form
I. Address (1:1–9)	I. Greeting (1:1–3)
II. Disorders in the Corinthian Community (1:10—6:20)	II. Thanksgiving (1:4–9)
A. Divisions in the Church (1:10—4:21)	III. Body Text (1:10—16:12)
B. Moral Disorders (5:1—6:20)	IV. Closing (16:13-24)
III. Answers to the Corinthian's Questions (7:1—11:1)	
A. Marriage and Virginity (7:1–40)	
B. Offerings to Idols (8:1—11:1), etc.[45]	

Figure 2: Outline and Form

Describing the Genre. The second step in this criticism places the identified form in a specific genre. Genres are «the conventional and repeatable patterns of oral and written speech, which facilitate interaction

---

[43] G.M. TUCKER, *Form Criticism of the Old Testament*, 11.
[44] J. BARTON, «Form Criticism: OT», 839.
[45] Cf. the New American Bible.

among people in specific social settings»[46]. Inclusion in a certain genre does not follow hard-fast rules, rather it is based on general similarities in structure and purpose. The genre in the above example is that of the NT letter. The general pattern of the letter genre is greeting – body – closing. Genres can be large units such as gospel, letter, apocalyptic, or can be as small as proverb, psalm, and saying. OT genres include the following: myth, historical narrative, proverb, poetry, apocalyptic, oracle, legal codes, call narrative, commissioning, covenantal formula, credal statements. NT genres include the following: gospel, letter, parable, hymn, infancy narrative, miracle story, speeches, greeting and benedictions, prayers, vice and virtue list, apocalyptic, and travel narrative.

Identifying the Sitz im Leben. The third step in genre criticism is the identification of the *Sitz im Leben* of a passage. As mentioned above, the existence of a genre presupposes a social setting in which it developed.[47]. The exegete, at this point of the study, will attempt to recover that setting. The social setting is neither the setting in which the text was written nor the historical circumstances mentioned in the passage but rather the context for which the form was created. The following simple guideline is helpful in this regard — a form can be used over and over again for situations that fit the social setting. Psalm 122 is used here as an example. The psalm is characterized as a *psalm of ascent.* The social setting of an ascent psalm is the ancient Jewish custom of pilgrimage to Jerusalem. The psalm could be used over and over again anytime someone would make a pilgrimage to the holy city. The psalm was probably sung and committed to memory, it would have been communicated from generation to generation in this oral form even after it reached the written form in the Bible. The NT letters provide another example. Characteristics of the social setting of the NT letter genre include the following: the leader of a community writes to either the people or a particular person in the community concerning matters of the faith; the actual or implied author is usually absent from the community; the community has a respect for the leader; and the leader has a great concern for the welfare of the community to whom he writes.

---

[46] J.L. BAILEY, «Genre Analysis» 200.

[47] M. Bakhtin notes the following four principles of the connection between genre and social setting: a) genres emerge from repeated social interactions within specific arenas of life and are normally employed within the same or similar social contexts, b) most cultures exhibit a rich repertoire of genres, offering a wide range of particularized visions of reality, c) genres take shape over generations and even centuries, d) changes in "real social life" can modify a genre to such an extent that a new genre emerges. see J.L. BAILEY, «Genre Analysis», 200-203.

Stating the Intention of the Genre. The final step is to state the intention of the genre. The exegete, at this point in the study, is not concerned with the author's intention in using or incorporating the genre but with the intention of the genre itself. The intention or function of the genre can be described in general terms for the genre itself and in particular terms for the genre as specified through a particular passage. The examples mentioned in above will serve as example. The general intention of an *ascent psalm* is for the community to give praise to God at the time of national pilgrimage. The intention of the genre particularized by Psalm 122 is to express this praise once inside the city. The general intention of at NT letter is to communicate a teaching on the faith.

6. Tradition Criticism

What is tradition criticism?[48] Tradition criticism is the study of a biblical text seeking to identify the traditions that underlie the text in its final form. Tradition means «handing on» — the handing on of beliefs, stories, prayers etc. from one generation to another. The «handing on» takes place on two levels, written and oral. Thus, tradition criticism focuses on the pre-history of the text[49].

The principle promoters of this approach were the OT scholars G. von Rad and M. Noth[50]. The methodology attempts to trace the history of the text prior to its final form. The study is especially important in the work of OT exegesis for two reasons: because of the strong indications of a pre-literary oral tradition in the ANE; and because the movement from oral tradition to written tradition to the final edition of a text occurred, in some cases, over hundreds of years. The study is not utilized as much in NT studies due to the short period of oral tradition prior to the written form.

---

[48] Handbooks on tradition criticism include: R.C. CULLEY, «Oral Tradition and the Old Testament Studies»; B. GERHARDSSON, *Memory and Manuscript*; W.H. KELBER, *The Oral and Written Gospel*; D.A. KNIGHT, «Tradition and Theology in the Old Testament»; E. NIELSEN, *Oral Tradition*; W.E. RAST, *Tradition History and the Old Testament*.

[49] This criticism is only valid for writings of the Bible that seem to have a pre-history. In other words, those writings that seem to be composed by a single individual at a single point in time for a specific situation would not be analyzed by this procedure.

[50] For further reading on the history of the method see: R.C. CULLEY, «Oral Tradition and the Old Testament Studies»; T.J. FARRELL, «Kelber's Breakthrough»; D.A. KNIGHT, *Rediscovering the Traditions of Israel*, D.A. KNIGHT, «Tradition History», *ABD* VI.

The specific goals of tradition criticism are the following: to make inquiries about the community or group responsible for the shaping and transmission of a particular tradition; to identify the geographical location on which the tradition was developed; to identify the sociological, political or cultural influences on the tradition; and to study the various themes of the OT[51].

The text will have already been examined in a literary and genre analysis so individual units in the text will be apparent. Utilizing the results of these two criticisms, tradition criticism a) identifies the layers of traditional material within a text, and b) determines the history of the pre-tradition.

Identifying Layers of Traditional Material. The first step in tradition criticism involves identifying the different layers of traditional material within a text. The unit to be studied will be read and compared with other similar passages. Then the differences will be noted and a conjecture will be made to identify the layers of traditional material.

Determining the History of the Pre-tradition. The exegete, after identifying the different layers in a tradition, will attempt to construct a history of the development of that particular tradition. The exegete is aware of the hypothetical nature of this type of study. Questions that he will attempt to answer are: why were certain passages lengthened or shortened? why was certain material reformulated? does the reformulation add a new meaning to the text? and how was the handing-on influenced by the historical situation?

Having at least a minimal understanding of the pre-history of the biblical texts will help the exegete to determine the author's intentions. A knowledge of the pre-history of the material contained in the text will enable the exegete to make a comparison with the final text to see the contribution of the final author/redactor.

7. Redaction - Composition Criticism

What is redaction criticism?[52] Redaction criticism is the study of the biblical text that seeks to identify «the theological motivation of an author as this is revealed in the collection, arrangement, editing and modification of traditional material, and in the composition of new material or the crea-

---

51 W.E. RAST, *Tradition History and the Old Testament*, 19-32.

52 For further reading and some examples of redaction criticism see: J. BARTON, «Redaction Criticism: OT»; ID., *Reading the Old Testament*; 45-60; R.F. COLLINS, *Introduction to the New Testament*; 196-230; N. PERRIN, *What is Redaction Criticism?*; R.H. STEIN, «Redaction Criticism: NT».

tion of new forms within the traditions of early Christianity (or Judaism)»[53].

The critical procedures used prior to redaction criticism sought to determine the historical development of the text. Redaction criticism studies and analyzes the text in its final form; that is, the text that has been deemed authoritative and canonical. In other words, the methodology moves from a diachronic to a synchronic approach.

Redaction criticism developed in reaction to some of the practices of literary criticism. As stated above, literary criticism in its earlier development concentrated on the identification of sources. As sources were identified theories concerning the composition of the text developed. The initial theories viewed the final editor (or redactor) as not much more than a «collector» of sources. Gradually it became more and more apparent that in many works the redactor was much more than a «collector». He was a theologian, who expressed in his work a particular theology. So the question was raised, «what title should be used for the last person who works on the text — editor, or author/composer?» The proposed answers are reflected in the titles used for this final step in the HCM. Willi Marxsen coined the term *Redactiongeschichte* which is translated *redaction criticism*. The use of this term suggests the final worker on the texts was an editor. E. Haenchen suggests *composition criticism*, recognizing that the final editor did not just combine or edit someone else's material but he actually composed or wrote some of the material himself and placed his own creative-mark on the work as a whole. Although *composition criticism* is probably the better term, we will use *redaction criticism* as this is the term most commonly used.

Redaction criticism comprises the following two steps: a) analyzing the composition of the text and b) identifying the theological content in a text/s.

Analyzing the Composition. An exegete would have already identified sources, forms and traditions that might have been used in the composition of a text. He now studies these seeking to determine how and why they were incorporated into the final text. While conducting this study, the exegete may notice passages for which there is no «back-ground» material. He will make a judgment concerning the authorship of such passages by comparing the theological themes of the author, the style of his language and grammar, etc. Some questions he may ask are the following: did the final redactor compose the passage? does the passage indicate a source not identified through source criticism? if the redactor did com-

---

[53] N. PERRIN, *What is Redaction Criticism?*, 1.

pose the additional material, what insights can be gained into his theology?

An exegete working on the Gospels will be greatly aided by a synopsis. The synopsis arranges parallel gospel passages in columns for easy comparison. This tool is a good place to start the redactional analysis. Comparing the passages, the exegete will look for deletions, additions, changes in vocabulary, basically those things that are different between the texts. He will then start to consider possible reasons for the differences.

Studying of the Theological Context. The position of a text in a certain place in the work may also give an indication of authorial intent. The exegete will now study the passage as situated in the complete text — immediate and broad contexts are considered. The rearrangement of passages by the editor can give a nuance or a different meaning to a passage. The theological purposes of a particular author begin to become apparent as the redaction critic evaluates the text. Identifying and describing this theology will complete the study of the redaction.

Redaction criticism brings the exegete to the final goal of his work - making an interpretation of the text. He formulates this interpretation on his understanding of the text in its original context with particular regard for what the author of the text was trying to accomplish through his writing. In other words the exegete expresses the meaning intended by the author. The meaning expressed can be on the level of verse, pericope or complete work. For most texts redaction criticism completes the process of the historical critical analysis of a text. One further evaluation, historical criticism, is made for those texts that claim to give historical witness.

8. Historical Criticism

What is historical criticism?[54] Historical criticism is the study of texts that may provide historical information on persons or events of the past. The texts are evaluated to make a judgment on their claim of historical witness. In other words the accuracy of the reporting is either verified, clarified or denied.

Historical criticism should not be confused with the HCM. The HCM is a methodology for the study of an ancient text with the purpose of understanding the meaning of the text. History is involved in this study, such as the history of textual transmission, the history of composition, the development of traditions, etc. The goals of this method, however, are not

---

[54] For bibliography see: A.K. GRAYSON – T.L. THOMPSON – D. LATEINER, «Historiography», 205-219.

necessarily to study the texts as sources of history. *Historical criticism* is a method that is used in conjunction with HCM when either a text in the historical genre is being studied or when a text is thought to contain historical information.

Three considerations should be made when working with historical criticism. First, the exegete will have to be aware of the different methods of writing history. The ancient practice of writing history is different than the practices used by authors today. For example there were certain liberties involved in the presentation of historical material that would not be found in the accepted writing practices of today. Second, the exegete will have to have an in-depth knowledge of the ancient world. The knowledge will include: a history of the ANE, of the Greek and Roman empires, of early Christianity, background information on the social structures and practices of those worlds, the important personages of the times, systems of dating important events, political and religious systems, etc. Third, the exegete will have to work with a certain philosophy of history while doing his research. Procedures and techniques for historical criticism vary too greatly to list generally accepted practices here.

9. The HCM as Practiced Today – Summary

The HCM is used today by many biblical scholars and exegetes. The goal of the method is understanding the *literal sense* of the biblical text. This understanding is expressed in an interpretation. The presentation of this interpretation will vary greatly with the intentions of the exegete. Influences which they will consider are the following: level of scholarship, intended audience, intended setting (pastoral, spiritual, or academic), etc. Generally speaking, the interpretation of a text using HCM will give the meaning expressed in the final text as understood in its original historical setting. The method uses both diachronic and synchronic approaches.

The purpose of this chapter has been to introduce the reader to the HCM. The techniques, procedures, practices, and rationale of the HCM has been presented according to the general practices of today (see chart 2). The reader is once again reminded that these are general descriptions. In practice exegetes modify and shape the method to the text they are studying. In this regard there is a great flexibility to the method. The chapter has also been attentive to clarify the terminology used in historical-critical exegesis. In the next chapter the dissertation will examine the roots of the HCM in the early church.

Summary of the Principle Components of the HCM

Description of the Criticisms	Procedures, Techniques, Practice
Introduction is the technical term used to describe the study of background material for understanding the biblical texts.	1. General Introduction - history of ANE, literature of the ANE, geography of the Holy Land, social studies, archeology, Greco-Roman history, etc. 2. Introduction for a Particular Book - author, date, intended audience/place of composition, etc.
Textual Criticism is the study of ancient documents for which the original text is no longer in existence with the two-fold goal of determining the original reading of specific passages as well as the history of transmission for a particular work.	1. compiling a list of variants for a particular passage, and eliminating variants which can be explained by transcriptional errors 2. examining and comparing the variants to determine the best reading 3. emmending of the text when necessary (primarily in OT studies)
Grammatical Criticism is a scholarly evaluation of the philological and semantic elements in a passage.	1. evaluating the words in a passage for lexical and contextual meaning, 2. evaluating the grammatical constructions in a passage 3. evaluating any idiomatic expressions in the passage.
Literary Criticism is «the study of literature, especially from the point of view of what in French is called explication de text: the attempt to read the text in such a way as to bring out its inner coherence, the techniques of style and composition used by the author, all that makes it a piece of literary art»	1. delimiting the textual units, 2. establishing the internal coherence among the individual units 3. identifying any particular literary styles or devices used by an author 4. investigating for sources when the text gives evidence of composite material
Genre Criticism is the study of the text as a reflection of patterns and conventions used in oral and written communication with the goal of gaining an insight into the social setting in which the genre developed The study was originally called form criticism	1. analyzing the structure and form 2. describing the genre 3. identifying the *Sitz im Leben* 4. stating the intention of the genre
Tradition Criticism is the study of a biblical text seeking to identify the traditions which underlie the text in its final form.	1. identify the layers of traditional material 2. determining the history of the pre-tradition
Redaction Criticism is the study of the biblical text that seeks to identify «the theological motivation of an author as this is revealed in the collection, arrangement, editing and modification of traditional material, and in the composition of new material or the creation of new forms within the traditions of early Christianity (or Judaism)».	1. studying the composition of the text 2. identifying the authors theological intentions in the arrangement of the material in a text/s.
Historical Criticism is the study of texts which may provide historical information on persons or events of the past. The texts are evaluated to make a judgment on their claim of historical witness. In other words the accuracy of the reporting is either verified, clarified or denied.	*Procedures and techniques for historical criticism vary too greatly to list generally accepted practices. The following are given for general guidelines.* 1. the exegete should be aware of the different methods of writing history. 2. the exegete should have a in-depth knowledge of the ancient world. 3. the exegete will work with a certain philosophy of history while doing his research.

Figure 3: The Principle Components , Procedures, and Techniques of the HCM

CHAPTER II

The Roots Of The Historical Critical Method
in Patristic and Medieval Literature

Interpretation of the Bible in the Church presents the necessity and limits of the HCM within the larger framework of Catholic biblical interpretation. The 1993 document, while discussing the history of the method, briefly notes that the roots of the method can be identified in the exegesis of the early church. The Commission includes this statement as a response to recent arguments that call for replacing the HCM with a «spiritual exegesis» similar to that of the patristic and medieval periods. The PBC wishes to show that certain elements of the method have been recognized as important and necessary for proper exegesis even in the formative years of Christianity. Although the HCM only formally develops following the Renaissance, its roots are in the exegesis of the patristic and medieval periods.

This chapter seeks to identify elements of the HCM in the literature of these periods. The chapter contains three sections. The first section examines the hermeneutical basis of the HCM, the *literal sense*. The presentation surveys the development of the *literal sense* in this period. The second section identifies elements of the HCM found in the patristic and medieval writings[1]. The elements include the following: techniques used

---

[1] The study does not aim to be a complete catalog of the HCM in patristic and medieval literature nor will it be a history of Catholic exegesis. The chapter provides representative examples from the literature available. Examples from the patristic period are much more numerous than those from the medieval period. There are two reasons. First, biblical studies and theological studies were united more closely in the patristic period so that the literary output associated with the Scriptures was greater. Second, the study of the Bible during the medieval period was more associated with the *gloss* than with the text (see below, page 51).

in the study of ancient texts; tools that developed as an aid for critical study; and the recognition of problems in the text that required critical investigation. The third section, the conclusion, summarizes necessity and limits of the HCM as understood during this period. In this way the chapter will identify the place of the HCM in the early Church.

1. The Hermeneutical Basis of the HCM

Hermeneutical principles provide the basic guidelines for biblical interpretation. The theological basis for the principles is the belief that the Scriptures are inspired. In other words, the text has both divine and human dimensions. This unique nature of the biblical text requires special terminology to describe its meaning. The terms used in biblical hermeneutics are the *senses of Scripture*. The complexities in biblical interpretation can be seen in the various formulas for these *senses*. The basic senses are the *literal sense* and the *spiritual sense*, although the number and definitions have varied over time.

In the early church, Origen saw the *spiritual sensé* as the primary sense; all other senses collapsed into it. By the time of Aquinas, however, the *literal sense* became the foundational sense for biblical hermeneutics. All other senses were defined in relationship with the *literal sense*. The following section will survey the ascendancy of the *literal sense* to its position as the principle of unity for biblical interpretation. The survey will begin with Origen's three senses and concludes with Aquinas' treatment

---

For further reading on the history of exegesis see: W.D. BOER, «Hermeneutic Problems»; W.J. BURGHARDT, «On early Christian Exegesis»; A. CUNNINGHAM, «Reading the Scriptures»; H. DE LUBAC, *Exégèse médiévale*; B. DE MARGERIE, *An Introduction* ; D.S. DOCKERY, *Biblical Interpretation*; F.W. FARRAR, *History of Interpretation*; E. FERGUSON, «The Bible in the Early Church»; D.S. FERGUSON, «Biblical Hermeneutics»; T. FINAN – V. TWOMEY, *Scriptural Interpretation in the Fathers*; E. FLESSEMAN VAN LEER, *Tradition and Scripture in the Early Church*; K. FROEHLICH, *Biblical Interpretation*; R. GRANT – D. TRACY, *Short History of Interpretation*; R.M. GRANT, *Heresy and Criticism*; R.A. GREER, «The Christian Bible»; R.P.C. HANSON, «Biblical Exegesis»; M.L. LAISTNER, «Antiochene Exegesis»; G.W.H. LAMPE, «To Gregory the Great»; J. LECLERCQ, «From Gregory the Great to St. Bernard»; R. LOEWE, «The Medieval History»; ID., «The "Plain" Meaning of Scripture»; B.M. METZGER, «Textual Criticism among the Church Fathers»; H. NASH, «The Exegesis»; F. O'FEARGHAIL, «Philo and the Fathers»; J. ROGERSON – C. ROWLAND – B. LINDARS, *Study and Use of the Bible*; J.W. ROGERSON – W.G. JEANROND, «Interpretation, History of»; F. SADOWSKI, *The Church Fathers on the Bible*; M. SIMONETTI, *Biblical Interpretation*; Id., *Lettera e/o Allegoria*; B. SMALLEY, «The Exposition», ID., *The Bible in the Middle Ages*; C. STEINMETZ, *The Bible in the Sixteenth Century*; J.F. BOYLE, «Faith Seeking Understanding».

of multiple senses. This study is intended to be a brief introduction to the *literal sense*. It is not intended to be an extensive treatment of the hermeneutical principles of these periods[2].

1.1 *Origen's Three Senses*

Origen was the first exegete to speak in terms of multiple senses for a biblical passage. He recognized three senses: the *literal*, the *moral* and the *spiritual*. The three were modeled after the Platonic concept of the person. According to this concept, the person was composed of body, soul and spirit. Origen built his hermeneutical theory on this concept; thus, the *literal sense* represents the body, the *moral sense* represents the soul and the *spiritual sense* represents the spirit[3]. Origen emphasized the *spiritual sense* in his biblical interpretations. The *spiritual sense* was the highest sense representing a deeper meaning to the text that only the perfect man could understand[4]. According to Origen, the *literal sense* is the lowest of the senses representing a meaning that can be understood by simple men[5]. It is primarily associated with historical meaning (words reflecting real events of the past). In reference to the legal codes, however, it is the meaning expressed directly by the words themselves; in other words, the obvious meaning[6].

---

[2] An extensive treatment is not needed here, for such studies see the bibliographic references in footnote 1. The HCM of later periods use the *literal sense* as its base. A general understanding of its development is helpful as background for the latter debates.

[3] G.W.H. LAMPE, «To Gregory the Great», 175, notes, however, that more often than not «the spiritual sense crowds out the moral, or the two are fused together».

[4] ORIGEN, *De Principiis*, IV.1.11. English trans.: ANFa, 366.

[5] For further reading see G. WATSON, «Origin and the Literal Interpretation».

[6] ORIGEN, *De Principiis*, IV.1.19. English trans.: ANFa, 368, «But that no one may suppose that we assert respecting the whole that no history is real because a certain one is not; and that no law is to be literally observed, because a certain one, understood according to the letter, is absurd or impossible; or that the statements regarding the Savior are not true in a manner perceptible to the senses; or that no commandment and precept of His ought to be obeyed; we have to answer that, with regard to certain things, it is perfectly clear to us that the historical account is true; as that Abraham was buried in the double cave at Hebron (Gen 25:9), as also Isaac (Gen 35.29) and Jacob (Gen 50: 13), and the wives of each of them; and that Schechem was given as a portion to Joseph (Gen 48:21-22); and that Jerusalem is the metropolis of Judea, in which the temple of God was built by Solomon; and innumerable other statements. For the passages that are true in their historical meaning are much more numerous than those which are interspersed with a purely spiritual sense. And again, who would not say that the command which enjoins to «honor your father and your mother, that it may be well with you» (Exod 20:12), is useful, apart from all allegorical meaning, and ought to be observed, the apostle Paul (Eph 6:2-3) also having em-

Origen had several reasons for his negative view of the *literal sense*. He viewed the *literal sense* as placing limitations on the meaning of a text especially regarding the unity of the OT and NT[7]. Furthermore the *literal sense* on its own could not explain certain problems in the text including the following: contradictions to common sense and reason, the portrayal of God in some passages as immoral, and anthropomorphism in the text. These problems as well as his high views on inspiration[8] and his appreciation of the mysterious nature of the biblical text led Origen to emphasize a *spiritual sense*. This *spiritual sense* was described through alle-

---

ployed these very same words? And what need is there to speak of the prohibitions, «You shall not commit adultery», «You shall not kill», «You shall not steal», «You shall not bear false witness» (Exod 20:13-16)? And again, there are commandments contained in the Gospel which admit of no doubt whether they are to be observed according to the letter or not: e.g. that which says, «But I say unto you, Whoever is angry with his brother» (Matt 5:22), and so on. And again, «But I say unto you, Swear not at all» (Matt 5:34). And in the writings of the apostle the *literal sense* is to be retained: «Warn them that are unruly, comfort the feeble-minded, support the weak, be patient towards all men» (I Thes 5:14); although it is possible for those ambitious of a deeper meaning to retain the profundities of the wisdom of God, without setting aside the commandment in its literal meaning. The careful reader, however, will be in doubt as to certain points, being unable to show without Long investigation whether this history so deemed literally occurred or not, and whether the literal meaning of this law is to be observed or not. And therefore the exact reader must, in obedience to the Savior's injunction to «search the Scriptures» (John 5:39), carefully ascertain how far the literal meaning is true, and how far impossible; and so far as he can, trace out, by means of similar statements, the meaning everywhere scattered throughout the Scripture of that which cannot be understood in a *literal sense*».

[7] See J. ROGERSON – C. ROWLAND – B. LINDARS, *Study and Use of the Bible*, 32-33. Despite Origen's heavy emphasis on an allegorical interpretation, H. CROUZEL, «Origen», *EEC* II, 621, calls him «the greatest literal exegete of antiquity».

[8] ORIGEN, *De Principiis*, IV.1.8. English trans.: ANFa, 355-356, writes: «Then, finally, that the Scriptures were written by the Spirit of God, and have a meaning, not such only as is apparent at first sight, but also another, which escapes the notice of most. For these words which are written are the forms of certain mysteries, and the images of divine things. Respecting which there is one opinion throughout the whole Church, that the whole law is indeed spiritual, but that the spiritual meaning which the law conveys is not known by all, but to those only on whom the grace of the Holy Spirit is bestowed in the word of wisdom and knowledge». M. SIMONETTI, *Biblical Interpretation*, 41, notes that Origen «does not limit himself to thinking of Scripture as a book inspired by the Holy Spirit, but as the divine word he effectively identifies it with Christ (= the Logos), the Word of God; the letter of the sacred text functions, like the human body assumed by Christ, as the envelope which encloses the divine Logos (C. Celsum VI 77; Comm.Ser. in Mt. 27): Sacred Scripture is the permanent incarnation of the Logos».

gory[9]. Emphasis on the *spiritual sense* became the accepted and preferred mode of interpretation for several hundred years. Three abuses led to its demise — excesses in the method, complex and exaggerated allegoriza- tion, and Gnostic utilization depriving the text of historical value. The An- tiochenes reacted to these abuses with an emphasis on the *literal sense*[10].

1.2 *The Antiochene Use of the Literal Sense*

The debate concerning hermeneutical principles of the patristic period, in past scholarship, was defined in terms of the Alexandrian School and the so-called Antiochene school[11]. The Alexandrians represented the alle- gorical approach. The Antiochenes represented the literal approach. Today the distinction is not so clearly defined. The generalizations of past schol- arship do not suffice for categorizing individual writers along the lines of a *strictly* allegorical or *strictly* literal approach to biblical interpretation. The differences regarding biblical interpretation may better be expressed in terms of *emphasis* or, even better, the relationship between these two approaches. Origen, as mentioned above, emphasized the allegorical ap- proach and the *spiritual sense*. This does not eliminate the *literal sense*

---

9 Origen's emphasis on the *spiritual sense* was also a reaction to the millenarianists who used literal interpretations to predict the end-time. R. GRANT – D. TRACY, *Short History of Interpretation*, 61 notes that the allegorical approach was indicative of Ori- gen's desire to show the intellectual respectability of the biblical texts to the well edu- cated pagans of his era.

10 An earlier critic of the allegorical method was Tertullian. He feared that the alle- gorical method would lead to a de-historicizing effect. G.W.H. LAMPE, «To Gregory the Great», 172, notes that Tertullian thought the use of allegory «might resolve the plain truth of Scriptures into vague speculation, particularly in the exposition of the NT, whose clear teaching about such matters as the resurrection of the body and final judgment must be taken at face value».

11 The School of Alexandria was established in Alexandria by Clement. It developed under Origen, moved with him to Caesarea in Palestine, and continued there after his death. The School of Antioch never existed. The name was associated with a group of bishop-theologian-exegetes who lived in or near Antioch. Lucian of Antioch, Diodore of Tarsus, Theodore of Mopsuestia, John Chrysostom and Nestorius are generally in- cluded in this group.

Tertullian is an early figure in biblical studies who does not fit into either group. He was perhaps the first exegete to set down specific rules for interpreting a text. The principles he used in approaching a text were: «progress from the known to the un- known, from the certain to the less certain; explain the obscure passages by the others which are generally clear in meaning; do not stop at the written word, but seek to know the spirit of the text; find in the NT the meaning of difficult OT passages». See A. CUNNINGHAM, «Reading the Scriptures», 194; and T.P. O'MALLEY, *Tertullian and the Bible*.

but only supersedes it. The Antiochenes on the other hand emphasized the *literal sense* as the foundational meaning. This does not eliminate other meanings but any extended meaning had to be rooted in or related to the *literal sense*.

Origen had identified the *literal sense* as either a verbal or historical meaning. The Antiochenes began to incorporate the notion of the author's intention with the earlier understanding of the *literal sense*[12]. «According to the Antiochenes, whatever God wished to reveal to us in the Scriptures was also understood in some way by the inspired authors, and therefore any higher meaning given to a passage must be solidly based on the direct, literal meaning of the passage»[13]. As a result, any theological or doctrinal development would be based on their exegetical work[14].

Although the Antiochenes emphasized the *literal sense* as the basis for interpretation they also recognized a *spiritual sense* in the biblical texts. The term used to describe the Antiochene approach to the *spiritual sense* is *theoria*[15]. According to the *theoria*, the *spiritual sense* of a passage will flow out of the *literal sense*. In other words it will be based on the *literal sense*. So that the *spiritual sense* is in reality an aspect of the *literal sense*. «The *theoria* would be used especially to explain the prophecies of Christ

---

[12] D.S. DOCKERY, *Biblical Interpretation* , 103, considers Theophilus of Antioch as the earliest representative of the historical approach. Theophilus' method is reflected in his letter to Autolycus. When he comments on Genesis 3:8, he is confronted with an anthropomorphism. He explains that «God walking» must refer to the second person of the Trinity. He refuses to make an allegory in favor of a literal-historical interpretation of the text. The pattern continues throughout his work. See THEOPHILUS, *To Autolycus*, 2.22. English trans.: ANFa 2, 103.

[13] L.F. HARTMAN, «St. Jerome as an Exegete», 50. Hartman continues his comments with a contrast: «According to the Alexandrians, on the other hand, God's message to us in the inspired books often surpassed the understanding of the human author of those books: and therefore, since God's meaning need not be tied down so rigorously to the direct sense as intended by the human authors, a passage may often be interpreted in a figurative way (tropologically or allegorically they called it) so that we may arrive at the fuller, higher meaning intended by God». W.J. BURGHARDT, «On early Christian Exegesis» 88, notes that Theodore of Mopsuestia's first rule in exegesis was discovering the author's intention.

[14] D.S. DOCKERY, *Biblical Interpretation*, 127; M.F. WILES, «Theodore of Mopsuestia», 192.

[15] For further reading on *theoria* see D.S. DOCKERY, *Biblical Interpretation*, 107; B. DE MARGERIE, *An Introduction,* 165-187; B. NASSIF, «The "Spiritual Exegesis" of Scripture» 438-456; A. VACCARI, «La θέωρια antiochena nella scuola esegetica di Antiochia».

in the OT»[16]. The basis of this emphasis was the belief that the biblical passages «could never be separated from the institutions and events to which they refer, rather they should be studied precisely in context, in the light that these events and institutions supply»[17]. The basics of this concept continued through the patristic period to the medieval period.

1.3 *Augustine*

Augustine developed his principles for studying the Scriptures in *De doctrina Christiana*[18]. He did not use the term *literal sense*; however, he did acknowledge the importance of the author's intention. He elaborated on this in the following passage:

> Whoever understands in the Sacred Scriptures something other than what the writer had in mind is deceived, although they do not lie. Yet, as I began to say, if he is deceived in an interpretation by which, however, he builds up charity (which is the end of the precept), he is deceived in the same way as is someone who leaves the road through error, but makes his way through the field to the place where the road leads. Nevertheless, he must be corrected and shown how it is more advantageous not to leave the road, lest by a habit of deviating he may be drawn into a crossroads or even go the wrong way. By rashly asserting something which the author did not intend, he frequently runs into other passages which he

---

16 B. DE MARGERIE, *An Introduction to the History of Exegesis*, 169, notes that Chrysostom in his *Sixth Sermon on Penance*, 4, distinguishes between verbal prophecy and a typical prophecy. «Prophecy in type is that which takes place in deeds or in historical realities; the other prophecy is one in words. For God has persuaded some by highly insightful words, while he has bolstered the certitude of others, the less sophisticated, through the vision of events». L. PIROT, *L'oeuvre exégètique de Theodore de Mopsueste*, as quoted by DE MARGERIE, Ibid., 266, gives another example. Commenting on Chrysostom's exegesis of Matthew 2:14-15 which quotes Hosea 11:1 «Out of Egypt I have called my son», Pirot notes: «In the literal sense there is absolutely no doubt that Hosea's prophecy is alluding to the departure from Egypt; but in the typical sense, we must understand it as referring to Jesus Christ, of whom Israel was a figure». See B. DE MARGERIE, Ibid.,173, n. 23.

17 B. DE MARGERIE, *An Introduction*, 186.

18 A notable contemporary of Augustine was Jerome. L.F. HARTMAN, «St. Jerome as an Exegete», describes Jerome's hermeneutics as eclectic. The three primary influences on his work are Origen, the Antiochenes and the Rabbi's. Jerome incorporates elements from these three influences so that his exegesis includes allegorical, literal and rabbinical-style interpretations. His use of the *literal sense* can be found in his *Commentary on the Letter to Philemon*. Jerome's concept of the *literal sense* is that of the author's intention. Hartman, in part two of his article, discusses these three influences with examples from Jerome's writings. See also P. JAY, «Saint Jérôme et le triple sens de l'Écriture» and J.N.D. KELLY, *Jerome*.

cannot reconcile to that interpretation. If he agrees that these latter are true and definite, then the opinion which he had formed concerning the former cannot be true, and it happens, in some way or the other, that by loving his own opinion he begins to be more vexed at Scripture than at himself. If he allows this error to creep in, he will be utterly destroyed by it. «For we walk by faith and not by sight»[19].

Augustine later clarified cases where the authorial intention is difficult to ascertain. His basic rule in these cases was that an interpretation may be given as long as its meaning is derived from another Scripture passage[20]:

> Besides, not only one but perhaps two or more interpretations are under-stood from the same words of Scripture. And so, even if the meaning of the writer is unknown, there is no danger, provided that it is possible to show from other passages of the Scriptures that any one of them is in ac-cord with truth. A man who thoroughly examines the Holy Scriptures in an endeavor to find the purpose of the author (through whom the Holy Spirit brought Holy Scripture into being), whether he attains this goal or whether he elicits from the words another meaning which is not opposed to the true faith, is free from blame, if he has proof from some other pas-sage of the Holy Scriptures. In fact, the author perhaps saw that very meaning, too, in the same words which we are anxious to interpret. And, certainly, the Spirit of God who produced these words through him also foresaw that this very meaning would occur to the reader or listener; further, He took care that it should occur to him because it also is based upon truth. For, what could God have provided more generously and more abundantly in the Holy Scriptures than that the same words might be understood in several ways, which other supporting testimonies no less divine endorse?[21]

In *On the Profit of Believing* (*De Utilitate Credendi*), Augustine distinguishes between the *literal sense* as meaning tied to the words and the *figurative* sense as meaning tied to the intention. He notes the necessity of identifying the kind of language used in a passage before attempting to interpret it. If the text is figurative it should be interpreted figuratively, if

---

[19] AUGUSTINE, *De doctrina Christiana*, I.36-37.41. PL 34, 34-35. English trans.: FOC 4, 57-58. See also AUGUSTINE, *De consensu Evangelistarum*, I.2.4. PL 34, 1044. English translation NPNF, Series I.6, 78. Augustine uses authorial intention to explain the differences between Matthew and Luke's infancy narratives. He says that Matthew presented the «record of the Incarnation according to royal lineage» while Luke «occupied himself with the priestly lineage and character of the Lord». For text see footnote 130.

[20] Similar to Tertullian's rule of explaining the unknown by the known.

[21] AUGUSTINE, *De doctrina Christiana*, III.27.38. PL 34, 80. English trans.: FOC 4, 147.

the text is a literal text it should be interpreted literally[22]. In these cases the author's intention while writing is the basis of the distinctions[23].

1.4 *The Beginning of the Medieval Period*

Gregory the Great speaks of three steps in exegesis. The first step is the identification of the literal-historical sense of a text. From this point the typical sense can be identified and expounded upon and finally the moral sense should be elaborated. Gregory's principles show that by the end of the patristic period the *literal sense* was becoming the starting point and foundation for biblical interpretation.

The medieval period witnessed a decline in exegetical studies[24]. The study of Scriptures, as well as education in general, moved into the monastery during this period. Charlemagne started a revival in education with his organization of schools. This eventually led to the establishment of universities in the twelfth century. The two main developments for biblical studies in this period are the *gloss* and the *questio*.

The *gloss* were collections of comments or reflections of the Fathers that would be written in-between or surrounding the sacred text. The biblical text was then studied from a Patristic perspective[25]. Critiques of the

---

[22] AUGUSTINE, *On the Profit of Believing*, 5. PL 42, 68. NPNF, Series I, III, 349. Augustine states: «All that Scripture therefore, which is called the OT, is handed down fourfold to them who desire to know it, according to history, according to ætiology, according to analogy, according to allegory [...] Thus (for example) it is handed down according to history, when there is taught what hath been written, or what hath been done; what not done, but only written as though it had been done. According to ætiology, when it is shown for what cause any thing hath been done or said. According to analogy, when it is shown that the two testaments, the old and new, are not contrary to one another. According to allegory when it is taught that certain things which have been written are not to be taken in the letter, but are to be understood in a figure».

[23] It is best to avoid categorizing Augustine's exegesis as either literal or spiritual. As with most Fathers, the lines between literal and spiritual interpretations are not always that clear. See Augustine's various commentaries on the *Book of Genesis* for examples.

[24] J. LECLERCQ, «From Gregory the Great to St. Bernard», 185.

[25] B. SMALLEY, «The Exposition», 204, uses the following quote from a prologue to the glossed Apocalypse to show the authority of the gloss:

And full knowing of mickle truth, That now is his, its great truth;
What they mean in their kind, Witness the gloss and ye shall find
It as a key that will unlock, The Door that is full fast stuck.

The chief figures of this period were: Alcuin, Rabanus Maurus, and Walufrid Strabon. B. SMALLEY, *The Bible in the Middle Ages*, 43 notes that during this period the study of Hebrew began to revive.

gloss by Robert of Melum and others eventually lead to is disuse[26]. The *questio* was a method that subjected the text to a series of questions seeking to identify all the possibilities for meaning. In some cases the *questio* was used to ascertain the *literal sense* of the text. For example, Drogo, Lanfranc, and Berengar «use dialectic in order to tunnel underneath their text; they attempt to reconstruct the logical process in the mind of their author»[27].

A revival in Scripture studies comes in the twelfth century primarily with the work of the Victorines, monks of the Abbey of St. Victor in Paris. Hugh was the first Victorine to have an impact on Scripture studies. As a result of his contact with Jewish commentators of the day, he began a revival of Scripture studies. These studies were based on the *literal sense*. For example, Hugh believed that the OT should be studied

> with the help of Hebrew and with the aid of all that could be known about the history of the biblical world, its geography and the manners and customs then in force. He believed that the text thus studied provided a sacred history and that the sacred history provided the framework in terms of which theology and doctrine should be studied[28].

Hugh carefully made the distinction between the *literal* and *spiritual senses*, teaching his students not to consider the *spiritual sense* until the *literal sense* was first established[29]. For Hugh the *literal sense* is «not the word, but what it means; it may have a figurative meaning; and this belongs to the *literal sense*. To despise the *literal sense* is to despise the whole of Sacred literature»[30]. Hugh's pupil, Andrew of St. Victor, continued the work of his teacher in the development of the *literal sense* as the basis for exegesis. All other senses were considered secondary to the *literal sense*.

---

[26] B. SMALLEY, *The Bible in the Middle Ages*, 229, states: «Robert analyzes the various ways in which an excerpt from authority can be made. You can abridge your original, retaining both the sense and the diction; you can retain the sense, while altering the diction; or you can alter both. The glosses, he complains, do often differs from their originals in sense, in diction and in sequence. Further, by removing a passage from its context you may alter its meaning, even if you keep the diction intact. And you do violence to your author if you change his words, even if you retain the sense. To quote the emphatic conclusion: the glosses have no authority from the mere fact of being glosses: «Hence we deny that a person expounding the sense of an author and changing his words is the spokesman of authority».

[27] B. SMALLEY, *The Bible in the Middle Ages*, 72-73.

[28] J. ROGERSON – C. ROWLAND – B. LINDARS, *Study and Use of the Bible*, 68.

[29] B. SMALLEY, *The Bible in the Middle Ages*, 230.

[30] B. SMALLEY, «The Exposition», 93.

Albert the Great emphasized the *literal sense* to the point of dismissing allegorical interpretation as logically absurd; his understanding of the *literal sense* was tied to the intention of the author[31]. Smalley gives an example from Albert's exegesis:

> In commenting on the temptation of our Lord in the wilderness to change stone into bread, he says «this is the literal truth», and goes on to reject the conventional comparisons between the hard stone and the Law, or the sinner's heart: «I think it an absurd exposition, and contrary to the mind of the author»[32].

Toward the end of the patristic period the *literal sense*, although it was certainly not the exclusive sense, was beginning to have a foundational role in the interpretation of the Scriptures. During the medieval period, the question of the meaning of Scriptures and the senses of Scripture continued to be discussed and questioned, especially regarding the relationship between the senses. Although many saw the *literal sense* as the basis of the other senses, the question was by no means closed.

1.5 *Thomas Aquinas*

Thomas Aquinas argued in favor of the *literal sense* when discussing the senses of Scripture[33]. He first mentioned the four senses which scholars at that time were applying to the Scriptures (historical or literal, allegorical, tropological or moral, and anagogical)[34]. The result of this type of exegesis was the emergence of multiple meanings for a single passage. Thomas critiqued the practice as a source of confusion and deception.

He rather saw the meaning of a text as tied to the *literal sense*. Thomas began with a distinction between words and things. He noted that words have meaning as do the things they represent. He then distinguished the *literal sense* from the *spiritual senses*. The *literal sense* represents the basic meaning of the words. The *spiritual sense* represents the meaning

---

[31] J. ROGERSON – C. ROWLAND – B. LINDARS, *Study and Use of the Bible*, 287.

[32] B. SMALLEY, *The Bible in the Middle Ages*, 299.

[33] THOMAS AQUINAS, *Summa Theologica*, Ia.10.1-3. The English translation cited here is from T. GILBY, *Summa Theologica*, 36-41.

[34] R. GRANT – D. TRACY, *A Short History of Interpretation*, 85. The traditional grouping is based on a short Latin verse «*littera gesta docet, quid credas allegoria, moralis quid agas, quo tendas anagogia*» — «the letter shows us what God and our fathers did; the allegory shows us where our faith is hid; the moral meaning gives us rules of daily life; the anagogy show us where we end our strife».

signified by the things represented by the words. Thomas further noted that the *spiritual sense* «is based on and presupposes the *literal sense*»[35].

The *spiritual sense* is divided into three distinct senses: the allegorical, the moral, and the anagogical. The *allegorical sense* «is brought into play when the things of the old law signify the things of the new law». The *moral sense* describes «the things done in Christ and in those who pre-figured him are signs of what we should carry out». The *anagogical sense* signifies «the things that lie ahead in eternal glory»[36].

The *literal sense* is the meaning that the author intends, «and the author of Holy Scripture is God who comprehends everything all at once in his understanding». Aquinas while referring to Augustine notes the possibility of multiple meanings for the *literal sense* in three points.

First, the possibility for multiple meaning does not set up «ambiguity or any other kind of mixture of meaning», because the multiplicity is not based on the terms but the things they signify. This things can be signs of other things. «Consequently holy Scripture sets up no confusion, since all meanings are based on one, namely the *literal sense*... for nothing neces-sary for faith is contained under the *spiritual sense* that is not openly con-veyed through the *literal sense* elsewhere»[37].

Second, the *literal sense* has three aspects: historical, etiological, and analogical. Aquinas, referring to Augustine's explanation, states: «you have history when any matter is straight forwardly recorded; etiology when its cause is indicated, as when our Lord pointed to men's hardness of heart as the reason why Moses allowed them to set aside their wives; analogy when the truth of one Scriptural passage is shown not to clash with the truth of another»[38].

Third, «the parabolic sense is contained in the *literal sense*, for words can signify something properly and something figuratively». In these cases the *literal sense* refers to the object signified. Aquinas gives the following example: «When Scripture speaks of the arm of God, the *literal sense* is not that he has a physical limb, but that he has what it signifies, namely the power of doing and making»[39]. Here Thomas placed Augustine's distinction between words and things from *De doctrina Christiana* in an Aristotelian framework[40]. God is the principal author of

---

[35] THOMAS AQUINAS, *Summa Theologica*, Ia.10.1-3. English trans., 37.
[36] THOMAS AQUINAS, *Summa Theologica*, Ia.10.1-3. English trans., 37.
[37] THOMAS AQUINAS, *Summa Theologica*, Ia.10.1-3. English trans., 39.
[38] THOMAS AQUINAS, *Summa Theologica*, Ia.10.1-3. English trans., 39.
[39] THOMAS AQUINAS, *Summa Theologica*, Ia.10.1-3. English trans., 41.
[40] B. SMALLEY, «The Exposition», 215, explains «The Aristotelians thought in terms of causality rather than reflections. God, pure action, is the first mover, who

Holy Scripture who expresses meaning by «things», in other words historical events. On the other hand, human writers express meaning through words. So the *literal sense* is «what the human author expressed by his words; the *spiritual senses* are what the divine author expressed by the events which the human author related. Since the Bible is the only Book that has both a divine and human authorship, only the Bible can have both a *literal* and *spiritual sense*»[41]. So Aquinas safeguarded «the *spiritual sense* of Scripture, seeing them as senses intended by God but he allowed the *literal sense* to come fully into its own»[42]. The *literal sense* described in terms of the author's intention was considered the foundational sense of biblical interpretation from this time forward[43].

---

moves the inferior causes from potentiality to act. Just as the body won a new dignity, so the inferior causes won a power of action which they had not possessed in the Augustinian tradition and also reacted on Bible study. As God is the "first mover" of the universe, so he is the "first author" of Scripture; the sacred writers are authors too, chosen by God as instruments of his revelation, and acting under his motion but choosing their own words and their own material. Scripture began to seem less like a mirror of universal truth and more like a collection of works whose authors intended to teach particular truths; so exegesis was bound to resolve itself into the scientific study of these authors. The exegete fastened his attention on the letter, which represented the words chosen by them or by their translators as the apt test to express their meaning».

[41] B. SMALLEY, *The Bible in the Middle Ages*, 300.

[42] J. ROGERSON – C. ROWLAND – B. LINDARS, *Study and Use of the Bible*, 73. F.W. FARRAR, *History of Interpretation*, 269, would disagree. He notes that Thomas in his exegesis spent more time on the speculative and «he is meager in the explanation of the literal sense, but diffuse in speculative discussion and dialectic developments». Farrar, 290, further suggests that the greatest fault of the exegesis of this period was «the assumption that every part of Scripture admitted of a multiplex intelligence». He also criticizes the tying of Scripture to philosophy noting a comment by Erasmus that «if Jerome or Augustine could have come to life again they would have been derided for their ignorance, because they could not have understood such portentous words as "instances, relations, amplifications, restrictions, formalities, haecceiteies, and quiddities"».

[43] The exegetes who followed Thomas up to the time of the Renaissance and Reformation continued the stress on the *literal sense*. Nicholas of Lyre was heavily influenced by the work of the rabbis particularly Ibn Ezra and Rashi. F.W. FARRAR, *History of Interpretation*, 276, notes that Ibn Ezra distinguishes five different methods of biblical commentary: the verbal which dwells on every separate word; the subjective which pays no attention to tradition; the allegory which reads mysteries into the sacred text; the kabbalistic develops secrets out of letters, numbers and symbols; and the literal which confines itself to developing the actual meaning of the writers.

2. HCM Procedures in Patristic and Medieval Literature

Chapter I described the HCM as a collection of individual criticisms used in conjunction with one another. The criticisms attempt to solve problems in the biblical text and to explain difficult passages. In other words, the critical approach seeks to answer questions raised by the biblical text. The critical approach incorporates techniques or procedures to study a text and develops tools to aid that study. Elements of the critical approach have their root in the exegetical studies of the early Church. The elements include the following: techniques used to study the text; recognition of problems in the text that require critical investigation; and tools developed as an aid to a critical study of the texts.

The following section provides examples of these elements that are found in the literature of the Fathers and Scholars. The presentation will follow the outline of the HCM as described in the first chapter: introduction, textual criticism, philological analysis, literary criticism, genre criticism, and historical criticism. Tradition criticism and redaction criticism will be excluded since they developed based on the results of the source and form criticisms as practiced in the nineteenth and twentieth centuries. The first chapter noted that sometimes critical procedures can overlap. Some of the examples listed below may be applicable to more than one type of criticism. Citations will be used only once to avoid unnecessary repetition and to provide more variety in the examples. Cross-references will be provided when appropriate.

2.1 *Introduction*

The following section examines elements of the modern *Introduction* that are found in the patristic and medieval periods. The presentation discusses three aspects of the *Introduction*: a) the literary background for the modern *Introduction*, b) the question of «authorship» and its effect on biblical studies, c) the role of the intended audience and d) the importance of general background information for understanding biblical texts.

Literary Background for the Introduction. The *Introduction* developed as a technical text beginning with the work of Michaelis in the seventeenth century. In the patristic and medieval periods, however, literary forms developed that in content were similar to the modern *Introductions*. The roots of this type of presentation are found in the works of Theodore of Mopsuestia, Jerome, Hadrian, Cassiodorus, and Isidore of Seville. An even closer resemblance to the modern *Introduction* is found in the medieval period when Scripture scholars imitated the *Introduction* as used in the study of secular literature.

Theodore of Mopsuestia in the prefaces to his commentaries prefixes «a general introduction in which he discussed each book of the Bible as a whole. The authorship, date and content were carefully studied. The actual motives and insights of the writers were investigated, and great care was displayed in placing books in the correct historical settings»[44]. In a similar way, Jerome in his *Prologue to the Commentary on the Letter to Philemon* discusses the authorship question and the date of the composition[45].

Hadrian in his *Introductions* (ἐισαγωγη εἰς τὰς θείας γραφάς) gives guidelines for OT studies. Soggin views this work as the basis for the modern *Introduction*. In fact, the English term *introduction* is a translation of the Latin *introducio* which in turn is a translation of Hadrian's title, εἰσαγωγη[46]. Hadrian presents aspects of Hebrew thought, style and composition as expressed in the language of the OT. Included in the work is a discussion on biblical anthropomorphism from a linguistic perspective and a enumeration of literary devices with examples from the Scriptures (i.e. metaphor, parables, comparisons, synechdoche, paraphrase, recapitulation, allegory, irony, enigma)[47].

Cassiodorus' *The Institutes of Divine Literature* (*Institutiones divinarum litterarum*) is characterized as a «sort of introduction to the Scriptures and profane literature»[48]. Cassiodorus mentions the works of Tyconius, Augustine, Hadrian, Eucherius, and Julius Africanus as models for his presentation[49]. The work basically covers four areas. First, units of the Bible, the books along with their notable commentators, are listed according to sections (the Octateuch, the Prophets, the Psalms, etc.). Second, the canonical lists of Jerome, Augustine, and the LXX are presented.

---

[44] D.Z. ZAHAROPOULOS, *Theodore of Mopsuestia on the Bible*, 125-126. See also footnote 141.

[45] JEROME, *Prologue to the Commentary on the Letter to Philemon*. PL 26, 599-602. For an in-depth bibliography on Jerome and his work see D. BROWN, *Vir Trilinguis*, 203-231.

[46] J.A. SOGGIN, *Introduction to the Old Testament*, 3.

[47] PG 98, 1271-1312. V. NAZZARO, «Hadrian», 369, notes: «This work, which reveals a fine sense of language and originality in the distinction of rhetorical figures, is a passably good instrument for the interpretation of Scripture».

[48] M.L. ANGRISANI SNFILLIPPO, «Cassiodorus», 149. The second part of the *Institutes* deals with secular literature see PL 70, 1149-1218.

[49] CASSIODORUS, *Institutiones*, I.10.1. PL 70, 1110. W.G. KÜMMEL, *Introduction to the New Testament*, 26, regards these works as expositions and not true introductions. He is correct from this later vantage point. However, in this still early period of biblical exegesis these works provided basic information that would help the reader to understand the text — the same concept underlying the formalized *Introduction*.

Third, problems with the text such as transcriptions and orthography are discussed. Fourth, important figures of church history are identified.

Isidore of Seville was noted for his *Introductions (Prooemia)* to the Scriptures. The work presents the main elements of the biblical text in a very brief summary statement or list. The *prooemia* of Exodus, for example, includes the following items: the slavery of the Hebrews, the plagues in Egypt, the liberation from Egypt, the crossing of the Red Sea, the bestowal of the Decalogue, the establishment of the covenant[50]. Isidore treats the four *Gospels* as a unit as he does with the *Letters* of Paul. He notes, however, some of the distinctive characteristics of individual gospels. For example, he notes that Matthew was written in Judea, Mark in Italy, Luke in Achaia, and John in Asia Minor[51]. The identification of the «place of writing» is an important element in the later *Introduction*.

As the schools developed in the Middle Ages, the Bible became a subject for study along with other works of antiquity. The procedures used in lectures on these ancient texts, biblical and secular, included the *Introduction*. Smalley uses a lecture on the *Aeneid* as an example stating, «A lecturer on the *Aeneid* would begin with an account of the authorship, place, date and purpose of the poem; he would then go through it line by line or word by word, explaining the grammar and the allusions to history, mythology and geography to be found there»[52]. The material covered in this medieval type of introduction would be the basic format formalized in the work of Michaelis.

The Authorship Question. The identification of the authors of the individual biblical books has its root in tradition. For example, Moses was traditionally considered the author of the *Pentateuch*. This tradition is reflected in the Scriptures themselves. Ezra 6:18, for example, presumes mosaic authorship — «Finally, they set up the priest in their classes and the Levites in their divisions for the service of God in Jerusalem, as is prescribed in the book of Moses»[53]. Although questions concerning Mosaic authorship were not raised until the medieval period (see below page 77), the Fathers did question the authorship of other books traditionally associated or attributed to notable figures of salvation history. The discussion of biblical authorship was usually raised in association with canonical questions. Nevertheless, the discussions led to a study of authorship based on style and composition of the biblical text, similar in principle to

---

[50] ISIDORE, *Introductions*, 19. PL 83, 159.
[51] ISIDORE, *Introductions*, 91. PL 83, 176.
[52] B. SMALLEY, «The Exposition», 209.
[53] See also Ezra 3:2; Neh 8:1; 13:1; and Acts 28:23.

the *Introduction* of the HCM[54]. Examples of such questions are provided from Hippolytus, Clement, Origen, Dionysius, Jerome and Augustine.

Hippolytus in his *Commentary on the Psalms* (εἰς τοὺς ψαλμούς) breaks with the traditional view of Davidic authorship of the *Psalms*. He does not deny Davidic authorship altogether but rather suggests multiple authors for individual psalms in the collection:

> The Hebrews give the book the title *Sephra Thelim* (*Book of Praises*) and in the *Acts of the Apostles* it is called the *Book of Psalms* (the words are these, «as it is written in the Book called *Psalms*» Acts 1:20), but the name of the author in the inscription of the book is not found there. And the reason of that is, that the words written there are not the words of one man, but those of several together; Ezra, as tradition says, having collected in one volume, after the captivity, the psalms of several, or rather their works, as they are not all psalms. Thus the name of David is prefixed in the case of some, and that of Solomon in others, and that of Asaph in others. There are some also that belong to Jeduthun; and besides these there are others that belong to the sons of Korah, and even to Moses. As they are therefore the words of so many thus collected together, they could not be said by anyone who understands the mater to be by David[55].

Clement of Alexandria discusses the authorship of *Hebrews* in his *Hypotyposeis*[56] ('Υποτυπώσεις). Clement sees similarities of style shared between *Hebrews* and *The Acts of the Apostles*. He concludes that the Greek edition was a Lucan translation of a Pauline original written in Hebrew:

> And as for the *Letter to the Hebrews*, he says indeed that it is Paul's but that it was written for Hebrews in the Hebrew tongue, and that Luke, having carefully translated it, published it for the Greeks; hence, as a result of this translation, that same complexion of style is found in this *Letter* and in the *Acts*: but that the (words) «Paul an apostle» were naturally not prefixed. For, says he, «in writing to Hebrews who had conceived a prejudice against him and were suspicious of him, he very wisely did not repel them at the beginning by putting down his name[57].

---

54 Later investigations would reveal different meanings of «author» in the ancient world such as the actual writer of a particular work, the editor/compiler of earlier works, or the inspiration behind a written work.

55 HIPPOLYTUS, *On the Psalms*, 1. PG 10, 608. English trans.: ANFa 5, 199.

56 EUSEBIUS, *HE*, VI.14.1. In this paper, all English quotations from the *HE* are taken from K. LAKE – J.E.L. OULTON, *Eusebius: Ecclesiastical History*, I-II.

57 Clement as quoted by EUSEBIUS, *HE*, VI.14.1. Clement later modifies his views concerning the reason for Paul's name not being attached to the letter. He sees the ab-

Origen, in his *Homilies* ('ομιλίαι), also questions the authorship of *Hebrews*. After noting differences between this *Letter* and other Pauline writings based on language and style, he sees similarity among the writings based on theological content. He states:

> That the character of the diction of the epistle entitled *To the Hebrews* has not the apostle's rudeness in speech, who confessed himself rude in speech, that is, in style, but that the epistle is better Greek in the framing of its diction, will be admitted by everyone who is able to discern differences in style. But again, on the other hand, that the thoughts of the epistle are admirable, and not inferior to the acknowledged writings of the apostle, to this also everyone will consent as true who has given attention to reading the apostle.... But as for myself, if I were to state my own opinion, I should say that the thoughts are the apostle's, but that the style and composition belong to one who called to mind the apostle's teachings and, as it were, made short notes of what his master said. If any church, therefore, holds this epistle as Paul's, let it be commended for this also. For not without reason have the men of old time handed it down as Paul's. But who wrote the epistle, in truth God knows. Yet the account which has reached us (is twofold), some saying that Clement, who was bishop of the Romans, wrote the epistle, others, that it was Luke, he who wrote the *Gospel* and the *Acts*[58].

Dionysius of Alexandria discusses the authorship of *Revelation* in the second book of *On Promises* (Περὶ ἐπαγγελιῶν). The discussion comes as a response to those who would reject the canonical status of *Revelation* by denying apostolic authorship. Traditionally *Revelation* was associated with the Johannine writings (*Gospel* and *Letters*). Dionysius defends the canonical status but insists that authorship is an open question[59]. The question is approached in three ways. First, Dionysius dis-

---

sence of Paul's name in «deference to the Lord and because he wrote to the Hebrews out of his abundance, being (primarily) a preacher and apostle of the Gentiles».

[58] EUSEBIUS, *HE*, VI.25.13. All copies of Origen's original work are lost. Fragments are preserved through quotations and references by other authors. The authorship and canonical status of the *Letter to the Hebrews* caused much discussion in the early Church. Tertullian questions the authorship of *Hebrews* in his *On Morality* (*De pudicitia*). Though traditionally associated with Paul, Tertullian suggests Barnabas. No reasons are listed. For a discussion on Augustine's thought on the authorship of Hebrews see, R.F. COLLINS, «Augustine of Hippo», 137; A.-M. LA BONNARDIERE, «L'Épître aux Hébreux dans l'oeuvre de saint Augustin». For a general discussion on the canonicity of *Hebrews* see H.Y. GAMBLE, *The New Testament Canon*, 50-56.

[59] EUSEBIUS, *HE*, VII.25.4. All copies of Dionysius' original work are lost. Fragments are preserved in quotations and references by other authors. See *HE*, VII.4-7. 24-25.

cusses authorship on the basis of specific references to authorship in the books. *Revelation* identifies John several times as its author while the *Gospel* and *Letters* have no proper identification of their author. Dionysius concludes that *a* John wrote *Revelation* because the author says so, but he is not necessarily the author of the *Gospel* and *Letters*. Second, Dionysius discusses authorship based on the content of the works. He notes the similarities between the *Gospel* and *Letters*[60] then concludes that neither the *Gospel* nor the *Letters* contain any mention of nor thought contained in *Revelation*[61]. Third, Dionysius compares the style of writing in each work and suggests different authors:

> One can estimate the difference between the *Gospel* and *Letters* and the *Apocalypse*. For the former are not only written in faultless Greek, but also show the greatest literary skill in their diction, their reasonings, and the constructions in which they are expressed. There is a complete absence of any barbarous word, or solecism, or any vulgarism whatever. For their author had, as it seems, both kinds of word, by the free gift of the Lord, the word of knowledge and the other of speech. But I will not deny that the other writer had seen revelations and received knowledge and prophecy; nevertheless I observe his style and that his use of the Greek language is not accurate, but that he employs barbarous idioms, in some places committing downright solecisms. These there is no necessity to single out now. For I have not said these things in mockery (let no one think it), but merely to establish the dissimilarity of these writings[62].

Jerome identifies the authors of several biblical books in his *On Illustrious Men (De viris illustribus)*. When listing the Apostles he notes the literary works ascribed to them. Regarding *The Letters of Peter*, Jerome

---

[60] Dionysius as quoted in EUSEBIUS, *HE*, VII.25.20-23, states: «For indeed a mutual agreement between the Gospel and the Epistle, and they begin alike. The one says: "In the beginning was the Word"; the other: "That which was from the beginning". The one says: "And the Word became flesh, and dwelt among us (and we beheld his glory, glory as of the only-begotten from the Father)"; the other, the same words slightly changed: "That which we have heard, that which we have seen with our eyes, that which we beheld, and our hands handled, concerning the Word of life; and the life was manifested"..... But the attentive reader will find frequently in one and the other "the life", "the light", "turning from darkness"; continually "the truth", "the grace", "the joy", "the flesh and blood of the Lord", "the judgment", "the forgiveness of sins", the love of God toward us", "the commandment that we should love one another", "that we should keep all the commandments"; "the conviction of the world", of "the devil", of the "antichrist"; the promise of the Holy Spirit; the adoption of the sons of God; the faith that is demanded of us throughout; "the Father" and "the Son": these are to be found everywhere».

[61] EUSEBIUS, *HE*, VII.25.24.

[62] EUSEBIUS, *HE*, VII.25-27.

states «He (Peter) wrote two *Letters* which are called *Catholic*, the second of which, on account of its difference from the first in style, is considered by many not to be by him»[63]. The reference demonstrates once again that the style of writing was used as a criteria to determine authorship.

Augustine discusses the authorship of Wisdom and Qoheleth while considering their canonicity. The works were traditionally associated with Solomon but Augustine sees ben Sirach as the author.

> As to the two books, one of which is entitled *Wisdom* and the other *Ecclesiasticus*, these are said to have been Solomon's, because of a certain likeness of style. Yet Jesus the son of Sirach is asserted most consistently to have written them. However, they must be counted among the prophetical books, because they have deserved recognition for their authority[64].

The Role of the Intended Audience. The role of the intended audience is also addressed in the modern *Introduction*. The audience can affect the selection of material or contents to be included in the text as well as the manner by which an author presents his material. This understanding is also found in the patristic period. Chrysostom notes differences in the content and presentation among the four Gospels in his *Homily on the Gospel of Matthew* (see page 82). He recognizes the role of the intended audience on the author of a writing by suggesting that Matthew and Mark were solicited by the community to write their gospels. The influence of the audience can be seen in the language and content of the composition. Chrysostom states:

> Of Matthew again it is said, that when those who from among the Jews had believed came to him, and besought him to leave to them in writing those same things, which he had spoken to them by word, he also composed his Gospel in the language of the Hebrews. And Mark too, in Egypt, is said to have done this self-same thing at the entreaty of the disciples. For this cause then Matthew, as writing to the Hebrews, sought to show nothing more, than that He was from Abraham, and David; but Luke, as discoursing to all in general, traces up the account higher, going on even to Adam. And the one begins with His generation, because nothing was so soothing to the Jews as to be told that Christ was the off-

---

[63] JEROME, *De viris illustribus*, I. E.C. RICHARDSON, *Liber de viris illustribus*. English trans.: LNPF, Ser. 2, III, 359.
[64] AUGUSTINE, *De doctrina Christiana*, II.8.13. English trans.: FOC 4, 71.

spring of Abraham and David: the other doth not so, but mentions many other things, and then proceeds to the genealogy[65].

General Background For Understanding the Texts. Several of the Fathers showed an interest in the historical and geographical backgrounds to the Scriptures, material that is included in modern *Introductions.* Eusebius and Jerome both had *onomastica* that cataloged the place names of the holy land contained in the Scriptures giving the locations of such places and their names at that time[66]. D. Brown suggests that Jerome's interest in the geography and topography of the land was «to assist him in a correct understanding of the *literal sense* of Scripture»[67]. Jerome gives his own argument on the importance of biblical geography in understanding the sacred texts:

> Just as those understand Greek history better who have visited Athens, and appreciate better the *Third Book of Virgil* who have sailed for Troy, passed Leucates and Aeroceraunum, to Sicily, and from there to the mouth of the Tiber, so also will he have a clearer perception of the sense of Holy Writ who gazes on Judea with his own eyes and recalled at their own sites the stories of its ancient cities, whose names are either still the same or have been changed[68].

---

[65] CHRYSOSTOM, *Homily on the Gospel of Matthew*, I.7. PG 57, 22. English trans.: NPNF, Series I, X, 3-4.

[66] EUSEBIUS, *Onomasticon.* PG 23, 903-976. JEROME, *Onomasticon.* CCh.SL 72, 57-161. Jerome used Eusebius' *Onomasticon* as the basis for his first part, the *Liber locorum.* He included additional locations and made corrections to the earlier work. He also added a second book, the *Liber nominum,* which listed all the proper names in the Scriptures and endeavored to explain their etymological roots. Some of the etymological explanations were a good philological analysis others were more speculative. For further reading and bibliography see J. QUASTEN, *Patrology,* III, 336; IV, 228; T.D. BARNES, «The Composition of Eusebius' Onomasticon'». In a later era, the Venerable Bede wrote his own collection of biblical names. See *De nominibus locorum quae leguntur in libro Actuum Apostolorum* PL 92, 1033-1040; PL 23, 1297-1306; and *De locis sanctis,* PL 94 1170-1190.

[67] D. BROWN, *Vir Trilinguis,* 137. See also J. WILKINSON, «L'Apport de saint Jérôme».

[68] JEROME, *Preface to the Chronicles (Paralipomenon).* PL 29, 401-402. L.F. HARTMAN, «St. Jerome as an Exegete», 75, notes that even though Jerome had an appreciation for the historical aspect of Scriptures especially in his later years, he «never completely abandoned the allegorical method, not merely because it was in vogue in those days and was expected of him by his readers, but also because he himself was convinced of the utility or even necessity of such exegesis. For him the Bible was not meant to be the plaything of man's minds; it was a heaven-sent manna for men's hearts and spiritual nourishment for their souls».

2.2 *Textual Criticism*

Textual problems have been recognized throughout the history of the church[69]. Despite the disputes about methodology in the patristic period between the Alexandrians and Antiochenes and in the current period between exegetes supporting diachronic methodology and those supporting synchronic methodologies, a general consensus exists recognizing the importance of textual criticism. This section presents examples of textual criticism from the works of Justin, Theodotus, Julius Africanus, Origen, Eusebius, Lucian of Antioch, Theodore of Mopsuestia, Jerome, and Augustine. It concludes with a short summary of the practices in the medieval period.

Justin Martyr's *Dialogue with Trypho* provides an early example of a textual problem. Justin, in his discussion with Trypho, defends Jesus' messiahship by quoting Isa 7:10-17. Justin argues: «Now it is evident to all, that in the race of Abraham according to the flesh no one has been from of a virgin, or is said to have been born of a virgin, save this our Christ»[70]. Trypho responds to Justin's arguments: «The Scripture has not, "Behold, the virgin shall conceive, and bear a son", but "Behold, the young woman shall conceive, and bear a son", and so on, as you quoted»[71]. Trypho is alluding to a discrepancy between the Hebrew text and the LXX. The LXX version of Isa 7:14 uses the word παρθένος which is translated «virgin», while the Hebrew has העלמה which is translated «young girl or maiden». Trypho recognizes this difference in the texts and is making his argument based on this difference. In a sense this argument is calling for a text critical study of the passage. Though the problem is not acknowledged by Justin, it is one of the earliest writings to display a textual problem at the root of a theological debate[72].

---

[69] Using the current scientific terminology could pose some problems if the usage is misunderstood. In no way should it be suggested that the Fathers or theologians of the Middle Ages were text critics in the modern sense. The vocabulary would not have been used, and the definition that we use today would apply only in a limited sense. This should not be viewed as a negative judgment. The resources that are available today such as the catalogued and reproduced copies of the MSS were not available in the early church.

[70] JUSTIN MARTYR, *Dialogue with Trypho*, 66. PG 6, 480. English trans.: ANFa I, 230.

[71] JUSTIN MARTYR, *Dialogue with Trypho*, 67. PG 6, 482. English trans.: ANFa I, 231.

[72] For a discussion of the problem from a philological approach see JEROME, *Liber Hebraicarum quaestionum* PL 23, 973-974; *Commentarius in Isaiam prophetam*, PL 24. 107-110.

Theodotus' awareness of textual problems and the need for careful study is evident from a passage in the *HE*. Eusebius mentions his role in the reproduction of sacred texts. The passage gives witness to several elements of textual criticism from this period including the recognition of numerous copies of the Scriptures, the need to collect and compare the texts, the recognition of discrepancies among the copies, the need for correcting texts with care, and the practice of emendation (which Eusebius discourages)[73].

Julius Africanus and Origen, in their *Correspondences*, discussed textual problems proposed by the use of the LXX. The questions raised by Julius and discussed by Origen concern not only possible mistranslation in the Greek text but also differences between the two texts regarding content. Julius, for example, mentions the last two passages from *Daniel* which are not «received among the Jews». Origen acknowledges the differences and notes that there are many other discrepancies between the two texts[74]. After giving numerous examples, he then concludes that it is important to study both texts and to note the various readings[75].

Origen is the first Father to designate principles for textual criticism when «in his commentaries he refers to NT readings that are supported by the *few, many*, or *most*, manuscripts accessible to him»[76]. His greatest contribution to textual studies was the *Hexapla*. The *Hexapla* was a book containing the text of the OT in six parallel columns. The first column contained the Hebrew text, the second column contained a transliteration of the Hebrew text into Greek characters, the third and fourth columns contained the Greek translations of Aquilla and Septimus Severus respectively, the fifth column contained the LXX translation and the sixth column contained the Greek translation of Theodotian. Included in the LXX column were the first symbols used for indicating textual problems. The «÷» or «obelus» was used to signify material added to the text, the addition concluded with «:» or «metobelus». The «✕» or «asterisk» signified missing material that was supplied from one of the other translations[77]. The *Hexapla* was held in the library at Caesarea and available to the monk-scholars working there. The early Scripture scholars, including

---

[73] EUSEBIUS, *HE*, V.28.16-19.

[74] ORIGEN, *To Julius Africanus*, 2. PG 11, 49. English trans.: ANFa 4, 386.

[75] ORIGEN, *To Julius Africanus*, 5. PG 11, 53. English trans.: ANFa 4, 390.

[76] E.J. EPP, «Textual Criticism: New Testament», *ABD* VI, 427. See also B.M. METZGER, «Explicit References in the Works of Origen».

[77] J. QUASTEN, *Patrology,* 44-45. See also S.P. BROCK, «Origen's Aims»; EUSEBIUS, *HE*, VI.14.1-10; R.W. KLEIN, *Textual Criticism of the Old Testament*, 7-10.

Jerome, would have been able to consult the various texts noting the similarities and differences so that they could determine the best reading[78]. Many scholars hold that only one copy existed due to the enormous size of the work. It is non-existent today except for a few fragments[79].

Eusebius' *Life of Constantine* (*Vita Constantini*) gives an important historical element regarding the transmission of the biblical text. Constantine wishing to provide copies of the Scriptures for the Diocese of Constantinople wrote to Eusebius asking for fifty copies. Constantine asks that the Scriptures be copied on parchment in a portable form by professional scribes[80]. Eusebius living at Caesarea used Origen's LXX version for the OT text. Some scholars, including Tischendorf, speculate that the Codex Sinaiticus and the Codex Vaticanus may have been two of the copies ordered by Constantine[81].

Lucian of Antioch also recognized problems posed by the various texts and translations of the Scriptures. Lucian, having a good knowledge of Hebrew, made his own corrections of the LXX text from the Hebrew text. J. Quasten notes that «This revision of the Septuagint was adopted by the greater number of churches of Syria and Asia Minor from Antioch to Byzantium, and was highly esteemed»[82].

Theodore of Mopsuestia occasionally makes reference to textual difficulties. Wiles points out that although Theodore considered the Hebrew text as fundamental[83], «he falls short of modern scholarly standards in not being led on by that conviction to the acquisition of a working knowledge of the Hebrew language for himself»[84]. Theodore's use of the LXX, however, was on a critical level. Zaharopoulos notes Theodore's excellent use of textual criticism of the LXX in his *Commentary on the Psalms*[85]. Re-

---

[78] See JEROME, *Prologue to the Commentary on Daniel*. CCh.SL 75a, 773-775.

[79] The series of textual notations are preserved in a Syriac translation of the fifth column of the *Hexapla* which has survived. For a modern reconstruction of the *Hexapla* see, F. FIELD, *Origenis Hexapla*. For bibliography see J. QUASTEN, *Patrology*, II, 45. J. GRIBOMONT, «Hexapla», 390.

[80] EUSEBIUS, *Vita Constantini*, 4. PG, 20, 953. English trans.: NPNF, Series 1, I, 549.

[81] J. BENTLEY, *The Secrets of Mt. Sinai*, 119-120.

[82] J. QUASTEN, *Patrology*, II, 142. Also see JEROME, *Ad Rufinium*, 2.27; B.M. METZGER, «Lucian and the Lucianic Recension».

[83] See Theodore's *Commentary on the Psalms*.

[84] M.F. WILES, «Theodore of Mopsuestia», 496.

[85] D.Z. ZAHAROPOULOS, *Theodore of Mopsuestia on the Bible*, 118. «He frequently introduced variant readings borrowed from Symmachus, Aquila, and Theodotion. Theodore, as usual, followed the text of the Septuagint which stands as the basis of his study of the Psalter, and apart from a certain number of instances in

garding the NT, Theodore occasionally notes a textual variant and his choice of reading[86].

Jerome's greatest contribution to textual studies was his Latin translation of the Scriptures, the *Vulgate*. Particularly important is his translation of the OT from the Hebrew texts. Prior to this translation the LXX was the primary text used in OT studies[87]. Jerome, however, thought the original language text, the Hebrew, should be the basis for any translation[88]. Jerome's arguments for the original text are summarized by Semple in five points. First, numerous LXX manuscripts were full of variations making the original version impossible to recover. Second, the LXX, even if one had the original translation, is still a translation. Third, the NT has at least five quotations from the OT that are not in the LXX but are in the Hebrew. Fourth, some of the respect shown the LXX was based on fable[89]. Fifth, «the principle of direct translation from the Hebrew had al-

---

which he accorded equal probability to the readings of the other Greek versions of the OT, the Mopsuestian did not seem to depart from the Alexandrian version».

[86] M.F. WILES, «Theodore of Mopsuestia», 497. See Theodore's *Letter to the Ephesians* in H.B. SWEETE, *Epistolas B. Pauli Commentarii*.

[87] The reasons for its high status include the following: the NT when citing the OT frequently uses the LXX text; some books in the LXX were not contained in the Hebrew text yet more often than not were considered canonical; and the Greek language was better known than Hebrew — in the East it was actually the spoken language.

[88] The LXX was so respected in the early Church that Augustine strongly objected to Jerome's use of the Hebrew text as the basis of his translation. However, he eventually dropped his objections. He informed Jerome in a letter: «As to your translation, you have now convinced me of the benefits to be secured by your proposal to translate the Scriptures from the original Hebrew, in order that you may bring to light those things which have been omitted or perverted by the Jews» (AUGUSTINE, *Letter* 82.5). See also R.F. COLLINS, «Augustine of Hippo», 140.

[89] Semple refers here to the legendary origin of the LXX. Eusebius quotes Irenaeus' account of these origins (EUSEBIUS, *HE*, V.8.3): «For before the Romans established their government, while the Macedonians still possessed Asia, Ptolemy, the son of Lagus, being very anxious to adorn the library, which he had founded in Alexandria, with all the best extant writings of all men, asked from the inhabitants of Jerusalem to have their Scriptures translated into Greek. They, for they were at that time still subject to the Macedonians, sent to Ptolemy seventy elders, the most experienced they had in the Scriptures in both languages, and God thus wrought what he willed. But Ptolemy, wishing to make trial of them in his own way, and being afraid lest they should have made some agreement to conceal by their translation the truth in the Scriptures, separated them from one another and commanded them all to write the same translation. And this they did in the case of all the books. But when they came together to Ptolemy, and compared each his own translation, God was glorified and the Scriptures were recognized as truly divine, for they all rendered the things in the same words and the same names, from beginning to end, so that even the heathen who were present knew that the Scriptures had been translated by the inspiration of God».

ready been accepted by the Church when it allowed Theodotian's translation to replace the LXX in parts of Job and Daniel»[90]. Jerome's appreciation of the Hebrew can be seen in his *Homilies on the Psalms*. In these
homilies, Jerome makes many references to the Hebrew text. He also
makes comments, sometimes elaborate, based on the titles that are found
only in the Hebrew text.

Jerome's guidelines for textual criticism are found in his biblical commentaries. Hulley outlines these principles. He categorizes thirteen types
of textual error familiar to Jerome: faulty word-division, faulty accentua-
tion, faulty punctuation, confusion of number signs, confusion of similar
letters, confusion of abbreviations, dittography and haplography, metathesis of letters, assimilation, omissions, transpositions, conscious emendation, and interpolations[91]. Hulley's article is a thorough review of these
principles with numerous examples from Jerome's writings that illustrate
them. Through these examples it is easy to recognize Jerome's excellence
in textual criticism. D. Brown notes that this excellence «was unmatched
in the early Church, even by Origen»[92].

Augustine's principles for textual criticism can be seen in his treatment
of Matt 27:9-10. The passage reads: «Then was fulfilled what had been
said through Jeremiah the prophet, "And they took the thirty pieces of
silver, the value of a man with a price on his head, a price set by some of
the Israelites and they paid it out for the potter's field just as the Lord had
commanded me"». The OT quotation poses a problem; it is not in *Jeremiah* but in *Zechariah*. In *De consensu Evangelistarum*, Augustine notes
the problem and attempts a solution using textual evidence. He begins by
noting that differences exist in the manuscripts, some readings have the
name Jeremiah and others have «spoken by the prophet». He acknowledges that it may be possible to argue that the reading without the name is
authentic. Augustine however supports reading the text with the name. His
reasons include the following. First the majority of manuscripts include
the name. Second, «those critics who have studied the Gospel with more
than usual care in the Greek copies, report that they have found it stated so
in the more ancient Greek exemplars». Third, the removal of the name is
more readily explained than an addition[93].

---

[90] W.H. SEMPLE, «St. Jerome as Biblical Translator», 237.

[91] For examples see K.K. HULLEY, «Principles of Textual Criticism», 89-101.
Also see B.M. METZGER, «St. Jerome's Explicit References».

[92] D. BROWN, «St. Jerome as a Biblical Exegete», 142.

[93] AUGUSTINE, *De consensu Evangelistarum*, III.7.29. PL 34, 1174; English
trans.: NPNF, Series 1, VI, 191. See also Testament, 153-154.

Text critical studies declined toward the end of the patristic period and the beginning of the medieval period due to a similar decline in Greek and Hebrew studies. The beginning of the decline can already be seen in Jerome's lifetime — neither Theodore nor Augustine knew Hebrew, and, Augustine struggled with Greek. Within this context the *Vulgate* eventually became the «set text» of the Western church, if not by definition certainly by usage[94]. As the *Vulgate* was becoming the standard text, text critical studies based on the original text suffered.

The textual critical work on the Scriptures during the medieval period was based on the *Vulgate* text[95]. Hugh of St. Victor, for example, makes a «literal Latin translation» when he was not satisfied with Jerome's translation[96]. An additional factor in the decline of textual criticism was the shift in emphasis from the study of the biblical text to the study of the *gloss* (see above page 51). In a certain sense the study of the Scriptures was being replaced with the study of the Fathers.

Although textual criticism was at a «low point» in the history of its development, one notable contribution was made during this period — the collection of lists of variant readings. The variants were collected in a literary work called *correctorium*.

> The *correctoria*, or lists of corrections and alternative readings, which were first introduced by the Dominicans, represented a specialization and systematization of the textual criticism in Stephen Langton's lectures. Their continuity with earlier scholarship appears in the frequent quotations of Andrew of St. Victor and Langton by Hugh of St. Cher in his correctorium[97].

The «return to the sources» of the Renaissance brought a resurgence in the study of Greek and Hebrew and the corresponding study of the origi-

---

[94] B. SMALLEY, *The Bible in the Middle Ages*, 197. See also, J. LECLERCQ, «From Gregory the Great», 183-184.

[95] J. LECLERCQ, «From Gregory the Great», 183, notes that versions other than the *Vulgate* were scarcely known in this period. Textual criticism in this era grappled with the variants among *Vulgate* manuscripts. By the late sixteenth century there were numerous editions of the *Vulgate*. The problems with numerous variants was recognized at the Council of Trent. The problem was solved by the call for one authorized version of the *Vulgate* to be used for public study and prayer. See *Decreta de sacris Scripturis*, II.61-64. *EB* 28.61-64. For text critical studies of the *Vulgate*, see R. LOEWE, «The Medieval History of the Latin Vulgate»

[96] B. SMALLEY, *The Bible in the Middle Ages*, 102. .

[97] B. SMALLEY, *The Bible in the Middle Ages*, 335.

nal language manuscripts[98]. Momentum in these studies increased with the invention of the printing press, and the publication edited versions of the Bible in the ancient languages.

2.3 *Philological Analysis — Grammatical Criticism*

Philological analysis or grammatical criticism is the third stage of the HCM as it is practiced today. The study is based on the original language texts of the OT and NT. The language studies are important not only for understanding the text in its original setting but also for accurately translating the text into modern languages. The roots of this study are found in the early church, especially in the patristic period, which is evident in several examples of the previous section. Although most of the early Fathers agree on the need for such studies[99], the importance an exegete places on language studies varied. This section presents examples from the patristic and medieval periods concerning the need for philological studies. The presentation will treat the following topics: a) hermeneutical principles and philological study, b) Jerome's appreciation of philology, and c) philological studies in the medieval period.

Hermeneutics and Philology. The previous section introduced the hermeneutical debates of the early church concerning the *senses of Scripture*. The hermeneutical approaches became a major determinant for the use of philological and grammatical analysis of a text. In fact it is on the philological level that the literal and allegorical approaches to interpretation have their most basic difference.

The literal approach sees the meaning of the words rooted in a concrete literary-historical framework. The meaning of a word is tied to the way it is used in its literary context — in a particular phrase, sentence, or passage. Theodore of Mopsuestia notes the importance of such meaning

---

[98] B. SMALLEY, *The Bible in the Middle Ages*, 218, notes two events that fostered the study of ancient languages. First, the translation of the *Koran* sponsored by Peter of Cluny in 1141-43. Second, the establishment of chairs of Greek and oriental languages in the principal schools and universities of Christendom ordered by the Council of Vienne in 1311-12.

[99] Most fathers appreciated the need for these studies, even those who had a limited knowledge of Hebrew and Greek. Augustine, for example, did not know Hebrew but saw its importance for understanding the meaning of the text. AUGUSTINE, *De doctrina Christiana*, II.11. PL 34, 42-43. English trans.: FOC 4, 73, states: «Men who know the Latin language, whom I have now begun to teach, have need of two others in order to understand the Sacred Scriptures. These are Hebrew and Greek, by which they may turn back to the originals if the infinite variances of Latin translators cause any uncertainty».

when he identifies his primary task in exegesis as explaining the «words that most people find difficult»[100].

Gen 1:29-30
«God also said: "See, I give you every seed-bearing plant all over the earth and every tree that has seed-bearing fruit on it to be your food; and to all the animals of the land, all the birds of the air, and all the living creatures that crawl on the ground, I give all the green plants for food." And so it happened».

Origen's Literal Interpretation	Origen's Allegorical Interpretation
The historical meaning, at least, of this sentence indicates clearly that originally God permitted the use of foods from vegetation, that is, vegetables and the fruits of trees. But the opportunity of eating flesh is given to men later when a covenant was made with Noah after the flood. The reasons for this, of course, will be explained more appropriately in their own places[101].	But allegorically the vegetation of the earth and its fruit which is granted to men for food can be understood of the bodily affections. For example, anger and concupiscence are offshoots of the body. The fruit of this offshoot, that is, the work, is common to us who are rational and to the beasts of the earth. For when we become angry justly, that is, for the reproach of one who is transgressing and for correction for his salvation, we eat of that fruit of the earth and the corporeal wrath with which we restrain sin, with which we restore justice, becomes our food[102].

Figure 4: Origen's Literal and Allegorical Interpretation's of Gen 1:29-30

The allegorical approach sees the contextual meaning of a word as less important than an allegorical meaning that can be attached to the word[103]. The meaning of the word, according to this approach, is determined by the interpreter within a larger framework of doctrine and tradition. The context for meaning in the allegorical approach is much broader than the literal approach with almost no limits to possible interpretations. A comparison will help clarify the differences in approach. Origen, while discussing

---

[100] THEODORE OF MOPSUESTIA, *Introduction to the Commentary of John*.

[101] ORIGEN, *Homily on Genesis I*, 17. PG 12, 161. English trans.: FOC 71, 69-70.

[102] ORIGEN, *Homily on Genesis I*, 17. PG 12, 161. English trans.: FOC 71, 70.

[103] M. SIMONETTI, *Lettera e/o Allegoria*, 19, notes the tendency to attribute diverse allegorical senses to one and the same Scripture passage was one of the distinctive characteristics of the Alexandrians. R.P.C. HANSON, «Biblical Exegesis», 412 noting the Jewish influence on this approach states: «every verse was regarded as potentially independent of the other and capable of interpretation without any reference to its context».

Gen 1:29-30, gives a literal interpretation followed by an allegorical inter-pretation. (see figure four above)

The analysis of the term «vegetation» is used here as an example. The literal interpretation of this text treats the words in their historical-literary context. The words represent a meaning rooted in the text itself. Thus the term «vegetation» refers to food that comes from plants. The allegorical interpretation separates the term from its contextual meaning and suggests an alternate meaning. In this case, the term «vegetation» refers to «affections of the body». The example serves to point out the difference between an allegorical and literal approach regarding philological studies. Exegetes who use a literal approach will have a greater need for philological analysis than exegetes using the allegorical approach.

Jerome's Appreciation of Philology. Jerome had an appreciation for philological studies that was evident in many of his works. He himself explains the importance of philological study while defending the Hebrew text of the OT in the *Preface to the Quaestiones Hebraicae in Genesim,*

> Therefore it shall be my concern both to rebut the errors of those who make different kinds of conjectures about the Hebrew books, and to re-store to their proper authority those things which in the Latin and Greek codices seem to burst forth in abundance; and to make plain through consideration of the native language the etymologies of objects, of names, and of territories which have no meaning in our own language. And so that the improvement be more easily recognized, we shall show, by comparison with what follows, what in them is either less, or more, or different.[104]

Jerome's appreciation of philology is most evident in his transla-tions[105]. Particularly significant is his translating the sense of a passage

---

[104] JEROME, *Preface to the Hebrew Questions in Genesis.* PL 23, 936. English trans.: C.T.R. HAYWARD, *Hebrew Questions on Genesis*, 29.

[105] For example see JEROME, *Homily 3*, 1. English trans.: FOC 48, 25. Several studies have discussed the extent of Jerome's proficiency in Hebrew. L.F. HARTMAN, «St. Jerome as an Exegete» suggests Jerome had a good speaking knowledge of He-brew. J. BARR, «St. Jerome's Appreciation of Hebrew», 290-91, disagrees suggesting Jerome had a total lack of conversational Hebrew because of the quickness of the trans-lation (the translation of Tobit was done with the aid of a translation of the Aramaic to Hebrew), and the detailed arguments on linguistic grounds that suggest Jerome got help with the difficult parts of the text.

For further reading on Jerome's knowledge of Hebrew and his translations see: E.P. ARNS, *La Technique*; J. BARR, «St. Jerome and the Sound»; J.H. BERNARD, «The Greek MSS»; D. BROWN, «St. Jerome as a Biblical Exegete»; E. BURNSTEIN, «La competence de Jérôme en Hébreu»; J.T. CUMMINGS, «St. Jerome as translator and

based on a contextual meaning of the words. In *Letter 57* he argues for such translations quoting several notable translators including Homer. In another work, the *Preface to the Chronicles of Eusebius*, he states:

> It is difficult in following lines laid down by others not sometimes to diverge from them, and it is hard to preserve in a translation the charm of expressions which in another language are most felicitous. Each particular word conveys a meaning of its own, and possibly I have no equivalent by which to render it, and if I make a circuit to reach my goal, I have to go many miles to cover a short distance. To these difficulties must be added the windings of hyperbola, differences in the use of cases, divergence of metaphor; and last of all the peculiar and if I may so call it, inbred character of the language. If I render word for word, the result will sound uncouth, and if compelled by necessity I alter anything in the order of the wording, I shall seem to have departed from the function of a translator[106].

Barr notes the significance of this principle: «by his translation for the *sense*, and abandoning the attempt to reproduce similarities in Hebrew verbal form, he often succeeded in escaping from the literalistic and etymological traps to which earlier translators had often fallen victim»[107].

Philology in the Middle Ages. No significant advances were made in philological studies during the medieval period[108]. The development of the *distinctio*, however, would help advance philological studies in a later period. The *distinctio* was a prelude to dictionaries and lexicons. A word was listed followed by examples of how the word has different meanings in different contexts usually related to the senses of Scripture. It helped the reader to understand literary devices in the Scriptures such as metaphor, allegory, symbol, and image[109]. Smalley uses the entry for «bed» as

---

exegete»; H. GOELZER, *Étude lexicographique* ; J.E.O. PREUS, *St. Jerome's Translation Terminology.*

[106] JEROME, *Letter 57*, 5. NPNF Ser. 2, VI, 114.

[107] J. BARR, «St. Jerome's Appreciation of Hebrew», 301.

[108] F.W. FARRAR, *History of Interpretation*, 286, notes that only one or two scholars had a «smattering» of Hebrew and the vast majority were ignorant of Greek.

[109] B. SMALLEY, *The Bible in the Middle Ages*, 246-247. Although F.W. FARRAR, *History of Interpretation*, 287 could refer to this practice as «a mere abuse of imaginary verbal resemblances», the practice did lead to a deeper appreciation for the various meanings a word could have in different contexts. The importance for our study is that the *distinctio* prepares the way for lexicons that catalog the various meanings of words including the figurative.

The first dictionary specifically intended for the NT was published in 1522. This version was a seventy-five unnumbered page work attached to the *Complutensis Polyglot*. W. BAUER – F.W. GINGRICH – F.W. DANKER, *A Greek-English Lexicon*, v,

an example. The entry includes the following uses: (the bed) of Scripture
— *Our bed is flourishing* (Canticles 1:15) representing the historical
sense, in other words the literal meaning of the Canticle is metaphorical;
of contemplation — *There shall be two men in one bed* (Luke 17:34) represents allegorical senses; of the Church — *Three score valiant ones sur-
rounded the bed of Solomon* (Canticles 3:7) represents an allegorical
sense; of conscience — *Every night I will wash my bed* (Psalm 7:7) represents the moral sense; of carnal pleasure — *You that sleep upon beds of
ivory* (Amos 6:4) represents the moral sense; of eternal punishment — *I
have made my bed in darkness* (Job 17:13) represents the anagogical
sense; of eternal blessedness — *My children are with me in bed* [Luke
11:7] represents the anagogical sense.

The resurgence in philological studies began in the fifteenth century.

> The same century (fifteenth) witnessed a marked development in philol-
> ogy, especially in the scientific pursuit of Hebrew and Greek grammars,
> lexicons, and texts of ancient authors were increasingly available, and the
> humanism of the day with its intense interest in the literature of pagan
> and Christian antiquity, seriously cultivated these languages[110].

2.4 *Literary Criticism*

The current practice of literary criticism did not develop until the nineteenth century. Elements of modern literary criticism that find their roots
in the patristic and medieval periods include the following: a) dividing the
text into smaller units, b) identifying elements of style and c) identifying
possible sources.

Division of the Text. The first step of modern literary criticism, as mentioned in Chapter I, is to divide the text into smaller units. In other words,
to make an outline of the text on the basis of content. The original texts
had no chapter and verse divisions; so the exegete would try to discern the
inner structure that an author gave to his work.

---

notes: «the incompleteness, inaccuracy, and elementary character of the glossary reflect
the low state of Greek studies at the time it was first published but it was the first and
useful succession of NT lexical works» The first NT dictionary with "scholarly preten-
sions" was *Lexicon Graeco-Latinum in Novum Testamentum* by Georg Pastor in
1619, followed by *Dictionarium Novi Testamenti* by Ludovicus Lucius in 1640.

110 R.E. MCNALLY, «The Council of Trent», 206. The development of grammars
and dictionaries helped foster the philological and grammatical analysis of the scriptures. The development of Greek and Hebrew grammars was preceded by Isidore of
Seville's *Etymologiarum*. This work is an early Latin grammar which uses numerous
examples from the biblical text. See W.M. LINDSAY, *Isidori: Etymologiarum*.

Pamphilius of Caesarea, in his *Exposition of the Acts of the Apostles*, provides an early example of dividing the text into units[111]. He divides the text into chapters and smaller subdivisions. He explains, «We make this exposition, therefore, after the history of Luke, the evangelist and historian. And, accordingly, we have indicated whole chapters by letters of the alphabet, and their subdivisions into parts we have noted by means of the asterisk»[112]. The following is an example:

C. Of the divine descent of the Holy Spirit on the day of Pentecost which lighted on them who believed. In this we have also * the instruction delivered by Peter, and * passages from the prophets on the subject, and * on the passion and resurrection and assumption of Christ, and the gift of the Holy Spirit; also * of the faith of those present, and their salvation by baptism; and, further, * of the unity of spirit pervading the believers and promoting the common good, and of the addition made to their number[113].

Biblical manuscripts also witness the division of texts into units and sub-units[114]. References to biblical passages, prior to standardization, were made by citing the first words of a passage or line. Chapter divisions were not added to the biblical texts until the thirteenth century. The work began in the Abbey of St. Victor in Paris. Eventually divisions became standardized. Division into verses did not occur until the sixteenth century. The systematic division of the text into units reflects an awareness of an inner structure to the text. The division into chapters and verses prepares for the development of concordances which give easy reference to words used in different contexts[115].

Literary Styles and Devices. One aspect of literary criticism, as practiced today, is the identification of style and devices in a particular work or corpus. Style was already described as an aid in determining authorship (see page 58). This section will present examples from the patristic and medieval periods demonstrating how the identification of style and literary

---

[111] The attribution of this work to Pamphilus is not universally acknowledged.

[112] PAMPHILUS, *Introduction to an Exposition to the Acts of the Apostles*. English trans.: ANFa VI, 166.

[113] PAMPHILUS, *Introduction to an Exposition to the Acts of the Apostles*. English trans.: ANFa VI, 166. The division eventually becomes Chapter 2 of Acts.

[114] B. METZGER, *The Text*, 22-23. The chapter divisions are called κεφάλαια. The oldest are preserved in the margins of the Codex Vaticanus. τίτλοι or chapter titles are another type of marker .

[115] J. ROGERSON – C. ROWLAND – B. LINDARS, *Study and Use of the Bible*, 283-284.

devices can help the exegete to determine the meaning of a text. Examples will be given from Jerome, Augustine, and Aquinas.

Jerome has a keen awareness of literary techniques such as assonance which many times was lost in translations, and etymological word plays. He mentions Jerome's analysis of the call of Jeremiah (Jer 1:11ff): «he was able to enjoy and explain the word play of *"saced"*, *"nux"* ("nut tree") and *"soced"*, *"vigilia"* ("watch")». His analysis of Isa 5:7-8 notes «that a word-play between *"mesphat"* and *"mesphaa"*, and between *"sadaca"* and *"saaca"* (judgment and bloodshed, justice and shouting), has produced what he (Jerome) calls an *"elegans structura sonusque verborum"*»[116].

Augustine discusses the art of rhetoric in the Scriptures in Book Four of *De doctrina Christiana*. Two examples are provided. First, Augustine recognizes the classical rhetorical device of *gradatio* or *climax* in Rom 5:3-5: «Not only that, but we even boast of our afflictions, knowing that affliction produces endurance, and endurance, proven character, and proven character, hope, and hope does not disappoint, because the love of God has been poured out into our hearts through the Holy Spirit that has been given to us»[117]. Second, he detects three distinct styles in the *Letter to the Galatians*—subdued, moderate, and grand[118]. In *De consensu Evangelistarum*, he notes differences in style and theme of the evangelists. For example he suggests that Matthew and Mark wished to emphasize the kingly aspect of Jesus when they arranged their material, while Luke wished to emphasize a priestly image (see below page 79)[119].

Thomas Aquinas', in the *Summa Theologiæ*, notes different types of speech in the Scriptures. He mentions poetry, allegory, metaphorical language, similes, and parables that affect the way one understands the text and the *literal sense* (see above page 53)[120].

---

116 See J. BARR, «St. Jerome's Appreciation», 292-293.

117 AUGUSTINE, *De doctrina Christiana*, IV .7.11. PL 34, 100-101. English trans.: FOC 4, 177.

118 AUGUSTINE, *De doctrina Christiana*, IV.20.44. PL 34, 110. English trans.: FOC 4, 213. After citing an example of the «grand» style in Galatians 4, Augustine asks: «In this passage have antithetical words balanced each other, have any words been joined to one another in a climax, or did *caesa, membra*, or periods ring in our ears? Nevertheless, not on that account is there any diminution in the stirring emotion with which we feel it vibrate».

119 AUGUSTINE, *De consensu Evangelistarum*, III.1.5. PL 34, 1048.

120 THOMAS AQUINAS, *Summa Theologica*, Ia.10.1-3. See T. GILBY, *Summa Theologica*, 36-41.

Background to Source Critical Approaches. Source criticism developed primarily in the nineteenth century with studies on the *Pentateuch* and *Synoptic Gospels*. Though the formal study of sources was a relatively late development, elements of that study can be found in the patristic and medieval periods.

The Church Fathers, along with the Jewish Rabbis basically accepted Mosaic authorship of the Pentateuch[121]. In the Middle Ages, discrepancies in the text raised some doubts concerning Mosaic authorship. These discrepancies included the following: Moses is spoken of in the third person; the *Pentateuch* includes an account of Moses' death (Deut 34); the Edomite kings list in Gen 36:31-39 includes kings who lived after Moses; the text «the Canaanite was in the land» (Gen 12:6; 13:7) reflects authorship at a time long after Moses, when the Canaanites no longer were the dominant people of the land, with the author informing a much later audience of a prior state of affairs; Moses is speaking «across the Jordan» (Deut 1:1), indicating authorship in Israel referring to Moses in the land of Moab; and «The *Pentateuch* reports that Moses "was very humble, more than every human on the face of the earth" (Num 12:3). It is difficult to imagine the humblest man on earth writing these words»[122]. The first detailed examinations of the text regarding Mosaic authorship were conducted later by Hobbes and Spinoza.

Synoptic studies in the nineteenth and twentieth centuries focused on the relationship between *Matthew*, *Mark* and *Luke*. Eventually it was established that a literary relationship of dependence exists among them. During the patristic period, comparisons were made between similar gospel passages seeking to determine their relationship (especially where differences occurred) and the effect that relationship has on the meaning of the text. Examples are provided from Julius Africanus, Eusebius, and Augustine.

Julius Africanus, in his *Epistle to Aristides*,[123] discusses the two genealogies of Jesus (Luke 1:5–2:52; Matt 1:1–2:23). The genealogies contain some differences both in content and presentation. Julian recognizes the differences and attempts to verify the historical accuracy of the text. He explains that Jewish family lines could be traced either through blood or legal lines. This would account for the two different presentations in the NT. He concludes:

---

[121] Jerome was the only notable exception. He held that Ezra compiled the Pentateuch from the notes of Moses.

[122] R.E. FRIEDMAN, «Torah», 618.

[123] Recalled by Eusebius in *HE*.

Thus neither of the evangelists is in error, as the one reckons by nature and the other by law. For the several generations, viz., those descending from Solomon and those from Nathan, were so intermingled by the raising up of children to the childless and by second marriages, and the raising up of seed, that the same persons are quite justly reckoned to belong at one time to the one, and at another time to the other, i.e. to their reputed or to their actual fathers. And hence it is that both these accounts are true, and come down to Joseph, with considerable intricacy indeed, but yet quite accurately[124].

Synoptic studies today are aided by a *synopsis*. A *synopsis* lists parallel Gospel passages as an aid for comparison (see above page 18). The first extensive comparison of parallel passages in the Gospels was done by Ammonius of Alexandria however no copies of the work have survived[125]. An early forerunner of the *synopsis* is Eusebius's *Evangelical Canons*[126]. The work was utilized by many of the Fathers including Jerome and quickly became a standard reference work in the study and use of the Scriptures[127]. Quasten explains Eusebius' organization of the gospel material:

He first divided the Gospels into small sections which were numbered in succession. He then prepared a table of ten canons, each containing a list of passages in the following order:

Canon I   passages common to all four Gospels;
Canon II   those common to the synoptics;
Canon III   those common to *Matthew, Luke* and *John*;
Canon IV   those common to *Matthew, Mark* and *John*;
Canon V   those common to *Matthew* and *Luke*;
Canon VI   those common to *Matthew* and *John*;
Canon VIII   those common to *Luke* and *Mark*;
Canon IX   those common to *Luke* and *John*;
Canon X   those peculiar to each Gospel: first to *Matthew*, second to *Mark*, third to *Luke* and fourth to *John*.

---

[124] JULIAN AFRICANUS, *To Aristides*, I.2. PG 10, 54. English trans.: ANFa VI, 126.

[125] See Eusebius, *HE*, VI.19. Eusebius used Ammonius' work while composing the *Evangelical Canons*.

[126] PG 22, 1275-1292.

[127] Jerome, for example, concludes *The Preface to the Vulgate Version of the New Testament* with a translation and transliteration of Eusebius' *Canons*. See PL 29, 562-764.

These tables used in combination with the numbers of the sections in the text of the Gospels enable the reader to discover at a glance the parallel passages[128].

Augustine's study on the relationships between the four gospels is titled *De consensu Evangelistarum*. In the preface to this work he establishes the principle that *Mark* was a summarization of *Matthew* — a theory that becomes the basis of synoptic studies for over 1000 years[129]. Augustine gives the order of gospel composition as *Matthew* first, followed by *Mark*, *Luke* and *John*. He suggests that *Matthew* was written in Hebrew then translated into Greek while the other evangelists originally wrote in Greek. Similarities and differences are also noted in the content of the four gospels[130]. The significance of this work, for this study, is that it recognizes differences among the gospels that require reasonable explanation.

2.5 *Genre - Form Criticism*

Although the formal study of genre and forms did not develop until Herman Gunkel's work in the late nineteenth century, elements exist in earlier exegesis such as identifying and categorizing literary patterns in a text. The major differences in the later development were the systematic approach to the study and the theory that an oral tradition underlies the text that connected it with a particular social setting. The following section will present examples from Theodore of Mopsuestia, Jerome and Augustine.

---

[128] J. QUASTEN, *Patrology*, III, 335.

[129] *De consensu Evangelistarum* is a «harmony» of the four gospels. A «harmony» interweaves the four gospels attempting to provide a unified chronological presentation. For a concise history of the «harmony» as a literary form, see M.B. RIDDLE, «Introductory Essay», 67-70. Harmonies were done before Augustine such as Titian's *Diatessaron*, and Ammonius' *Harmony*.

[130] AUGUSTINE, *De consensu Evagnelistarum*, I.2.4. PL 34, 1044. «For Matthew is understood to have taken it in hand to construct the record of the incarnation of the Lord according to the royal lineage, and to give an account of most part of His deeds and works as they stood in relation to his present life of men. Mark follows him closely, and looks like his attendant and epitomizer. For in his narrative he gives nothing in concert with John apart from the others: by himself, separately, he has little to record; in conjunction with Luke, as distinguished from the rest he has still less; but in concord with Matthew, he has a very large number of passages. Much, too, he narrates words almost numerically and identically the same as those used by Matthew, where the agreement is either with that evangelist alone, or with him in connection with the rest. On the other hand, Luke appears to have occupied himself rather with the priestly lineage and character of the Lord».

Theodore of Mopsuestia, while discussing the canonical status of the *Song of Songs*, classifies it as a specific type of writing. He identifies the *Song* as a marriage poem and associates it with a historical setting[131]. Theodore accepts the tradition that the *Song* was composed by Solomon on the occasion of his marriage to an Egyptian. However, he rejects the canonical status of the *Song* seeing that the material (marriage between Solomon and a pagan woman) was unacceptable[132].

Jerome notes different literary forms (not in the technical sense) in his *Preface to Daniel*. He calls the Susanna story a history, the *Song of the Three Young Men* a hymn, and the story of *Bel and the Dragon* a fable[133].

Augustine, in *De doctrina Christiana,* notes the importance of recognizing patterns in the written form. He says:

> Furthermore, learned men should know that our authors have used all the modes of expression which grammarians call by their Greek name, *tropes*, and they have employed them in greater numbers and more eloquently than those who do not know these writers, and have learned the figures in other works, can suppose or believe. Yet, those who know these tropes recognize them in the Holy Scriptures, and the knowledge of them is a considerable aid in understanding the Scriptures[134].

2.6 *Historical Criticism*

Historical criticism as practiced today seeks to determine certain facts about people, places, and events from the past. The procedures attempt to judge evidence (written, traditional, or archeological) on their claim of historicity. This type of critical approach was not practiced in the patristic or medieval periods. However, the literature of these periods do give evidence that the Fathers and Scholars had an appreciation of the Bible as a valid and somewhat reliable historical source. The primary difference between the ancients and current scholars regarding biblical history center around the goals of historical research. Whereas historical scholars today seek accurate factual information, the earlier exegetes sought to identify

---

[131] Form critical studies, which developed much later, are more concerned with the *social* setting in which the *Song* was used rather than a *historical* setting that might be reflected in the text.

[132] D.S. DOCKERY, *Biblical Interpretation*, 110. Theodore suggests the Song be used for personal reading rather than for public proclamation.

[133] JEROME, *Preface to Daniel*, PG 28, 1292.

[134] AUGUSTINE, *De doctrina Christiana*, III.29, 40. PL 34, 82. English trans.: FOC 4, 148.

the role of history in the interpretation of the text. Examples are presented from Origen, Theodore, Chrysostom and Augustine.

Origen's exegesis, although containing a large amount of allegorical interpretation, defends the historical context of the Scriptures[135]. In *Contra Celsum*[136], for example, he defends the historicity of the miracles performed by Jesus and his disciples against arguments raised by Celsus. In the same work, he defends the historicity of the Holy Spirit's appearance as a dove. At the same time Origen recognizes the difficulties in making historical judgments from any piece of literature:

> Before we begin our reply, we have to remark that the endeavor to show, with regard to almost any history, however true, that it actually occurred, and to produce an intelligent conception regarding it, is one of the most difficult undertakings that can be attempted, and is in some instances an impossibility. For suppose that some one were to assert that there never had been a Trojan war, chiefly on account of the impossible narrative interwoven therewith, about a certain Achilles being the son of a sea goddess Thetis and of a man Peleus or Sarpedon being the son of Zeus, or Ascalaphus and Ialmenus the sons of Ares, or Æneas that of Aphrodite, how should we prove that such was the case, especially under the weight of the fiction attached, I know not how, to the universally prevalent opinion that there was really a war in Ilium between Greeks and Trojans? And suppose, also, that some one disbelieve the story of Œdipus and Jocasta, and of their tow sons Eteocles and Polynices, because the sphinx, a kind of half-virgin, was introduced into the narrative, how should we demonstrate the reality of such a thing? And in like manner also with the marvelous event interwoven with it, or with the return of the Heracleidæ, or countless other historical events. But he who deals candidly with histories, and would wish to keep himself also from being imposed upon by them, will exercise his judgment as to what statements he will give his assent to, and what he will accept figuratively, seeking to discover the meaning of the authors of such inventions, and from what statements he will withhold his belief, as having been written for the gratification of certain individuals. And we have said this by way of anticipation respecting the whole history related in the Gospels concerning Jesus, not as inviting men of acuteness to simple and unreasoning candor in those who are to read, and of much investigation, and so to speak of in-

---

[135] Philo whose allegorizations had a heavy influence on Origen's work also appreciated the historical significance of the text. For examples, see his treatment of the destruction of Sodom (*De Abrahamo* 137-141), the flood (*De Vita Mosis II* 60-65), Abraham's separation from Lot (*De Abrahamo* 212-216), and the divine visitation to Abraham (*De Abrahamo* 118ff.)

[136] ORIGEN, *Contra Celsum*, I.37-38. PG 11, 729-32.

sight into the meaning of the writers, that the object with which each event has been recorded may be discovered[137].

Theodore of Mopsuestia emphasizes the Scriptures as a source for history[138]. According to Wiles, Theodore considers

the Bible as the record of a divinely intended and guided historical development. The Old Testament is to be read primarily as the account of God's gracious acts embodied in Israel's history. And the ultimate importance of that history is that it was designed in the purposes of God to provide setting for God's supremely gracious act in Christ, by which the new age was realized as God's salvation made available universally[139].

When studying the Prophets, Theodore begins with the original historical situation of the prophet then and proceeds with a «shrewd historical judgment in assessing those situations»[140]. When analyzing the Psalms, he attempts to identify the historical setting which prompted its composition[141]. When dealing with the historicity of NT passages, he relies heavily on the attributed author. Regarding the gospels he judges Matthew and John as more precise because they «were eyewitnesses»[142].

Chrysostom defends the Gospels as a source of historical information in his *Homily on the Gospel of Matthew*[143]. He disagrees with those who

---

[137] ORIGEN, *Contra Celsum*, 1.42. PG 11, 738. English trans.: ANFa IV, 414.

[138] R. DEVREESSE, *Essai sur Theodore de Mopsueste*, 73. D.S. DOCKERY, *Biblical Interpretation* , 109, describes Theodore as the «most consistent in emphasizing historical exegesis».

[139] M.F. WILES, «Theodore of Mopsuestia», 508.

[140] M.F. WILES, «Theodore of Mopsuestia», 501. D.Z. ZAHAROPOULOS, *Theodore of Mopsuestia*, 126 remarks: «Under Theodore's system of exegesis the prophetic literature is closely related to Hebrew history, and the OT prophets are set within the historical framework provided by their oracles. Theodore concluded that each prophet was called at a particular time to become an authentic herald of the divine revelation». For example, Theodore writes: «The blessed prophets Hosea, Joel, Amos, and Micah addressed their sayings to the entire nation of Israel, both to the ten tribes whose reigning city was Samaria, and likewise to the tribe of Judah and the inhabitants of Jerusalem. They denounced the people for their religious sins and for the moral transgressions which they were committing in many ways. And they also added to these sayings the list of impending evils which would come if the people continued to be unrepentant over their sins; I mean the disaster of the ten tribes which was caused by the Assyrians, and the events which happened to the tribe of Judah at the hands of the Babylonians».

[141] M.F. WILES, «Theodore of Mopsuestia», 498. The traditional notion of Davidic authorship was the starting point for Theodore's historical treatment.

[142] M.F. WILES, «Theodore of Mopsuestia», 494.

[143] CHRYSOSTOM, *Homily on the Gospel of Matthew*, 1.6. English trans.: NPNF, Series I, X, 3.

see the differences among the Gospels as a basis for denying historicity. The differences, he argues, are indicative of the truth contained in the sacred writings. For if the evangelists «had agreed in all things exactly even to time, and place, and to the very words, none of our enemies would have believed but that they had met together, and had written what they wrote by some human compact; because such entire agreement as this cometh not of simplicity». Chrysostom also makes an important distinction between major truths and minor details in the Gospels. He says:

> But if there be anything touching times or places, which they have related differently, this is nothing that injures the truth of what they have said. And these things too, so far as God shall enable us, we will endeavor, as we proceed, to point out; requiring you, together with what we have mentioned, to observe, that in the chief heads, those which constitute our life and furnish out our doctrine, nowhere is any of them found to have disagreed, no not ever so little.

> But what are these points? Such as follow: That God became man, that He wrought miracles, that He was crucified, that He was buried, that He rose again, that He ascended, that He will judge, that He hath given commandments tending to salvation, to the Old Testament, that He is a Son, the He is only-begotten, that He is a true Son that He is of the same substance with the Father, and as many things as are like these; for touching these we shall find that there is in them a full agreement[144].

Augustine's approach to history is reflected in *The City of God*. Chapters XII to XVIII trace the actions of God through the OT to the time of Christ. Through this presentation he prepares the way for much later studies on salvation history. Rogerson notes:

> For all this, the impressive thing about *The City of God* is that it is an attempt to take the OT seriously as history, and to consider how secular and sacred history are to be regarded in relation to each other. In some respects, it is an anticipation of the notion of *Heilsgeschichte* (Salvation History) of the nineteenth century, but without the philosophical assumptions of the latter. Indeed, Augustine's view that biblical history's main function is to give a clue to the hidden divine imperatives that are at work in secular history, is remarkably modern[145].

---

144 CHRYSOSTOM, *Homily on the Gospel of Matthew*, 1.6. English trans.: NPNF, Series I, X, 3. Chrysostom continues the discussion speaking on the historicity of the Gospels. He mentions the authors as being influenced by the audience to whom they write as having an effect on the method they choose to present the material.

145 J. ROGERSON – C. ROWLAND – B. LINDARS, *Study and Use of the Bible*, 52. The view that the OT prepared for the NT was commonly held in the early Church.

The Fathers recognized the sacred texts as a source for history. This should be evident in the examples given above as well as in the discussion on the *literal sense* in the first section of the chapter. God's interaction with his people are recorded and reflected in the biblical writings. This recognition was neither naive nor simplistic. Thus although the text was seen as generally reliable, historical inconsistencies in the texts needed to be addressed.

3. The Place of the HCM in Patristic and Medieval Exegesis

Interpretation of the Bible in the Church notes that the elements of the HCM can be found in the exegesis of the early church particularly in the work of Origen, Augustine, and Jerome. This chapter has identified the roots of the HCM in the literature of the early church. The roots include the hermeneutical basis of the method along with several of its exegetical procedures. The conclusion will analyze the place of these roots in the exegetical theory of the early church. First, the hermeneutical basis for the critical procedures is discussed. Second the necessity and limits of the critical procedures are identified as they are understood in this period.

3.1 *The Hermeneutical Basis for Critical Procedures*

The first section of this chapter presented a survey of biblical herme- neutics during the patristic and medieval periods. The survey gave special attention to the ascendancy of the *literal sense* because it became the un- derlying hermeneutical principle of the HCM. Recent debates among exe- getes and theologians have pointed out certain inadequacies of the *literal sense* in identifying meaning in the biblical texts. The inadequacies are partly rooted in absolutizing the *literal sense* as the only principle for bib- lical interpretation. Although the *literal sense* rose to a foundational posi- tion in the patristic and medieval periods, it never entirely excluded the possibility for multiple meanings. Five conclusions can be made from this brief survey regarding the *literal sense*.

First, the *literal sense* can be nuanced according to three aspects: verbal, historical, and authorial. The literal-verbal aspect is an interpretation based on the actual words of the text carefully respecting their lexical and con- textual meanings. The literal-historical aspect is an interpretation of the

---

The NT itself interprets the OT in terms of prophecy fulfilled, the Church as the con- tinuation of Israel (in Luke-Acts), promises fulfilled, etc. Other approaches that evalu- ate the relationship between the testaments included: *testimonia*, apologetics, and ty- pological interpretations. Augustine added the concept of salvation history.

text based on the principle that the text is reflective of an actual historical situation. The literal-authorial aspect is an interpretation based on the intention of the author as he wrote the text. Gradually the authorial intention became the primary meaning of the *literal sense*[146], but there has always been a certain amount of flexibility when referring to a *literal sense*.

Second, the *literal sense* became the principle of unity in biblical hermeneutics. The previous section outlined the ascendancy of the *literal sense* as the principle of unity in biblical hermeneutics. The need for a unifying principle is to prevent arbitrary interpretation. In other words, there is a need to identify the locus of meaning for interpretation. Origen had identified the locus of meaning in the *spiritual sense*. The *spiritual sense* continued to be the primary sense until the excesses of allegorical interpretation proved this untenable. The rise of the *literal sense* began in reaction to the excesses of allegory. That ascendancy continued as the meaning of the *literal sense* became more and more identified with authorial intention.

Third, the *literal sense* allows multiple meanings provided the additional meaning is related in some way to the literal meaning. The Antiochenes saw the *literal sense* as the most important, yet their practice of *theoria* allowed for multiple meanings to emerge from the *literal sense*. Aquinas noted the importance of the *literal sense* as the foundational meaning of the text but it was not the only meaning. Other senses were permitted provided they were based on or related to the *literal sense*. The importance of the *literal sense* did not eliminate the possibility of other meanings for a text (such as other senses) but required that the additional meanings be in some way related to the *literal sense*. Thus the unity expressed by the *literal sense* did not prohibit a multiplicity of meaning. Rather it provided a guideline for avoiding arbitrary or contradictory interpretations.

Fourth, the *literal sense* is not always readily identifiable. Identifying the *literal sense* defined as the author's intention can be problematic. Augustine's solution for such a case is an appeal to the canon. The meaning of a difficult passage may be discovered through recourse to other biblical passages.

Fifth, the hermeneutical principle of the *literal sense* is the basis for using critical procedures. The *literal sense* roots the text in its original historical context whether the *sense* is formulated as the verbal meaning,

---

146 Once again it should be stated that the ancients had a deep respect for the historicity of the biblical text. As the authorial-intention became the primary meaning of the *literal sense*, the historical aspect was deemed included in the author's intention.

the historical meaning or the author's intention. The necessity and limits of the critical procedures are identified in the following sections.

3.2 Why are the critical procedures necessary?

The second section of this chapter noted numerous examples of procedures used by the HCM that were used in the patristic and medieval periods. The necessity of the individual procedures should be evident from this presentation. Three general statements, however, are given here by way of summary.

Problems in the text require critical evaluation. The Fathers and Scholars recognized problems proposed by the biblical texts that require a critical (i.e. reasonable) solution. The following questions provide examples of the problems: what text is authoritative, not only are manuscripts different but versions are different in content (e.g. LXX or Hebrew text); how are conflicting passages to be explained (e.g. synoptics, historical accounts)?; who are the authors of the various texts (e.g. Psalms, Johannine literature, Pauline literature)?; how is symbolic language to be understood?; what is the significance of geographical references?

Understanding the original language texts require critical procedures. The need for language studies was recognized albeit to varying degrees in these periods. Figures such as Origen, Jerome, Chrysostom, Eusebius, and Augustine all recognized the importance of the original language texts. The study of these texts require the knowledge of the ancient languages. Language studies were needed to understand the imagery, idiom, and style of these texts.

Determining the literal sense requires critical methodology. The *literal sense*, as discussed above, has three different aspects: the literal-verbal, literal-historical, and the literal-authorial intention. Regardless of which aspect is stressed each implies the need for critical evaluation of the text. The literal-verbal understanding required the analysis of words, phrases, imagery etc. Comparative studies between texts were need for troubled passages. These studies lead to an analysis based on style and literary form. The literal-historical meaning required that historical questions be answered when text contains conflicting reports. As the *literal sense* became the foundational sense for biblical interpretation, the need to identify the author became important. The question was not always easily solved. Reliance on tradition provided a ready answer but as noted above not all texts could resort to tradition (e.g. *Hebrews, Revelation*). The critical evaluation of style was one response to these difficulties. Another response, albeit limited, was the attempt to determine the role of the audience on the author's intention.

3.3 Why are the critical procedures limited?

Critical procedures have a narrow focus. The critical procedures mentioned in the previous section tend to focus on very particular questions or problems. Although these can be helpful in understanding the whole of the text (e.g. authorship question, language studies), the techniques do not lend themselves to defining a global theological vision. For this reason the procedures were not used in isolation but often within a broader theological understanding of the text. This understanding is represented by the *senses of Scripture* or the *theoria*.

The literal sense can not always be determined. The *literal sense* defined as the author's intention is not always readily discernible. St. Augustine acknowledged this and suggested an interpretation in view of the canon in these situations. Origen also noted the limits of the *literal sense* when he described it in relationship to the «deeper meaning» accessible through the Spirit.

Critical procedures are not very helpful in identifying senses other than the literal. In the first section of this chapter it was pointed out that the ascendancy of the *literal sense* did not eliminate other *senses*. Critical procedures do not aid in determining these other senses.

Critical practices tend toward the technical and not towards the pastoral. During the patristic age exegetical studies were heavily influenced by a pastoral concern. Although critical practices were deemed necessary, their limitation regarding pastoral interpretations relegated their importance to a very specific and confined area, that is problematic texts.

Thus, the roots of the HCM had a necessary but limited role in the exegetical studies of the early church. The limits of the method can further be detected in the exegetical writings of this period. Practically speaking, the exegesis of this period simply went beyond the *literal sense*, sometimes disregarding it completely (e.g. extremes of allegorical interpretation), but many times addressing the consequences of *literal sense* (e.g. *theoria* of Antioch, Aquinas's approach). The attention given to this meaning in effect prohibited an absolute value being placed upon the *literal sense* or the critical procedures used in the study of the text. Although they were necessary and helpful they could not exhaust the meaning of the text.

CHAPTER III

Church Documents in the Nineteenth and Twentieth Centuries

The HCM developed formally in the period of humanism that followed the Renaissance (see Introduction). Catholic involvement was sparse. The church's reluctance to sanction the use of scientific methods lasted until the pontificate of Leo XIII in the late nineteenth century. Leo's encyclical *Providentissimus Deus* inaugurated the era of Catholic critical biblical scholarship. The time from Leo to the present can be divided into three periods represented by major ecclesial documents on biblical interpretation. The first period is marked by an initial opening to critical biblical studies in the encyclical *Providentissimus Deus* (1893) and the full acceptance of critical methodology in *Divino Afflante Spiritu* (1943). The second period is primarily represented by the conciliar constitution *Dei Verbum* (1965). The third period is represented by the PBC document *Interpretation of the Bible in the Church* (1993)[1].

These documents can be used to evaluate the HCM regarding its validity within the Catholic interpretive enterprise. A proper evaluation of the HCM in these documents should take four criteria into consideration: the pastoral and scholarly situation that prompted the church's official re-

---

[1] Chronological order is used to follow the development of the Catholic response to critical methodology. The doctrinal weight of these documents vary. *Dei Verbum* carries the most weight followed by the papal encyclicals. The PBC decisions carry the least weight cf. Chapter IV, footnote 1.

General bibliography on these documents include the following: «Venticinque anni dopo l'enciclica Providentissimus»; I. ANTONIUTTI, «Celebration du cinquantieme anniversaire»; J. ASURMENDI, «Cien anos»; M.C. CARLEN, *A Guide to the Encyclicals (1878-1937)»*; G. COLOMBO, «Bibbia e teologia»; R. FABRIS, «Bibbia e magisterio»; V. FUSCO, «Un secolo di metodo storico»; U.E. PARE, «Church and the Bible»; P. LAGHI – M. GILBERT – A. VANHOYE, *Chiesa e Sacra Scrittura*.

sponse, the Church's response to the situation, the general content of the
document under consideration, and finally the HCM as presented in the
document.

This chapter will evaluate the place of the HCM in the ecclesial documents of the first period of Catholic critical biblical scholarship (1893-
1943). Subsequent chapters will treat the other periods. This chapter is
divided into five sections, the first four correspond to the principal documents of this period: *Providentissimus Deus*, The PBC Decrees: 1905-
1915, *Spiritus Paraclitus*, and *Divino Afflante Spiritu*[2]. The four criteria
mentioned in the previous paragraph will provide the structure for each
section. The final section concludes the chapter by identifying the necessity and limits of the HCM as understood in this period.

1. *Providentissimus Deus*[3]

Catholic studies in the seventeenth and eighteenth centuries avoided the
use of critical methodology because of its rationalist tendencies. Consequently after the work of R. Simon (1638-1712) and J. Astruc (1684-
1766) there was no significant Catholic involvement in biblical scholarship until the nineteenth century[4]. Leo XIII gave the first formal authorization for the use of critical methods in his encyclical *Providentissimus
Deus*, which he issued on November 18, 1893.

---

[2] Unless otherwise indicated, citations for the documents will be taken from the
Enchiridion Biblicum hereafter *EB*. English translations and reference numbers will be
taken from J.J. MEGIVERN, *Official Catholic Teachings: Biblical Interpretation*, hereafter *OCT*. Documents of lesser significance will be mentioned in summary statements
or charts at the appropriate places in the text.

[3] Bibliography for *Providentissimus Deus* includes: «Venticinque anni dopo l'enciclica *Providentissimus*»; I. ANTONIUTTI, «Célébration du cinquantième anniversaire»;
S.M. BRANDI, *La questione biblica*; M.T. COCONNIER, «L'encyclique *Providentis-
simus Deus*»; J.J. COLLINS, «*Providentissimus Deus*»; A.C. COTTER, «Antecedents
of *Providentissimus Deus*»; M.J. GRUENTHANER, «Fiftieth anniversary»; S.
HARTDEGEN, «Influence of *Providentissimus Deus*»; J.C. HEDLEY, «Pope Leo XIII
and the Bible»; J.A. HOWLETT, «The Higher Criticism and Archeology»; H.J.T.
JOHNSON, «Leo XIII»; M.J. LAGRANGE, «*Providentissimus Deus*»; J.L. LILLY,
«Fiftieth anniversary of *Providentissimus Deus*»; A.J. MAAS, «A Negative View»; E.
MAGUIRE, «Encyclical of Pope Leo XIII»; L. MURILLO, «Las letras apostólicas»;
W.L. NEWTON, «*Providentissimus Deus*»; B. PRETE, «L'enciclica *Providentissimus
Deus*»; E.F. SIEGMAN, «Influence of the encyclical *Providentissimus Deus*»; F.
SPADAFORA, *Leone XIII e gli studi biblici*; E.F. SUTCLIFFE, «Golden jubilee of
Providentissimus Deus».

[4] Catholic scholars of the nineteenth century include: E. Renan, F. Vigouroux, R.
Cornely and M.J. Lagrange.

1.1 *The Scholarly and Pastoral Situation and The Church's Response*

The development of critical methodology continued in the nineteenth century: textual criticism became an independent discipline[5], significant advances were made in OT and NT literary (source) criticism[6], and the first scientific survey of the Holy Land inaugurated the discipline of biblical archeology[7]. Yet critical scholarship continued to be heavily influenced by philosophical trends, especially that of rationalism[8]. Hegel's idealism also exerted influence on biblical studies of this period. Although the Hegelians[9] sought to defend biblical authority from rationalist assaults, their method led to its further erosion, especially regarding historical events. Some of their conclusions illustrate the negative effects of this philosophical influence. For example, H.E.G. Paulus in his *Life of Jesus* (1828), concludes that angels are phosphorescence, narratives of healing omit their natural causes, and the transfiguration was the product of sleepy disciples who saw Jesus talking with two unknown persons during a

---

[5] As mentioned in the Introduction, the *textus receptus* had become the dominant text of the NT. Its de-thronement began with the work of Griesbach. His published editions of the NT (1774-1807) included changes from the *textus receptus*, a radical change at that time. The changes adopted were based on his fifteen canons of textual criticism. From this point on textual criticism developed slowly abandoning the *textus receptus* in favor of better manuscripts. Patristic citations and ancient versions began to be used as witnesses of the original text. Tischendorf published his edition in 1862 based on the *Codex Sinaiticus* (one of the best preserved uncial manuscripts), which he discovered at St. Catherine's Monastery, Mt. Sinai in 1844. Wescott and Hort published their edition of the NT in 1881, a companion volume identified the principles they used for textual criticism.

[6] In OT studies J. Wellhausen formulates the Documentary Hypothesis (1883) concluding that the promulgation of the law took place after the Babylonian exile. In NT studies K. Lachmann (1835) and C.H. Weisse (1838) establish the literary priority of Mark and H.J. Holtzmann (1863) formulates the Two-Source Theory.

[7] G.W. VAN BEEK, «Archeology», 207. Archeological studies of the biblical lands began with the work of Edward Robinson and Eli Smith in 1938. The two journeyed through Palestine studying the countryside and identifying biblical sites. From 1872 to 1878 C.R. Conder and H.H. Kitchener conducted studies under the auspices of the Palestinian Exploration Fund. In 1884, G. Schumacher made a survey of Hauran and Northern Transjordan. Although the science was only in its beginning stages and later developments would yield more reliable results, the work of these forerunners opened the door for new insights into the biblical text.

[8] R. GRANT – D. TRACY, *A Short History of Interpretation*, 111, states «One of the most striking features of the development of biblical interpretation during the nineteenth century was the way in which philosophical presuppositions implicitly guided it».

[9] For example, F.C. Baur and W. Vatke.

beautiful sunset[10]. F. Schleiermacher, in his *Leben Jesus* (1838), interprets the resurrection as a recovery from lethargy while the ascension was
Jesus' second and genuine death. The Quest for the Historical Jesus and
the History of Religions School also developed during this period and
likewise came under the influence of these philosophical systems.

Questions on biblical authority regarding the physical sciences and
history led to a discussion among Catholic theologians concerning biblical inerrancy and inspiration. A. Rohling suggested dividing the biblical
material into three categories: faith and morals, historical facts on which
faith and morals depend, and profane matters. Inerrancy is limited to the
first two categories. The sacred writers could err regarding the profane
material since they were «wholly left to their own resources». F. Lenor-
mant, an archeologist, proposed limiting inspiration to matters of faith and
morals based on the supposition that science and religion belonged to two
different planes. He also made a distinction between faith and revelation,
stating that everything in the Bible is inspired but not all is revelation.
Cardinal Newman included faith, morals and historical narratives under
inspiration but excludes *orbiter dicta* such as scientific data, or matters
such as Paul's greetings in his letters. S. di Bartolo distinguished three
degrees of inspiration: the highest applies to material regarding faith and
morals, the intermediate applies to historical data related to matters of faith
and morals, and the lowest applies to details of fact and in non-religious
matters such as «geography, chronology, science, perhaps even philosophy». The lowest degree does not guarantee inerrancy. In such cases the
error is ascribed to the human author not to God. J. Didiot suggested that
the magisterium had no basis for authoritative pronouncements regarding
profane history or the sciences, because inspiration did not preserve the
writers from error in these regards. A. Loisy suggested that a new definition of truth would help reconcile historical and scientific errors found in
the texts. His concept of biblical truth was «economical», «proportional»,
and «relative» so that historical and scientific data could be reconciled
with the text[11].

The state of biblical scholarship along with the inerrancy/inspiration
question provide the general context for *Providentissimus Deus*. The specific occasion that prompted the encyclical was an article by M. d'Hulst,
rector of the *Institute Catholique* of Paris in *Le Correspondant*[12]. The

---

[10] J. ROGERSON – C. ROWLAND – B. LINDARS, *Study and Use of the Bible*, 338.

[11] A.C. COTTER, «Antecedants of *Providentissimus Deus*», 117-124.

[12] The title «Le Question Biblique» became the term used to describe the debate
concerning the inerrancy/inspiration question and the use of critical methodologies.

article dated January 25, 1893 categorizes the theories on biblical inspiration as right, left and center. The right represents traditionalists and rigorists who defend the absolute inerrancy of Scripture. The left represents those holding to plenary inspiration «yet willing to admit inaccuracies and possibly errors in the Bible». The center represents those who distinguish between inspiration and revelation. While they admit the «theoretical possibility of errors in the Bible», they are very slow in making definite assertions concerning specific passages. The task of the apologist, according to d'Hulst, was to determine whether «the Bible really contained things which seemed to be errors or impossibilities and then, if certain difficulties with regard to alleged facts still remained insoluble, to ask whether inspiration was in fact incompatible with certain inexactitudes of expression in scientific and historical matters»[13].

Until 1893 the church's response to the development of scientific biblical criticism had been confined to short restrictive statements. In 1779, Pius VI defended the virgin birth against propositions made by rationalist criticism. In 1816, Pius VII urged the use of the Vulgate and the avoidance of vernacular translations[14]. In 1844 and 1846, Gregory XVI and Pius IX respectively wrote against the *Biblical Societies*. In 1864, the *Syllabus of Errors* defended the historical value of prophecies and miracles saying that they could not be dismissed as poetic fictions[15].

The church's response to the debate on biblical inspiration was first formulated in Vatican I's *Dei Filius* (1870). The Council condemned two theories of biblical inspiration that effectively removed God's role in the composition of the text. The first theory held by Sixtus of Sienna suggested that inspiration is retroactive, taking place only when the Church declares the text canonical. The second opinion proposed by Johann Jahn

---

[13] H.J.T. JOHNSON, «Leo XIII», 412. Johnson also mentions an earlier article in *Le Correspondant* (October 25, 1892) published shortly after Renan's death where d'Hulst comments on the hiatus between Catholic apologetics and modern knowledge so evident in Renan's seminary days. He suggested that Renan's defection, though not caused by the gap, might have been facilitated by it. The article may indicate the mood among Catholic scholars seeking direction from the magisterium on scientific biblical criticism.

[14] *OCT*, §281-283.

[15] PIUS IX, *Syllabus of Errors*, VII. *EB* §75; *OCT*, §281-283. The errors include the following: «The prophecies and miracles set forth in the narration of the Sacred Scriptures are poetical fictions; the mysteries of the Christian faith are the outcome of philosophic reflections; in the books of both testaments mythical tales are contained; Jesus Christ Himself is a mythical fiction».

held that God would interfere only if the human authors were going to commit a serious error in their composition[16]. Vatican I states in response:

> The church holds (the biblical texts) to be sacred and canonical, not because, having been carefully composed by mere human industry, they were afterwards approved by her authority, nor merely because they contain revelation with no admixture of error, but because, having been written by the inspiration of the Holy Spirit, they have God for their author and have been delivered as such to the church herself[17].

The pontificate of Leo XIII brought a renewal in Catholic education along with an opening toward critical study of the Bible. In 1878, Leo encourages the study of history and archaeology noting that they «have the magic power of causing stones to speak out their tales and to plead the cause of faith»[18]. In 1879, Leo encourages the study of scholastic philosophy in his encyclical *Aeterni Patris*[19]. In 1892, Leo authorizes and commends the foundation of the École Biblique in Jerusalem, the first Catholic school specifically dedicated to the critical study of the Bible[20].

1.2 *The Contents of* Providentissimus Deus

Providentissimus Deus is the first magisterial document to seriously consider critical biblical studies. The work responded to rationalist exegesis that attacks the divine character of the Scriptures but it also opens the door to modern biblical scholarship. The contents of *Providentissimus Deus* are discussed under the following themes: a polemic against rationalism, inspiration—inerrancy—authorship, the book of the Spirit and the book of the church, and Scripture studies in the church.

---

[16] A. NICHOLS, *The Shape of Catholic Theology*, 119-120.

[17] VATICAN I, *Dei Filius*, II.57. *EB* §77; *OCT*, §191.

[18] R.T. MURPHY, «Teaching of Providentissimus Deus», 125.

[19] The Roman Academy of St. Thomas Aquinas was established in the same year. Two years later a chair of Thomistic philosophy was also established in the Louvain followed by Laval, Freiburg, and Catholic University.

[20] Leo XIII, *Hierosolymae in coenobio*. The letter was issued on September 17, 1892. F.M. BRAUN, *The Work of Pere Lagrange*, 13, notes that the founding of the school was actually prompted by Leo who had urged Lecomte to establish a center for theological studies in the Holy Land. Lagrange established the school and used a critical approach for his studies. BRAUN, 16, states that Lagrange «was fully aware of the importance of ancient languages, and devoted the greater portion of his program to Semitic philology. In the early days he himself taught Hebrew, Arabic, Assyrian, general introduction to the Bible, history of the Ancient East, and biblical archaeology. Besides these there were courses in epigraphy, topography, Palestinian geography, and exegesis».

Polemic Against Rationalism. Leo responded to the critical exegesis of the day with a polemic against rationalism[21]. Rationalist exegesis, as mentioned above, sought to study the Bible devoid of its divine character. Leo's critique of rationalist exegetes include the following points: they begin their studies with flawed presuppositions that deny revelation and inspiration; they treat the Scriptures as «fables and falsehoods», holding that prophecies are made up after the event, miracles are not from God but products of natural law or tricks of myth, and apostolic authorship is denied to the Gospels; they force their conclusions on the world as the results of a «free science», results which they are constantly modifying and changing; and they propagate their views among the faithful in books, pamphlets, newspapers, public addresses rather than keeping it a scholarly discussion with men of learning and judgment[22].

Inspiration–Inerrancy–Authorship. Leo defended the divine character of the scriptures through an affirmation of divine authorship, inspiration, and inerrancy. He began the encyclical with a reaffirmation of Vatican I's teaching on inspiration[23]. Later in the document he rejected theories that limit inspiration to faith and morals, claiming a theory of inspiration based on God's intention rather than the words of the text[24]. Leo stressed that inspiration can not be isolated to parts of the text. Here he draws a connection between the inspiration of the authors' understanding and the words which express it. He stated:

---

[21] Leo's style of presentation may be distracting for readers today because of the polemical language. Leo's quote of Chrysostom, *EB*, §117; *OCT*, §327, is used as an example: «Wherefore it is needful that the man who has to contend against all should be acquainted with the engines and the arts of all — that he should be at once archer and slinger, commandant and officer, general and private soldier, foot-soldier and horsemen, skilled in sea-fight and in siege; for unless he knows every trick and turn of war, the devil is well able, if only a single door be left open, to get in his fierce bands and carry off the sheep». Other examples of the polemical language include the following: defense, attack, oppose and contend against, tactics and arms, champions in so momentous a battle, hostile attack, adversaries, fight, contest, enemy, weapons.

[22] *EB*, §100-101; *OCT*, §309-311. Leo argued that «men of the gospel» (i.e. preachers, ministers) who are influenced by this type of exegesis are undermining the Scriptures. He also criticized professors of other sciences who urge the attack on the Bible by their intolerance of revelation. His final critique decried the ridicule and «scurrilous jesting» of the church brought on by rationalists.

[23] *EB*, §81; *OCT*, §289.

[24] *EB*, §124, *OCT* §337. «... (as they wrongly think) in a question of the truth or falsehood of a passage, we should consider not so much what God has said as the reason and purpose which He had in mind in saying it — this system cannot be tolerated».

Hence, the fact that it was men whom the Holy Spirit took up as his instruments for writing does not mean that it was these inspired instruments — but not the primary author — who might have made an error. For, by supernatural power, He so moved and impelled them to write — He so assisted them when writing — that the things which He ordered, and those only, they, first, rightly understood, then willed faithfully to write down, and finally expressed in apt words and with infallible truth. Otherwise, it could not be said that He was the Author of the entire Scripture[25].

The affirmation of inspiration is given while treating the inerrancy and authorship questions. These three themes are inter-related. God is the author of the Scriptures in that he inspires the human author to write; therefore the text can contain no error. In this formula all three elements are necessary. If one principle is violated the whole concept becomes unreasonable. For example, if one holds for error in the text, and if God is the author of the text, then God is the author of error. If the Bible is a «letter from God» to mankind, and if this «letter» contains error, then God is a deceiver. Since God can neither be the author of error nor a deceiver then God must not be the author of the Scriptures.

As noted above, studies in the physical sciences provoked questions regarding inerrancy. The results of scientific research conflicted with data from the Bible. Leo proposed that since science and theology have different concerns no real discrepancy will be found between the two provided that each scholar remains within his area of competence. Exegetes should not evaluate the Scriptures as though the authors were trying to teach «the essential nature ... of the visible universe», for this was beyond their intention. Consequently, exegetes must consider the authors' use of «figurative language», the use of terms commonly available to the writers, and the possibility that the writers wrote according to appearances[26].

Leo affirmed divine authorship by referring to God as the author, describing the text as a product of divine composition, and describing the

---

[25] *EB*, §126, *OCT* §339. The theory of inspiration that Leo presented reflected that of Cardinal Franzelin which is described as «content inspiration». R.F. COLLINS, *Introduction to the New Testament*, 337, summarizes this theory: «According to Franzelin, the dogma of inspiration must be derived from the dogmatic statement of God's authorship. In his exposition the Jesuit professor...not only used the notion of instrumental causality developed by the Schoolmen, but also made a deft distinction between the formal and material components of the scriptural books. By assigning the material parts to the human authors, Franzelin allowed sufficient contributions from the human author as to allow for some affirmation of human authorship. By ascribing the content and the truths of Scripture (*res et sententiae*) to God, Franzelin specified the notion of principal instrumental causality and highlighted the *Deus auctor* formula».

[26] *EB*, §121; *OCT*, §333.

inspiration through which the books were written[27]. The human author is relegated to a subordinate role. Elements of the dictation theory[28] and the instrumental causality theory are present in the document[29]. Although Leo suggested studying the text from the perspective of the human author for apologetic reasons, his emphasis is clearly on the divine[30]. The emphasis on the divine is Leo's response to rationalist attacks on the divine character of the Scriptures. From the current perspective, the role of the divine author may seem out of proportion to that of the human authors. The role of the human author however was not directly attacked in rationalist exegesis[31]. Thus Leo presented an affirmation of the divine character of the Scriptures, not an explanation of the relationship between the divine and human authors.

Book of the Spirit and the Book of the Church. Leo noted that interpretation of the biblical text should take into consideration its divine character. Scripture is inspired by the Holy Spirit; thus, the Holy Spirit must be the primary guide for interpretation: «...Sacred Scripture is not like other books...To understand and explain such things there is always required the "coming" of the same Holy Spirit»[32]. Furthermore the Bible is the book of the church and authentic interpretation will only come from within the church. The guidelines for this interpretation are: the magisterium[33], the Fathers[34], and the analogy of faith[35].

---

[27] See the following paragraphs for examples: *EB*, §84, 91, 97, 114, 121, 129; *OCT*, §294, 305, 307, 324, 333, 343.

[28] *EB*, §124; *OCT*, §338.

[29] *EB*, §81, 121, 124; *OCT* §291, 333, 338. See also footnote 25.

[30] *EB*, §116; *OCT*, §326.

[31] One of the effects of critical exegesis was that the text was studied as a human document. In spite of the concentration on the human element, the role of the human author/s were gradually dismissed (e.g. in the extremes of source criticism). For this reason I say «not directly» when speaking of the attack of rationalist exegesis on the biblical text. Greater attention is given to the role of the human author in the later development of the HCM (especially in redaction and tradition criticisms).

[32] *EB*, §89; *OCT*, §302.

[33] *EB*, §109; *OCT*, §319. «The first and dearest object of the Catholic commentator should be to interpret those passages which have received an authentic interpretation either form the sacred writers themselves, under the inspiration of the Holy Spirit (as in many places in the NT), or from the church, under the assistance of the same Holy Spirit, whether by her solemn judgment or her ordinary and universal magisterial — to interpret these passages in that identical sense, and to prove, by all the resources of science, that sound hermeneutical laws admit of no other interpretation».

[34] *EB*, §110; *OCT*, §321. «The holy Fathers "to whom, after the Apostles, the Church owes its growth — who have planted, watered, built, governed and cherished it", the holy Fathers, We say, are of supreme authority, whenever they all interpret in

Scripture Study in the Church. Leo responded to the ridicule of the rationalists[36] with a defense of Catholic biblical scholarship. He charts the significant Catholic contributions to biblical studies from the early church to the current day[37]. Leo, using apologetic language, encouraged biblical studies in the church. The defense of the scriptures and doctrine is the basis for such studies[38]. To this end the use of scientific methodology is encouraged[39]. *Providentissimus Deus* §17 presents the general guidelines for using critical procedures. Studies will proceed with caution giving due respect to that which has been defined. Free investigation is allowed for open questions. The goals are to prove, expound and illustrate doctrine, to maintain the Bible's full authority in cooperation with the magisterium of the Church, and to freely investigate those passages that have not been defined by universal agreement of the Fathers nor solemnly proclaimed by the Magisterium. The apologetic and polemical aspects of the document help explain the cautious approach.

Leo also presented plans for Scripture studies in seminaries[40]. First, the initial course in the Scripture curriculum should be an *Introduction*. In this course, the student will be taught the goals of Scripture studies: to defend the integrity and authenticity of the scriptures, to investigate the true sense of the text and to refute the objectors[41]. Lessons in the methods of interpretation are the basis of the introduction. For practical reasons select texts are studied. The goal is to teach the methodology so well the student can make a personal study of the books not covered in the class. The *Vulgate* is to be the text used yet recourse to original texts is permit-

one and the same manner any text of the Bible, as pertaining to the doctrine of the faith or morals; for their unanimity clearly evinces that such interpretation has come down from the Apostles as a matter for Catholic faith».

[35] *EB*, §109; *OCT*, §319. «In the other passages the analogy of faith should be followed, and Catholic doctrine, as authoritatively proposed by the Church, should be held as the supreme law; for seeing that the same God is the author both of the Sacred Books and the doctrine committed to the Church, it is clearly impossible that any teaching can, by legitimate means, be extracted from the former, which shall, in any respect, be at variance with the latter».

[36] *EB*, §100-101; *OCT* §309-311.

[37] *EB*, §91-99; *OCT*, §305-307.

[38] *EB*, §119; *OCT*, §330.

[39] *EB*, §108; *OCT*, §318.«By this most wise decree the Church by no means prevents or restrains the pursuit of biblical science, but rather protects it from error, and largely assists its real progress».

[40] *EB*, §103-132; *OCT*, §312-345. He began by noting the need for dedicated professors who have received proper training. Something very important at that time since it was only the beginning of Catholic involvement in critical studies.

[41] *EB*, §104-107; *OCT*, §314-315.

ted. Second, the relationship between Scripture and theology will be presented[42]. The professor is to remind the students that the divine-human character of the biblical text sometimes requires a unique understanding: «For the language of the Bible is employed to express, under the inspiration of the Holy Spirit, many things that are beyond the power and scope of the reason of man — that is to say, divine mysteries and all that is related to them». Finally, the student is to be taught the means for defending the Sacred Scriptures through the use of a critical approach[43].

1.3 *The HCM as Exposed in* Providentissimus Deus

The HCM is not mentioned by name in *Providentissimus Deus* for the term, as understood today, was not in use at this time. Leo critiques the use of *higher criticism* preferring to speak of *the art of true criticism*[44]. He criticizes *higher criticism* for two reasons. First, it judges the origin, integrity and authority of the biblical books based on «internal evidence» alone. Second, the method is imbued with rationalist presuppositions that deny anything beyond the natural. Leo also laments the fact that there are those who study the ancient monuments and documents with the goal of discrediting the biblical accounts[45]. He does not describe *the art of true criticism* explicitly; however, the meaning can be inferred from the encyclical. The term refers to the use of critical methodologies within the framework of Catholic theology. When considering historical questions such as the origin or transmission of the text precedence should given to the historical witnesses of the text rather than internal evidence[46]. Furthermore, the guidelines described in the discussion on physical sciences and biblical studies can also be applied to historical studies (see above). This section will consider the following elements of the HCM as presented in *Providentissimus Deus*: hermeneutical principles, introduction, textual criticism, original language studies, and literary criticism.

Hermeneutical Principles. The hermeneutical basis for interpretation is the *literal sense*. The *literal sense*, as described in the encyclical, refers to the verbal or historical meaning of a text. The exegete must «not to depart from the literal and obvious sense, except only where reason makes it un-

---

[42] *EB*, §108-117; *OCT*, §316-328.

[43] *EB*, §118-131; *OCT* §329-343.

[44] *EB*, §119; *OCT*, §330. The term *higher criticism* was discussed in Chapter I footnote 2. It was first coined by Eichhorn for studies of the text other than textual criticism.

[45] *EB*, §123; *OCT* §336.

[46] *EB*, §119; *OCT*, §330.

tenable or necessity requires»[47]. The divine mysteries contained in the books require additional senses — «There is sometimes in such passages a fullness and a hidden depth of meaning which the letter hardly expresses and which the laws of interpretation hardly warrant. Moreover, the *literal sense* frequently admits other senses, adapted to illustrate dogma or to confirm morality»[48]. Thus allegorical interpretation has a proper place when justified by the *literal sense*[49]. The references to the additional senses however are more a defense of patristic exegesis than a discussion on their relationship. Moreover, the relationship between the senses of scripture and critical methodology are not discussed.

Introduction. While giving his program for seminary studies, Leo mentioned the *introduction*. The term seems to be used in the technical sense, The content of this *introduction* was described above, in the previous section.

Textual Criticism. Leo praised the various printed editions of the Vulgate, LXX, and other ancient versions in his defense of Catholic biblical scholarship[50]. He noted the need for textual criticism: «It is true no doubt, that copyists have made mistakes in the text of the Bible; this question, when it arises, should be carefully considered on its merits, and the fact not too easily admitted, but only in those passages where proof is clear»[51]. The statement acknowledges the science of textual criticism and accepts its use for troublesome texts; however, it does not elaborate on the principles used in the study[52].

Original Language Studies and Philology. Leo recommended study of the original language texts twice. First, while speaking of seminary scripture studies. He acknowledged the Tridentine decree calling the *Vulgate* the «authentic» version for use in «public lectures, disputations, preaching and exposition». This is the text to be used by the students. However, «wherever there may be ambiguity or want of clearness, the "examination of older tongues", to quote St. Augustine, will be useful and advanta-

---

[47] *EB*, §112; *OCT*, §322.

[48] *EB*, §108; *OCT*, §316.

[49] *EB*, §112; *OCT*, §322. Leo stated: «Neither should those passages be neglected which the Fathers have understood in an allegorical or figurative sense, more especially when such interpretation is justified by the literal, and when it rests on the authority of many».

[50] *EB*, §94-99; *OCT*, §306-307.

[51] *EB*, §123; *OCT*, §336.

[52] *EB*, §106; *OCT*, §315. While discussing the recourse to original languages Leo noted «The question of "reading" having been, when necessary, carefully discussed, the next thing is to investigate and expound the meaning».

geous»[53]. The second reference to language studies is more explicit: «... it is most proper that professors of sacred scripture and theologians should master those tongues in which the sacred books were originally written; and it would be well that ecclesiastical students also should cultivate them, more especially those who aspire to academic degrees»[54]. To this end Leo encouraged the establishment of «chairs» or faculties in universities to provide for studies of the biblical and Semitic languages as well as related subjects[55].

Literary Criticism. Leo mentioned «figurative language» used by the author and «terms commonly available to the writers»[56]. *Literary criticism* is required to understand these terms and images. The exegete «while weighing the meanings of words, the connection of ideas, the parallelism of passages, and the like, should by all means make use of such illustrations as can be drawn from apposite erudition of an external sort; but this should be done with caution». The suggestions including the reference to comparative ANE literature are meant to aid the understanding of words, phrases and ideas contained in the text. Caution is expressed to prevent biblical studies from becoming lost in ANE studies. The caution is also intended as a warning against equating Judeo-Christian religion with other religions of the ANE or Greco-Roman world.

2. The Decrees of the PBC 1905-1915

The church was now moving ahead, albeit cautiously, into the field of scientific biblical criticism[57]. Leo established the PBC due to the increased

---

[53] *EB*, §106; *OCT*, §315.

[54] *EB*, §118; *OCT*, §329.

[55] Leo did not indicate what these studies should include, leaving some room for development.

[56] Leo refered to Aquinas' theory of sensible appearances to explain scientific discrepancies (cf. *EB*, §121; *OCT* §333).

[57] H.J.T. JOHNSON, «Leo XIII», 414, noted the criticism of *Providentissimus Deus* by Charles Gore, a respected Anglican theologian of the period who interpreted the document as requiring a strictly historical interpretation of the scriptures (along the lines of a fundamentalist approach). JOHNSON assails his views as unfounded. J.A. HOWLETT, «The higher criticism and archeology» discusses the criticisms of *Providentissimus Deus* and concludes with a positive appraisal of the encyclical. He sees it as a moderate teaching that rather than overly restricting Catholic biblical scholarship gave it room to expand. In this regard, he was proven right. W.L. NEWTON, «*Providentissimus Deus*», 123, notes: «Even the decrees of the Council of Trent, fundamental as they are, scarcely outweigh this encyclical; for it was issued in times more critical than the Protestant revolt, and it is more detailed in the positive direction it gives to Catholic exegesis. From the past the document gathers into one earnest ex-

Catholic participation in biblical studies. The Commission would gather and issue decisions on various biblical questions raised in current scholarship[58]. Between the years 1905 and 1915 fourteen decisions regarding biblical questions were issued by the Commission.

2.1 *The Scholarly and Pastoral Situation and The Church's Response*

Following *Providentissimus Deus* Catholic scholars began incorporating elements of the scientific methods into their studies. The two most noted Catholic biblical scholars of the period were M.J. Lagrange and A. Loisy. Lagrange was the founder of the *École Biblique* and the *Revue Biblique*. In 1897, while giving a lecture in Fribourg, he suggested accepting aspects of the source theory for the Pentateuch (although he still held to Mosaic authorship)[59]. In 1902, he spoke positively of critical methodology at a conference in Toulouse[60]. Loisy's work, on the other hand, eventually led him to reject the notion of biblical inspiration as well as Christ's intention to found the church. Several of his thoughts were condemned in the *Lamentabili*[61]. He was excommunicated in 1908, his views being characterized as modernist.

Pius X, in *Pascendi Dominici Gregis*, described the modernist movement as a mixed system of all sorts of heresies unified by the belief in the spirit of the times and a rejection of immutability in doctrine. In the early

pression our Catholic faith in the divine origin of the Scriptures; and for the future it establishes principles upon which that faith may be defended».

S. HARTDEGEN, «Influence of *Providentissimus Deus*», 141-47 notes the influence of the encyclical on Catholic biblical Studies of the period. He lists Catholic scholars, translations of the biblical texts, versions, commentaries, periodicals and biblical societies that developed after the publication of the encyclical. See also C.P. GRANNAN, «A program of biblical studies», and H.J. HEUSER, «The encyclical *Providentissimus Deus*» for the development of a university Scripture curriculum based on the encyclical.

[58] The PBC was established through the Apostolic Letter *Vigilantiae*, issued on October 30, 1902. *EB*, §137-148; *OCT*, §350-366. Leo noted three functions of the Commission. The first function was to analyze the intellectual trend of the day regarding biblical sciences and to employ those discoveries that are useful — special mention is made of the study of philology and similar sciences. The second function was to exercise «active vigilance and unremitting assiduity» regarding the authority of the Scriptures. The third function was to focus attention on biblical interpretation as a source for spiritual nourishment for the faithful. For futher reading on the history of the PBC see A. VANHOYE, «Passé et présent de la Commission Biblique».

[59] Subsequently published in the *Revue Biblique*: M.J. LAGRANGE, «Les sources du Pentateuque».

[60] M.J. LAGRANGE, «Bulletin».

[61] The Holy Office published the *Lamentabili* on July 3, 1907.

part of the twentieth century critical biblical scholarship came under suspicion of being part of this movement[62]. The challenge to traditionally held beliefs and the popularization of critical scholarship naturally led to confusion and consternation among the faithful raising an additional concern for the magisterium.

The church responded to this crisis with a very conservative approach toward scripture studies. The results of scientific criticism would be scrutinized very closely for tenents of «modernism» and anything suspicious would be curtailed. Magisterial concerns at this time were not so much a serious evaluation of biblical methodology as a criticism of its results. Critical scholarship was sacrificed for the pastoral well-being of the Church. The PBC decisions, the *Lamentabilli* and part of the encyclical *Pascendi Dominici Gregis* contain the church's response to biblical studies at this time. The PBC decisions are considered below[63].

2.2 *The Content of the PBC Decisions*

The PBC issued fourteen decisions regarding biblical scholarship between 1905-1915. The first two decisions deal with biblical history, the remaining twelve consider individual sections of the Bible. The PBC presents each decision as either a positive or negative response to a question. The decisions are restrictive for the most part. Some decisions, however, are ambiguous leaving room for more discussion. General characteristics of the decisions include the following: the affirmation of ecclesial authority regarding biblical studies; the non-critical acceptance of tradition and the testimony of the fathers; the support for critical methods when they support traditional beliefs (for example, authorship and sources) and an indiscriminate endorsement of biblical history. The contents of the documents are summarized in figure five below[64].

---

[62] *Pascendi Dominus Gregis* was published on September 8, 1907. For further reading on biblical studies during the pontificate of Pius X see: A. BEA, «Il modernismo biblico»; A. BEA, *San Pio X;* «C. THEOBALD, «L'exégèse catholique»; A. VACCARI, «Pio X e gli studi biblici»

[63] The *Lamentabilli* and *Pascendi Dominici Gregis* are not presented in this thesis. The content regarding biblical studies is similar to that of the PBC decisions.

[64] R.F. COLLINS, *Introduction to the New Testament*, 365, notes that the first decision came in response to two theories regarding implicit citations. Ferdinand Prat insisted that it was possible for the author to cite sources with which he did not agree without making any explicit reference to the fact that he was quoting. Bonaccorsi held that the sacred author was responsible for the truth of his quotations only when he stated his agreement with them.

2.3 *The HCM in the PBC Decisions*

The intention of the PBC decisions is not so much scholarly as it is pastoral. The primary concern was the curtailing of rationalism and modernism, not the formulation of a biblical methodology. The decisions do not specifically refer to the HCM nor do they identify any particular scholars associated with the theories that they criticize. They do, however, deal with the results of historical-critical studies. The elements of the HCM that can be detected in these decisions will be identified below. First hermeneutical principles will be presented followed by elements of the individual criticisms.

Hermeneutical Principles. The PBC was ambiguous regarding the *literal sense.* On the one hand scientific data may be explained by the author using common parlance of the day with no intention of expressing scientific data[65]. On the other hand, the author's intention may not be used to deny biblical history[66]. While addressing the interpretation of Genesis, the Commission states that allegorical interpretation is permitted so long as it is tied to the literal/historical meaning[67]. The PBC decisions also seek to preserve the integrity of the canonical collection, especially regarding the relationship between the OT and the NT. For example, it is unacceptable to hold that the prophet always addressed a local situation, for sometimes he predicts the future[68]. The same principle applies to the psalms[69].

Introduction. The PBC decisions made several observations regarding authorship and dating of individual works. The decisions defend the traditional authorship of Isaiah, Matthew, Mark, Luke and John[70]. The evidence used in support of traditional authorship is external to the biblical text[71]. More flexibility is noticed with the Psalms. Several psalms are required to be Davidic, others are left undecided. The psalms that are affirmed as Davidic specifically mention his name, either in the psalm itself or in another biblical book[72]. Other than this, no principles are given for

---

[65] *EB*, §330; *OCT*, §407.
[66] *EB*, §189; *OCT*, §383.
[67] *EB*, §386; *OCT*, §433-434.
[68] *EB*, §277; *OCT*, §387.
[69] *EB*, §339; *OCT*, §425.
[70] *EB*, §280,394,409; *OCT*, §391,450, 379.
[71] cf. *EB*, §187; *OCT*, §379.
[72] *EB*, §335; *OCT*, §417.

Contents of the PBC Decisions 1905-1915

Date Location	Title Contents of the decision
Feb 13, 1905 EB, 160 OCT, 367-368	*On explaining historical presentation as an «Implicit Quotations»* The implicit citation theory attempted to explain historical problems in a text on the grounds that that the inspired author quoted a non-inspired source which contained an error. The PBC rules that it is unacceptable except when it can be proved that the sacred author really cites another source and the author's integrity is not violated when positing a source used - in other words when he uses a source he makes it his own.
June 23, 1905 EB, 161 OCT, 369-370	*On explaining historical presentation as «historical appearance»* Historical problems in a text can be explained as «historical appearance» only when it can be proved that the author had no intention of giving historical fact when he wrote the text. In other words his intention had to be to use it as a parable or allegory distinct from the literal or historical significance of the words.
June 27, 1906 EB, 181-184 OCT, 371-378	*On the Mosaic Authorship of the Pentateuch* The PBC states the following: Moses is author of Pentateuch and it was not compiled in a period after his death; it is possible that someone wrote at the dictation and/or direction of Moses; it may be postulated that Moses used written or oral sources in his composition; and textual emendations whether additions (i.e. death of Moses) or modifications (i.e. language changes in translations) may have been added after the death of Moses by either glosses or the work of an inspired author.
May 29, 1907 EB, 187-189 OCT, 379-384	*On the Author and Historicity of the Gospel of John* Authorship: The Apostle John was the author of the Fourth Gospel as based on external evidence such as testimony of the Fathers, its title in the canons and catalogues, as well as ancient manuscripts and early liturgical texts. Internal evidence may be used to support this identification. Comparison with Synoptics: Differences between John and the other gospels can be reasonably solved considering the diversity of time, scope and hearers to whom the author wrote.
June 28, 1908 EB, 276-280 OCT, 385-394	*On the Book of Isaiah* The PBC decided the following: The prophecies in the *Isaiah* are the foretelling of future events, they are not to be considered narratives composed after the event nor are the supernatural elements to be removed from the prophecies; The fulfillment of messianic and eschatological prophecies are not to be isolated to an immediate fulfillment within the prophet's own life time; The prophecies may be of events much later than the prophet's lifetime without requiring a second author (ie. Isaiah 40-66); It is not permitted to use philological argument for a plurality of authors; nor may cumulative arguments be used.

Figure 5a: The PBC Decisions 1905-1915

Contents of the PBC Decisions 1905-1915

Date Location	Title Contents of the decision
June 30, 1909 EB,324-331 OCT, 395-410	*On the Historicity of Genesis 1-3* The PBC rejects the opinions of various exegetical systems which try to exclude a historical meaning for the first three chapters of Genesis. The events of these chapters are rooted in real, objective and historical events. They may not be explained away through the use of myth, fable, or cosmologies of other ancient notions. Furthermore they may not be explained as being presented under the appearance of history to explain a religious or philosophical truth. As long as the literal sense is not denied, allegory may be used following the example of the Fathers. It is not necessary to seek scientific accuracy in the text. The historicity of several specific items is mentioned: «special creation of man, the formation of the first woman from man, the unity of the human race, the original happiness of our first parents in a state of justice, integrity, and immortality, the divine command laid upon man to prove his obedience, the transgression of that divine command at the instigation of the devil under the form of a serpent, the fall of our first parents from their primitive state of innocence and the promise of a future redeemer». However, the word *yôm* may mean a natural day or a space/period of time.
May 1, 1910 EB,332-339 OCT, 411-426	*On the Psalms* David does not have to be considered the author of all the psalms; however, the following must be regarded as Davidic: 2,15,17,31,68, and 109. The titles in the Alexandrian text should not be questioned except for serious reason. They can be considered as from an ancient Jewish tradition or the authors themselves. The theory that certain psalms were modified or altered after they were originally written (for liturgical or musical reasons or by the error of copyists) is permitted. A late date i.e. after Ezra or Nehemiah based on internal evidence may not be held. A messianic nature must be recognized in some of the psalms.
June 19, 1911 EB,383-389 OCT, 427-440	*On the Gospel of Matthew* Matthew the Apostle is the author of the first Gospel. That it was written in Aramaic or Hebrew is sufficiently supported by the tradition. It is not to be held that the gospel was written after the destruction of Jerusalem. It was not originally a collection of sayings by an anonymous author. The Greek Matthew is identical in substance with the original. The arrangement of material for dogmatic or apologetic purposes does not necessarily violate the historicity of the events described in the Gospel. Passages peculiar to *Matthew* are not to be considered devoid of historicity just because they are only in the first gospel (i.e. chapters 1-2; primacy of Peter, power to Baptize given to Apostles, universal mission entrusted to the Apostles, the Apostles' profession of faith in the divinity of Christ)

Figure 5b: The PBC Decisions 1905-1915

Contents of the PBC Decisions 1905-1915

Date Location	Title Contents of the decision
June 26, 1912 EB, 399-400 OCT, 459-462	*On the Synoptic Problem* Scholars may discuss the problem of the differences among the three synoptics. However, they may not subscribe to the Two Source Theory, which says Matthew and Luke writing independently used Mark and Q as literary sources.
June 12, 1913 EB, 401-406 OCT, 463-474	*On Acts of the Apostles* Luke is the author of the third gospel and the Acts of the Apostles. Internal considerations particularly the two prologues are used as evidence. Acts of the Apostles is the work of one sole author. The we-passages confirm the unity of composition and its authenticity. The PBC denies that Acts was written later than Paul's captivity and rejects the theory that explains the abrupt ending of Acts as due to another book either written or planned. Luke used his sources including Paul accurately, honestly, and faithfully; so historical accuracy may be claimed.
June 12, 1913 EB, 407-410 OCT, 475-482	*On the Pastoral Epistles (I and II Timothy; Titus)* The Pastoral Epistles were written by Paul and should be considered genuine and canonical. The *Fragmentary Theory* is rejected (The theory states that the Pastoral epistles were made of fragments from other non-paulinte epistles now lost. The letters were written between the period of liberation from the first imprisonment and Paul's death.
June 24, 1914 EB, 411-413 OCT, 483-488	*On the Letter to the Hebrews* The epistle is a genuine epistle of Paul. Paul mus te retained as the author but the question of whether he planned and composed the letter in its final form is still open for discussion. The canonicity and authority of the letter is also affirmed.
June 18, 1915 EB, 414-416 OCT, 489-494	*On the Parousia and Second Coming* Problems concerning the parousia cannot be explained by holding that the writer was expressing a human view which was erroneous. Paul has said nothing concerning the Parousia which was out of harmony with the ignorance of the time. 1 Thess.4:15-17 (esp. ἡμεῖς οἱ ζῶντες περιλειπόμενοι) should not be interpreted as meaning Paul thought he would live to see the Parousia.

Figure 5c: The PBC Decisions 1905-1915

evaluating the identity of the author. The date of composition is also discussed for several works. Determination of the latest date is based on traditional grounds[73]. The only principle given is phrased in a negative way: if internal evidence is used in dating, it cannot be the only evidence used[74].

Textual Criticism. The need for textual criticism is acknowledged indirectly. While discussing the Pentateuch, the Commission mentions modifications in the text. The variants can be explained by the following: the translation of older words with a more recent expression, an addition to the text by an inspired author; an error of amannensis; and the addition of glosses[75]. The titles of the psalms are seen as part of the text based on witness of the Hebrew text and are older than the LXX. This may be questioned for solid reason[76]. While the PBC affirmed the longer ending of Mark as authentic, it gives no reasons. The commission acknowledged a textual problem in Luke 1:46 (some MSS have the Magnificat attributed to Elizabeth instead of Mary). Appeal is made to the overwhelming support of other manuscripts as well as the context of the passage to solve the problem[77].

Philology. The decision to treat *yôm* as a period of time notes an appreciation for the use of philology in the study of the Bible[78]. In another decision, the we-passages of the Acts of the Apostles are described as a philological support for the historicity of the events described therein[79].

Literary/Source Criticism. Source criticism is allowed with the Pentateuch as long as Mosaic authorship is preserved[80]. However, the Two-Source theory is rejected for the Synoptics as well as the «fragmentary hypothesis» for the pastoral letters[81]. Results of literary criticism are used to support the single authorship of Luke-Acts. Studies of the prologues indicate the unity of Luke-Acts based on language, style, method of narration, the scope of doctrine[82].

---

[73] E.g. Acts had to be composed around the time of Paul's captivity. The Pastoral Epistles were written prior to Paul's death.

[74] *EB*, §338; *OCT*, §423.

[75] *EB*, §184, *OCT*, §377.

[76] *EB*, §335; *OCT*, §417. The decision does not elaborate what it means by «solid reason».

[77] *EB*, §393; *OCT*, §447.

[78] *EB*, §331; *OCT*, §409.

[79] *EB*, §403; *OCT*, §467.

[80] *EB*, §181-183; *OCT*, §371-375.

[81] *EB*, §400; *OCT*, §461.

[82] *EB*, §401; *OCT*, §463.

Genre/Form Criticism and History of Religions. The results of form criticism are viewed very negatively. Biblical history cannot be dismissed as a result of literary form[83]. Texts may not be explained as fables or cosmologies borrowed from ancient religions. Genesis 1–3 may not be explained as legend[84]..

Historical Criticism. Although the decisions do not specify principles for the study of history, general guidelines can be deduced from the different decisions. When considering biblical history, the exegete must consider: references in other parts of the bible[85]; continual witness of the Jewish people[86]; the tradition of the church[87]; internal arguments from the text[88]; the witness of the canon, catalogues, manuscripts, codices, and liturgical texts (re: supporting authorship of biblical texts); and the unanimous decisions of the fathers[89].

The PBC decisions curtailed the use of critical methodology by Catholic exegetes. The reasons were more pastoral than scholarly. The value of these statements today is historical. The ambiguity used to express these decisions is perhaps an indication of a willingness to open up areas for more discussion at a latter period. This willingness can also be seen in Pius XII's *Divino Afflante Spiritu*, and even more explicitly in the letters of Miller and Kleinhans in 1955 (see below page 130).

3. *Spiritus Paraclitus*

The PBC decisions had the effect of restricting Catholic biblical studies[90]. Yet even during this period the church encouraged the cautious development and use of critical methods. In 1906, Pius X issued directives for biblical studies in seminaries. He suggested that courses stress inspiration and canonicity while incorporating scientific methodology. The following studies should be included in the curriculum: the study of the original texts and important versions, the history of both testaments; the history of the Hebrew people and their relations with other oriental na-

---

[83] *EB*, §161, 189; *OCT*, §370, 383.

[84] *EB*, §277; *OCT*, §387 . Possibly a reference to Gunkel's work on Genesis in either *Schöpfung und Chaos* (1895) or *Commentary on Genesis* (1901).

[85] *EB*, §191; *OCT*, §371.

[86] *EB*, §181, 325; *OCT*, §371, 397.

[87] *EB*, §181, 325, 383; *OCT*, §371,397,427.

[88] *EB*, §181; *OCT*, §371.

[89] *EB*, §383; *OCT*, §427.

[90] As did Pius X's *Praestantia Sacrae Scripturae* (October 7, 1907) EB §268-273; 0CT, §584-589, which reinforced the authority and decisions of the PBC.

tions[91]; the study of the ancient languages (for the more promising students) — Hebrew, Greek, Syriac, Arabic and other Semitic languages[92]; the study of biblical exegesis, archaeology, geography, chronology, theology, and history[93]. In 1909, Pius X established the Pontifical Biblical Institute (PBI). Pius' instructions for the curriculum included the following elements of the HCM: the introduction, archeology, history, geography, and philology. He furthermore suggests the formulation of a methodology that is used with scientific rigor[94].

Although the Catholic church was committed to further scientific research, the cautious approach was favored and the results of scientific exegesis were carefully monitored. This is perhaps best seen in the removal of Père Lagrange from the École Biblique in 1912 under the suspicion of heresy[95]. The cautious approach was also reflected in the 1917 Code of Canon Law. The Code placed restrictions on publishing books on the Scriptures without ecclesial approval[96] as well as forbidding the publication of modern language editions of the Bible[97]. Additional restraint on Catholic biblical scholarship was evident in Benedict XV's encyclical *Spiritus Paraclitus* issued on September 15, 1920.

3.1 *The Scholarly and Pastoral Situation and The Church's Response*

The fifteenth centenary of the death of St. Jerome was the immediate occasion for *Spiritus Paraclitus*. In fact the encyclical was issued on September 15, the feast of St. Jerome. Another issue that prompted the letter was a dispute concerning the directives in *Providentissimus Deus* regarding the study of history. *Providentissimus Deus* had noted that the same principles used for evaluating scientific data in the Bible could be applied to the study of history[98]. This principle was interpreted along the

---

[91] *EB*, §167; *OCT*, §500.

[92] *EB*, §172; *OCT*, §505.

[93] *EB*, §173; *OCT*, §506. The dogmatic formulations of the church provide the framework for using such studies.

[94] *EB*, §291.

[95] The foundation of the PBI was viewed, at that time, as a corrective to the École Biblique that was under suspicion concerning their exegetical method. In 1912, Lagrange was recalled from Jerusalem. A year later, after having faithfully submitted and explained his views, he was invited to return to the École by Pius X. See F.M. Braun, *The Work of Père Lagrange*; M. GILBERT, «Cinquant'anni di magistero romano », 24. For further reading on Catholic biblical studies of this period see footnote 62.

[96] *EB*, §435.

[97] *EB*, §436.

[98] *EB*, §123; *OCT*, §336.

following lines: if problems regarding scientific data in the text could be explained by saying that the author wrote what sensibly appeared to him, then problems concerning historical data could be explained by saying that the author wrote what was commonly accepted in the community at the time he wrote. Historical error in the text may result from the author expressing the common thought of the age. For example, during the period when the NT was written, Moses was considered the author of the Pentateuch. The reasoning would follow that when Luke wrote Acts mentioning the Book of Moses he was reporting the belief as it was commonly known at the time not making a definitive proclamation that Moses wrote the Pentateuch. *Spiritus Paraclitus* responds to this theory on interpreting historical data.

3.2 *The Contents of Spiritus Paraclitus*

The contents of the encyclical are framed within a commentary on the life and work of St. Jerome[99]. *Spiritus Paraclitus* basically affirmed the teaching of *Providentissimus Deus*[100]. The work, however, developed the inspiration-inerrancy-authorship question. Theories regarding biblical inerrancy were checked. Benedict rejected the following positions: truth is limited to religious elements in the text, truth is expressed according to external appearance, and the notion that it is not important what God said as why he said it[101].

Regarding the authorship of the Bible, *Spiritus Paraclitus* spoke in terms of a divine-human partnership. The human author, however, is still viewed as an instrument of the divine. God is the author through his illumination of the writer's mind even to the point of editing; yet the individual writers have full freedom under the divine influence[102]. The presenta-

---

[99] Benedict spoke on the life of Jerome in §591-599. The encyclical contains many references to Jerome's life and work that are beyond the scope of this thesis and will not be considered in the presentation.

[100] Benedict followed *Dei Filius* and *Providentissimus Deus* in affirming the inspiration and inerrancy of the scriptures as tied to divine authorship. See *EB*, §450-452; *OCT*,§606-609. He also echoed *Providentissimus Deus* regarding the guides for the exegete: the Holy Spirit, the Fathers of the Church and magisterium. See *EB*, §469-473; *OCT*, §630-633.

[101] *EB*, §454; *OCT*, §612-614.

[102] *EB*, §448; *OCT*, §600. «You will not find a page in his writings (Jerome) which does not show clearly that he, in common with the whole Catholic church, firmly and consistently held that the sacred books — written as they were under the inspiration of the Holy Spirit — have God for their author, and as such were delivered to the church. Thus he asserts that the books of the Bible were composed at the inspiration, or suggestion, or even at the dictation of the Holy Spirit; even that they were

tion did not solve the question of this relationship, rather it presented the fundamental elements in the tension, any theory that does not respect both elements will be unacceptable.

Benedict briefly mentioned the relationship between the OT and NT. The unity of the two testaments is Christ, for «every single page of either testament seems to center around Christ...»[103].

3.3 *The HCM as Exposed in Spiritus Paraclitus*

Benedict praised scholars who sought to find new ways of explaining the difficulties in the Bible through the use of critical methods. He warned them, however, that they «will come to miserable grief if they neglect our predecessor's (Leo) injunctions and overstep the limits set by the Fathers»[104]. This section will consider the following elements of the HCM as presented in *Spiritus Paraclitus*: hermeneutical principles, textual criticism and philology, and historical criticism.

Hermeneutical Principles. The defense of biblical historicity heavily influenced Benedict's thoughts on exegesis. He noted that Jerome's first rule of exegesis is the study of the actual words: «he was most careful to consult the original text, to compare various versions, and if he discovered any mistake in them, to explain it and thus make the text perfectly clear»[105]. Benedict following Jerome described the *literal sense* as the basis of interpretation. Here, the *literal sense* is almost equated with an *historical sense*. Benedict states:

---

written and edited by Him. Yet he never questions but that the individual authors of the books worked in full freedom under the divine afflatus, each of them in accordance with his individual nature and character. Thus he is not merely content to affirm as a general principle — what indeed pertains to all the sacred writers — that they followed the Spirit of God as they wrote, in such sort and that God is the principal cause of all that Scripture means and says; but he also accurately describes what pertains to each individual writer. In each case Jerome shows us how, in composition, in language, in style and mode of expression, each of them uses his own gifts and powers; hence he is able to portray and describe for us their individual character, almost their very features...This partnership of God and man in the production of a work in common Jerome illustrates by the case of a workman who uses instruments for the production of his work; for he says whatsoever the sacred authors say, 'Is the word of God, and not their own; and what the Lord says by their mouths He says, as it were, by means of an instrument'». Cf. *EB*, §448; *OCT*, §601, God «illumines the writer's mind regarding the particular truth, which in the person of God, he is to set before men...».

103 *EB*, §491; *OCT*, §680.
104 *EB*, §453; *OCT*, §611.
105 *EB*, §485; *OCT*, §655.

Jerome then goes on to say that all interpretation rests on the *literal sense*, and that we are not to think that there is no *literal sense* merely because a thing is said metaphorically, for «the history itself is often presented in metaphorical dress and described figuratively» Indeed, he himself affords the best refutation of those who maintain that that certain passages have no historical meaning: «We are not rejecting the history, we are merely giving a spiritual interpretation of it»[106].

After noting Jerome's insistence on establishing the *literal sense*, Benedict spoke of a deeper or hidden meaning (*spiritual sense*)[107]. He also suggested caution not to violate the historical sense in favor of the mystical: «... he (Jerome) repudiates many mystical interpretations alleged by ancient writers; for he feels that they are not sufficiently based on the literal meaning»[108]. He noted the absence of a spiritual meaning of much exegesis of the day and suggests:

> if they would pass from the literal to the more profound meaning in temperate fashion, and thus lift themselves to a higher plane, they would, with St. Jerome, realize how true are St. Paul's words: «All Scripture is inspired by God and useful for teaching, for reproving, for correcting, for instructing in justice»[109].

Textual Criticism and Philology. Benedict accepted the important and necessary role of textual criticism in an exegete's work[110]. Appreciation for philological study is reflected in Benedict's statements on the *literal sense*.

Historical Criticism. Benedict criticized those who apply Leo's principles for the physical sciences to history. Specifically those who hold that historical portions of Sacred Scripture «do not rest on absolute truth ... but on relative truth, namely what people then commonly thought». His critique is very strong and almost contradicts *Providentissimus Deus*.

> After all, what analogy is there between physics and history? For whereas physics is concerned with «sensible appearances» and must consequently square with phenomena, history, on the contrary, must square with facts, since history is the written account of events as they actually occurred[111].

---

106 *EB*, §486; *OCT*, §657.
107 Here Benedict seems to refer to the *spiritual sense* without using the term. The expression «deeper meaning» or «hidden meaning» is similar to those used by Origen.
108 *EB*, §486; *OCT*, §659.
109 *EB*, §486; *OCT*, §661.
110 *EB*, §446-447, 485; *OCT*, §595-598, 655.
111 *EB*, §455; *OCT*, §615.

Benedict went on to say that even if Leo's principles apply, it is not a universal law, and are only to be used for refuting fallacies and the defense of historical truth[112]. Benedict gave no principles for determining historicity because everything in the text is to be taken as historical. He also criticized the use of several critical procedures that result in destroying the historical value of a text. Specifically mentioned are: implicit quotations, the identification of a text as «pseudo-historical», and the «kinds of literature» theory[113]. The notion of «implicit quotations» was discussed above (see footnote 64). The other two can be considered part of genre-form criticism. The form cannot be used to dismiss historicity.

4. *Divino Afflante Spiritu*[114]

Twenty-three years passed before another encyclical was written regarding scripture studies. Restrictions continued to be placed on Catholic biblical scholars during this period. The magisterial statements issued between the two encyclicals are listed on figure six. The PBC Letter to the Bishops of Italy in 1941 was the first indication of a new openness to critical biblical studies. The door to modern studies was fully opened with the encyclical *Divino Afflante Spiritu*.

4.1 *The Scholarly and Pastoral Situation and The Church's Response*

The HCM continued to develop becoming further defined and specialized as the twentieth century progressed. Criticisms began to be identified as individual disciplines. At this point the HCM consisted of several approaches: textual criticism, philology-grammatical criticism, source criticism and form criticism. Form criticism was particularly influential during this period. It had developed earlier in the century as a reaction to over zealous source criticism[115]. The goal of form criticism was to identify the oral traditions and

---

[112] *EB*, §456; *OCT*, §616.

[113] *EB*, §461; *OCT*, §619.

[114] For further reading see: «*Divino Afflante Spiritu*; encyclical»; W.M. ABBOTT, «Pius XII's Encyclical»; B. AHERN, «Textual Directives»; A. BEA, «*Divino Afflante Spiritu*»; ID., «L'enciclica *Divino Afflante Spiritu*»; E. GALBIATI, «I generi letterari»; G. HAMILTON, «*Divino Afflante Spiritu*»; A. KLEINHANS, «De progressu doctrine et praxi ecclesiasticae»; J. LLAMOS, «La enciclica *Divino Afflante Spiritu*»; J.A. O'FLYNN, «*Divino Afflante Spiritu*»; U.E. PARE, «Church and the Bible»; A. RoMEO, «L'enciclica *Divino Afflante Spiritu*»; E.F. SUTCLIFFE, «*Divino Afflante Spiritu*»; P. VANUTELLI, «Dopo l'enciclica *Divino Afflante Spiritu*».

[115] Gunkel developed *form criticism* for the OT while Bultmann, Dibelius and Schmidt developed it for the NT.

the *Sitz-im-Leben* from which the written sources originated. For some exegetes form criticism renewed a confidence regarding biblical history, for others it confirmed the notion that historical reconstruction was futile and impossible.

Catholic biblical scholarship during the twenties and thirties continued along a cautious path. The magisterium continued to defend the inspiration and inerrancy of the scriptures as they had been traditionally understood. Any theory that seemed to violate the traditional formulation of inerrancy or inspiration was seen as an attack on the authority of the Scriptures and the Church. The attitude began to change in the late thirties and into the forties.

The beginning of change can be seen as early as 1929 when P.J. Levie published «*La crisi dell'Antico Testamento*»[116]. Levie raises the question of whether Catholics should use scientific investigation including archeology and comparable ANE literature in the study of the Bible. Another indication of an openness to the HCM came in 1935 when A. Bea attended, with the authorization of Pius XI, a conference on the study of the OT in Göttingen organized by Protestant exegetes[117]. At the same time there was a movement in the Church that did not favor the critical study of the Bible. In 1941 an anonymous pamphlet titled *A Most Grave Danger for the Church and for Souls. The Critical-scientific System of Studying and Interpreting Holy Scripture, Its Evil Misconceptions and Aberrations* was distributed to the entire episcopacy of Italy[118]. The letter heavily criticized the use of scientific-critical methods in biblical exegesis. The pamphlet reflects a growing fundamentalist outlook regarding biblical interpretation during this period[119]. The PBC responded to the pamphlet calling it «a virulent attack against the scientific study of the Holy Scriptures»[120] (see figure six). Such was the general state of affairs just prior to *Divino Afflante Spiritu*. Although these events helped prepare for the encyclical, the immediate occasion was the fiftieth anniversary of *Providentissimus Deus*. The encyclical was issued by Pius XII on September 30, 1943.

---

116 J. LEVIE, «La crise de l'Ancien Testament».

117 M. GILBERT, «Cinquant'anni di magistero romano», 24-26.

118 The author of the pamphlet is unnamed, however, it is believed to have been written by Dolindo Ruotolo under the pseudonym Dain Cohene.

119 Fundamentalism began in the United States as a Protestant reaction to rationalist exegesis. The movement spread to parts of Europe and had an influence on many Catholics. Though the intention is to defend the divine character of the biblical text as well as the historicity of the text, the result is a separation between the divine and the human as well as between faith and reason. The system ends up in naive fideism.

120 *EB*, §523; *OCT*, §697.

Ecclesial Documents Regarding Biblical Studies 1921–1943

Date Location	Title Contents of the decision
Nov 17, 1921 PBC EB, 496	*On the variant readings to the OT and NT of the Vulgate* The PBC permits the publication of variants in the Vulgate versions of the NT and OT. Notes for scholarly purposes such as St. Jerome's Prefaces may be added.
Dec 12, 1923 Holy Office Merry de Val EB, 497-504	*On the condemnation of the «Manuel Biblique»* The Vigouroux-Bacuez-Brassac manual «Manuel Biblique ou Cours d'Ecriture Sainte a l'usage des Seminaires» is condemned. The reasons center on inspiration and inerrancy regarding historicity. The decision states that it is impermissible to separate essence and detail when dealing with inspiration.
April 27, 1924 Pius XI EB, 505-512	*On the training of Bible Professors* Gives guidelines for the training of professors in Sacred Scriptures. The regulations include a requirement for seminary professors to take the license or doctorate from the PBC or PBI.
April 2, 1925 Holy Office EB, 512a	*The Italian Bible translated by Giovanni Luzzi* The Holy Office forbids the use of Luzzi's (a Waldensian) Italian translation by the faithful. The document cites Canon 1399 n.1 that states only theology students or Scripture scholars are permitted to use editions or translations by non-Catholics.
July 1, 1933 PBC EB, 513-514 OCT, 689-692	*On two false interpretations of the Biblical text* 1. It is not permitted to exclude the resurrection of Jesus Christ from an interpretation of Ps 15:10-11. 2. It is not permissible to hold that in the literal sense Matt 16:26 and Luke 9:25 refer to only the temporal life of man and not his soul.
Feb 27, 1934 PBC EB, 515-519	*On the work called «Die Einwanderung Israels in Kanaan»* «Die Einwanderung Israels in Kanaan» written by Federico Schmidtke of Bratislava is censured. The PBC notes the following points made by Schmidtke with which it finds difficulty: the patriarchal narratives do not contain the history of particular individuals but of the tribes, that Jacob is not a son of Isaac but a representative of a certain Aramean tribe and that not all the Israelites went down to Egypt but only a part of the people namely the tribe of Joseph.

Figure 6a: Significant Ecclesial Documents Regarding Biblical Studies, 1921-1943

Ecclesial Documents Regarding Biblical Studies 1921–1943

Date Location	Title Contents of the decision
April 30, 1934 PBC EB, 520	*On the use of the translations of the Sacred Scriptures in the Church* Responding to a question raised by the Bishops of Holland regarding the use at liturgical functions of a vernacular version of the Epistles and Gospels from the original languages. The PBC responds that it is not permissible, only the Vulgate should be used in liturgy.
March 14,1937 Pius XI AAS, XXIX, 145-167 Carlen, *Papal Encyclicals 1903-39*, 525-536	*Mit brennender Sorge* Pius defends the canonicity and authority of the OT. Pius states (paragraphs15-16): «The sacred books of the OT are exclusively the word of God, and constitute a substantial part of his revelation, they are penetrated by a subdued light in harmony with the slow development of revelation, the dawn of the bright day of redemption. This should be expected in historical and didactic books, they reflect in many particulars the imperfection, the weakness and sinfulness of man. But side by side with innumerable touches of greatness, they also record the story of the chosen people, bearers of the Revelation and the Promise, ...Whoever wishes to see banished from church and school the Biblical history and wise doctrines of the OT blasphemes the name of God, blasphemes the Almighty's plan of salvation and makes limited and narrow human thought the judge of Gods design over the history of the world: he denies his faith in the true Christ...»
July 16, 1939 PBC EB, 521	*Letter of the PBC to the Bishops of Italy* The PBC responds to a pamphlet sent anonymously to all the bishops of Italy with the title: *A Most grave danger for the church and for souls. The critical-scientific system of studying and interpreting Holy Scripture, its evil misconceptions and aberrations.* The anonymous author attacks all levels of the critical method proposing a spiritual or meditative exegesis in its stead. The PBC rebukes the arguments under four topics: a) the literal sense, b) the teaching of Trent does not exclude recourse to the original text; c) textual criticism; and d) the study of oriental languages and auxiliary sciences. In each of these areas the PBC defends current Catholic approaches using critical investigation. The Commission rebukes the author in all his arguments especially the superficiality of the statements. Moreover, the letter is published under the approval of the Holy Father (Pius XII).

Figure 6b: Significant Ecclesial Documents Regarding Biblical Studies, 1921-1943

4.2 *The Contents of Divino Afflante Spiritu*

Divino Afflante Spiritu is sometimes referred to as the «Magna Charta» of Catholic exegetes. The encyclical marks a significant turning point for Catholic biblical studies. The period of cautious restraint was over. Now scholars were encouraged to use critical methodologies. The contents of *Divino Afflante Spiritu* will be discussed under the following topics: the affirmation of the teachings of previous documents, inspiration-inerrancy-authorship, new developments in biblical studies, guides to biblical studies, and pastoral issues regarding the Bible.

Affirmation of the Teachings of Previous Ecclesial Documents. Pius XII began his encyclical on biblical studies with a reaffirmation of canonicity, inspiration and divine authorship as defined by the documents of Trent, Vatican I, and Leo XIII[121]. This is followed by a commemoration of the fiftieth anniversary of *Providentissimus Deus* and an acclamation of Leo's defense of biblical inerrancy[122]. Pius calls the encyclical the «supreme guide in biblical studies»[123]. He then traced the major accomplishments of Catholic biblical scholarship from the pontificate of Leo XIII and began with praise for the *École Biblique* and the foundation of the PBC[124]. Following this, he listed the successive pontiffs and their contributions in the promotion of biblical studies[125]. Notably absent is the mention of any restraints placed on biblical scholarship through the decisions of the PBC and other magisterial documents in the first part of the century.

Inspiration-Inerrancy-Authorship. Pius affirmed the earlier documents regarding inspiration and inerrancy but focused attention on the authorship question. In *Providentissimus Deus*, Leo had placed emphasis on the divine author's role in the composition of the Scriptures as a response to rationalist attacks. In *Spiritus Paraclitus*, Benedict described the relationship between the divine and human authors as a «partnership», yet he too emphasizes the divine character. In *Divino Afflante Spiritu*, Pius affirmed both human and divine authorship as his predecessors did, but emphasizes the role of the human author. As Leo defended the divine character of the Scriptures from assault by the rationalists, Pius defended the human character from attacks by the fundamentalists.

---

[121] *EB*, §538; *OCT*, §718.
[122] *EB*, §539; *OCT*, §720.
[123] *EB*, §538; *OCT*, §719.
[124] *EB*, §541; *OCT*, §722.
[125] *EB*, §542-545; *OCT*, §723-728.

Pius described the human author as a «living and reasonable instrument of the Holy Spirit» who «uses his faculties and powers, (so) that from the book composed by him all may easily infer 'the special character of each one and, as it were, his personal traits'». At the same time the author is described as «inspired» and he is an «instrument of the Holy Spirit»[126]. The more vivid description of authorship is found in §37, where the interplay of the divine and human is described with Christological imagery. Pius stated: «for as the substantial Word of God became like to men in all things, "except sin", so the words of God, expressed in human language, are made like to human speech in every respect, except error»[127].

The human author is reasonable and free. He uses his creativity and speaks a language conditioned by time and place in his composition of the biblical text. The human aspect of the word requires a critical study of the text so that the message of the text can be understood. The hermeneutical principle underlying the study is the *literal sense* defined as the author's intention (see below). Then inerrancy is redefined in terms of the *literal sense*. Difficulties in the text regarding both the physical sciences and history can be explained through the *literal sense*[128]; the human author cannot be taxed with error when the intention of his communication was not the conveyance of historical or scientific matter[129].

New Developments in Biblical Studies. Pius noted the developments in biblical studies that were only in their initial stages when Leo wrote *Providentissimus Deus.* He specifically mentioned excavations in Palestine and the discovery «of written documents, which help much toward the knowledge of the languages, letters, events, customs, and forms of worship in ancient times»[130]. He also noted the discovery and study of ancient manuscripts, advances in patristic studies as well as advances in ancient language studies and textual criticism.

The Scriptures: Book of the Church. Pius reminded commentators that the care for and interpretation of the scriptures has been confided to the Church. He followed Leo in calling for interpretations that take into con-

---

126 *EB*, §555; *OCT*, §750.

127 *EB*, §559; *OCT*, §754.

128 *EB*, §560; *OCT*, §755. «Not infrequently — to mention only one instance — when some persons reproachfully charge the Sacred Writers with some historical error or inaccuracy in the recording of facts, on closer examination it turns out to be nothing else than those customary modes of expression and narration peculiar to the ancients, which used to be employed in the mutual dealings of social life and which in fact were sanctioned by common usage».

129 *EB*, §560; *OCT*, §756, cf. 758-9

130 *EB*, §546; *OCT*, §728.

sideration the teaching of the magisterium, the interpretations given by the Fathers and the «analogy of faith»[131].

Pius specifically addressed the role of patristic exegesis. First, he defended patristic exegesis against attacks calling it uncritical[132]. Second, Pius expressed hope that current scholarship can make a deeper and more accurate interpretation using the information that is available today that was not available to the Fathers[133]. Third, he noted the vast field for study in reference to ecclesial authority: «there are but a few texts whose sense has been defined by the authority of the Church, nor are those more numerous about which the teaching of the Holy Fathers is unanimous»[134]

Pastoral Issues and Biblical Studies. Pius stated that the purpose of the Scriptures is not to satisfy intellectual curiosity but to «instruct us to salvation, by the faith which is in Christ Jesus», so «that the man of God may be perfect, furnished to every good work»[135]. Prayerful reading of the Bible is proposed as a vehicle to know Christ and to build reliance on Him. Pius quoted St. Jerome: «to be ignorant of the scriptures is to be ignorant of Christ», and «if there is anything in this life which sustains a wise man and induces him to maintain his serenity amidst the tribulations and adversities of the world, it is in the first place, I consider, the meditation and knowledge of the Scriptures»[136]. To this end, he called on the

---

[131] *EB*, §551; *OCT*, §741. «With special zeal should they apply themselves not only to expounding exclusively these matter which belong to the historical, archaeological, philological and other auxiliary sciences... (but) they should set forth in particular the theological doctrine in faith and morals of the individual books or texts so that their exposition may not only aid the professors of theology in their explanations and proofs of the dogmas of faith, but may also be of assistance to priests in their presentation of Christian doctrine to the people»

[132] *EB*, §554; *OCT*, §745. «For, although sometimes less instructed in profane learning and in the knowledge of languages than the scripture scholars of our time, nevertheless by reason of the office assigned to them by God in the Church, they are distinguished by a certain subtle insight into heavenly things and by a marvelous keenness of intellect, which enables them to penetrate to the very innermost meaning of the divine word and bring to light all that can help to elucidate the teaching of Christ and promote holiness of life».

[133] *EB*, §555; *OCT*, §748. «How difficult for the Fathers themselves, and indeed well nigh unintelligible, were certain passages, is shown, among other things, by the oft repeated efforts of many of them to explain the first chapters of Genesis; likewise by the reiterated attempts of St. Jerome so to translate the Psalms that the *literal sense*, that namely, which is expressed by the words themselves, might be clearly revealed ».

[134] *EB*, §565; *OCT*, §764.

[135] *EB*, §566; *OCT*, §766.

[136] *EB*, §568; *OCT*, §774.

clergy to promote the reading and study of the sacred texts among the faithful. Vernacular versions should be made available (with ecclesiastical approval) and the faithful should be informed about public conferences, dissertations, periodicals on biblical subjects. Furthermore, bishops should see that seminaries are particularly suited with biblical faculties that instill in their students a love for the sacred scriptures. Exegetical «explanation should aim especially at the theological doctrine, avoiding useless disputations and omitting all that is calculated rather to gratify curiosity than to promote true learning and solid piety»[137]. Scripture professors should aim to have their students' hearts set on fire as the word is interpreted and expounded[138].

4.3 *The HCM as Exposed in* Divino Afflante Spiritu

Of all the documents considered in this chapter, *Divino Afflante Spiritu* contains the clearest endorsement of the HCM. Pius encouraged the use of diachronic studies in general when he stated: «...the interpreter must, as it were, go back wholly in spirit to those remote centuries of the East and with the aid of history, archaeology, ethnology, and other sciences, accurately determine what modes of writing, so to speak, the authors of that ancient period would be likely to use, and in fact did use»[139]. The HCM in *Divino Afflante Spiritu* is discussed in the following sections: hermeneutical principles, philology and textual criticism, and literary criticism and auxiliary sciences.

Hermeneutical Principles. Pius spoke of both the *literal sense* and *spiritual senses* of the Scriptures. The *literal sense* is the sense intended by the human author[140]. Since the biblical texts were composed in particular historical settings, critical methodology will aid in determining the human author's intention. The *spiritual sense* must also be identified provided it be «clearly intended by God»[141]. Pius specifically mentioned the use of the OT to prefigure the NT as an example of the *spiritual sense* —

---

137 *EB*, §567; *OCT*, §771.
138 *EB*, §567; *OCT*, §772. The goal of a seminary scripture professor should be to have their students experience what happened to the disciples on the way to Emmaus. The disciples having heard the words of the Master, they exclaimed, «Was not our heart burning within us, whilst he opened to us the Scriptures». Cf. Luke 24:13-35.
139 *EB*, §558; *OCT*, §752.
140 *EB*, §550; *OCT*, §740.
141 *EB*, §552; *OCT*, §743.

for God alone could have known this spiritual meaning and have revealed it to us. He also cautioned against using other figurative senses[142].

Philology and Textual Criticism. Pius praised the renewed study of the original language texts that began in the Renaissance[143]. He called for Catholic biblical scholars to engage in ancient language studies so that he may support the interpretation «by the aids which all branches of philology supply»[144]. The language studies allow access to the original texts, texts that carry more weight than any translation. The use of a skilled literary criticism will foster a deeper understanding of the text[145].

Study of the original texts necessitates a textual critical study. After noting St. Augustine's insistence on using a corrected text, Pius called for the restoration of the text[146]. He noted that the «preconceived notions» of the past have been replaced with established and secure rules. He greeted the discovery of new biblical and ANE texts and codices as sources for fruitful study regarding the transmission of the texts. He furthermore called for the use of textual criticism by Catholic students so that new original language editions may be published[147].

Pius also clarified the place of the Vulgate in relation to the original texts. He noted that the Council Fathers of Trent called for editions of the text in Latin, then Greek and Hebrew. He suggested that the call was never realized due to the difficulties of the times. Trent taught that the Vulgate should be used as authentic but this only applies to the Latin Church.

---

[142] *EB*, §553; *OCT*, §744. «It may indeed be useful, especially in preaching, to illustrate, and present the matters of faith and morals by a broader use of the Sacred text in the figurative sense, provided this be done with moderation and restraint; it should, however, never be forgotten that this use of the Sacred Scripture is, as it were, extrinsic to it and accidental, and that especially in these days, it is not free from danger, since the faithful, in particular those who are well-informed in the sacred and profane sciences, wish to know what God has told us in the Sacred letters rather than what an ingenious orator or writer may suggest by a clever use of the words of Scripture».

[143] *EB*, §547; *OCT*, §731-732.

[144] *EB*, §547; *OCT*, §733.

[145] *EB*, §547; *OCT*, §733. «... having been written by the inspired author himself, (the original language text) has more authority and greater weight than any, even the very best, translation, whether ancient or modern; this can be done all the more easily and fruitfully, if to the knowledge of languages be joined a real skill in literary criticism of the same text».

[146] *EB*, §548; *OCT*, §735. The text should «as perfectly as possible, be purified from the corruptions due to the carelessness of the copyists and be freed, as far as may be done, from glosses and omissions, from the interchange and perdition of words and from all other kinds of mistakes, which are wont to make their way gradually into the writings handed down through many centuries».

[147] *EB*, §548; *OCT*, §736.

Furthermore it only applies to the public use of scriptures and in no way limits the value of the original texts. The Vulgate text was recognized on the basis of use not for critical reasons. The text is not threatened by the use of the original texts nor of translations in the vernacular[148].

Literary Criticism and Auxiliary Sciences. Pius used the term *literary criticism* but its meaning is not clear. It seems to best fit genre-form criticism as described in the first chapter[149]. Pius also mentioned the need to understand such items as idioms, forms of speech, poetic description, legal forms, methods of recording fact and history[150]. Scripture study should incorporate comparison with the other literature of the ANE. While doing so the exegete should pay due consideration to inspiration and the religious purpose of the texts[151]. Pius stressed the importance of such literary studies — the interpreter should «be convinced that this part of his office cannot be neglected without serious detriment to Catholic exegesis»[152].

In order to conduct a proper literary study, exegetes must be aware of the peripheral sciences that will help them understand the cultural, social, and historical conditions of the ANE. The sciences are tools that cannot be neglected — «let them (exegetes) neglect none of those discoveries, whether in the domain of archaeology or in ancient history or literature, which serve to make better known the mentality of the ancient writers, as well as their manner and art of reasoning, narrating, and writing»[153].

5. The Place of the HCM in Catholic Exegesis
   from *Providentissimus Deus* to *Divino Afflante Spiritu*

The nineteenth and twentieth centuries witnessed the formalization of critical techniques and procedures into the disciplines or «criticisms» that constitute the HCM. For the most part this process developed outside the Catholic church. Catholic participation in critical biblical scholarship began in 1893 when Leo XIII opened the door for the cautious use of critical methodologies. The movement into the twentieth century saw restraints placed on scholarship due to the modernist crisis. As the critical methodologies became more credible the church responded with encouragement

---

148 *EB*, §549; *OCT*, §737-739.
149 cf. *EB*, §558-559; *OCT*, §752-754.
150 *EB*, §558; *OCT*, §753.
151 *EB*, §558; *OCT*, §753.
152 *EB*, §560; *OCT*, §755.
153 *EB*, §561; *OCT*, §757.

for their use by Catholic biblical scholars. In 1943 Pius XII granted Catholic scholars the formal call to utilize the developing methodologies.

The ecclesial documents studied in this chapter give the rationale and guidelines for the use of critical biblical scholarship in Catholic exegesis. The guidelines are presented within the broader context of a Catholic understanding of the Bible. The result is that the guidelines were broad directives that the biblical scholar can work with in generating his own method. In other words, the guidelines do not present a method nor do they propose a «step by step» process for interpretation, rather they aid in the formalization of a methodology. The guidelines also aid exegetes, theologians, and even the faithful in evaluating biblical scholarship from a Catholic perspective.

The theological principle that provides the starting point for a Catholic exegete when approaching a text is that the Bible has both a divine aspect and a human aspect. Pius XII best described this using christological imagery. The duel character of the Bible requires the exegete to respect a tension that exists in his studies. The refusal to include either aspect in exegesis will result in deficient and possibly faulty exegesis, such as happened with rationalist exegesis or fundamentalist exegesis. The central problem of rationalist exegesis is that the text is stripped of its divine character. The central problem with fundamentalist exegesis is the stripping of the text of its human character. A balanced approach is necessary.

This chapter of the dissertation has evaluated the ecclesial documents dealing with biblical interpretation. The documents have been studied according to the historical circumstances in which they have developed. Different historical settings have led to different emphases with regard to biblical interpretation. The conclusion of this chapter will summarize the hermeneutical basis of the HCM reflected in the ecclesial documents of this period, then evaluate the place of the HCM in this period by noting the necessity and limits of the method as presented in the documents of the period.

5.1 The Hermeneutical Basis of the HCM

The ecclesial documents issued in this period regarding biblical studies mention the hermeneutical principles which underlie the use of any methodology.

Providentissimus Deus describes the *literal sense* as the obvious sense. In other words the meaning is the verbal or historical meaning. The divine nature of the Bible require other senses. Leo notes that the *literal sense* itself allows other senses when it is adapted to illustrate dogma or morality. The use here seems to refer to the figurative use of language.

Spiritus Paraclitus notes that the *literal sense* is the basis of all interpretation. The *literal sense* here is almost equated with a historical sense. At the same time a deeper meaning is allowed and should be sought. The deeper meaning is hidden behind the words. Benedict seems to be referring here to the *spiritual sense* without specifically mentioning it by name. Care must be taken however not to use a *mystical sense* that invalidates the historical information in the text or *literal sense*.

Divino Afflante Spiritu defines the *literal sense* as that sense intended by the author. Other senses may and do exist but should be firmly rooted in the *literal sense*. The *spiritual sense* is particularly evident in dealing with the OT prefigurations of the NT. Pius notes that the *spiritual sense* needs to be identified provided it is from God. No guidelines are presented to determine this *spiritual sense*.

The three primary documents of this period operate under the principle that the *literal sense* is important; however, there is a certain amount of ambiguity to the *literal sense* in the earlier documents. *Divino Afflante Spiritu* has the clearest presentation of the *literal sense* as the basis for exegetical studies and biblical interpretation. The reader is reminded that the purpose of these documents was not to explicitly give a teaching on the *literal sense*, so the treatments will vary. The earlier documents, stressing the divine aspect of the text give less attention to the *literal sense*. *Divino Afflante Spiritu* stresses the human aspect of the Scriptures as representative of the divine, so the *literal sense* is stressed. Throughout the development of Catholic guidelines to critical approaches, the *literal sense* was viewed as the basis for historical critical research and interpretation. The degree to which this type of exegesis was allowed and/or encouraged depended upon the value and definition of the *literal sense*.

5.2 *Why is the HCM necessary?*

The HCM is needed to help determine the literal sense. Even though the *literal sense* was described differently in the documents of this period (either as the obvious meaning, the historical meaning, or the author's intention), it still required some use of the HCM. By the time of *Divino Afflante Spiritu* the method had made significant advances in its own development. The idea of inspiration as divine-human cooperation required that respect be paid to the human author of the text and the meaning he was trying to communicate through the text. The significance of this document or theory should not be underestimated. The basis of much Catholic exegesis from this time onwards, really the entry of Catholics into the field of critical exegetical studies, begins with this concept and principle.

The HCM is needed for the study of the original language texts. Provi-dentissimus Deus and *Divino Afflante Spiritu* both require and encourage the study of the ancient oriental languages. The language studies are required based on the principle that the original language texts are better than any translation. These texts are the substance of any biblical study. *Providentissimus Deus* also sees the need for language studies as an aid in understanding the historical condition of the text, especially regarding the relationship between the text and the physical sciences. *Divino Afflante Spiritu* notes the need for language studies so that recently discovered texts in Palestine can be read and understood.

Discovery of ancient texts and manuscripts necessitate textual criticism. The discovery of ancient texts and manuscripts necessitate textual and historical criticism. Textual criticism is required to facilitate the management, investigation and explanation of the numerous manuscripts and their variant readings. Consequent questions concerning the history of textual transmission and the development of variants needed to be explained. Furthermore, comparison of texts and stories shared between ancient Israel and other nations of the ANE beg explanation. Critical approaches such as historical criticism and literary criticism can aid in explaining the significance.

Archeological discoveries require historical critical methodology. The archeological discoveries in the various excavations that took place during this period required historical criticism. Excavations took place, remains were evaluated and explanations were offered concerning the life and events related to biblical history. These events require the use of historical criticism to explain the texts in relationship to these findings. This is not to say that the documents state that the archeological findings needed to be verified or denied, only that they could not be ignored and needed to be considered when dealing with the biblical texts.

The historical condition of the text requires literary criticism to understand the language. Related to the study of languages is the study of literary criticism. The use of language as a force for communication through symbol, ideas, concepts, images, idiom etc. necessitates a critical study of these items so that the text may be understood. This comes as a natural consequence of studying the original languages and the original texts.

5.3 *Why is the HCM limited?*

The critical methodology has been tainted with rationalist philosophy. Providentissimus Deus pointed out that some of the critical exegesis practiced at that time was tainted with rationalist philosophy that denies the divine aspect to the text or at least diminishes it to insignificance. Critical methodology when used with a rationalist philosophy is tainted and rendered useless for Catholic biblical studies.

The literal sense is limited. The *literal sense*, which was discussed above, is limited in determining the meaning of the text. The degree to which the limits are expressed vary. Leo notes that reason calls the reader to go beyond the *literal sense* (verbal-historical) to a deeper meaning. Pius refers to the *spiritual sense* which is necessitated by the limits of the literal. The *spiritual sense* is needed to explain the relationship between the OT and the NT.

The art of true criticism receives validity within larger framework. Providentissimus Deus while criticizing the practices of rationalist exegesis calls for the art of true criticism. The term, as mentioned above, is not clearly defined nor described. However, it seems to point to the use of critical methodology within a larger framework or understanding of the biblical text that would recognize a divine aspect, an inspired nature to the text, and the text as the book of the Church. Critical exegesis can be used and developed within this larger context. The method is thus limited by the context in which it is used and by the Catholic understanding of the biblical text. *Providentissimus Deus* and *Divino Afflante Spirit* would see several guidelines as providing the framework for Catholic exegesis: the magisterium, the Fathers of the Church and the analogy of faith.

Absence of spiritual meaning in the exegesis of the day (PD). Leo notes a void in the exegesis of his day regarding the spiritual significance of the text. The rationalist approach deprived the text of spiritual significance. Critical methodology without seeking to address the spiritual significance can effectively ignore it. Pius similarly warns that the purpose of exegesis needs to be carefully watched. The exegete cannot do his work to satisfy curiosity but should aim at determining the theological significance of the texts under consideration.

The HCM is thus seen as necessary and limited during this period. The *literal* sense, its underlying hermeneutical principle, requires this methodology. The historical contexts for the ecclesial documents from *Providentissimus Deus* to *Divino Afflante Spiritu* and their various purposes influenced the degree to which the method was accepted or required. The next chapter will consider the second period of Catholic critical exegesis. This period is represented by two documents *Sancta Mater Ecclesia* and *Dei Verbum*.

CHAPTER IV

Dei Verbum

Divino Afflante Spiritu opened the door for full Catholic participation in critical exegesis. The document was eagerly received by Catholic biblical scholars and a renaissance began in biblical scholarship. The period of openness to these methods lasted until the end of Pius XII's reign, at which time a new movement emerged in opposition to critical exegesis. A debate began concerning the value, place and practice of critical exegesis within the church. This debate coincided with the Second Vatican Council's discussions on revelation which culminated in the publication of *Dei Verbum.*

The introduction to the previous chapter identified three periods of Catholic biblical scholarship in this century. The periods are identified by ecclesial documents that responded to questions regarding biblical interpretation. The second period is represented by *Dei Verbum* and *Sancta Mater Ecclesia.* These ecclesial documents provide us with a source for evaluating the church's response to the development and use of critical methodology in this period. As in the last chapter, four factors will be considered in the evaluation: the pastoral or scholarly situation which prompted the church's official response; the church's response to the situation; the general content of the document under consideration; and the HCM as presented in the document.

This chapter will be similar in presentation to Chapter III modified, however, for the shared historical background of the two documents. The chapter is divided into four sections. The first section addresses the pastoral and scholarly situation between the promulgation of *Divino Afflante Spiritu* and *Dei Verbum.* The second and third sections will evaluate *Sancta Mater Ecclesia* and *Dei Verbum* regarding the content of the documents and the HCM as exposed in them. The final section of the chapter will evaluate the place of the HCM in Catholic exegesis in terms of its necessity and limits according to these documents.

1 The Pastoral and Scholarly Situation and The Church's Response

During the reign of Pius XII biblical scholarship developed along the lines set by *Divino Afflante Spiritu*[1]. The official documents released at the beginning of this period reflect the encouragement offered to Catholic scholars using critical methods (see figure seven, page 131).
Catholic biblical scholars and theologians began to question the authority of the 1905-1915 PBC decisions in the years following *Divino Afflante Spiritu*. In 1956, A. Miller and A. Kleinhans, the Secretary and Undersecretary of the PBC, lifted the restrictions imposed on biblical scholarship by the earlier decisions[2]. Pius XII's encouragement for the use of critical methodologies in Catholic biblical scholarship and his call

---

[1] For information on the work of Catholic biblical scholars during this period see the following: B.M. AHERN, «Gathering the Fragments»; D. STANLEY, «Biblical Theology of the New Testament»; C. STUHLMUELLER, «Catholic Biblical Scholarship».

[2] E.F. SIEGMAN, «The Decrees of the PBC», 24. Miller, commenting on a recent edition of the *EB* states: «As long as these decrees (of the PBC) propose views which are neither immediately nor mediately connected with truths of faith and morals, it goes without saying that the scholar may pursue his research with full liberty, provided always that he defers to the supreme teaching authority of the church. Today we can hardly picture to ourselves the position of Catholic scholars at the turn of the century, or the dangers that threatened Catholic teaching on Scripture and its inspiration on the part of liberal and rationalistic criticism, which like a torrent tried to sweep away the sacred barriers of tradition. At present the battle is considerably less fierce; not a few controversies have been settled and many problems emerge in any entirely new light, so that it is easy enough for us to smile at the narrowness and constraint that prevailed fifty years ago».
Siegman remarks that even though the document is not delivered as an official document it carries the spirit of the PBC and is consistent with the official statements of Rome which followed *Divino Afflante Spiritu*. In addition to the Suhard letter he notes the PBC decision in 1941 to remove the Decrees of the PBC from the SSL and SSD examinations. Cardinal Ratzinger, *Observatore Romano*, July 2, 1990, 5, giving examples of prudential judgments as statements which are authoritative only for a particular period states: «In this regard one can refer to the statements of the Popes during the last century on religious freedom as well as the anti-modernistic decisions of the Biblical Commission of that time». For further reading on this type of magisterial statement see the CDF *Instruction on the Ecclesial Vocation of the Theologian*, 24; A. DULLES, *The Craft of Theology*, 108-111.

Ecclesial Documents Regarding Biblical Studies: 1943-1963

Date Location	Title Contents of the document
March 24, 1945 Apostolic Letter *EB*, 571-575 *OCT*, 782-792	*In Cotidianis Precibus* The letter praises the new edition of the Latin Psalter for its use of the original language texts. The previous text called the Gallican Psalter was based on Jerome's pre-Vulgate translation of the Psalms. The Psalter had been approved by Pius V. In this letter Pius XII praises the work of Catholic exegetes and translators. - «For recent times have witnessed remarkable progress in the mastery of oriental languages, particularly Hebrew, and in the art of translation. Scholarly research into the laws of meter and rhythm governing oriental poetry has advanced apace. The rules for what is called textual criticism are now seen in clearer light». *EB*, 572; *OCT*, 784.
Jan 16, 1948 PBC - Letter James M. Voste *EB*, 577-581 *OCT*, 796-801	*Letter of the PBC to Cardinal Suhard* PBC responds to Suhard's questions regarding sources in the Pentateuch and the historicity of Genesis 1-11. The letter signed by Voste with the approval of Pius XII makes three important points. The first regards the PBC decisions regarding these topics (EB 161; 181-184; 324-331). In light of *Divino Afflante Spiritu* «these answers are in no way opposed to further and truly scientific examination of these problems in accordance with the results obtained during these last forty years» (*EB* 579; *OCT* 798). The second regards sources. «There is no one today who doubts the existence of these sources or refuses to admit a progressive development of the Mosaic Laws due to social and religious conditions of later times, a development which is also manifest in the historical narratives» since the questions raised are very complex and undecided the Catholic scholar is encouraged to take part in the scholarly investigations» (*EB*, 580; *OCT* 799). The third regards literary forms in Genesis 1-11. The study can be obscure and complex since there are no corresponding forms in Greco-Roman literature. The scholar should continue to study «all the literary, scientific, historical, cultural and religious problems connected with these chapters; one should then examine closely the literary processes of the early oriental peoples, their psychology, their way of expressing themselves and their very notion of historical truth; in a word, one should collate without prejudice all the subject matter of the palaeontological and historical, epigraphic and literary sciences». (*EB*, 581; *OCT*, 800).

Figure 7a: Ecclesial Documents Regarding Biblical Studies: 1943-1963

Ecclesial Documents Regarding Biblical Studies: 1943-1963

Date Location	Title Contents of the document
May 13, 1950 PBC - Instruction A. Miller *EB*, 582-610 *OCT*, 802-838	*On the Proper Way to Teach Sacred Scripture in the Seminaries and Colleges* The document begins suggesting thorough training for seminary professors. Directives are given concerning Scripture studies in seminaries. The goal of the professor is to excite and foster in the students an active and abiding love for the Scriptures together with a proper knowledge of them. *EB*, 591; *OCT*, 814. Regarding critical methodology the document gives the following guidelines: a) students should be taught how to base their explanations of the biblical text on valid scientific foundations; b) a general introduction should include «the doctrine of inspiration, the truth of Sacred Scripture and laws of interpretation (hermeneutics); a special *Introduction* should include setting forth the theme of each book, its purpose, authorship and date *EB*, 596; *OCT*, 815 ; c) encouragement for the professor to offer courses in biblical languages, biblical theology, history, archeology, or any auxiliary discipline for select students of greater talents *EB*,605 ; *OCT*, 832.
August 12, 1950 Pius XII Encyclical *EB*, 611-621* *OCT*, 839-846* *excerpts	*Humani Generis* The encyclical makes the following observations regarding biblical scholarship: a) it critiques those who «speak of a human sense of the Scriptures, beneath which a divine sense, which they say is the only infallible meaning, lies hidden»; b) refutes those seeking to have the literal sense yield to a new exegesis called symbolic or spiritual; c) allows for the discussion of evolution of the body so long as it comes from living matter and that judgments are submitted to the church; d) teaching on polygenism can not be reconciled with the church's teaching on original sin; e) restates the statements regarding the historicity of Genesis 1-11 in the PBC letter to Cardinal Suhard. The historical narratives of the OT even though at times similar to ANE narratives are still inspired and thus are in a different category of literature.
June 9, 1953 PBC - Declar. *EB*, 621	*On the book «On Psalms» by Bernard Bonkamp* Short statement saying that the book is not suited for use in seminaries or the colleges of religious because it does not follow the guidelines for Catholic hermeneutical practice and its conclusions are based largely on subjective criteria.
Dec 15, 1955 PBC - Instruc. *EB*, 622-633 *OCT*, 851-865	*On Biblical Associations and on Biblical Conventions and Meetings* Guidelines are set forth for meetings and associations of biblical scholars which should be subject to proper ecclesial authority. The rules are given in reaction to abuses by those claiming a «spiritual or symbolic» exegesis and their teaching these things to a group not formally educated in these matters.

Figure 7b: Ecclesial Documents Regarding Biblical Studies: 1943-1963

for broader use of the Bible among Catholics continued throughout his pontificate.

Signs of a change, however, did appear toward the end of the pontificate. In April 1958, the Congregation for Seminaries «expressed displeasure with volume I of the *Introduction á la Bible* just published under the editorship of A. Robert and A. Feuillet»[3]. Indications of a new debate regarding critical biblical scholarship continued in the early years of John XXIII. On February 17, 1960, he addressed the faculty of the PBI on the occasion of the fiftieth anniversary of its foundation. After praising the work of the institute and its faithfulness to the church, John remarked: «Unfortunately, in all ages, there are always a few dark clouds, arising from certain notions that have little to do with true science, cluttering up the horizon whenever men attempt to see the Gospel in all its clear and radiant splendor»[4]. He went on to caution the use of scientific critical methods[5]. Once again the place of critical scholarship in the church was being called into question.

The stress on the *literal sense* in Catholic biblical interpretation coupled with the use of critical methodology following *Divino Afflante Spiritu* led to questions concerning the unity and integrity of the Bible, especially regarding the relationship between the OT and the NT. The questions were debated among exegetes and theologians alike. Scholars took two different approaches attempting to solve this problem. The first approach was referred to as *spiritual exegesis*. This approach is similar to the typological interpretations of the patristic period[6]. The second approach used the *sensus plenior* (fuller sense) to preserve the integrity of the Bible. R.E. Brown defines the *sensus plenior* as «additional, deeper meaning intended by God but not clearly intended by the human author, which is seen to exist in the words of a biblical text (or group of texts or even a whole book) when they are studied in the light of further revelation or develop-

---

[3] R.E. BROWN – T.A. COLLINS, «Church Pronouncements», 1167.

[4] *AAS* 52, 155; *OTC*, §875.

[5] *ASS*, 52, 156-157; *OTC*, §886. He concludes: «In this light, you can easily understand the need, already mentioned above, which exists for absolute adherence to the sacred deposit of Faith and to the Magisterium of the church. The charter of the Biblical Institute entrusts to you the delicate task of promoting sound biblical scholarship "according to the mind of the Catholic Church", that is "in conformity with norms already established or to be established by the Apostolic See"».

[6] J.L. MCKENZIE, «Problems of Hermeneutics», 201. The two foremost proponents of this type of interpretation were Jean Daniélou and Henri de Lubac.

ment in the understanding of revelation»[7]. It should be noted that the basis of this discussion was not so much the «fact» of biblical integrity but rather how to describe it taking into consideration credible biblical scholarship. The debate was nothing new in the church. The early church had discussed the problem in the various formulations of the senses of Scripture. At this point however the debate revealed a gap between Catholic biblical scholarship and dogmatic theology. The way in which the Scriptures had been used in dogmatic theology was called into question thus heightening the debate[8].

The debate over the use of critical methodology reflected a growing dispute between exegetes and theologians[9] as well as ecclesial institutions and officials. This debate that eventually is referred to as *the Roman Controversy*[10] was intertwined with the preparations for the Second Vatican Council and the document which eventually became *Dei Verbum*[11].

---

[7] R.E. BROWN, *The Sensus Plenior*, 92. An extensive bibliography on the *sensus plenior* can be found in his dissertation. For further clarification see: R.E. BROWN, «The Problem of the *Sensus Plenior*», «The *Sensus Plenior* in the Last Ten Years»; and B. VAWTER, «The Fuller Sense».

[8] J.L. MCKENZIE, «Problems of Hermeneutics», 203, states: «But hitherto theology has had no difficulty in admitting that the liturgy, theology, and ecclesiastical documents, with varying degrees of restraint, can and do employ biblical texts by accommodation and extension and illustration rather than by interpretation of the genuine meaning and by strict logical demonstration». See also: L. ALONSO-SCHÖKEL, «Argument d'Écriture et théologie biblique».

[9] Exegetes appealed to *Divino Afflante Spiritu* and argued that critical methods were necessary for understanding the texts. Some theologians argued that critical methodologies were destructive of revealed dogma and doctrine. For a sample of this school see: C.E. RUFFINI, «Literary Genres and Working Hypotheses in Recent Biblical Studies» and «The Bible and its Genuine Historical and Objective Truth». Ruffini admits the quest for knowledge of the human author's intention is a principle which «can have a legitimate and generally accepted interpretation». However, «the use made of it has the effect of undoing a good part of the traditional exegesis, which has always shown respect for the *germana veritas historica et objectiva sacrae Scripturae*, to use the expression of the Supreme Congregation of the Holy Office in its Monitum of June 20, 1961».

[10] See J.A. FITZMYER, «A Recent Roman Scriptural Controversy».

[11] The student today has the advantage of more historical data from ante-preparatory documents, diaries and journals, as well as institutional records which had not been previously available due to the standard practice of keeping such items and information private until a suitable time period has past. For a recent history of the Vatican Council and its preparation see: G. ALBERIGO – J.A. KOMONCHAK, *The History of Vatican II*. Of a projected three volumes the first two are available in Italian and English. For further reading on the history of this period see: X. RYNNE, *Letters from Vatican City*; ID., *Vatican II*; S. SCHMIDT, *Augustine Bea*; A. STICKLER, «Pontifical Universitas Romana». For American involvement in the Roman Controversy and in Vatican II

The preparations for Vatican II revealed the brewing debate over critical biblical scholarship[12]. The ante-preparatory solicitations from the bishops and academic institutions indicated concern from some to restrict the use of critical methods. The bishops *vota* regarding the study and use of the Scriptures in the life of the church were numerous; and the issues raised for consideration were varied and broad. From the *vota* one notices the obvious impact biblical studies were having on the life of the Church. Bishops were seeking clarification on questions raised in biblical studies regarding history, inerrancy, inspiration, texts and versions, interpretation and methodology, literary genres, and the authority of the PBC[13].

The concerns regarding the use of critical methodology were evident in these *vota*. Some of the concerns dealt with the results of critical studies while not specifically mentioning the methodology. For example the *vota* regarding the historicity of biblical accounts. The question of historicity had been raised in the critical scholarship of earlier periods and was still an issue of concern. One votum mentioned the defense of the miraculous

---

regarding biblical questions see: G.P. FOGARTY, *American Catholic Biblical Scholarship*, 281-350.

[12] John XXIII had been elected pope in October, 1958. Three months later on January 25, 1959 in a speech to a group of Cardinals at St. Paul's Outside-the-Walls he declared his intentions: «Trembling a little with emotion but at the same time humbly resolute in my purpose, I announce to you a double celebration which I propose to undertake: a diocesan synod for the city and a general council for the universal church». The planning of the council was a major undertaking. The study and use of the Bible in the church was only one of the many pastoral and theological topics discussed in the planning.

The planning of Vatican II involved two phases: antepreparatory and preparatory. As part of the ante-preparatory work comments and opinions called *vota* would be solicited from the bishops of the world, from the Curia, and from the universities. The *vota* would contain items or issues which the contributor thought needed addressing by the council. Following this the antepreparatory commission would synthesize the material into *questiones* for the preparatory commission to use in planning the Council. The final role of the commission was to present names for proposed committee membership.

The preparatory phase would take the *quaestiones* and divide them up for discussion among 16 commissions and secretariats. A central planning commission would coordinate the efforts headed by the Pope. The role of the committees was to formulate working documents to be used in the Council.

For an in-depth discussion on the preparations for Vatican II see G. ALBERIGO - J.A. KOMONCHAK, *The History of Vatican II*. For discussion on the Scriptures and the development of the preliminary documents see pages: 138-139; 162-164; 190-192; 229-230; 272-285; 306-308; 354-355.

[13] *Conspectus Analyticus* in *Acta et Documenta*, Ser I vol 2, 15-31.

against demythologization[14]. Others dealing with historicity sought clarification on the origins of the world as described in the Pentateuch, the genealogies and the lifespans of the Patriarchs, and the flood narrative. These *vota* did not directly attack or criticize critical methodology but recommended a clarification in the propositions of critical studies[15].

There were *vota*, however, that were more directly suspicious of critical methodology. One *vota* suggested that the council address the compatibility of form criticism with the dogma of inspiration[16]. Others asked the council to identify the principles Catholic exegetes should use in their studies[17], to emphasize the divine aspect of the scriptures[18]; to address the authority of the Church in the interpretation of the Scriptures[19]; to determine the relationship between theology and Scriptures[20]; to identify clear standards and norms for exegesis so that liberal, rationalist, or materialist interpretations may be avoided[21]; and to follow traditional teachings and to avoid innovations[22].

On the other hand there were *vota* that encouraged the careful use of scientific method. One *votum* suggested that the scientific conclusions of Catholic exegetes be kept in mind while explaining the Scriptures with specific reference to literary genres and documents (i.e. sources) in inspired books[23]. Other *vota* suggested that liberty must be conceded to all historical, scientific, and archaeological investigations in exegetical work[24]; similarly freedom should be granted to exegetes who work under the authority of the bishops following the norms of *Divino Afflante Spiritu*[25]; that church document should not make assertions with which scientific study has shown discrepancies (e.g. the series of years in the Martyrology)[26], and that the primacy of the literal sense should be declared[27].

---

[14] *Conspectus Analyticus* V.1.2, in *Acta et Documenta*, Ser I vol 2, 15.

[15] Cf. *Conspectus Analyticus* V.1.1-9, in *Acta et Documenta*, Ser I vol 2, 15-16.

[16] *Conspectus Analyticus* V.2.7, in *Acta et Documenta*, Ser I vol 2, 17.

[17] *Conspectus Analyticus* V.5.1, in *Acta et Documenta*, Ser I vol 2, 20.

[18] *Conspectus Analyticus* V.5.2, in *Acta et Documenta*, Ser I vol 2, 21. Cf. V.5.8 which seeks an emphasis on the divine aspect and the role of the Church in interpretation because of the «many false notions» current in that day.

[19] *Conspectus Analyticus* V.5.3, in *Acta et Documenta*, Ser I vol 2, 21.

[20] *Conspectus Analyticus* V.5.6, in *Acta et Documenta*, Ser I vol 2, 21.

[21] *Conspectus Analyticus* V. 5.19-20,25 in *Acta et Documenta*, Ser I vol 2, 23-24.

[22] *Conspectus Analyticus* V. 5.28, in *Acta et Documenta*, Ser I vol 2, 25.

[23] *Conspectus Analyticus* V. 5.23, in *Acta et Documenta*, Ser I vol 2, 24.

[24] *Conspectus Analyticus* V. 5.26, in *Acta et Documenta*, Ser I vol 2, 25.

[25] *Conspectus Analyticus* V. 5.27, in *Acta et Documenta*, Ser I vol 2, 25.

[26] *Conspectus Analyticus* V. 5.9, in *Acta et Documenta*, Ser I vol 2, 22.

Other *vota* were open to the use of critical methodology but stressed the care with which they should be used. One suggested that the role of the Spirit must be considered in making interpretations and the effect of interpretation on the pastoral use of the Scriptures[28]; another suggested clarifying the teaching on literary genres so to prevent abuses[29].

The university *vota* also reflected the debate regarding the Bible and biblical studies. The three universities considered here are the Pontifical Biblical Institute, the Gregorian University, and the Lateran University[30].

The Biblicum's *votum* is the most extensive of the university *vota*. Following the preliminary *votum* which commends the study and use of Scriptures in the Church, the document is divided into two parts. The first part concerns doctrinal issues and suggests the following: a clearer description of the relationship between Scripture and Tradition; a clearer description on the role of faith in the process of salvation; a discussion on the role of the efficacious Word of God in the sacred books in the sanctification of Christians; a discussion on the historicity of the Gospels and avoiding anti-Semitism[31]. Of these doctrinal *vota* the one most relevant to critical methodology is the fourth — that dealing with the historicity of the Gospels.

This particular *votum* is divided into two sections. The first suggests that the Council reaffirm those truths of faith that govern the interpretation of the Scriptures. Three important truths are mentioned: Christian faith is founded on divine activity within historical circumstances (especially the incarnation, life, death and resurrection of Jesus Christ); revelation was not completed before the close of the apostolic age; and since the four gospels are inspired they enjoy inerrancy (this notion of inerrancy must be joined to the notion of historicity). The second suggests that the Council leave it to Catholic interpreters (lead by the magisterium) to further determine what type of historicity is to be attributed to the Gospels or to individual pericopes[32]. This particular *votum* regarding historicity requires the use of historical-critical methodology in the interpretation of the

---

[27] *Conspectus Analyticus* V. 5.12, in *Acta et Documenta*, Ser I vol 2, 22. Cf. V.5.11.

[28] *Conspectus Analyticus* V. 5.24, in *Acta et Documenta*, Ser I vol 2, 24.

[29] *Conspectus Analyticus* V. 6.1, in *Acta et Documenta*, Ser I vol 2, 25.

[30] The dates of these three *vota* are as follows: *PBI Votum*, April 24, 1960; *Gregorian University Votum*, April 7, 1960; and the *Lateran University Votum*, May 4, 1960.

[31] *PBI Votum*, in *Acta et Documenta*, Ser I vol 4, par I-1, 123-132.

[32] *PBI Votum*, in *Acta et Documenta*, Ser I vol 4, par I-1, 128.

Scriptures because of the historical conditioning of revelation and inspiration.

The second part of the Biblicum's *votum* makes four suggestions dealing with disciplinary issues: a) that the norms given by Pius XII in *Divino Afflante Spiritu* for the study and interpretation of the Scriptures should be solemnly commended and adopted as the Council's own especially regarding the use of the original texts, the application of critical method, genres and literary forms, the theological meaning of the texts and the ecclesial tradition; b) that the free examination of those issues addressed in earlier PBC decisions be permitted under the guidance of the magisterium so long as those decisions did not regard faith and morals; c) that no Roman congregation should issue anything related to the Bible without first being reviewed by the PBC which should comprise the best experts who are best able to decide biblical questions; and finally d) that a more careful consideration of scholars' reputation when their works are called into question (particularly if the author's books are prohibited, precise and not general reasons should be communicated to him)[33].

The section on biblical hermeneutics of the Gregorian University's *votum* suggest that the norms for biblical hermeneutics set forth specifically in *Divino Afflante Spiritu* be accepted by the Council[34]. The *votum* suggest clarification on several paragraphs of earlier ecclesial documents. First, from *Providentissimus Deus* regarding the analogy of faith and the relationship between Scripture and doctrine, the place of Patristic exegesis, and the place of later Catholic commentators[35]. Second, from the *Oath Against Modernism* which states: «Equally I reject any way of judging and interpreting Holy Scripture which takes no account of the Church's Tradition, of the analogy of faith and the norms laid down by the apostolic See; which adheres to the theories of the rationalists, and presumptuously and rashly accepts textual criticism as the only supreme rule»[36]. Third, from *Divino Afflante Spiritu* regarding theological exegesis that while considering the historical, archaeological, and philological sciences is aimed toward assisting professors of theology, priests and the faithful[37]. Fourth, from *Divino Afflante Spiritu* regarding the identification and study

---

[33] *PBI Votum*, in *Acta et Documenta*, Ser I vol 4, par I-1, 133-136.

[34] *Gregorian University Votum*, in *Acta et Documenta*, Ser I vol 4, par I-1, 9.

[35] *Gregorian University Votum*, in *Acta et Documenta*, Ser I vol 4, par I-1, 9-10. Cf. *Providentissimus Deus*, *EB* §109-113. English trans. §320-323.

[36] *Gregorian University Votum*, in *Acta et Documenta*, Ser I vol 4, par I-1, 10. Cf. *Sacrorum Antistitum*, *EB* §109-113. English trans. *The Christian Faith*, 143/9, 53.

[37] *Gregorian University Votum*, in *Acta et Documenta*, Ser I vol 4, par I-1, 10. Cf. *Divino Afflante Spiritu*, *EB* §551. English trans. §741.

of the literary forms used by the sacred authors[38]. Following this the *votum* suggests a clarification on the status of the Vulgate and the use of the original language texts in biblical studies[39].

Whereas the Biblicum and Gregorian *vota* promoted a continued course for using critical methodology as outlined in *Divino Afflante Spiritu* the Lateran *votum* stressed an absolute inerrancy for the Scriptures which would eliminate the need for historical critical studies[40]. The document insists that absolute inerrancy has already been solemnly defined through past encyclicals (quoting *Providentissimus Deus* and *Spiritus Paraclitus* as well as *Divino Afflante Spiritu*), in the Fathers of the Church and in the Scriptures themselves. Spadaforra, the author, attacks several French exegetes including d'Hulst, Robert, Feullet, Barucq, and Cazelles for recent works on the topic of inerrancy. No solution to the difficulties in the biblical text can be ascribed to the appearances theory. Spadafora suggests that the council solemnly and infallibly define the doctrine[41].

Meanwhile in the Roman academic circles the debate over the HCM became heated and public. The debate can be seen through several articles published at this time. In 1960, L. Alonso-Schökel, a professor at the PBI, published an article titled «*Dove va Esegesi Cattolica*». He noted the current crisis indicated by John XXIII's speech. Alonso-Schökel defended the use of critical methodology drawing on *Divino Afflante Spiritu* and a speech that Pius XII gave six months before he died. He argued that the cause of the crisis was not the use of critical procedures but their misuse. He suggested that some exegetes have handled historical questions insufficiently and have popularized their results with little regard for prudence or charity. Antonio Romeo, a professor at the Lateran, responded to Alonso-Schökel's article in «*L'Enciclica* "Divino Afflante Spiritu" *e le* "Opiniones Nouveau"» published in *Divinitas*, a publication of the Lateran. In this article Romeo not only attacked the opinions of Alonso-Schökel but the state of current Catholic biblical scholarship especially the work of the Biblicum[42]. He held that *Divino Afflante Spiritu* made no

---

[38] *Gregorian University Votum*, in *Acta et Documenta*, Ser I vol 4, par I-1, 10. Cf. *Divino Afflante Spiritu*, *EB* §560. English trans. §755.

[39] *Gregorian University Votum*, in *Acta et Documenta*, Ser I vol 4, par I-1, 9-11. Cf. *Divino Afflante Spiritu*, *EB* §549. English trans. §738-739.

[40] *Lateran University Votum*, in *Acta et Documenta*, Ser I vol 4, par I-1, 363-370.

[41] *Lateran University Votum*, in *Acta et Documenta*, Ser I vol 4, par I-1, 370.

[42] A. ROMEO, «L'enciclica *Divino Afflante Spiritu*». The work attacked several noted Catholic scholars along with the PBI. The scholars include: L. Alonso-Schökel, M. Zerwick, J. Levie, A. Vogtle, P. Benoit, and A. Descamps. É. FOUILLOUX, «The Announcement of the Council», 137, comments: «Once John XXIII turned the Roman

change in the direction of biblical studies and he attacked those Catholic scholars who used critical methods. Ernest Vogt, the rector of the PBI, wishing to defend the Biblicum from these attacks attempted to publish a rebuttal in *Divinitas* but was refused the opportunity. In early 1961, the Biblicum published a response «*Pontificium Institutum Biblicum et recens libellus R.miD.ni A. Romeo*»[43]. Following this article, the Holy Office ordered the question to be reserved for their consideration[44].

On June 20, the Holy Office issued a monitum that seems to be a response to the debate. The monitum «warns against those who bring into doubt the genuine historical and objective truth of the Sacred Scriptures, not only of the OT, but even of the NT, even to the sayings and deeds of Christ Jesus»[45]. The result was further debate[46]. Two additional actions of the Holy Office further indicated their intention: the listing of Jean Stein-

---

college where he had done his ecclesiastical studies into a full-fledged university (May 17, 1959), the Lateran appointed itself the watchdog of Catholicism, as was shown by its attack on the Biblical Institute. Moreover, it provided itself with the weapons for this attack: its journal *Divinitas* was also the vehicle for the Pontifical Academy of Theology, an organization that served as a rallying point for *zelanti* (zealots) of every kind».

[43] P.I.B., «P.I.B. et recens libellus R.mi.D.ni A. Romeo», 3-17.

[44] J.A. KOMONCHAK, «The Preparation of Vatican II», 279, quotes Vogt in footnote 419. «Msgr. Romeo's article, from the time of its publication, has been widely and quite freely circulated for seven months. But as soon as our simple correction was published, the sale of the two abstracts was forbidden (for both parties, it is true). But then other violent articles against us were published, without any impediment. We have not replied lest we descend to the same level and to avoid a formal controversy and so as not to expose ourselves to a new prohibition». KOMONCHAK, 279, also recounts the hierarchy's reaction to the Roman Controversy. «On 19 Jan 1961 Tromp learned about Romeo's article from Garofalo who found it "defamatory and unjust". Two days later Tromp told Ottaviani of his concern that the TC might be considered to be involved, since four of the moderators of *Divinitas* were among its members; in his journal Tromp noted that the editor had not consulted him and that he had not yet read the article. Bea wrote Piolanti an energetic letter of protest, to which Pizzardo replied that Romeo's article had been published without his knowledge and represented the views only of the author. Three days later Tromp reported in his journal that the Pope had telephoned the rector of *Civiltà Cattolica* to inform him and the rector of the PBI that he had read Romeo's article "with displeasure and disgust". On 2 March *OssRom* announced the E. Vogt, rector of the PBI had been appointed to the TC. Finally, on 5 March the consultors to the PBC including Cerfaux composed a statement, sent to Vogt three days later, in which they deprecated Romeo's article and declared their solidarity with the PBI».

[45] *EB*, §634; *OCT,* §894.

[46] See: P.G. DUNCKER, «Biblical Criticism»; G.T. KENNEDY, «The Holy Office Monitum»; ID., «A Reply to Fr. Moran»; W.L. MORAN, «Father Kennedy's Exegesis».

mann's book *La vie de Jesus* on the Index and the suspension of S. Lyonnet and M. Zerwick from the Biblicum faculty[47]. John XXIII was getting annoyed with the controversy. He expressed «irritation at the PBC's silence during the ongoing debate and threatened to dissolve it if it did not fulfill its duties»[48].

At this point the debate shifted to the Preparatory Commissions for the council. The commissions dealing with the Scriptures and interpretation were the Theological Commission (TC) and the Secretariat for Christian Unity (SCU)[49]. The discussions were filled with tension[50]. The work of the TC resulted in the basic schema, *de fontibus revelationis*. Five points can be noted regarding biblical interpretation and the use of the HCM in this document. First, inspiration is viewed «in a univocal sense, as the divine action in the biblical author while he writes». The emphasis on the divine in this description of inspiration heavily restricts the role of the human author. The final redactor is seen as the inspired author. Second, inerrancy is defined as «absolute immunity of the entire sacred Scripture from error»; keeping this in mind the critic may explore the text in terms that the author used language and concepts of their time — the exegete must do so for apologetic reasons. Third, the OT is seen as proof of the NT and as a preparation for the gospel. Fourth, the Gospels reproduce the historical words and events of Jesus. Every attempt of biblical scholars to weaken the historicity is condemned. The only concession granted is that the ancients had an understanding of history and historical records which is different from ours. Fifth, the Vulgate is declared the authentic version.

---

47 J.A. KOMONCHAK, «The Preparation of Vatican II», 280, gives the details: «In September, Ruffini wrote to the new Secretary of State, Cicognani, to inform him that Tardini, shortly before his death, had indicated that two or three professors would be removed from the Biblicum. This appears to refer to S. Lyonnet and M. Zerwick, two of the scholars most vigorously attacked by Romeo; their suspensions from teaching, however, although it had long been sought, did not occur until the end of the academic year 1961-1962. Ottaviani made a similar effort, this time unsuccessful, to remove Myles Bourke professor of the NT and another of Romeo's targets, from the faculty of the archdiocesan seminary of New York».

48 J.A. KOMONCHAK, «The Preparation of Vatican II», 281, 354-355.

49 J.A. KOMONCHAK, «The Preparation of Vatican II», 191. The committee on Seminaries and Studies also submitted a proposal to the CPC. Komonchak summarizes: «The second chapter is devoted to the teaching of Scripture, which should begin with the divine origin of the sacred books, their inspiration, inerrancy, and historical and objective truth. Teachers of the Bible should focus on the *literal sense,* which is to be interpreted in light of magisterial statements, the Fathers and the analogy of faith». Cf. *Acta et Documenta,* Ser I, vol 3, 328-333.

50 See J.A. KOMONCHAK, «The Preparation of Vatican II», 233 esp. footnotes 282, 283.

The Development of *Dei Verbum*

First Draft	Second Draft	Third Draft	Fourth Draft	Fifth Draft
De fontibus revelationis	De divina revelatione	De divina revelatione	De divina revelatione	De divina revelatione
Nov. 14, 1962 Presented for discussion Nov. 20, 1962 Vote Nov. 21, 1962 John XXIII intervenes calling for a revised text by a mixed commission - Theological Commission and the Secretariat for Christian Unity.	March 1963 - draft produced Sent to bishops for their opinions No discussion at Second Session of Council; however, more opinions were solicited at the end of the session.	April 1964 - TC completes third draft Fall 1964 (beginning of Third Session) general schema approved	Revisions made from observations made at the beginning of the Third Session Fall of 1965 the Forth Draft was presented for voting in the Fourth Session.	Revisions were again made from the modi submitted during the Fourth Session November 18, 1965 the Fifth Draft was voted on, approved and promulgated.
Outline Chapter I: The Twofold Source of Revelation Chapter II: The Inspiration, Inerrancy, and Composition of Scripture Chapter III: The Old Testament Chapter IV: The New Testament Chapter V: Holy Scripture in the Church	Outline Chapter I: The Revealed Word of God Chapter II: The Divine Inspiration and Interpretation of Sacred Scripture Chapter III: The Old Testament Chapter IV: The New Testament Chapter V: The Use of Scripture in the Church	Outline Chapter I: Revelation Itself Chapter II: The Transmission of Divine Revelation Chapter III: Divine Inspiration and terpretation of the Holy Scriptures Chapter IV: The Old Testament Chapter V: The New Testament Chapter VI: Holy Scripture in the Life of the Church		

Figure 8: The Development of *Dei Verbum*

Principle Source for this imformation was G. Baum "Vaiican II's Consitution on Revelation

These points serve to illustrate the movement against the critical study of the Bible.

De fontibus was presented to the Central Planning Commission (CPC) in October, 1961 and discussed on November 9. A vote was taken after some serious criticisms were raised by the Committee. Seventy members voted *placet juxta modum* which meant the document had to be revised. Written observations were submitted but only minor modifications were made to the document[51]. Once again the debate would move to a new forum, this time the Second Vatican Council[52]. (See figure 9 on the previous page for a summary of the development of *Dei Verbum*).

Vatican II opened on October 11, 1962. The first session lasted until December 8, 1962. *De fontibus* was presented for discussion on November 14. In five sessions the fathers presented their general opinions on the text. After a number of interventions, the council president accepted a proposal for a vote[53]. The vote would decide whether to continue the discussion. A vote against further discussion would require a major re-writing of the document. The vote was taken on November 20. 62% voted to end the discussion which would effectively reject the document[54]. However, since a two-thirds majority was not achieved, Archbishop Felici, Secretary General of the Council, announced that discussions on Chapter I would begin the following day. Pope John XXIII, however, intervened and set up a

---

[51] J.A. KOMONCHAK, «The Preparation of Vatican II», 284. After the CPC discussions, Cardinal Bea had his Secretariat (SCU) work on a parallel text to *De fontibus*. The SCU had a final draft by April 1962. It offered a positive exposition of the Word of God as a source of life for the church and for individual Christians. Revelation was presented as God's ongoing conversation with man through his Word.

[52] G.P. FOGARTY, *American Catholic Biblical Scholarship*, 323, notes that on the eve of the council F. Spadafora, a professor at the Lateran, published «a pamphlet attacking Lyonnet and Zerwick for denying the historicity of the Gospels. It was rapidly distributed to many of the council fathers. It prompted a reply from the Biblical Institute, "A New Attack against Catholic Exegesis and against the PBI". Printed in French, German, Spanish, and English, it was distributed to all the bishops. The institute also distributed reprints of JA Fitzmyer's article, which had been published in TS in 1961, and which summarized the earlier attacks of Romeo on Scripture scholarship and on the institute. Both sides on the biblical question were trying to influence the bishops on the schema».

[53] G.P. FOGARTY, *American Catholic Biblical Scholarship*, 323 notes that Cardinal Bea in his intervention spoke of the document as the work of a particular school of theology, «not what the better theologians today think». In all the references to biblical scholars, he continued, only one was positive. He called for the schema to be redone to make it shorter, clearer, and more ecumenical». See *AAS* I, III, 48-51.

[54] The actual vote on continuing discussion was 1368 to end, 822 to continue.

commission headed jointly by Cardinals Bea and Ottaviani. That afternoon

> the Biblical Institute held a dissertation defense by Norbert Lohfink on Deuteronomy. Twelve cardinals, 150 bishops and numerous other visitors were present — so many in fact that the defense had to be moved from the Biblical Institute to the main hall of the Gregorian University across the street. William Moran, who had drawn the fire of Fenton for his efforts to challenge Kennedy, was the director of the dissertation. The defense had been made public, in order to show the council fathers that the Institute was not trying to undermine the faith. Though all the cardinals had been invited, Ottaviani did not attend. After the defense, Moran recalled, there was a formal reception for all the distinguished visitors, after which the Biblical scholars moved back across the street to the Biblicum where they had a real celebration[55].

John XXIII died in the period between the first and second sessions. Paul VI on the day after his election announced that the Council would continue. Meanwhile in March of 1963 the mixed commission had produced a second draft titled *De divina revelatione*. It was not a total reworking of the first draft but an abridgment and corrected version[56]. This second draft consisted of five chapters. A prologue was added including a quotation from John 1:2-3 that suggested «revelation is the communion-creating self-disclosure of God»[57]. Baum notes some of the significant changes: more attention is given to the role of the Scriptures in the mediation of Revelation, Scripture and Tradition are presented as ordered toward one another, both divine and human authorship are affirmed along, a distinction is made between «God's self-revelation in His action and word in Israel and the Spirit-inspired record of these events in the writings of the OT», «the sentences in which all attempts to reject or weaken the historicity of the Gospels are condemned have been eliminated», and the necessity of the Scriptures for the spiritual life of all Christians is mentioned[58].

The second session opened on September 29, 1963. There was no discussion on this draft at this session but the bishops were asked to submit comments in writing. These comments were coordinated and the draft revised accordingly into a third draft. The PBC document *Sancta Mater Ec-*

---

[55] G.P. FOGARTY, *American Catholic Biblical Scholarship*, 325. Citing X. RYNNE, *Vatican II*, 90 see also 35-37.

[56] G. BAUM, «Vatican II's Constitution on Revelation», 52. For a full text synopsis and all important interventions see G. HELLIN, *Concilii Vaticani II Synopsis*.

[57] G. BAUM, «Vatican II's Constitution on Revelation», 55-58.

[58] G. BAUM, «Vatican II's Constitution on Revelation», 57.

clesia treating historical questions regarding the transmission of the Gospel was issued between the second and third sessions. This document was another influence on the third draft. This draft was presented in the third session of the council (September 14 to November 21, 1964). Significant changes were noted in a *relatio* prepared by the TC and read by Archbishop Florit. A new first chapter on revelation was added. Baum summarizes:

> Revelation, the *relatio*, goes on to say, is «theocentric», that is, God reveals Himself. It must be clear that revelation cannot be equated with the communication of divine teaching. Revelation is «historical», that is, it takes place in history. God Himself intervenes in history to save man. This saving action of God achieves its full power only through His Word, which gives meaning to the action and renders witness to it. Revelation has thus a «sacramental» structure: it operates in the unity of action and word. The *relatio* distinguishes very clearly, though in an unusual terminology, between the «primary object» of revelation, namely, God as disclosing Himself in saving act and prophetic Word in history, and the «secondary object» of revelation, namely, the Word of God understood as the testimony through which God's self-disclosure is mediated to us in power. It is expressly stated that this witness to truth is not exhausted in the order of knowledge and understanding. «Since God becomes for us in Christ brother and mediator, this truth is in no way exhausted in the intellectual order; what is, in fact, demanded is that in and through Christ this truth becomes action through communion with the Most Holy Trinity. This is really an interpersonal communion». Salvational truth mediates interpersonal communion. The authors of the Constitution, the TC, were conscious of the fact, and did not conceal it form the Council Fathers, that the understanding of revelation proposed by them would lead to a new theological epistemology and a new understanding of Christian truth ... Revelation happens in the total person of Christ. Jesus Christ, the Son of God made flesh, is at the same time the «supreme act» of revelation and its «principal object»[59].

Other changes in the draft include the description of the apostolic transmission of revelation in the Church as «basically twofold, namely, both as oral preaching and religious practice and as the written word of Scripture»; and the concept of tradition has been deepened[60]. This third draft was accepted in principle, however, finer points were still being discussed. The fourth draft was presented in the fourth session (September 14 to December 8, 1965). After final modifications were made, the Coun-

---

59 G. BAUM, «Vatican II's Constitution on Revelation», 58-59.
60 G. BAUM, «Vatican II's Constitution on Revelation», 60.

cil fathers approved the fifth draft by a vote of 2344 to 6. Paul VI promulgated it as *Dei Verbum* on November 18, 1965.

2. *Sancta Mater Ecclesia*[61]

Toward the end of 1962, John XXIII asked the PBC to study form criticism and its application to the history of the gospels. The study began in 1963 and resulted in *Sancta Mater Ecclesia* which was issued on April 21, 1964. The document deals with the transmission of the Gospel from the time of Jesus to the time of the sacred writers. The clarification of the relationship of history to the written Gospel in the various NT accounts was an aid in understanding the role of the human authors of the Gospels and the use of critical methodologies in biblical studies.

2.1 *The Contents of Sancta Mater Ecclessia*

Following the introduction, the short document addresses exegetes, teachers in seminaries and universities, preachers, publishers and biblical associations. The document is divided into three sections which are discussed below.

The History of the Gospel. The document identifies «three stages of tradition by which the doctrine and the life of Jesus have come down to us»: the age of Jesus Christ — his life, ministry, passion, death and resurrection; the age of the apostles; and the age of the sacred writers[62].

The first stage in the transmission of the gospel is the age of Jesus. The document states that the life and ministry of Jesus was historically conditioned. Jesus spoke to his disciples in manner which they could understand: «He followed the modes and reasoning and of exposition which were in vogue at the time. He accommodated Himself to the mentality of His listeners and saw to it that what He taught was firmly impressed on the mind and easily remembered by the disciples». In this way, the disciples «were equipped to be witnesses of His life and doctrine». The document also notes that the disciples understood the miracles as deeds performed so that men would «believe in Christ and embrace the doctrine of salvation»[63].

---

[61] For general reading see Chapter III, footnote 1. For additional reading regarding *Sancta Mater Ecclesia* see: S. CIPRIANI, «*Presupposti dottrinali*»; G.A. KEARNS, «The Instruction on the Historical Truth of the Gospels»; J.A. FITZMYER, «Commentary».

[62] *SME*, §2. *EB*, §648; *OCT*, §927.

[63] *SME*, §2. *EB*, §649; *OCT*, §928.

The second stage in the transmission of the gospel is the age of the apostles. «The apostles proclaimed above all the death and resurrection of the Lord, as they bore witness to Jesus». This preaching occurred following the resurrection when Jesus' divinity was clearly recognized. *Sancta Mater Ecclesia* comments on the historical relationship between this stage and the previous: «After Jesus rose from the dead and His divinity was clearly perceived, faith far from destroying the memory of what had transpired, rather confirmed it, because their faith rested on the things which Jesus did and taught». As the apostles handed on the memory of Jesus they used modes of speaking which were «suited to their own purpose and the mentality of their listeners»[64].

The third stage in the transmission of the gospel is the age of the sacred writer. Each evangelist composed his work based on the «primitive instruction» that was first handed on by word of mouth. «From the many things handed down they selected some things, reduced others to a synthesis, (still) others they explicated as they kept in mind the situation of the churches». The message was communicated with a particular purpose so that the words and deeds of Jesus were explained «now in one context, now in another, depending on (their) usefulness to the readers». The document states that this purpose is knowable: «... anyone with pious diligence may seek the reason and with divine aid will be able to find it»[65].

Biblical Scholarship in the Church. The document notes the freedom in which the Catholic exegete conducts his work. The relationship is mentioned in terms of service to the magisterium and the church. The exegete owes obedience to the magisterium by virtue of its apostolic office that is under the guidance of the Holy Spirit. The same Spirit who guided the apostles and evangelists also guides the magisterium. Exegetes should also pay proper respect to the work of the Fathers.

Prudence in Preaching and Publishing. The Commission suggests prudence for preachers and publishers. Preachers are encouraged to be aware of current biblical scholarship as they prepare sermons, yet they should «refrain entirely from proposing vain or insufficiently established novelties»[66]. Publishers «should exploit all the real advances of biblical science that the diligence of recent (students) has produced. But they are to avoid entirely the rash remarks of innovators».

---

[64] *SME*, §2. *EB*, §650; *OCT*, §929.
[65] *SME*, §2. *EB*, §651; *OCT*, §930.
[66] *SME*, §4. *EB*, §655; *OCT*, §934.

2.2 *The HCM as exposed in Sancta Mater Ecclesia*

The document makes reference to several elements of the HCM and encourages their utilization by exegetes. The tone is positive and encouraging to scholars[67]. The endorsement of critical methodology is clear:

> He (the exegete) will diligently employ the new exegetical aids, above all those which the historical method, taken in its widest sense, offers to him — a method which carefully investigates sources and defines their nature and value, and makes such helps as textual criticism, literary criticism, and the study of languages[68].

Additionally, the Commission encourages the identification of literary genres so that the meaning intended by the author may be understood. Form criticism, however, should be used with caution.

> But let him (the exegete) be wary, because quite inadmissible philosophical and theological principles have often come to be mixed with this method, which not uncommonly have vitiated the method itself as well as the conclusions in the literary area. For some proponents of this method have been led astray by the prejudiced views of rationalism[69].

The use of the HCM is guided by the principles elaborated in the first part of the document (described above). The Gospel, in each stage of its transmission, was communicated to a particular people of a specific age in a specific part of the world within a specific cultural setting. Language, images and ideas were utilized that could be understood by those receiving the message. Thus, the apostles and sacred writers communicated the Gospel message of Jesus according to forms both spoken and written that were in use at that time, such as «catecheses, stories, testimonia, hymns, doxologies, [and] prayers». The exegete studies these forms while seeking out «the meaning intended by the Evangelist in narrating a saying or a deed in a certain way or in placing it in a certain context»[70]. Thus, the goal of the method is determining the intention of the human author, in other words, the *literal sense*. Through seeking the human author's intention, the exegete may identify God's intention in the composition:

---

[67] *EB*, §645; *OCT*, §923. The document refers to exegetes as «faithful sons of the church in great numbers who are experts in biblical matters...following the exhortations of the Supreme Pontiffs and are dedicating themselves wholeheartedly and untiringly to this serious and arduous task». They should be treated with «equity and justice by other scholars as well as with great charity».

[68] *SME*, §1. *EB*, §646; *OCT*, §925.

[69] *SME*, §1. *EB*, §647; *OCT*, §926.

[70] *SME*, §2. *EB*, §651; *OCT* §930.

... let them not pursue it as an end in itself, but that through it they might more plainly perceive the sense intended by God though the sacred writer. Let them not stop, therefore half-way, content only with their literary discoveries, but show in addition how these things really contribute to a clearer understanding of revealed doctrine, or if it be the case, to the refutation of errors[71].

3. Dei Verbum

Dei Verbum was promulgated on November 18, 1965 following five years of debate[72]. The debate and discussions mentioned above regarding biblical scholarship went hand in hand with the new way of describing revelation. The contents of *Dei Verbum* as well as the HCM exposed in the document are considered below.

3.1 *The Contents of Dei Verbum*

The Prologue of *Dei Verbum* begins with a proclamation of faith in God the father and Jesus his Son quoting I John. The theme of the document is then set forth «divine revelation and its transmission». The constitution contains six chapters.

Chapter One: Divine Revelation. Dei Verbum describes revelation as God's self communication with humanity. The revelation is transmitted through words and deed which are intrinsically bound up with one another[73]. It occurs in history beginning with God's «manifestation to our first parents», then to Abraham and the patriarchs, followed by Moses and the prophets. The fullness of God's revelation comes through Jesus: «For he sent his Son, the eternal Word who enlightens all men, to dwell among men and to tell them about the inner life of God[74]. He communicates di-

---

[71] *SME*, §3. *EB*, §654; *OCT*, §933. The immediate context of this statement is the address to teachers in seminaries.

[72] For further reading on *Dei Verbum* see the following: B.M. AHERN, «On Divine Revelation»; ID., «Scriptural Aspects of *Dei Verbum*»; G. ALBERGO – J.A. KOMONCHAK, *History of Vatican II*; L. ALONSO SCHÖKEL, «La Constitucion *Dei Verbum*»; ID., «La Palabra de Dios»; ID., «Unità e composizione»; B.D. DUPUY, *La Révélation Divine*; R. LATOURELLE, *Vatican II*, I, 123-382; S. LYONNET, *La Bibbia nella Chiesa*; G. O'COLLINS, «At the Origins of *Dei Verbum*»; ID., «Dei Verbum and Biblical Scholarship»; B. ORCHARD, «*Dei Verbum*»; I. DE LA POTTERIE, «La verità della S. Scrittura»; J. RATZINGER – A. GRILLMEIER – B. RIGAUX, «Dogmatic Constitution on Divine Revelation»; M.G. SANCHEZ, «Inspriación e interpretación»; M. ZERWICK, «De S. Scrittura».

[73] *DV*, §2. *EB*, §670; *OCT*, §952.

[74] *DV*, §4. *EB*, §672; *OCT*, §954.

vine revelation «by the total fact of his presence and self-manifestation —
by words and works, signs and miracles, but above all by his death and
glorious resurrection from the dead, and finally by sending the Spirit of
truth»[75]. The revelation is ongoing and not merely a voice from the past.
This revelation in Christ is «more and more profoundly understood»
through the continuous presence of the Holy Spirit[76]. Faith expressed
through obedience is required as a response to the revelation.

Chapter Two: The Transmission of Divine Revelation. The transmission of revelation is centered in Jesus Christ, «in whom the entire revelation of the most high God is summed up (cf. Cor 1:20; 3:16–4:6)»[77]. The
handing on of this revelation continued through his apostles by their
preaching, through their example and in their establishing of institutions.
Dei Verbum describes the transmission in terms of Tradition, Scripture,
and the Magisterium. «Sacred Tradition and Sacred Scripture make up a
single sacred deposit of the Word of God, which is entrusted to the
church»[78]. The role of authentically interpreting this Word of God is
given to the Magisterium who completes its task through the help of the
Holy Spirit. «Yet this Magisterium is not superior to the Word of God,
but is its servant». Thus,

> it is clear, therefore, that, in the supremely wise arrangement of God, sa-
> cred Tradition, sacred Scripture, and the Magisterium of the church are
> so connected and associated that one of them cannot stand without the
> others. Working together, each in its own way under the action of the one
> Holy Spirit, they all contribute effectively to the salvation of souls[79].

Chapter Three: Sacred Scripture: Inspiration and Interpretation[80].
The divine-human cooperation in authorship is affirmed[81]. The inerrancy
question is turned around so that the question deals with truth instead of
error — «we must acknowledge that the books of Scripture, firmly, faithfully and without error, teach that truth which God, for the sake of our sal-

---

[75] *DV*, §4. *EB*, §672; *OCT*, §954.

[76] *DV*, §5. *EB*, §674; *OCT*, §956.

[77] *DV*, §7. *EB*, §677; *OCT*, §959.

[78] *DV*, §10. *EB*, §683; *OCT*, §965.

[79] *DV*, §10. *EB*, §685; *OCT*, §967.

[80] The hermeneutical principles contained in this chapter are discussed below (page
153).

[81] Inspiration is not addressed specifically. B.M. AHERN, «*On Divine Revelation*»,
561, a member of the TC, suggests that not enough theological reflection had taken
place to make a decision on this matter. For more on views circulating at that time on
inspiration see: L. ALONSO SCHÖKEL, «El proceso de la inspiración»; ID., *The Inspired Word*.

vation, wished to see confided to the sacred Scriptures»[82]. The chapter also describes the implications of the divine-human authorship for interpretation (which is discussed below). The Scriptures are described as «the marvelous "condescension" of eternal wisdom». The purpose of this condensation is «that we may come to know the ineffable loving-kindness of God and see for ourselves how far he has gone in adapting his language with thoughtful concern for our nature». At the same time the Scriptures are inspired by the Spirit and must be read in this Spirit.

Chapter Four: The Old Testament. The Council affirms the integrity of the biblical text, specifically the OT and the NT. The framework for understanding the OT is salvation history. The books of the OT have a permanent and a lasting value. «The economy of the OT was deliberately so orientated that it should prepare for and declare in prophecy the coming of Christ, redeemer of all men, and of the messianic kingdom (cf. Luke 24:44; John 5:39; 1 Pet 1:10), and should indicate it by means of different types (cf. 1 Cor 10:11)». Even though the books contain matter which are imperfect and provisional, «nevertheless show us authentic divine teaching»[83]. Regarding the relationship with the NT books, *Dei Verbum* states: «God, the inspirer and author of the books of both testaments, in his wisdom has so brought it about that the new should be hidden in the old and that the old should be manifest in the new»[84].

---

[82] *DV*, §11. *EB*, §687; *OCT*, §969. The first intervention in favor of reformulating the «inerrancy» terminology was put forth in discussions on the third draft by Cardinal Köenig («saving truth»). G. BAUM, «Vatican II's Constitution on Revelation», 71, summarizes the discussion: «To avoid the idea that the adjective "saving" intended to limit inspiration to certain parts of Scripture, the TC was willing to replace the adjective by a subordinate clause which expressed its meaning more clearly. In the final text of the Constitution we read that the Bible teaches "the truth which God for our salvation wished to be contained in the sacred writings firmly, faithfully, and without error". The object of inerrancy is thus clearly narrowed to the saving truth contained in each and every part of Scripture. One may not understand this as if only certain parts of Scripture teach truth without error. According to the teaching of the church, the entire Scripture is inspired in all its parts. It is the saving truth contained in all these parts that is communicated without error». See also B.M. AHERN, «*On Divine Revelation*», 562; L. LEGRAND, «The Authority of Scripture».

[83] *DV*, §15. *EB*, §693; *OCT*, §975.

[84] *DV*, §16. *EB*, §694; *OCT*, §976. S. LYONNET, «A Word», 164-168, makes three observations about this statement. First, the NT does not presuppose the OT simply because it is the fulfillment of the latter. It presupposes knowledge of the OT, and is addressed to people who were brought up on the OT. Second, the NT will often remain incomprehensible to the person who does not have the necessary knowledge of the OT. Third, only by comparing the NT with the OT can we understand the radically new contribution of the NT although it still remains in true continuity with the OT.

Chapter Five: The New Testament. The Council once again notes the centrality of Christ in the revelation of the Father. The revelation was first communicated to the apostles who have a special place in its transmission for

> this mystery was not made known to other generations as it has now been revealed to his holy apostles and prophets by the Holy Spirit (cf. Eph 3:4-6; Gk. text), that they might preach the Gospel, stir up faith in Jesus Christ and the Lord, and bring together the church. The writings of the NT stand as a perpetual and divine witness to these realities[85].

The gospels have a special place in the canon due to their apostolic origin. This origin is affirmed vaguely in terms of authorship: «they and others of the apostolic age handed on to us in writing the same message they had preached, the foundation of our faith; the fourfold Gospel...»[86]. The constitution stressed that the evangelists faithfully hand on what Jesus did and taught «for their eternal salvation»[87]. At the same time the sacred authors «in writing the four Gospels, selected certain of the many elements which had been handed on, either orally or already in written form, others they synthesized or explained with an eye to the situation of the churches, the while sustaining the form of preaching, but always in such a fashion that they have told us the honest truth about Jesus»[88]. Brief comments are made on the writings of St. Paul and «other apostolic writings composed under the inspiration of the Holy Spirit»[89].

---

[85] *DV*, §18. *EB*, §696; *OCT*, §978.

[86] *DV*, §18. *EB*, §697; *OCT*, §979. The reference to «others of the apostolic age» is most likely a reference to Mark and Luke. There is no intention here by the council to drop the notion of apostolic authorship. B. ORCHARD, «*Dei Verbum* and the Synoptic Gospels», 206, states «by employing the phrase "the sacred authors", a deliberate ambiguity is introduced into the text at this point. While the reader may be expected to understand the terms "sacred authors" or "evangelists" as "the Apostles and apostolic men" mentioned in §18 and the first two sentences of §19, it is logically and grammatically possible to interpret these terms without any difficulty in the remainder of §19 as referring instead to "post-apostolic authors", i.e. second-generation Christian writers and scribes».

[87] *DV* §19's statement — «whose historicity she unhesitatingly affirms» — must not be understood as history in the modern sense of the word. History for the ancient peoples was communicated much differently than today regarding facts, interpretation of facts, and presentation of information. The constitution speaks of the history of the transmission of the Gospel in similar terms as *Sancta Mater Ecclesia*. See J. CABA, «Historicity of the Gospels (Dei Verbum 19)», 300-311; B. RIGAUX, «Chapter V - The New Testament», 252-261.

[88] *DV*, §19. *EB*, §698; *OCT*, §980. Cf. *Sancta Mater Ecclesia*, *EB*, §651; *OCT*, §930.

[89] *DV*, §20. *EB*, §699; *OCT*, §981.

Chapter Six: Sacred Scripture in the Life of the Church. The constitution makes four points regarding the Scriptures in the life of the church. First, it acknowledges Scriptures and Tradition as the vehicles through which the Spirit speaks to the church. Reading the Scriptures is described as an encounter with the divine: «In the sacred books the Father who is in heaven comes lovingly to meet his children, and talks with them»[90]. Second, the council orders that «suitable and correct translations» be made in cooperation with the «separated brethren» so that the Scriptures may be accessible to the people. The translations should include suitable notes to facilitate reading of the text[91]. Respect should be shown to the ancient translations: the LXX, other Eastern translations, and especially the Vulgate. Third, the constitution reminds Catholic exegetes and theologians to consult the Fathers, the sacred liturgies, and the Magisterium as they examine and explain the biblical texts[92]. The goal of such studies is to prepare ministers for nourishing the flock. Theological studies should be based on the Scriptures: «... the "study of the sacred page" should be the very soul of sacred theology»[93]. Fourth, *Dei Verbum* addresses the role of the bishops, priests, deacons, catechists and other ministers of the Word. «Constant sacred reading and diligent study» of the sacred Scriptures is demanded for «ignorance of the Scriptures is ignorance of Christ»[94].

3.2 *The HCM in Dei Verbum*

Dei Verbum requires the use of historical critical methodology through the hermeneutical principles it sets forth. The document does not discuss the HCM per se, however elements of the method are mentioned. The following section examines the hermeneutical principles and methodological procedures of the HCM present in *Dei Verbum*.

---

[90] *DV*, §21. *EB*, §701; *OCT*, §983.

[91] *DV*, §25. *EB*, §707; *OCT*, §989. These notes may even be prepared by non-Catholics. S. LYONNET, «A Word», 181, remarks that a French ecumenical translation of the Letter to the Romans appeared in January of 1967. He says the notes in this edition were enough to be a full commentary.

[92] In, P. LAGHI – M. GILBERT – A. VANHOYE, *Chiesa e Sacra Scrittura*, 42, Vanhoye notes that prior to *Dei Verbum* the documents speak of the «use» of the Sacred Scriptures, now they speak of the «study» of the Scriptures, indeed as the soul of theology. He continues saying it is not enough to use the scriptures as *dicta probantia* to confirm theological theories, a methodological study is necessary. All the while the exegete has to be informed by theology so that one discipline enriches the other.

[93] *DV*, §24. *EB*, §704; *OCT*, §986.

[94] *DV*, §11. *EB*, §687; *OCT*, §987. Quoting St. Jerome

Hermeneutical Principles. DV §11 begins with an affirmation of biblical inspiration. The Scriptures have God as their author; yet God chose men to write the sacred texts. These men «made full use of their powers and faculties so that, though he acted in them and by them, it was as true authors that they consigned to writing whatever he wanted written and no more»[95]. The change from earlier ecclesial documents is significant — there is no mention of «instrumentality» nor «dictation theory». *Dei Verbum* describes the human author as a «true author» who «made full use of their powers and faculties» while «employed» by God. The reformulation of the traditional belief recognizes the creative human element in the composition of the Scriptures. At the same time it respects the divine character of the Scriptures, for the human authors were committed to writing only what God wanted and nothing more. All that the inspired authors affirm should be regarded as affirmed by the Holy Spirit so that «we must acknowledge that the books of Scripture, firmly faithfully and without error, teach that truth which God, for the sake of our salvation, wished to see confided to the sacred Scriptures»[96].

Dei Verbum's principles for interpretation follow its description of inspiration. First, since God speaks to men in human fashion, the interpreter, «if he is to ascertain what God has wished to communicate to us, should carefully search out the meaning which the sacred writers really had in mind, that meaning which God had thought well to manifest through the medium of their words». In other words the interpreter must determine the *literal sense*. Secondly, since the Scriptures should be read with the divine author in mind, «no less attention must be devoted to the content and unity of the whole of Scripture, taking into account the Tradition of the entire church and the analogy of faith...». *DV* §13 speaks of the condescension of eternal wisdom in the Scriptures. The description follows the Christological analogy of *Divino Afflante Spiritu*. «Indeed the words of God, expressed in the words of men, are in every way like human language, just as the Word of the eternal Father, when he took on himself the flesh of human weakness, became like man». Thus two hermeneutical principles can be derived from *Dei Verbum*: identifying the human author's intention and maintaining the integrity of the biblical collection.

Methodological Procedures. Dei Verbum mentions neither the term HCM nor «critical methodology» nor any of the individual criticisms by name. The document, however, does mention guidelines for study of the

---

[95] *DV*, §11. *EB*, §687; *OCT*, §987.
[96] *DV*, §11. *EB*, §687; *OCT*, §987.

text which require the HCM. The elements of the HCM as found in *Dei Verbum* are presented according to their individual criticisms: philology-grammatical criticism, textual criticism, literary-source criticism, genre-form criticism, and historical criticism.

Philology-Grammatical Criticism. *DV* §12 maintains that «due attention must be paid both to the customary and characteristic patterns of perception, speech and narrative which prevailed at the age of the sacred writer, and to the conventions which the people of his time followed in their dealings with one another». In order to do this a thorough study of philology is necessary as well as some elements of historical criticism and literary criticism. *DV* §22 calls for modern translations of the Scriptures from the original texts: «But since the Word of God must be readily available at all times, the church, with motherly concern, sees to it that suitable and correct translations are made into various languages, especially from the original texts of the sacred books». Such translations require the study of ancient languages and philology.

Textual Criticism. The constitution does not specifically mention textual criticism. The need for textual criticism had ceased to be a debated point by this time. Nevertheless, the document makes an allusion to textual criticism §22, while addressing the need for translations. Some of the ancient versions referred to are the LXX and the Vulgate. The existence of these various versions require textual criticism.

Literary - Source Criticism. *DV* §19 mentions the evangelists selecting material from the elements handed on either orally or in «written form». This reference acknowledges the possibility of pre-gospel writings and the presence of source material. Such possibility requires source criticism. Through such a study the author's use of sources can be identified and analyzed so as to better understand his intention.

Genre-Form Criticism. *DV* §12 following *Divino Afflante Spiritu* affirms the importance of recognizing literary forms. The reason for such study is «that truth is differently presented and expressed in the various types of historical writing, in prophetic and poetical texts, and in other forms of literary expression»[97]. In other words, there is no singular way of expressing truth in human language. The human author chose a means of communicating. Since language and literary forms are historically conditioned, the interpreter must attempt to identify these forms. The forms mentioned above are used as examples (history, prophetic, poetry). The references to an author's «determined situation» and the «circumstances

---

[97] *DV*, §12. *EB*, §689; *OCT*, §971.

of his time and culture» affirms the need to identify the *Sitz-im-Leben* of the form.

Historical Criticism. An interpretation based on the author's intention necessitates an historical study. The sociological, cultural, political, and religious life of the period must be studied in order to have a proper understanding of the language, images, and religious practices used or mentioned in the biblical texts. The process in which the gospel was handed on from the time of Jesus to the apostles to the sacred writers also necessitates historical criticism. The transmission occurs in time and through time (cf. §17-19). Here the constitution echo's *Sancta Mater Ecclesia*. The evangelists at times used a selective process choosing from elements which had been handed on to them either orally or in a written form. At other times, they synthesized or explained in light of the audience to which they were writing. Thus their communication of the «truth» was accomplished in a concrete historical setting which no doubt influenced their decisions in composing a text. Due consideration of this transmission is necessary in biblical studies. The document does not, however, call for a reconstruction of Jesus' life and ministry. Historical criticism is needed to understand the biblical writings and the Gospel message contained in and reflected through these writings.

4. The Place of the HCM in Catholic Exegesis according to Dei Verbum and Sancta Mater Ecclesia

The debates leading up to and included in the Vatican Council included the question of using historical critical methods in the study of the Bible. The debates helped shape the final document on revelation, *Dei Verbum*. The affirmation of the role of the human author in the work of composition necessitates the use of the HCM. The conclusion of this chapter will present the hermeneutical basis of the HCM as understood in this period. Following this the conclusion discusses the necessity and limits of the method according to the ecclesial documents of this period.

4.1 *The Hermeneutical Basis of the HCM*

More than any of the previous documents *Dei Verbum* contained an affirmation of the divine and human cooperation in the composition of the Scriptures. *Divino Afflante Spiritu* saw this cooperation in clear terms of the human author and the divine author. Mention is made of the *literal sense* through which the exegete seeks to identify the human author's intention. A spiritual sense exists which is the divine intention reflected in the text. There is a clear distinction between the two senses. Critical methods are used to understand the *literal sense* while the spiritual sense is discerned through recourse to the Magisterium, the Fathers and the analogy of faith. *Dei Verbum* removes the sharp distinction between the human and divine by representing inspiration in terms of God's communication with man, in human language. The human author rather than being the instrument is a true author. God works through his work. No longer are a *literal sense* or a *spiritual sense* mentioned. The clear isolation of divine and human is replaced by the unity of the divine and human. The Christological references are used in an analogous way to exemplify this unity. Distinctions are present but not to the point of breaking down the unity. The human author's intention is the pathway to the divine author's intention to teach salvific truth. The divine role is further reflected in the unity of the Testaments. Interpretation will be the search for the salvific meaning in the text understood first through the human authors intention from which a trajectory or development may take place guided by the Spirit[98].

4.2 Why is the HCM necessary?

The Gospel message is historically conditioned, it must be understood from an historical perspective. Sancta Mater Ecclesia along with *Dei Verbum* recognize and comment on the historical transmission of the Gospel. The three stages of this transmission involve many factors which effect the manner in which the gospel message is communicated to a particular audience. Jesus himself presented his Gospel in a manner that would be understandable to his disciples. The Apostles took this Gospel message, understood now in the light of the Resurrection, and communicated to a new generation of disciples of different cultures. Finally the sacred writers composed their texts under the inspiration of the Holy Spirit, in a manner which was understandable to their contemporaries. Each stage of this transmission is historically conditioned. One role of the exegete is to determine the meaning of the text as it was communicated in the third

---

[98] In J. RATZINGER – A. GRILLMEIER – B. RIGAUX, «*Dogmatic Constitution on Divine Revelation*», 239, Grillmeier notes two points on the importance of historical critical exegesis. First, because everything is seen from the point of view of the *salutis causa* of inspired Scripture, any scriptural statement which has been arrived at by critical historical work is a genuine *sensus pneumatic*. The pneumatic meaning of Scripture must not be separated from the historically established *sensus auctoris*. Second, all searching for the *sensus plenior* must start with the findings of critical historical research, which must proceed according to legitimate methods of theological scholarship. An interpretation that is detached from the genuine *sensus auctoris* is eisegesis, not exegesis.

stage. In order to do this the scholar must take into consideration the two stages prior to the final, not so much that the prior stages may be understood in themselves, but so that the final text may be understood in light of the earlier stages[99].

Determining the literal sense requires the use of the HCM. The *literal sense* is not mentioned by name in either of the documents considered above. Yet both documents clearly refer to it when it speaks of the human author's intention. *Dei Verbum* speaks of the human authors as «true authors» who freely use their talents and abilities while inspired by God. To understand their intentions in writing an historical approach is required. The intention of the sacred writer is influenced by his historical situation. *Sancta Mater Ecclesia* pointed this out in regard in the third stage of the Gospel transmission, but the principle may also be applied to other writings of the Bible. Each author was conditioned by time, place and audience. The HCM is used to evaluate the text in light of these historical conditions.

Modern translations of the Bible require the HCM. Dei Verbum §22 demands that modern language translations of the Bible be made so that the Word of God might be readily accessed by the people of the present age. Translation in itself requires the HCM. The translation of ideas, concepts, idiom, etc. require an historical knowledge of the period. Although philological-grammatical criticism has perhaps the most important role in translation, the other criticisms of the HCM can also aid in the process. For example poetic constructions will be better translated when understood after a genre-form critical study. Furthermore *Dei Verbum* suggests that explanatory notes be attached to the translations. The notes will help explain images, events, customs, historical situations which are not readily accessible to the modern reader. The practice is standard today in many modern translations. The material for such translations is often the result of historical-critical studies.

4.3 Why is the HCM limited?

Certain philosophical and theological principles taint form-criticism. Sancta Mater Ecclesia mentions that form-criticism may be used in the study of the Bible but should be used with caution. Care must be taken not to include philosophical or theological pre-suppositions imposed by a rationalist approach. The PBC cautiously encourages the use of form

---

[99] J.A. FITZMYER, «Historical Criticism», , notes that one of the most important roles of the Catholic exegete is to determine the relationship between Stage I and Stage III, between the ministry of Jesus and the final written form of the Gospels.

criticism. The statement points to the influence which the exegete brings to the method. The pre-suppositions with which exegetes use their method affect the value placed on it. The pre-suppositions of the exegete will be a major factor in the debates of the next period.

The HCM does not of itself take into consideration the canonical collection, the tradition of the church and the analogy of faith. Dei Verbum §12 noted that divine authorship must be kept in mind while giving an interpretation of the text. Consequently three elements which have to be considered are the canon, the tradition of the church and the analogy of faith. The HCM as a method does not specifically treat these elements of the text. Sometimes the consideration is made, other times it is effectively ignored. Therefore exegetes will have to include this consideration in their own application of the method.

CHAPTER V

The Scholarly and Pastoral Situation Preceding
Interpretation of the Bible in the Church

The third period of Catholic participation in critical biblical scholarship
is represented by the PBC document *Interpretation of the Bible in the
Church*. The evaluation of the document will be similar to the treatment of
ecclesial documents in the previous two chapters. Chapter Five presents
the scholarly and pastoral situation along with the church's response prior
to PBC publication. Chapter Six studies the contents of the document and
its treatment of the HCM. Chapter Seven presents the response of scholars and theologians to the document regarding biblical hermeneutics and
the HCM.

The question of biblical studies and the role of the scriptures in the life
of the church continued to be discussed in the years following the promulgation of *Dei Verbum*. T. Curtin evaluated this discussion in his doctoral dissertation *Historical Criticism and the Theological Interpretation
of Scripture*. The study extensively evaluated articles published between
1965-1983 regarding the principles and purpose of biblical studies. The
discussion from 1965-1975 was evaluated according to English[1], French[2]

---

[1] Curtin began his presentation noting that the American and English discussion
centered more on historical critical methodology than its hermeneutical implications.
Scholars during this period generally approved of scientific exegesis and the attempt to
identify the *literal sense*. He saw the acceptance of the HCM by American Catholic
scholars in the late 1960's reflected in the preface to the *JBC* which calls that work «a
visible monument to the victory in the great biblical battle». He also showed how
questions began to arise regarding the theological meaning of the Scriptures that eventually led to the discussion on the relationship between the divine and human intentions in the Scriptures as well as the relationship between exegesis and theology.

[2] The French concerns went beyond the use of the method to the subsequent implications for interpretation arising from its use. The HCM makes an interpretation based

and German language groups[3]. The period 1975-1983 was treated thematically[4].

Curtin summarized the discussion as involving three major areas of human thought and endeavor regarding the study of scriptures for the years 1958–1983: the historical and literary study of ancient texts, the philosophical question of what it means to interpret, and the Christian need to find the word of God[5]. The problem for biblical interpretation was «to reconcile the three areas in a way that would do justice to each, yet not prevent the others their full exercise and inquiry»[6], so that a «holistic interpretation» or «integral interpretation» would be possible. This integral interpretation will include the following: attention to both the divine and human authorship of the biblical text; attention to the canonical unity of the collection of individual works; an appreciation of the Scriptures as a book of the church; and an appreciation of the interpreter's role in the endeavor.

---

on the author's intention. French scholars during this period were concerned about the manner by which this meaning is communicated to the present. The discussions did not call for the dismissal of the HCM but a refinement that recognized the need to actualize. The end of this period saw the call for a more complete biblical hermeneutic. Curtin noted that «commentators agreed on the insufficiency of an historical-literary approach alone, but differed over its relationship to the needs of faith and whether exegesis was attending to them». Questions were raised concerning the value of the *literal sense* and newer methods including a canonical approach and structuralism were being encouraged.

[3] The period 1965-1968 began with articles on the acceptance of historical critical exegesis. Each author saw a value to historical critical research in aiming to identify the meaning for the text yet also recognized the need for the method to be complemented in some way. The discussion in the years 1968-1971 dealt with biblical interpretation within the church. The thought presented in this section regarded the connection between exegesis and faith experienced through the church and how the two interact. Curtin presented the reflections of Karl Lehmann on the role of hermeneutics in exegesis. 1972-1975 saw continued discussion on how to inter-relate historical criticism with theological interpretation. Suggestions included the study of tradition in relationship to the Scriptures, the study of patristic ecclesiology and its relationship with exegesis, the development of *Wirkungsgeschichte*.

[4] The individual discussions on historical criticism and theological interpretation in the individual language groups converged in the years 1976-1983. Curtin presents the discussions from this period under following five themes: the necessity and limits of historical criticism, the relationship between exegesis and theology, exegesis practiced within a broader context, the communal aspect of biblical interpretation, and the relationship between critical exegesis and the present meaning of scripture.

[5] T.R. CURTIN, *HCTIS*, 295.

[6] T.R. CURTIN, *HCTIS*, 295.

With regard to historical criticism in this endeavor Curtin summarized the lines of convergence that emerged in the latter part of the discussion as follows:

> a) Historical criticism has not come to an end despite its evident problems and limitations. The *literal sense* continues to claim an authority but within a larger perspective of biblical interpretation that recognizes there are other legitimate meanings of Scripture as well.
>
> b) It could be said that the aim of biblical interpretation is now the total word of Scripture. This includes the historical *literal sense* of the original inspired author, the *canonical sense* coming from the whole Bible in the relationship of the testaments and the centrality of Christ, and the present meaning as the church reads Scripture in the light of the times and her experience of Christ ... They demand the collaboration of different disciplines within a communion of faith.
>
> c) The authority of the *literal sense* is defined in protective terms. The *literal sense* sets the parameters for attributing a meaning to the text, but does not exhaust that meaning. It claims the authority of inspiration and constantly recalls biblical interpretation to the original event of divine revelation. The efforts to know and understand the original events of salvation are still required, but since these attempts can never finally be sure of their results then more than the *literal sense* is needed.
>
> d) In sound theology, biblical interpretation has to go further than the *literal sense*. God continues to make himself known.
>
> e) Suggestions for the actualization of Scripture go beyond the boundaries of critical, analytical study[7].

Curtin's dissertation identified the major elements of the discussions from 1965-1983. Many of the points raised by these scholars continued to be raised in the following period, 1984-1995. During this period there was much dissatisfaction with the trends in biblical exegesis especially regarding the use of the HCM. The dissatisfaction eventually is described as a crisis in biblical interpretation. It is this crisis that prompts the PBC to write *Interpretation of the Bible in the Church*.

This chapter describes the pastoral and scholarly situation that preceded *Interpretation of the Bible in the Church*. The chapter contains eight sections. Each section discusses a topic either related to or indicative of the developing crisis in Catholic biblical interpretation. The presentation in each section includes the summary of an article(s) that illustrates the topic.

---

[7] T.R. CURTIN, *HCTIS*, 306-307.

Additional bibliography for the individual topics is indicated in the foot-notes[8]. The final section concludes the chapter summarizing the primary concerns regarding the HCM raised in the debate.

1. *Birth of the Messiah* and the Movement Against Historical-Critical Exegesis

R.E. Brown published *The Birth of the Messiah*, a commentary on the infancy narratives of *Matthew* and *Luke*, in 1978. The work was a signifi-cant Catholic contribution to critical biblical scholarship. The CBQ noted its significance by including two reviews of the work breaking a long-standing policy of containing only one review of a work. The book spawned much discussion concerning biblical methodology; in fact it re-generated the debate in the Catholic church (as well as among Christians of other denominations)[9] regarding the use of the HCM in biblical stud-ies. Reviews of *Birth of the Messiah* reveal the tension and debates[10]. Brown defended his work and the use of the HCM in Catholic exegesis in several articles calling for a balanced and nuanced discussion. One such article is «Liberals, Ultraconservatives, and the Misinterpretation of Catholic Biblical Exegesis», published in 1984[11].

The article provides a witness to the debates of the period, the need for careful analysis of the method as well as an appraisal of some difficult issues in biblical interpretation. Brown argued that the discussion or cri-tique of Catholic exegesis cannot remain on the level of vague generalities.

---

[8] Numerous articles have been published on the topic of biblical interpretation for this period, many of which reiterate points made during the earlier period (see chart seven).

[9] J.D. Kingsbury in his review remarked «Brown's book is an ambitious undertak-ing, it would be curious indeed if a work of this magnitude did not evoke contrary opinions».

[10] Reviews that were mostly favorable were written by the following: M. Bourke, J.P. Dunn, J.D. Kingsbury, R.H. Fuller, N.J. McEleney, F.J. Moloney, R. North, G. O'Collins, and H. Wansbrough. Reviews that were mostly negative were written by the following: E. Black, L.T. Johnson, J. McHugh and M. Miguens. R. Laurentin and G.A. Kelly wrote full books criticizing Brown's methodology and results (R. LAURENTIN, *The Truth of Christmas*; G. A. KELLEY, *The New Biblical Theorists,* see also *The Church's Problem with Bible Scholars*). Brown's response to Laurentin is considered above.

[11] See: R.E. BROWN, «Biblical Exegesis»; J.A. FITZMYER – R.E. BROWN, «Danger Also from the Left»; J. MURPHY-O'CONNOR, «Again under Attack», re-sponds to a similar misrepresentation of Brown's work by G.A. KELLY, *The New Biblical Theorists*.

Rather the particular issues or questions raised in exegetical work need to be the basis of discussion.

Prior to examining the misrepresentations of Catholic biblical exegesis, Brown summarized the Catholic approach to biblical studies using critical methodologies as directed by the magisterium. However, the focus of Brown's discussion of misrepresentation centered on specific examples from the writings of Thomas Sheehan and Rene Laurentin. Brown described Sheehan as a liberal Catholic philosopher and Laurentin as a conservative Mariologist[12]. He saw both as intelligent scholars who have misrepresented Catholic biblical scholarship to their readers. A thorough argument was presented in each case.

Brown took issue with Sheehan's portrait of contemporary Catholic biblical scholarship in his review of Hans Küng's *Eternal Life?* entitled «Revolution in the Church»[13]. In his review, Sheehan presented an analysis of what he called a «liberal consensus» among Roman Catholics «that was undermining the classic presentation of church doctrine»[14]. Brown refuted Sheehan's opinions by dismantling the notion of «liberal consensus»[15], and by demonstrating Sheehan's misrepresentation of the scholarship he cites.

For example, Sheehan summarized the «liberal consensus» on the virginal conception is that «Jesus [did not] know that his mother, Mary, had remained a virgin in the very act of conceiving him... Most likely Mary told Jesus what she herself knew of his origins: that he had a natural father and was born not in Bethlehem but in Nazareth»[16]. In the footnotes,

---

[12] R.E. BROWN, «Liberals, Ultraconservatives», 314. Before he addressed Sheehan and Laurentin, Brown gave some general examples of misrepresentation. For example, biblical scholarship basically affirms that the disciples and early Christians «grew in an appreciation of Jesus and had to reinterpret language to suit his greatness». He noted with surprise both ultraconservative and liberal claims that most NT scholars deny that Jesus was the Messiah or that he knew who he was. «They even have "biblical scholars" affirming that Christians reshaped Jesus drastically to fit their own views, distorting the authentic Jesus». Brown stated that numerous examples could be given, many times they involve the following areas of theology: the virginal conception, the bodily resurrection, the sacraments, and mariology.

[13] T. SHEEHAN, «Revolution in the Church».

[14] R.E. BROWN, «Liberals, Ultraconservatives», 316.

[15] Sheehan grouped together the following theologians : R. Schnackenburg, R.E. Brown, R.E. Murphy, P. Benoit, J. Meier, J.A. Fitzmyer, D.M Stanley, R. Pesch, W. Kasper, D. Tracy, E. Schillebeeckx, and H. Küng. Brown noted the incongruity of such a group based on: different disciplines, different opinions within this group, and different approval ratings by ecclesial authority.

[16] R.E. BROWN, «Liberals, Ultraconservatives», 319. Concluding his remarks on Sheehan, Brown conceded that two recent Catholic exegetes (McKenzie and Schaberg)

he cited Brown's *The Birth of the Messiah* and *The Virginal Conception and Bodily Resurrection of Jesus* as supporting his presentation. Brown countered

> What he did not mention is that I wrote that the scientifically controllable evidence favors the historicity of the virginal conception, and that in my judgment the church teaches infallibly that Mary conceived as a virgin. I have indicated no support whatsoever for the suggestion that Jesus did not know that his mother had remained a virgin in the act of conception, and that Mary told Jesus that he had a natural father[17].

Brown also addressed the work of Rene Laurentin *The Truth of Christmas Beyond the Myths*[18]. Brown gave some historical background to Laurentin's theological work then appraised the new book. He found the book «openly hostile to modern historical-critical exegesis of the NT». Brown noted that Laurentin had suggested a rationalist consensus which beginning in the previous century «has been taken up belatedly by Catholics, so that today rationalists' presuppositions have won over a large part of the ecclesiastical intelligentsia»[19]. Brown challenged this representation of Catholic biblical scholarship in four ways: by dismantling

---

as well as Küng seem to dispense with the virginal conception. He insisted, however, that their conclusions are not representative of Catholic biblical scholarship.

[17] R.E. BROWN, «Liberals, Ultraconservatives», 319. Brown answered his critics in R.E. BROWN, *Birth of the Messiah*[2], 573-577. For a thorough examination of the virginal conception see, R.E. BROWN, *Birth of the Messiah*[2], 697-712. Other examples of Sheehan's misrepresentation refer to the resurrection and ecclesiology. Brown demonstrated that no consensus could be found among the 12 scholars in Sheehan's list regarding the details of the resurrection. For example, «Sheehan cites Küng and Schillebeeckx for the idea that Christian faith in the risen Jesus came from his appearances independently of the empty tomb. That is probably so; but unlike Küng and Schillebeeckx, I have written that the emptiness of the tomb gave an essential coloring to the preaching about the risen Jesus - «being raised» implied *bodily* resurrection; the one who appeared had a risen *body* that was no longer in the tomb». Brown also took issue with Sheehan's presentation of ecclesiology. Sheehan presented the «liberal consensus» on ecclesiology as teaching that «it seems he [Jesus] did not know he was supposed to establish the Holy Roman Catholic and Apostolic Church with St. Peter as the first in a long line of infallible popes». Brown refuted this statement and speaks of the development of the church stemming from Jesus' ministry through his death and resurrection, and the gift of the Spirit. «Sheehan's negative description quoted above presupposes a simplistic understanding of church foundation, involving explicit intention on Jesus' part during his ministry - an explicitness not necessarily part of Catholic doctrine on the subject».

[18] R. LAURENTIN, *The Truth*. Originally published in French in 1982.

[19] R.E. BROWN, «Liberals, Ultraconservatives», 320.

Laurentin's perception of a rationalist consensus[20]; by demonstrating the complexities of infancy narrative research regarding historicity[21]; by correcting a misquotation from his *Birth of the Messiah*[22]; and by calling into question the value of Laurentin's approach.

Brown concluded the article summarizing the positions of ultraconservatives and ultraliberals represented by Sheehan and Laurentin in their appropriation of Catholic biblical scholarship:

---

[20] R.E. BROWN, «Liberals, Ultraconservatives», 321. Brown critiqued Laurentin's list of rationalists that includes J.A. Fitzmyer and himself. He defended Fitzmyer and himself noting that their good standing has been acknowledged by Rome by virtue of their appointments to the PBC. Brown responded to Laurentin's accusation that rational exegesis denies the miraculous: «Unfortunately, he [Laurentin] does not document the claims that he makes about either the rationalist presuppositions or the denial of the miraculous; and so I for one am left astounded, since the well-known Catholics whom I associate with critical infancy narrative exegesis (Schnackenburg, Schürmann, Vögtle, Fitzmyer, Meier, Bourke, and Legrand) are not guilty of either. In my own *Birth of the Messiah* I stated that it was unscientific to presuppose that miracles are impossible; and so a critical exegesis of the infancy narratives, such as I have written, need have nothing to do with rationalist presuppositions».

[21] Brown observed that Laurentin made an effort to prove the historical events of the Infancy Narratives (Matt 1–2; Luke 1–2) and by doing this «he regards himself as defending the Catholic tradition against those modern Catholic NT exegetes who have reduced the narratives to fiction or theological creations». Brown countered this by describing the complexity of historical research regarding the infancy narratives. He said: «logically the historicity of the infancy narratives can be judged differently from the historicity of the rest of the Gospel». The later parts of the Gospels have the apostolic witness to give evidence. Yet Brown carefully notes that he is not saying details of the infancy narratives are *not* historical but «only that we have serious reason for questioning their historicity». Added to this difficulty is that fact that «the infancy narratives do agree on the Davidic descent of Jesus, on birth at Bethlehem, and on conception by a virgin without a male parent».

[22] R.E. BROWN, «Liberals, Ultraconservatives», 323. Laurentin criticized Brown regarding his presentation on the virginal conception, saying that he claims that the virginal conception is found only in the Gospels of the last third of the first century. Brown replied that this statement is «scandalously incomplete, since he does not tell his readers that I argue for a pre-Gospel tradition affirming this fact».

He continued with a defense of his work in *The Birth of the Messiah*: «The precision in matters of historicity might be useful but scarcely salvific. The truth, however, is just the opposite. In my *Birth of the Messiah*, if I may take myself as an example of the modern approach, I confined the historical debates largely to appendixes, and spent most of the work on a positive analysis of the tremendous wealth of the infancy narratives, so evocative of the OT and so brilliantly clear on the Christology of Jesus as the Son of God. I contented that the theological value of the infancy narratives did not depend on historical debates which often concern matters quite foreign to the emphasis of the evangelists themselves».

[Ultraconservatives] stunned by the new historical observations of a critical exegesis, interpret that exegesis as a rejection of Catholic dogmas
precisely because they identify the dogmas with the literalist scriptural
underpinning that was previously inculcated in Catholic circles. Ultraliberals also attempt to fit modern critical exegesis into a presculptured
mold. Often liberal ideas have been shaped by theologians whose primary source of reflection was not exegesis but philosophy or sociology,
or by theologians who have consciously or unconsciously chosen a radical, rather than a centrist, exegesis[23].

Brown noted that for the scholarly discussion to continue on a fruitful
course, proper representation of the views of Catholic exegetes is essential
for the discussion to progress. The discussion or critique of Catholic exegesis cannot remain on the level of vague generalities rather the issues involved especially the particular nuances in exegetical studies need to be
the basis of discussion.

Summary. The reaction to *The Birth of the Messiah* and the subsequent
debates regarding the use of the HCM mark the beginning of the crisis in
Catholic biblical interpretation. Brown's article demonstrates the need for
careful analysis of exegesis. The polarization noted by Brown is a hin-
drance to careful analysis of exegetical results and practices. This polarization reflects society at that time in categorizing thought or position in
political terms: ultraconservative or ultraliberal. Brown suggested any description of Catholic exegesis should be done in terms of a centrist position[24]. Although this is correct, a more adequate description of «centrist»
would be needed if the discussion on the Catholic use of HCM were to
advance. A thorough presentation of the Catholic understanding of critical
exegesis is provided by J.A. Fitzmyer in 1989 (see below, page 214).

2. The Rift between Academy and Church, Exegesis and Actualization

The second topic of this chapter considers the perceived rift between the
academy and the church. This rift is an indication of the crisis in biblical
interpretation. The problem had been noted in the earlier debate by Dreyfus in his article «Exégèse en Sorbonne, exégèse en Église». The question
focused on what the role of exegetical studies have with regard to the life

---

23 R.E. BROWN, «Liberals, Ultraconservatives», 325.
24 Brown used the term «centrists» to describe those practitioners of HCM who use
the method within the framework of faith recognizing the inspiration of the Scriptures,
the divine role in composition while seeking the meaning of the text in the *literal
senses.*

of the faithful. The question was considered by S. Schneiders and U. Vanni. Schneiders' «Church and Biblical Scholarship in Dialogue» discussed the rift in terms of intellectual pursuits and pastoral application. Vanni's «Exegesis and Actualization in the Light of *Dei Verbum*» discussed the rift in terms of exegesis and actualization.

S. Schneiders: Church and Scholarship in Dialogue, 1985. S. Schneiders pointed out a tension that exists between the scholar and the faithful[25]. The tension is based on the antagonistic relationship of faith and science that began in the Enlightenment. Today it finds expression between some scholars who regard the faith filled approach as «unscientific, dogmatic, and credulous» and believers who regard «the academy as a laboratory in which the sacred text is irreverently dissected and the Word of God mediated through the Scriptures is rendered sterile and irrelevant»[26]. Schneiders saw the tension as unnecessary. She proposed a solution based on the complementarity of the scholarly and pastoral approaches through four comparisons[27].

The first comparison regarded the understanding of the text. The historical critic sees the Bible as an ancient text, in other words, an artifact produced in a different age at a distant place. From this historical perspective it is clear that a great distance separates the reader from the text. The interpreter attempts to bridge this distance. The believer reads the text to have an encounter with God. The understanding of the text is that it is, to use Gadamer's terms, a «classic». A classic is seen as a work of art to be appreciated. Schneider saw the two views as complementary. The text

---

[25] Schneiders distinguished the scholar from the faithful reader. R.E. BROWN - S.M. SCHNEIDERS, «Hermeneutics», 1150. Brown added a further distinction among the faithful readers: the professional reader and the general reader. Professional readers are those who preach and teach (clergy, catechists, leaders of Bible classes). The study of history and language will help the professional reader to avoid anachronistic ideas and conceptions and to stay rooted in the text. General readers must acknowledge that some work is involved in the reading of Scripture. Effort is needed in acquiring scholarly information on the text to help one read the text for deeper understanding. The call for effortless reading based either on «better» translations or divine assistance in reading will not eliminate the need for effort on behalf of the reader. To assist the general reader Brown proposes that religious education should be taught in parallel with the general educational background of the reader. See C. BRYAN, «The Preachers and the Critics: Thoughts on Historical Criticism», for a discussion on the tension between the believer and the exegete from a Protestant perspective. See also: S. Brown, «New Directions in Biblical Interpretation» for a similiar presentation.

[26] S.M. SCHNEIDERS, «Church and Biblical Scholarship», 353.

[27] Schneiders acknowledges her indebtedness to the thought of Gadamer and Ricoeur. See S.M. SCHNEIDERS, «From Exegesis to Hermeneutics».

is one at the same time an object for study and a work of art to be appreciated[28].

The second comparison regarded the aims of the study. The scholar's primary concern is the meaning of the text in its original language and historical/cultural setting. «The scholar wants to explain the text, how it came to be, what and who produced it, how it "makes sense" as a text, what it says». Schneiders said the scholar's task is to maintain the distance between the text and the reader. The distance is necessary in recognition of its «otherness». A dialogue is then possible between the reader and the text. The aim of the non-professional believer is in Gadamer's terms a «fusion of horizons». The reader wants to understand «what the text means for the church community here and now». Schneiders explained the need for both approaches:

> Unless the scholar succeeds in keeping the text at least somewhat strange and unfamiliar, the believer will not be challenged and changed by its meaning. But conversely, unless, with the believer, the scholar finally enters into a genuine dialogue with the subject matter of the text, he or she will continue to contemplate an interesting but personally irrelevant record of ancient civilization[29].

The third comparison regarded the approach to the task. Scholars recognize problems in the text due to its historical/cultural remoteness, the ancient language of its composition, unfamiliar genres and sometimes strange subject matter. To solve these problems exegetes use a highly developed and refined methodology[30]. Believers approach the text seeking spiritual nourishment. They use the text as a starting point for meditation on the mystery of God's self-gift in revelation. They appropriate the text; in other words, they enter into a dialogue with the text situating themselves in relation to the biblical message. This appropriation is a necessary component of biblical interpretation. Both approaches are required. Exegesis is needed so that the reader can understand the text. Faith complements exegesis by «situating what individual texts say within the tradition as a whole, and thus to arrive at a meaning which is both critical and salvific»[31].

The fourth comparison regarded the role of tradition in interpretation. Schneiders commented that the scholar's approach to the tradition is usually a cautious approach because «historically, ecclesiastical authorities

---

28 S.M. SCHNEIDERS, «Church and Biblical Scholarship», 354.
29 S.M. SCHNEIDERS, «Church and Biblical Scholarship», 355-356.
30 S.M. SCHNEIDERS, «Church and Biblical Scholarship», 356.
31 S.M. SCHNEIDERS, «Church and Biblical Scholarship», 357.

have often invoked tradition to stifle research which did not seem to support church positions». Yet, at the same time the tradition supplies the exegete with the «presuppositions» with which he or she approaches the text. Schneiders advised finding ways to develop «the capacity to criticize the tradition, to unmask its ideological perversions». The believer on the other hand depends greatly on tradition. «It is knowledge of the tradition, immersion in it, that guides one's understanding, corrects one's naiveté, challenges one's over-eager self-justification»[32].

U. Vanni: The Rift between Exegesis and Actualization, 1987. Vanni's article is part of a collection commemorating the twenty-fifth anniversary of Vatican II. He identified a rift between actualization and exegesis that contrasts with the teaching of *Dei Verbum*[33].

Vanni began by evaluating *Dei Verbum*'s instructions regarding exegesis and actualization. Exegesis has an historical-literary and a pneumatic aspect. The historical-literary aspect recognizes the inspired author and his role in the composition. The pneumatic aspect recognizes the role of the Spirit in the writing and collection. Actualization refers to the scripture as experienced in the present life of the church. Two forms are mentioned: translation and «pastoral actualization» at the end of exegetical work. Exegesis and actualization are further distinguished when the constitution identifies the role of exegetes and those «whose task is bringing this work into contact with the people of God»[34]. The disciplines however are distinct but inter-dependent: «It is clear that exegesis and actualization do not merely exist side by side like two parallel lines, but are in fact in a relationship of dependency, inasmuch as exegesis is seen in function of actualization»[35].

---

32 S.M. SCHNEIDERS, «Church and Biblical Scholarship», 357.

33 U. VANNI, «Exegesis and Actualization», 345, refers to the work of Refoulé and Dreyfus and the now famous distinction: exégèse en Sourbonne, exégèsse en Eglise. I. DE LA POTTERIE, «Reading the Holy Scripture "in the Spirit"», 309 also acknowledges the significance of this distinction. He notes in footnote 3, «Dreyfus says that if he were to translate the title without the French allusion, it would be "Exegesis as Philosophy, Exegesis as Ministry in the Church"» (see below, page 174).

34 U. VANNI, «Exegesis and Actualization», 351.

35 U. VANNI, «Exegesis and Actualization», 352. Vanni stated: «Exegesis must retain its own specific character and perform its task with the tools proper to it. However, both the research and the explanation entailed in the task of exegesis must be carried out in such a way as to enable the immediate servants to carry out their task in an adequate manner». He reminded the reader that *Dei Verbum* called for all pastoral activity (liturgy, theology and study) to be nourished by the Scriptures: «We can sum up by saying that Scripture works to nourish the whole life of the church, penetrating its various aspects from within, and that it does so with the help and mediation of

Vanni then examined the relationship between exegesis and actualization as seen in operation. He made four observations. First, the relationship is such that both exegesis and actualization must completely retain their identity and function. Partial exegesis would be inadequate for actualization, for «when coming in contact with the life of the church it would fall back on itself». Partial actualization would not be able to absorb exegesis, for «if the material provided by exegesis were brought into contact with an ecclesial life that was chronically debilitated, it would be unassailable and would remain unassimilated»[36].

Second, a bond of continuity must exist so that a movement between exegesis and actualization may take place. The spirit is the source of this unity and makes movement between the two possible. «Were it not for this intentionality of life as brought by the Spirit, there would be a break between exegesis and actualization, or at best they would be merely parallel to one another»[37].

Third, this continuity suggests a «specific movement of the word of God which is thus interpreted by exegesis and enters into the everyday practice and life of the church»[38]. Fourth, the movement or path that is suggested by the written word of God, starts from exegesis and ends in actualization. He explained:

> It is in the framework of actualization that this movement is able to develop its multiple, dynamic potentialities, while retaining so to speak the form it has acquired in exegesis. And it is then, in the framework of actualization in the life of the church, that both tradition and that nucleus of lived truths, which make it possible to speak of the «analogy of faith», emerge and take on form. This sets up a reverse movement: the two elements of tradition and analogy of faith, which are brought about by the impact of the word of God on the life of the church, tend to move from actualization to exegesis, and far from acting as a restraint, they throw light on it and in particular foster what we have described as its pneumatic dimension. There is a movement of reciprocity between exegesis and actualization[39].

---

study. And the specific contribution of the exegete is to study with a view to actualization».

[36] U. VANNI, «Exegesis and Actualization», 353.

[37] U. VANNI, «Exegesis and Actualization», 353.

[38] U. VANNI, «Exegesis and Actualization», 354. Using the images of *Dei Verbum*, Vanni noted that exegetical content in actualization becomes «vigor, strength, illumination of the mind, strengthening of the will, renewed ardor, nourishment, renewal, etc.».

[39] U. VANNI, «Exegesis and Actualization», 355.

Thus both remain whole, and exist in a continuity of life guided by the Spirit that brings about a «type of influence of reciprocal causality»[40].

Vanni concluded his article evaluating the current situation regarding exegesis and actualization. First, he observed a broad current in actualization that follows the instruction of *Dei Verbum*. «This is demonstrated by, among other things, the many publications, including some of an exegetical character, that illustrate the liturgy of the word as this is laid down in the various cycles of readings». Yet at times actualization ignores exegesis preferring to «listen to the reading» directly on opening the book. He warned that this practice is in opposition to *Dei Verbum* and runs the risk of superficiality.

Second, Vanni recognized a gap between exegesis and actualization that has caused exegesis to fall back on itself in a state of crisis. He saw the HCM as part of this problem. *Dei Verbum* calls for an historical-literary and pneumatic exegesis. A more pneumatic element or rather more attention to this element would «have changed exegesis and certainly made it less distant from lived reality»[41]. Vanni suggested that the scientific aspect of exegesis needs to be reformulated more strictly by including the pneumatic element. Exegesis will not be truly scientific until it does. The scientific method usually seeks proof. Such proof is «extremely limited and indeed almost nonexistent with regard to literary research or even to historical research alone, except maybe when it can be oriented toward the past»[42]. Verification of exegesis, he proposed, takes place in actualization.

Third, he evaluated current questions regarding methodology. The continuity between exegesis and actualization becomes the criteria for evaluation. Vanni noted that the HCM is necessary but insufficient. «Whenever it is seen as an absolute that is complete and closed in on itself, its orientation toward the past cuts it off from the present of actualization». Structuralism is closer to actualization but it «entails a risk of turning in on itself if it does not bring the text as a whole into contact with the person to whom it is addressed, bringing out and highlighting his reaction to it, or if it follows the philosophical view that reduces man to a range of relationships — a view incompatible with that of the Bible». He concluded that a

---

[40] U. VANNI, «Exegesis and Actualization», 355. Vanni went on to note that this reciprocal relationship has been accepted and incorporated into the life of the church. This is demonstrated by «among other things, the many publications, including some of an exegetical character, that illustrate the liturgy of the word as laid down in the various cycles of readings. A number of journals deal specifically with this subject». He specifically mentioned the Italian publication *Servizio della Parola*.

[41] U. VANNI, «Exegesis and Actualization», 356.

[42] U. VANNI, «Exegesis and Actualization», 357.

Dei Verbum envisions an exegetical method that incorporates valid elements from the HCM and structuralism but moves beyond it. The broader vision «would be able to appreciate and make full use of the contribution of experience, of actualization, even on the methodological level»[43].

Summary. Schneiders and Vanni both described and evaluated the rift between the academy and the church. Schneiders addressed the question to a popular audience. The rift was described in terms of intellectual pursuit involving historical critical exegesis and pastoral application. The solution was seen in the complementary of the two approaches. Vanni described the rift in terms of exegesis and actualization. Historical critical exegesis has failed in the past due to a disregard for the pneumatic aspect of interpretation as well as a failure to address the present situation. He suggested broader vision of exegesis that includes both elements of the HCM and elements of structuralism as a possible solution. The gap between critical exegesis and the lived experience of the faithful identified in this section was one more indication of the crisis in biblical interpretation.

3. The Call for a Spiritual Exegesis

The crisis in biblical interpretation also involved the call for a more spiritual exegesis. Historical-critical exegesis was accused of neglecting the pneumatic or spiritual dimension of the Scriptures. Therefore exegesis was considered segmented or fragmented. Spiritual exegesis was seen as a solution that would provide a more integrated interpretation. This section considers three articles that call for a reform in exegetical practice based on pneumatic exegesis: I. de la Potterie, «Reading Holy Scripture "In the Spirit": Is the Patristic Way of Reading the Bible Still Possible Today?», D. Farkasfalvy, «The Case for Spiritual Exegesis», and M. D'Ambrosio, «Henri de Lubac and the critique of Scientific Exegesis».

I. de la Potterie: Reading in the Spirit, 1986[44]. I. de la Potterie described the problem of biblical exegesis in the contemporary age as fragmented. Exegetical studies place too much emphasis on the literal meaning with little regard for the spiritual. He argued that true interpretation of

---

[43] U. VANNI, «Exegesis and Actualization», 358.

[44] The article was written as a response to several articles that appeared in the 1980 *Concilium* edition titled *Conflicting Ways of Interpreting the Bible*. De la Potterie criticized these studies for failing to acknowledge the critiques of the HCM raised by Refoulé and Dreyfus and to appreciate the church's authoritative role in the interpretation of Scripture. For further reading on spiritual-pneumatic interpretation see: G. CHANTRAINE, «Exegesis and Contemplation»; F. DONAHUE, «Modern or Early Church Interpretation?»; H.U. VON BALTHASAR, «God is His Own Exegete»; C. KANNENGIESSER, «The Bible»; and M.A. MOLINA PALMA, «La interpretación».

Scripture can only be done in the church. A reading in the church must be a reading in the Spirit[45]. The article began with a general survey of exegetical history.

De la Potterie described patristic and medieval exegesis as a synthesis of the letter and the spirit. He noted that the synthesis was achieved based on the basic premise of patristic exegesis — the Scriptures were inspired by God and therefore have a divine sense deeper than the human sense. Vatican II pointed this out when it stated «one must read and interpret the Holy Scripture in the same Spirit with which it was written» (*DV* 12). According to de la Potterie this involves two aspects: subjective and objective. The subjective element entails that the interpretation be done «in the spirit» in other words in the light of faith. The objective element requires that the interpretation be done «in the same Spirit by whom it was *written*». In other words the interpretation must always consider the divine mystery represented by the text[46]. This synthetic exegesis was represented in the patristic period, especially in the works of Origen and Jerome, and continued in the middle ages[47].

---

[45] I. DE LA POTTERIE, «Reading the Holy Scripture», 309, quoted J.A. Moehler, *Die Einheit in der Kirche, oder das Prinzip des Katholizismus*. «Scripture should be interpreted according to the Spirit, because it is the work of the Holy Spirit; this Spirit is given to us by the church of Jesus, which has come down to us with a perfect continuity; whatever contradicts it should be considered erroneous ... Scripture should be interpreted spiritually, which is to say that one cannot find in it anything that contradicts the conviction of the church .... To interpret Scripture according to the doctrine of the church has never been considered as harming the exegete».

[46] I. DE LA POTTERIE, «Reading the Holy Scripture», 311-13. He clarified: «The connection is so deep in them that Manlio Simonetti could entitle his recent work on patristic exegesis *The Letter and/or Allegory*. Here "the letter" and "allegory" are presented in a dialectical relation (and/or); there is a certain tension between them. This tension helps to explain the rift between the two great schools of exegesis in antiquity: the school of Antioch and the school of Alexandria. The latter (including Clement, Origen, and others) certainly sinned by excess in allegorizing every detail of the biblical accounts. But the inverse tendency, that of the Antiochians, which granted an almost exclusive privilege to the letter and a single historical sense of the Bible, was perhaps even more dangerous for Christian faith».

[47] I. DE LA POTTERIE, «Reading the Holy Scripture», 315. The basic unity provided by the Spirit which was recognized in the patristic period was carried over into the medieval period. The hermeneutical principle was the four senses. However, rather than viewing them as four individual and separate senses, de la Potterie suggested they are four aspects of a singular reality. He quoted de Lubac, «Sur un vieux distique: La doctrine du "quadruple sens"», 357: «one must be careful not to speak of a plurality of biblical senses, which would lead to arbitrariness. In reality there is only one true "sense" of Scripture, because there is only one unique Mystery — "the Mystery of Christ, prefigured or made present by the events, interiorized Christ, prefigured or made

The modern period saw the patristic and medieval synthesis dissolve. The rupture began with a shift in intellectual life from the transcendent to the earthly. The result for exegesis was the move from theology to science bringing «the historical and rational method to the fore». Movements in philosophy encouraged this rupture. Spinoza and Kant were particularly influential. For Spinoza the governing idea «is the notion of immanence: every problem must be resolved by the resources of reason *alone*». Thus biblical sciences «became exclusively philological and historical sciences. The exegesis of texts can have no other rules: it must deny itself any other dimension, ignore all opening to transcendence, exclude the meddling of faith». The consequence was a rupture between scripture and faith. For Kant religion must be experienced within the limits of reason alone. This resulted in a rupture between Scripture and tradition. De la Potterie notes that as scholarship developed in the nineteenth century this rupture moved to separate history from reality by claiming history is reality witnessed by the distinction between «the so-called historical (*histroisch*) Jesus» and the true «historic (*geschichtlich*), biblical Christ»[48].

Following this historical survey, de la Potterie commented on the current state of biblical studies. He praised the use of the scriptures in prayer groups and in personal prayer through *lectio divina*. He also suggested that rationalist exegesis and historic scientism was «beginning its inexorable decline». While some recommend the newer methods of materialist and psychological readings, he proposed rediscovering the principle of «reading in the spirit».

He argued against those who say that the *spiritual sense* is not scientific by appealing to Ladriere who identified the hermeneutical sciences as the third category of scientific investigation. These hermeneutical sciences bring «into play the category of "meaning"». Exegesis falls into this

---

present by the events, interiorized in the soul of the individual, consummated in glory"».

[48] I. DE LA POTTERIE, «Reading the Holy Scripture», 316, correlates his criticism with the thought of Blondel. The problem was described in terms of the relationship between Christian *facts* (the history of salvation) and Christian *beliefs* (dogmas). Theology has often taken the abstract form of what Blondel calls «extrinsicism»: this consists in separating truth from history, in showing oneself indifferent to the human progress through the history of salvation and the concrete aspect of revelation. In theological studies two extremes were mentioned dogmatism and historicism. Dogmatism neglected history resulting in the reactionary movement of historicism. De la Potterie stressed the necessity of keeping event and word related and connected if theology and exegesis are to be well-founded: «The faith we profess depends on a revelation that forms part of history, and from which it is impossible entirely to separate it» (quoting Lagrange).

category. «Its role is to interpret Holy Scripture, to find "meaning" in it»[49]. This quest for meaning is not exclusively a philological or historical endeavor, it requires faith. Therefore the *spiritual sense* is scientific.

De la Potterie then made two observations regarding the relationship between exegesis and hermeneutics. First, he invoked Heidegger's definition of interpretation which is more «re-presentation» than explication or «representation». To interpret a text is to disclose the «virtualities» that it conceals, «to liberate its interior forces». He saw this as similar to the patristic practice of going beyond the letter to the spirit. Second, he proposed *Wirkungsgeschichte* (the study of the influence of the text) as a method for gaining a new appreciation for the role of tradition as the connection between history, faith and dogma.

He concluded that the

> faithful reading of the Holy Scripture and its Christian interpretation cannot be done except «in the Spirit». This requires, in reply to the question posed by my sub-title, that one distinguish between the letter and the spirit of Scripture. In the study of the letter, it goes without saying that one can't just go back to the methods and the procedures of the ancients, which are outdated in many respects. One ought here to take advantage of the immense resources of modern exegesis. Nonetheless one must recall the «patristic way of reading the Bible»: we should read and interpret in the spirit prescribed by the Fathers themselves, This is the way of the tradition. It is also the way that the church asks us to follow today, in the constitution *Dei Verbum*, 12....It is not a matter of looking for a *spiritual sense* beyond the *literal sense*, but of finding one within it. The aim is to arrive at an «interior penetration of the text, as it was written for believers by inspired believers., according to their experience of God»[50].

D. Farkasfalvy: The Rift between Exegesis and Theology, 1986. Farkasfalvy referred to a «crisis» in biblical scholarship among Catholics and other Christians. The crisis, he believed, signaled a change in eras from the period of critical biblical study to a «post-critical» age. This change is signified by a «genuine transcendence of the HCM — a transcendence gained not by discarding or rejecting the method, but by going beyond the limits of its horizon while fully retaining those features that proved themselves valid and valuable during the "critical" period»[51].

Farkasfalvy traced the history of exegesis in an effort to show how a «post-critical» period may proceed. He divided the history of exegesis

---

[49] I. DE LA POTTERIE, «Reading the Holy Scripture», 322.
[50] I. DE LA POTTERIE, «Reading the Holy Scripture», 324.
[51] D. FARKASFALVY, «In Search of a "Post-Critical" Method», 288.

into five periods: patristic and medieval exegesis[52], confessional exegesis in the sixteenth and seventeenth centuries[53], critical exegesis[54], Catholic biblicism after Vatican II and post-critical exegesis[55]. His treatment of the first three periods was similar to de la Potterie's description (see above).

The fourth period was described as the emergence of Catholic biblicism after Vatican II. Farkasfalvy had seen the period following *Divino Afflante Spiritu* as the turning point in Catholic biblical studies. In the post-war period, the renewal of biblical studies was part of a larger renewal that involved patristic and liturgical studies:

> the biblical movement and thus the acceptance of many of the conclusions and methods of critical biblical scholarship in Catholic circles became possible only because it was accompanied by a patristic and liturgical renewal. From the patristic renewal of the post-war years, this new Catholic biblicism obtained a theological framework which, at that time, appeared to be capable of absorbing and digesting the solid findings of critical exegesis. Studies on the unity of the two testaments, the historical

---

[52] D. FARKASFALVY, «In Search of a "Post-Critical" Method», 291-292. Farkasfalvy described the exegesis of this period in five points. First, the basis for the biblical text is salvation history, conceived as a chain of human events under divine initiative and divine intervention. Second, salvation history has a universal scope both geographically and historically. Third, salvation history operates by eliciting the response of faith, and thus not by abolishing or reducing, but by enhancing human freedom and bringing the human self to full growth in the process of self-understanding and self-possession. Fourth, in this hermeneutical framework two links are constantly presupposed: a horizontal linkage among the texts themselves as expression and explanation of the one and the same salvation plan; and a vertical linkage that connects the texts with events, and thus anchors the order of thought to an order of facts. Fifth, as a consequence, the exegetical practice of the church Fathers and their medieval disciples consciously and consistently operated on a variety of levels. Sixth, this ancient hermeneutical system was cultivated in close interdependence with a theory of inspiration that is as old as the canon itself. Because of the christological exegesis of the OT, the church Fathers extended and generalized the Jewish custom that referred to the authors of Scripture as «prophets».

[53] D. FARKASFALVY, «In Search of a "Post-Critical" Method», 292. Farkasfalvy described the period as «confessional biblicism» because «it turned the bible into a collection of *loci theologici*, a florilegium of biblical passages or, even better, into an arsenal of biblical weapons to be used for proving one's own doctrinal position and disproving the opponents' beliefs».

[54] D. FARKASFALVY, «In Search of a "Post-Critical" Method», 295-296. He noted four developments in modern intellectual life characteristic of the critical period: the development of linguistic studies; the development of natural sciences; the appearance of historiography as a scientific and rational discipline; and the development of the HCM in exegesis as a result of the new information obtained through the new studies.

[55] D. FARKASFALVY, «In Search of a "Post-Critical" Method», 298.

character of revelation, the interconnection of events and concepts, the historical and communitarian nature of biblical inspiration, the relationship of Bible and church, biblical reading and liturgical assembly, biblical proclamation and sacramental sign, and so on, abounded in those years, demonstrating that this new exegesis promoted faith and church rather than threatening it with harm or destruction. A biblical renewal was in the making with no intention of dissecting the Bible into historically disjoined facts or insights nor of operating only on the level of academic research.

Another characteristic of biblical scholarship of this period was the «flirting» with existentialism by Catholic philosophers and systematic theologians. Farkasfalvy concluded this section noting that «one was tempted to believe in those years that we had just reached the threshold of a new Golden Age of philosophical and theological synthesis»[56]. In the years following the Vatican Council, biblical research rapidly changed its character and tone and consequently its relationship to theology. On the positive side he recognized a growth in biblicism such as the use of the bible in ecclesial life (retreats, music, catechesis, devotions, etc.). On the negative side he saw a lot of «dead wood» in a great number of Catholic publications that he attributed to experimental zeal[57]. He furthermore lamented the end of the joint effort that had «one common aim — the renewal of theology at large, reaching deep into the subsoil of the sources and aiming at a fruitful dialogue with contemporary man struggling with his intellectual, spiritual, and temporal problems»[58].

The present period of biblical scholarship, according to Farkasfalvy, is witnessing the move to a post-critical exegesis. He attributed this move to a rejuvenation of the spirit that existed in the years just prior to the council. The following are the characteristics he used to describe the «post-critical» age of biblical scholarship:

a.) intellectual honesty with regard to all the tools and evidences of modern scholarship[59]

---

[56] D. FARKASFALVY, «In Search of a "Post-Critical" Method», 300.

[57] D. FARKASFALVY, «In Search of a "Post-Critical" Method», 300.

[58] D. FARKASFALVY, «In Search of a "Post-Critical" Method», 301-302.

[59] D. FARKASFALVY, «In Search of a "Post-Critical" Method», 302. Farkasfalvy notes that this requirement «is based on a sound theology of the biblical word which requires that the full humanity of the Bible be recognized and any trace of a biblical monophysitism be expelled». He explains his terminology as taken from Louis Bouyer, «Où en est le mouvement biblique?». He also notes R.E. Brown's corresponding terms «Chalcedonian» and «adoptianistic approaches» in his *The Critical Meaning of the Bible*.

b) the full recognition of the text as an expression of faith

c) the post-critical exegete interprets the biblical text in the context of the Bible as a whole: he sees in its canon the reflection of a unified and universal salvation history, centered on Christ.

d) in post-critical perspective there appears — horror of horrors! — a new quest for harmonization: unity and universality seen from the perspective of faith, capable of seeing beyond the contingent components of human history.

e) post-critical exegesis, by courageously entering the realm of faith, must be able to open the doors for a new spiritual exegesis of the Bible[60].

f) post-critical exegesis, if guided by the perspective of salvation history, must discover the organic rapport that exist between the individual and community in the order of salvation.

g) post-critical exegesis must exhibit a consciously cultivated positive relationship with theological anthropology[61].

In this article, Farkasfalvy identified a rift between exegesis and theology by placing the relationship in an historical context. He noted the present «crisis» as a turning point for Catholic exegesis that will now move beyond critical exegesis. The move would not eliminate critical exegesis but would place it within the broader framework of faith. Recalling the interaction of the patristic, liturgical and biblical movements in the mid-twentieth century he also suggested the need for cooperation among the theological disciplines.

D'Ambrosio: Re-visiting H. De Lubac, 1992. M. D'Ambrosio presented a study on the work of de Lubac and the question of spiritual exegesis. He demonstrated the roots of the current «post-critical» movement in the work of De Lubac. The study began by establishing de Lubac's support for critical exegesis[62], then proceeded to discuss his critique of the method by pointing out its limitations.

---

[60] D. FARKASFALVY, «In Search of a "Post-Critical" Method», 305, clarified the term «spiritual exegesis» as «an exegesis that sees the exegete and his word also as part of the unified and universal salvation history and thus about an exegesis that is capable of discovering valid analogies between the salvific meaning of the ancient text and the actual saving deeds of the same God through the same Christ».

[61] D. FARKASFALVY, «In Search of a "Post-Critical" Method», 302-307.

[62] M. D'AMBROSIO, «Henri de Lubac», 368-372. For example, in 1945 de Lubac wrote: «Recently there has been attributed to me some kind of opposition to scientific exegesis being accorded citizenship in the church, and similarly, to the work of my colleagues and to the spirit of our faculty [Catholic faculty of Lyons]. This rumor,

The underlying weakness of the method was its claim of objectivity and its inability to provide an integral interpretation. Three further weaknesses were also identified[63]. The first weakness was an «excessive fascination with facts which is characteristic of historical positivism»[64]. This led to a preoccupation with isolated texts and events. As a result, the exegesis failed to deal with a deeper and more synthetic apprehension of the truth — «the true subject matter of the various texts and the unified history they record»[65]. The second weakness was an unrecognized pre-understanding in many of the exegetes who used the method[66]. The unexamined pre-understanding led to a new dogmatism. He recalled Barth's work that showed how modern critical biblicists [Protestant], who rejected the Christian dogmatic tradition so as to be rooted only in the Bible, «freed themselves from the dogma of the church only to enslave themselves to

though absurd, has become so insistent, and has spread so far and wide that I find myself obliged to combat it. I am aware of finding myself thus in the most ridiculous position, namely that of the man who must defend himself from the charge of denigrating that very thing of which he has always been known to have been the warmest partisan».

De Lubac also recognized exegesis as a distinct discipline «whose relative autonomy ought to be preserved» yet whose results should be forged into a new unity of exegesis, dogmatic theology, and spirituality. D'Ambrosio explained: «He [de Lubac] believes that the role of exegetical specialists is more important than ever today and agrees with Oscar Cullmann that their "great and unique responsibility" is "to be faithful to the text in radical fashion, even if the exegetical result thereby obtained is a modest one and possibly seems, at first glance, useless for dogmatics or for the practical life of the church". Thus, de Lubac, parting ways with certain proponents of renewed spiritual exegesis, deems it excessive and unnecessary to oblige scientific exegetes to add spiritual exegesis to their already long list of exacting duties».

63 See M. D'AMBROSIO, «Henri de Lubac», 373-376, for his analysis of M. Blondel's influence on de Lubac's critique of historical-critical exegesis.

64 M. D'AMBROSIO, «Henri de Lubac», 377.

65 M. D'AMBROSIO, «Henri de Lubac», 377. De Lubac quoted Barth in this regard when he said that many commentators see the Bible «as a book which interests them, but which does not concern them».

66 M. D'AMBROSIO, «Henri de Lubac», 378, «Everybody has his filter, which he takes about him, through which, from the indefinite mass of facts, he gathers in those suited to confirm his prejudices. And the same fact again, passing through different filters, is revealed in different aspects, so as to confirm the most diverse opinions. It has always been so, it always will be so in this world. Rare, very rare are those who check their filter».

their own dogma and the dogma of their times»[67]. The third weakness was a «hyper-criticism» that resulted in a «philological massacre»[68].

D'Ambrosio summarized de Lubac's study of the history of exegesis as follows:

> Indeed, the fundamental goal of de Lubac's lengthy study of the history of exegesis is essentially to prove that, underlying all the different commentators of the centuries with their disparate terminologies, a single «traditional hermeneutic» can be identified which, in its basic outlines, can and must guide Christian interpretation of the Bible even today. Through it necessarily begins with an attempt to apprehend the literal or historical meaning of the Bible with the help of the best scientific tools available in a given epoch, this comprehensive hermeneutic invariably proceeds to search out the deeper *spiritual sense* of the biblical texts by means of a corresponding «spiritual understanding». This movement of spiritual understanding, often termed allegory, aims not merely at the interpretation of texts, but more fundamentally, the reinterpretation of the heritage of Israel, indeed of all history and reality, in the light of the Mystery of Christ which the Christian tradition unanimously identifies as the subject matter of both Old and New Testaments[69]

D'Ambrosio concluded his article correlating his study with the current discussion on critical exegesis. He recognized a movement in the last several decades to go «beyond the predominantly detached, critical, and analytical approach to reality that emerged in the Enlightenment to a more personal, synthetic, and holistic stance in the face of the world and its mysteries». This movement is often described as «post-critical». It recognized that although the HCM was «an indispensable tool in the interpretation of historical texts, [it] is of itself incapable of generating the kind of fruitfulness for human life that must be the final result of the interpretation of any great text, especially one that purports to be the Word of God». D'Ambrosio recognized de Lubac as a forerunner of this post-critical stage — for he «unhesitatingly accepted that method's validity,

---

[67] M. D'AMBROSIO, «Henri de Lubac», 380.

[68] M. D'AMBROSIO, «Henri de Lubac», 381. «Actually, when the critical function alone is active, it succeeds rather quickly in pulverizing everything. It makes it impossible to see what is invariable in the mind of man and in doctrinal tradition. It clouds over the continuity and the unity of revealed truth as seen in diverse cultural expressions which coincide with and follow one from another. As a result, divine revelation, inasmuch as it does not reach man except through signs, finds itself redacted to a series of thoughts and interpretation which are entirely human. Christian faith, in its first authenticity, becomes no more than a fact of culture, important surely, but as such outdated».

[69] M. D'AMBROSIO, «Henri de Lubac», 384-385.

had already anticipated several of the important, post-critical questions of hermeneutics that would dominate scholarly circles decades later. It was this foresight, and not some pre-critical hostility to the emerging exegetical science which inspired his lifetime study of ancient Christian exegesis»[70]

Summary. This section has considered the call for a more spiritual exegesis as suggested by de la Potterie, Farkasfalvy and D'Ambrosio. The call for the reform of Catholic exegetical practices is prompted by a dissatisfaction with the HCM. The authors criticize the philosophical background in which the method developed, its false claim to objectivity, the pre-occupation with the past, and the failure to address the present. Each author appeals to the exegesis of the Fathers that they refer to as integrated or synthetic. The basis of this integration is the unity of the letter and spirit. The call for a more pneumatic exegesis does not eliminate the need for historical criticism but means that it should be re-configured or re-formulated to consider the pneumatic aspect of interpretation.

4. Modern Hermeneutics and Exegesis

The development of modern hermeneutical studies and its relationship with exegesis was part of the debate regarding methodology that led to the crisis in biblical interpretation[71]. Numerous questions have been raised in hermeneutical studies that affect biblical methodology; singular or multiple meaning; the locus of meaning (text, author, interpreter); the interaction between reader and text; subject and object in the act of understanding; and the relationship between original meaning and latter understanding. The influence of modern hermeneutical thought has had its most profound affect on biblical studies in the development of multiple methodologies used in the study of texts (see below, page 188). P. Grech discusses the relationship between hermeneutics and exegesis in *The Dictionary of Fundamental Theology*[72]. The article contains five sections: an introduction, the history of biblical hermeneutics, modern hermeneutics, the theological dimension of modern hermeneutics, and consequences for fundamental theology.

---

[70] M. D'AMBROSIO, «Henri de Lubac», 387.

[71] For further reading on the influence of philosophical hermeneutics on biblical interpretation see the following: P. FRUCHON, «Exégèse biblique et tradition»; S.M. SCHNEIDERS, «Faith»; ID., «From Exegesis to Hermeneutics»; P. GRECH, «The Language of Scripture»; ID., *Ermeneutica e theologia biblica*.

[72] P. GRECH, «Hermeneutics».

Grech began the article demonstrating the origins of biblical hermeneutics in the biblical period itself. The period witnesses a hermeneutical principal that re-reads earlier events in the light of later situatons. Even before canonization «we find a continuous reinterpretation that adapts legal provisions to the circumstances of the day and rereads prophecies in the light of the latest events in the history of salvation by the method of *haggadah*». The practice of reinterpretation was also practiced in the interpretation of dreams and visions. «The authors' historical sense has value only insofar as it also speaks to the present». In the intertestamental period apocalyptic literature «sought to interpret its own times in the light of the biblical tradition with which it was linked, and to do so by means of references, implicit citations, or midrashic elaboration»[73]. Regarding NT interpretation, Grech stated:

> The literary technique adopted in rereading the OT is similar, but the content is completely different, although in line with the traditional pattern of reinterpretation found in the Bible, which rereads the texts with the understanding offered by the most recent events in the history of salvation. It is obvious that for Jesus the chief event is the advent of the Kingdom of God, while for the NT authors it is the coming of Christ, together with his death and resurrection, the fullness of God's work of salvation. Consequently, the Christ-event sheds light on the meaning of the biblical texts, which thereby receives its full significance. The NT thus offers certain types of hermeneutics that latter become models for patristic exegesis: literal explanation, midrashim, *midrash* of the *Peshitta*, allegory and typology.[74]

Grech continued the summary biblical hermenteutics noting the principles used by Irenaeus, Origen, the Antiochenes, Cappadocians, and Augustine and summarized the principals of interpretation as follows:

> We can say that we have a biblical text that contains within itself more possibilities for explanation that the historical author intended. The author's own intention will always be the primary meaning, but the community that reads the text, whether in synagogue or in the church, extracts other meanings from it, informed by the unfolding of history, in such a way that the text speaks continually to every succeeding generation. Text and community are thus inseparable, in that the community becomes the context in which the text is read, together with the actual moment in history. The way in which this continuous understanding is expressed or explained is influenced by the cultural atmosphere in which

---

[73] P. GRECH, «Hermeneutics», 416.
[74] P. GRECH, «Hermeneutics», 417.

it is read, which sometimes requires a translation or, better still, transfer from one cultural language to another, or from a language of the past to one of the present. When considering an inspired text, it is the Spirit working within the community that realizes the possibilities of the text in relation to the living out of the *regula fidei*[75].

Grech considered the topic of modern hermeneutics. He surveyed the major influences in its develpoment begining with M. Luther's separation of biblical interpretation from the tradition. He then considered the development of hermeneutical philosophy in the work M. Illiricus, J. Ernesti, F. Schleiermacher, W. Dilthey, and H. Gadamer. Grech summarized Gadamer's approach as follows:

Hermeneutics is understanding, but this understanding comes about when the reader, living in the present and thus heir to certain prejudices that reach the reader through the continuum of cultural history, is confronted with the text. The horizon of the text and that of the reader are founded the one within the other such that the former understanding is modified and becomes a new understanding. But even this is not absolute; it is still a link in the chain of different historical understandings of the past. The continuity of tradition is the *Wirkungsgeschichte* (the history of effects) of the texts at the beginnings of our culture and revealed in language, into which cultural values are inserted. Although the text is normative, its interpretation is a continuous process, and one cannot say that an interpretation is definitive because the act of comprehension renews itself from one generation to the next through each interpreter giving rise to a fresh truth; this truth itself becomes the object of interpretation. In Gadamer's view, tradition is the chain of explanations that gives rise concrete expression to understanding[76]

Following the treatment of modern hermeneutics Grech dealt with its theological dimension. He began with the theology of Bultmann noting that some serious problems raised by Bultmann need to be considered in fundamental theology: «the questioning of the historicity of the Gospels, the relevance of our knowledge of the historical Jesus to our faith in the Christ of the kerygma, and the question of the demythologization of the NT message»[77]. Bultmann removed the historicity of the Gospel relying on faith alone rather some cooperation with reason. Grech observed that for Bultmann

---

75 P. GRECH, «Hermeneutics», 418.
76 P. GRECH, «Hermeneutics», 420.
77 P. GRECH, «Hermeneutics», 421.

the traditional truths of Christianity can act as an initial understanding in order to arrive at such a faith, but they are not its proper object. They are formulated in a language that dates back two thousand years and that shows signs of the mystical vision of the Judeo-Hellenistic world. In order to be acceptable today they need to be translated anew, or demythologized, into a more modern language[78].

Bultmann's separation of history and faith «has been criticized from all sides: «because it removes the *extra nos* of salvation (Käsemann), because it smacks of gnosticism and docetism (Jeremias), and because there remains no criterion for judging the various post-resurrection Christologies (Robinson)»[79]. Grech explained that «demythologized hermeneutics did not fare too well» emptying Christianity of its «revelatory content».

Ricoeur spoke of «symbol» instead of «myth». He held that humankind must be studied through the cultural manifestations in its history which are «codified in signs, symbols, or myths that have a retrospective function toward their own origin and a theological dimension that looks forward to the maturation of the human being ... Myth is concerned with the outer shell of faith, not its core»[80].

E. Betti, E. Hirsch, and P. Szondi reacted against Gadamer's subjectivism insisting that he «did not leave a single means for verifying the truth or falsity of an interpretation because the subject comes to replace the author to such a degree that there is a lack of Hegelian total vision and a descent into historical fragmentation. The true meaning of a passage, so they maintain, is that intended by the author, and it is a closed and complete meaning»[81]. Grech pointed out that L. Pareyson gave a «substantial correction» to Gadamer.

> Pareyson gives an ontological foundation to interpretation, maintaining the unity of the truth and the plurality of its manifestations, in that truth of being reveals itself continuously or sporadically in important cultural events. Pareyson thus gives us a personal ontology. Finally, the literary criticism of Hirsch also gives rise to a school that, drawing together structural analysis and aspects of classical and modern rhetoric, seeks to discover what impact a text (especially scriptural texts) has had on its immediate readership. R. Jewett and other biblical scholars in the United States have applied this method of research[82].

---

[78] P. GRECH, «Hermeneutics», 421.
[79] P. GRECH, «Hermeneutics», 421.
[80] P. GRECH, «Hermeneutics», 422.
[81] P. GRECH, «Hermeneutics», 422.
[82] P. GRECH, «Hermeneutics», 422.

Grech, in the final section of this article, dealt with the consequences of modern hermeneutics for fundamental theology. He suggested that the area most affected by the controversies in modern hermeneutics is biblical exegesis. «Hitherto both Catholics and Protestant traditions have thought that the true meaning of Scripture, that inspired by the Holy Spirit, is the *literal sense*, namely, that intended by the author»[83]. He continued:

> We have seen that, with the strengthening of the role of the subject who is interpreter, the *mens auctoris* is in danger of disappearing. On the other hand, we have noted how certain OT texts have come to be used theologically in the NT, not according to their literal meaning, but read anew from the viewpoint of the latest events in the history of salvation. Thus the fathers drew allegorical meanings from the text that are by no means the fruits of pure fantasy. From these we may conclude that the text as such, as entrusted to the church, contains the greater possibilities of meaning than the meaning(s) foreseen by the human author, and that these meanings are realized by the historical process of God's saving activity in the church and in the world. History is thus a hermeneutical principle of interpretation of revelation in which the Spirit has inspired the initial author to continue speaking by his own words, surpassing the original historical limitation. The link with the original meaning, however, cannot be broken without going against the *mens auctoris* or the obvious meaning of the text[84].

Grech completed the presentation considering the implications of hermeneutics on the relationship between scripture and tradition, as well as other aspects of dogmatic theology and fundamental theology.

---

[83] P. GRECH, «Hermeneutics», 423. For further reading on the inadequacies of the older definition of *literal sense* see: X. LÉON-DUFOUR, «L'exégèse, trente ans après» (*HCTIS*, 170-174), «Teologia e Sacra Scrittura» (*HCTIS*, 247-250); N. LOHFINK, «Zur historisch-kritischen Methode» (*HCTIS*, 191); and P. GRECH, «The Old Testament», 131-134. R.E. BROWN – S.M. SCHNEIDERS, «Hermeneutics», 1148-1150 also recognized some difficulties and attempted to clarify the meaning of the *literal sense*. To this end Brown expanded the definition to «the sense which the human author directly intended and which the written words conveyed». Here he made the distinction between the biblical author (used in the ancient sense of authority) and the words used to convey meaning. The distinction enables the words to have a level of meaning on their own albeit within the framework provided by the author (context).

[84] P. GRECH, «Hermeneutics», 423. For a similar views see B.F. MEYER, «The Challenges»; J.R. RIGGS, «The "Fuller Meaning" of Scripture»; and C.J. SCALISE, «The "Sensus Literalis"».

5. The Multiplication of Methods

The 1960's and 1970's witnessed an increase in the different methods used to study and interpret the Scriptures. As the number and variety of methods increased confusion regarding interpretation increased. This was alluded to in the Vanni and de la Potterie articles considered above. In the 1980's and early 1990's questions circulated concerning the value and validity of these methods as well as their relationship one to the other[85]. This confusion regarding the multiplication of methods was another element that prompted the writing of *Interpretation of the Bible in the Church*[86]. R.E. Brown and S. Schneiders discussed the numerous methodologies in their article on hermeneutics in the *NJBC*[87]. In the *NJBC*, Brown modified his article on hermeneutics from the original article in the *JBC* to reflect the more recent discussions. The primary re-working comes in the attention given to contemporary approaches to the *more-than-literal senses*. In the previous edition the *more-than-literal* discussion covered the patristic and medieval senses followed by a treatment of the sensus plenior and typological interpretation. The present edition focuses on new methodologies that have been developing to study the *more-than-literal senses*. The article contained four parts: introduction[88], the

---

[85] See J. O'GRADY, «Biblical Methodologies».

[86] Cf. *EB*, §1268.

[87] The *NJBC* was published in 1990. In the preface, Carlo Cardinal Martini praises the work as a serious aid to Catholics and for the ecumenical movement. He applauded the use of scientific criticism used in the commentary and notes that «this contemporary approach is achieved without neglecting the long road that Christian tradition has traveled in dedicated, constant, and loving attention to the Word of God. This is the principal route recommended by the Second Vatican Council itself, lest the path of the Christian reader of the Bible be encumbered either by an arid literalism «that kills» (2 Cor 3:6) or by a reading that drifts off into generalized spiritual applications. In fact, the biblical message is, as is Christ himself, flesh and divine Word, history and transcendence, humanity and divinity».

[88] Brown began the «Introduction» with a presentation on hermeneutics. He noted that hermeneutics can refer to the interpretation by speech itself communicating what is in the mind, to the translation from one language to another, «a process that goes beyond the mechanical equivalents of words and enters into the issue of transference form one culture and world view to another», or to the process of commenting and explaining a text. He also mentioned difficulties in current hermeneutics due to the interaction among the philosophy of being, the psychology of language, and sociology. Added to the complexity is the long history of the development of biblical texts. Brown summarized this development beginning with the revelatory events on which the texts are based, moving through the composition of the texts, and ending with the interpretation of the texts in later periods.

literal sense, the *more-than-literal senses*, and further considerations[89]. The third section raised the question of multiple methods.

Brown and Schneiders classified the various methods used to study the scriptures according to their hermeneutical counterpart, the *literal sense* or the *more-than-literal sense*. The HCM although it is not explicitly described is the method used to determine the *literal sense*. Here Brown basically follows the original *JBC* article. He defined the *literal sense* as «the sense which the human author directly intended and which the written words conveyed»[90].

Brown clarified the definition. Authorship should be understood in the ancient sense which includes redactors. He added that at times authorship is attributed to a famous person according to ancient practice. The original authors wrote to convey a message to their readers. The present meaning of the text may be more abundant but it should have some relationship «*to what the text meant* to the first readers». Brown rejected the skepticism of literary critics who saw the determination of the *literal sense* as impossible. He did acknowledge, however, difficulties such as the difference between the «substantial writer» and the «editor or redactor». Brown suggested that the quest for the *literal sense* includes both the sense that «parts originally had before editing and the sense books had after the editing».

The author's intention is conveyed by the written words of the text. Brown insisted that interpretations have to be rooted in the inspired words of the text not in some notion of thought. «In the evangelists' interpretation we have understanding of Jesus' words that the Holy Spirit has inspired for the church — an inspiration that assures believers that even when the evangelists go beyond Jesus' own teaching, they have not seriously distorted Jesus». Implicit in the term is the comprehension of the audience/readers envisioned by the author. «Reflection on that factor may check over imaginative proposals about what the author meant. Interpretations based on elaborate relationship among widely scattered biblical words and passages (detected through concordances) must be judged on whether the ancient author could have expected his audience, who had no concordance, to make the connections». Brown acknowledged that the *literal sense* is not always easily discernible; however, this does not mean

---

[89] In this section, Brown discussed five issues regarding the relationship of exegesis to other areas of theology and ecclesial life: accommodation, authoritative interpretation by the church, academic freedom and exegetical inquiry, exegesis and the authority of the Fathers, and popular communication of modern critical views.

[90] R.E. BROWN – S.M. SCHNEIDERS, «Hermeneutics», 1148-1149.

that it should be avoided or replaced by another sense (or, in effect, another method). Brown accepted the idea that the bible is a «classic» and as such its beauty and truth make it accessible to people in all times and cultures. Yet it is not because of a literary value that the majority of people read it; they read it for religious purposes. Brown addressed the accusation that the HCM has made biblical scholarship irrelevant to the religious needs of people. He responded that the charge is untrue of Catholic practice since Vatican II. Over specialization can be a problem and educators should be aware of it when teaching. Brown also warned that each time there has been a movement that put emphasis on the primacy of the *literal sense* in Catholic biblical interpretation, the movement was swallowed by a more attractive movement that stressed the theological or the spiritual aspects of Scripture almost to the exclusion of literal exegesis. He warned those who teach and study the Scriptures not to be mislead into easier paths.

Although he did not give a descriptive account of the HCM, Brown defended several aspects of the method: genre-form, literary, and redaction criticisms. In order to determine the *literal sense* of a text it is important to identify the literary form used by the author. «A history and a novel may treat the same person or event, but we expect different degrees of fact and fiction from them, whereas in regard to poetry the issue of fact and fiction is irrelevant. Nevertheless, all three can convey truth, and sometimes one conveys a truth that the others cannot». The canonical sense of the bible treats it as one book; yet in its origins it has come together as a collection of books. Brown noted that there must be a serious endeavor to classify the books according to the type of literature they represent. Once a literary form is identified, «standards applicable to that for help to clarify what the author meant, i.e. the *literal sense*»[91]. Furthermore, the long history of editing or redaction that is involved in many biblical texts is studied, not for its own sake, but to help identify the *literal sense*. Using this process

90-95 percent of the Bible can be determined by a reasonable application of the ordinary rules of interpretation. There are some passages whose meaning eludes us because the text has been corrupted in trans-

---

[91] Brown saw two misconceptions regarding this approach. «Some conservatives regard the quest for literary form as an attempt to circumvent the historicity of biblical passages, and therefore they think it dangerous to apply the theory of literary forms to the more sacred sections of the Bible». Brown responded that if one correctly classifies a certain part of the Bible as fiction, one does not destroy the historicity because it was never written as history. Others think the identification of literary form challenges inspiration. To this Brown responded that Pius XII noted that God could inspire any literary form that was not deceitful or unworthy.

mission, because they use rare words, because the author expressed himself obscurely, or because we do not have sufficient knowledge about the context in which they were composed. Continued study constantly casts light even on passages such as these[92].

The problems raised by multiple methods was alluded to in Brown's treatment of the *literal sense* but it was much more explicit in the presentation on the *more-than-literal senses*. Brown first acknowledged the insufficiency of the *literal sense* to determine a meaning that may go beyond the human author's intention.

First, centuries after he wrote it, the author's book was joined in a collection called the Bible. This new arrangement, which scarcely could have been foreseen by the author, may have seriously modified his intent. Second, even after the canonical collection was stabilized, belief that Scripture had a divine «author» means that the Bible is God's word to audiences of all time. This continuing biblical engagement of readers/hearers with God (with or without the catalyst of preaching) uncovers meaning beyond that envisioned by the human author, in his local and limited circumstances[93].

Brown traced the history of the *more than literal senses* from the NT era up to the contemporary period. He gave special attention to the use of typology, the *sensus plenior*, and promise-fulfillment theology to explain the relationship between the two testaments but concluded that these approaches have been deemed inadequate for scholarship, evidenced by their lack of utilization by scholars and theologians[94]. He also warned that a fundamentalist approach is unacceptable. Brown acknowledged the role of the new hermeneutics before discussing the methods that developed under its influence. Specifically treated are literary criticism, canonical criticism, and miscellaneous contributions[95].

The discussion of *literary criticism* in the *NJBC* was presented by S. Schneiders. The term *literary criticism* was used in this discussion as it is

---

92 R.E. BROWN – S.M. SCHNEIDERS, «Hermeneutics», 1152.

93 Here we see a notable change from the original *JBC* article. Brown began this treatment noting that because of the long tradition of a *more-than-literal sense* it should not be lightly dismissed by scientific scholars. The presentation here is much more positive with regard to the *more-than-literal senses*. He urged scholars to examine these senses especially in their relationship to the *literal sense*.

94 R.E. BROWN – S.M. SCHNEIDERS, «Hermeneutics», 1157.

95 In a similar approach J. CABA, «Métodos exegéticos», analyzed four currents in NT studies regarding method: the HCM, redactional criticism, structuralism, literary criticism, rhetorical criticism, and midrashic analysis. After descriptions of each method, the values and limitations of each method were presented.

used in the study of secular literature[96]. The approach developed in biblical studies as a reaction to insufficiencies in redaction criticism. Schneiders saw this as a «paradigm-shift» in biblical studies. This shift was greatly influenced by the work of Gadamer and Ricoeur. Central to the approach is the dialogical nature of historical understanding. In biblical studies, the dialogue is between the reader and the text about the subject matter. Three questions are asked: «What is the subject matter or referent of the text? How does the text "work" to engage the reader? How does the subjectivity of the reader influence the process of interpretation?» Schneiders differentiated this approach from the historical-critical approach noting that *literary criticism* views the text «as a "mirror" reflecting a world into which the reader is invited» not «as a "window" onto an historical world (the events recounted or the community situation which the text was composed)».

Literary criticism is a generic term for a number of independent approaches or methods categorized as either non-contextual or contextual. Non-contextual methods focus attention on the text. Schneiders characterized the methods under two headings: structuralism and deconstruction.

Structuralism is a generic term which describes methods which view the text as a «closed system of signs that have meaning not in themselves or in reference to extra-textual reality but only in relation to one another. The model for the understanding of signs, whether minute textual units (e.g. words) or larger units (e.g., parables), is the semiotic model according to which a sign is composed of a signifier (expression) and a signified (content)».

Deconstruction challenges structuralism's metaphysics of presence. It rather «places the emphasis on the signifier, which is such only in relation to other signifiers rather than in relation to a determinate signified, for the signified is itself a signifier within another sign. In other words, the text is a bottomless series of references to other references which never comes to a rest in a «real» or determinate referent»[97].

Contextual approaches centered on the audience. Schneiders' described the various contextual approaches:

---

96 R.E. BROWN – S.M. SCHNEIDERS, «Hermeneutics», 1158. Schneiders argued for a theologically responsible use of literary criticism based on a «growing appreciation of language as mediation of being rather than as system of verbal labels and thus of intimate relationship of content to form in all texts, including canonical ones».

97 R.E. BROWN – S.M. SCHNEIDERS, «Hermeneutics», 1159. Schneiders went on to say that this theory has not gained much attention due to its stance of complete indeterminacy.

Rhetorical criticism treats the text not as the object of interpretation but rather as a poetic source for interaction with the reader so that no intrinsic or exclusive meaning may be withdrawn from the text Rhetorical criticism assumes the particular text is influencing a particular audience at a particular time. The method analyses communicative techniques reflected in the text. The method is influenced by Aristotelian and contemporary approaches to rhetorical analysis. Narrative criticism is the term used when rhetorical criticism is applied to narratives[98].

Sociological Criticism «seeks to investigate reading as an essentially collective phenomenon in which the individual reader is part of a "reading public" with particular socio-historical characteristics that influence the process of interpretation».

Psychological criticism «emphasizes the influence of personality and personal history on interpretation».

Phenomenological criticism studies the interaction between the reader and the text and how it is actualized or realized by the reader.

She concluded «the variety of literary-hermeneutical approaches to the interpretation of biblical texts precludes any totalitarian claims for any one approach». *Literary criticism* deals with the text in its final form, with the world in front of the text not the historical world behind it; and it understands that present meaning is mediated by language through interpretation. «Most literary-critical biblical scholars recognize the importance, even the necessity, of historical-critical exegesis for full understanding of the biblical texts; but they reject any understanding (or better misunderstanding) of the HCM as the sole, uniquely authoritative approach to biblical interpretation». Canonical criticism, another approach that deals with the text in its final form, is treated next.

The remainder of the article was written by Brown[99]. Canonical criticism is practiced in two different forms one developed by B.S. Childs, the other by J.A. Sanders. Childs studied the text in the final canonical form. For him this meant the final form of the linguistic text (e.g. Masoretic text), the collection (e.g. Pentateuch) and the individual book. «Only the final canonical form of text, book and collection is sacred Scripture for a community of faith and practice; and historical criticism has been a distraction with its isolation of individual books, its analysis of sources, and its concentration on the author's intent and circumstances». Sanders on

---

[98] R.E. BROWN – S.M. SCHNEIDERS, «Hermeneutics», 1160. Schneiders distinguished narrative criticism from narratology or structural analysis of the story.

[99] See footnote 87.

the other hand saw the criticism as «having evolved from the other critical disciplines, reflecting back on and informing them. Its unique contribution is in addressing questions of biblical authority by situating the Scriptures as word of God in the matrix of a believing community of readers and interpreters». Sanders was not as insistent on the final form of the text as Childs. He rather saw an ongoing canonical process «where early traditions that were deemed valuable were contemporized and adapted in new situations helping a community to find identity in an otherwise confusing world». Thus, «selectivity is at work in all stage of the process, and a richness of diversity in the canon (diachronically as well as synchronically) prevents later theological constructs from being imposed on the Bible»[100].

Before concluding this section of the article, Brown noted two additional types of *more-than-literal sense* exegesis. The first he called exegesis for personal transformation. W. Wink's approach is used as an example. This approach «proposes a psychoanalytically informed critique of the way we read the text ..... for instance in discussing Mark 2:12, Wink asks «who is the "paralytic" in you? or who is the "scribe" in you?»». The original authors intention did not usually cover such approaches because they were usually more concerned with community issues: ecclesial, doctrinal, and liturgical dimensions. The second is advocacy exegesis that studies the scriptures from the position of a cause such as liberation theology or feminism.

Brown concluded his presentation on the *literal* and *more-than-literal senses* in the *NJBC* article suggesting that «while an interpreter can concentrate on one or the other, these are not separable categories; for the total process of explanation and understanding involves the relationship

---

[100] R.E. BROWN – S.M. SCHNEIDERS, «Hermeneutics», 1161. Brown suggested that a judgment on canonical criticism is complicated by the tone of Childs' «claims imperiously dismissing the worth of recent commentaries». He did acknowledge, however, three important points from Childs' approach. First, many times HCM commentaries stop with parts of the book, not relating it to the whole. Second, since the books were written for believers and by believers, the context of the community is a worthy place for interpretation. Third, canonical criticism helps recall that the Spirit was active not only in the composition of the biblical texts but also in their reception and subsequent interpretation.

He also registered several concerns with canonical criticism. Overemphasis on the final form may cause a break in the continuity with the earlier community. The intentions of the original authors cannot be totally overridden by the canonical collection. The canon forming process was not always deliberate. Finally, Sanders' theory that the Christian community received its identity through the development of the canon has been deemed exaggerated.

between the two». Up to the present most biblical commentaries have concentrated on the *literal sense*. Two reasons were presented:

> a) there is broad agreement at least in theory on how to arrive at the *literal sense*; and b) the possibility of engaging the text in order to determine what it now can or should mean to the reader is complicated by the diversity of readership, so that many commentators choose to confine themselves to the task of explanation, expecting that the readers themselves will move to vital understanding. That supposition is a bit optimistic, and commentators cannot rest content with being archaeologists of meaning. Perhaps the situation will be helpful when the advocates of the various criticisms that uncover the *more-than-literal senses* will move from theory to practice and begin to write commentaries themselves. That would make some of the discussion less abstract[101].

Summary. R.E. Brown saw the *literal sense* as the basis for exegetical study and interpretation of the Scriptures. Yet this was insufficient due to the canonical collection of books that point to an intention beyond the human author. Patristic and medieval exegesis give insight into the *more-than-literal sense* but the methods used in these periods are inadequate today because they fail to take into consideration advances in modern studies. The newer approaches to the *more-than-literal senses* provide a methodological approach that can enable the study of the text from a critical standpoint. The approaches however are varied and insufficient in themselves. Brown and Schneiders suggest using the various methods in conjunction with the HCM. The cataloging of these methods in this article points to the next step in integration. The *literal sense* is determined using historical-critical methodologies. The *more-than-literal senses* are determined by the newer methodologies. The integration of the two will only come with time and practice to see if the validity of the multifaceted approach is feasible and non-contradictory. The catalogue of criticisms reflects the later catalogue in *Interpretation of the Bible in the Church*.

6. Critical Exegesis and Catholic Education

The crisis in biblical interpretation also involved the relationship between critical exegesis and Catholic education. This topic is addressed from a particularly American perspective. By 1983 the church was beginning to move into the second generation of post-Vatican II Catholics. Many adults who received updates in their religious education did so via their children's education. This plus the increased exposure to and use of

---

101 R.E. BROWN – S.M. SCHNEIDERS, «Hermeneutics», 1162.

the Scriptures in pastoral and religious education settings, the accessibility of reading material based on critical exegesis, the availability of formal classes and group study programs, the exposure to critical exegesis in homilies (albeit limited), and the presentation of exegetical results or ambiguities by the secular press contributed to a rising awareness of modern biblical approaches. Furthermore, there was the lingering problem of fundamentalism. The result in many cases was confusion and a tension. This section presents two articles that identify and propose solutions for these problems: D. Konstant, «The Use of the Bible within the Church» and R.E. Brown, «Communicating the Divine and Human in Scripture».

D. Konstant, «The Use of the Bible within the Church», 1991. The year 1990 witnessed the twenty-fifth anniversary of *Dei Verbum*. Numerous articles were written concerning the document and biblical studies[102]. Konstant studied the theme from a pastoral perspective in a lecture he delivered on November 17, 1990 marking the fiftieth anniversary of the Catholic Biblical Association of America. The primary focus of his presentation was a comparison on the use of Scripture in liturgy and education in the years 1940 and 1990[103]. Konstant's treatment on education is considered here.

---

[102] See also J.R. DONAHUE, «The Changing Shape»; F.J. MOLONEY, «Catholic Biblical Scholarship»; ID., «Whither Catholic Biblical Studies?»; G. O'COLLINS, «*Dei Verbum*»; and M. VIDAL, «The Relationship».

[103] M. VIDAL, «The Relationship» in a similar talk to the French Biblical Association *«Evangile et Vie»* noted similar changes in the church regarding the Bible and the church. One in particular that is not included in Konstant's presentation was that of Bible reading. Vidal quoted from two editions of *Lexikon für Theologie und Kirche* «On Bible Reading». The difference of approach in these two editions (1931-1951) will be obvious.

First, the 1931 edition stated: «The church, as always, rejected the assertion that Bible reading is necessary for everybody; it has done this in consideration of the Catholic rule of faith to prevent handing over Bible reading to subjectivism; it has done it out of respect for the Word of God... and has also done it for other reasons based upon the God-given exclusive competence of the ecclesial magisterium. The Catholic practice is justified by the history of errors, especially of the Protestant parties, that born from free Bible reading, undermined more and more the belief in the divine origin of Sacred Scripture».

Second, the 1951 edition stated «Jesus and Paul (Mt. 4:4; Rom 15:4) speak of the salvific value of Bible reading in such positive terms that obviously the early and medieval church also recommended Bible reading. Impartial research today admits that in the past, Bible reading in native languages was widespread, even in the middle ages». Although the information regarding the widespread knowledge of «native languages» is incorrect, the comparision of the two editions notes the difference in emphases on reading the Scriptures.

Konstant noted two major problems facing religious education: fundamentalism and the failure to recognize the sacramentality of the scriptures. He described fundamentalism as «a tendency, that is not restricted to scripture or to religious matters; it may be characteristic of an age that is in a constant state of flux — anything that can bring stability is likely to be welcomed». Regarding the reading of scriptures, nothing other than a literal meaning is permitted. Anything less will bring a refusal to listen or discuss. At the other end of the spectrum is the failure to recognize the sacramentality of the scriptures. In other words, the failure to recognize the «word of God» in the scriptures. Konstant proposed a solution to these problems — the recognition of the divine word in the Scriptures. He said: «the one who knows that Christ "is present through his word, in that he himself is speaking when scripture is read in the church", will not be over-anxious about the precise exegesis of a passage of Scripture, but will be happy to let the words and the spirit of those words soak in»[104].

After describing the differences in teaching the Scriptures to adults and children[105], Konstant advised teachers of the scriptures to reflect the word of God in their teaching. He gave three suggestions:

a) The natural and proper way to speak of revelation will be through the use of biblical language, thought, idiom and metaphor always in line with the tradition and teachings of the church. Faith and knowledge are required to do this effectively. *Lectio divina* was recommended as a method for prayer, study and reflection. This type of reading neither omits nor relies on scientific methodology in coming to understand the scriptures, for «the words of scripture have but one purpose, namely to reveal to those who have ears to hear the real presence of God; and to enable com-

---

104 D. KONSTANT, «The Use of the Bible», 11. Though this is true the more relevant issue is how to communicate this belief to a fundamentalist, a task that is probably beyond the competence of exegesis and in the realm of fundamental theology.

105 D. KONSTANT, «The Use of the Bible», 11. Teaching Scriptures to adults can take place under two models: formal education and group reflection. Since the council formal religious education has been available in every diocese. Teaching Scriptures to children needs to reflect adult catechesis. Konstant noted catechists coming to a new awareness of the levels of religious education. Each level has their own needs and capacities. He added that it is not necessary to cover everything in childhood. Selective use of the Bible in education is entirely appropriate as long as it is a balanced approach. He concluded his remarks on formal education: «We are coming to terms with the fact that the academic study of scripture, through of genuine value, is no more than one way of entering into the technicalities of the text. The *breath* of the text, for it is alive, is discovered only as we are able to let the word rest easily in the mind and heart».

munion between the listener and God — neither more nor less than that»[106].

b) God reveals himself through events as well as words so due attention should be given to salvation history.

c) The teacher should «ensure that the students come to an unworried appreciation of the importance and nature of literary form, understanding that scripture will remain deadlocked until this discriminating key is used. «Until this is grasped no understanding of scripture will ever be possible»[107].

Konstant concluded that for the ordinary Catholic «Scripture has been opened up in a marvelous way. For the first time they are seeing the word of God as they should: as normative and central; as in a special way a guide and source for their understanding of faith; as great nourishment for their holiness»[108].

R.E. Brown, «Communicating the Divine and Human in Scripture», 1992. On April 20, 1992, R.E. Brown addressed the National Catholic Educational Association (NCEA) on the relationship of critical exegesis to religious education[109]. The first topic Brown discussed is American Catholics and the Bible. Following Vatican II, the use of the Bible in the life of the church has increased greatly. While this was going on in the church, Catholics in the United States were being fully incorporated into American society. The incorporation meant that many Catholics were forming judgments on various issues similar to mainstream America despite «what we might desire by way of church guidance»[110]. Brown noted

---

106 D. KONSTANT, «The Use of the Bible», 13.

107 D. KONSTANT, «The Use of the Bible», 13.

108 D. KONSTANT, «The Use of the Bible», 14.

109 Brown noted the importance of the question in his division of the twentieth century according to Catholic biblical studies. He saw the first third of the century as marked by a rejection of critical methods. The second period was characterized by the acceptance and utilization of the methods. The third period, the present period, witnesses Catholics beginning to digest the import of this change [from a non-critical to a critical approach in biblical studies] for church and private life. Brown noted the development in his own work. He said that in the 1980's: «I began to concentrate on the necessity of seeing both the divine and the human in Scripture as a key to furthering the impact of a modern, centrist biblical approach on church life: the Scriptures seen as «the word of God in human words». He continues: «without an appreciation that the Scriptures are uniquely from God (a truth embodied in the term *inspiration*), one may veer toward dismissing their message as something of the past that no longer has to be listened to. Without an appreciation that every word in the Scriptures has been uttered by human begins in fixed circumstances to communicate a message, one may misread them, applying their words to solve problems to which they do not speak».

110 R.E. BROWN, «Communicating», 4.

the Bible is the source of authority for most Americans concerning religious beliefs and teachings, in fact it is «almost the only authority that is appealed to with any acceptance»[111]. He proposed that since the Bible has this authoritative weight for religious discussion in America, then Catholic educators should respond with the formation of Catholics «who are capable of exercising a balanced judgment about the way the Bible is used by the participants»[112].

The second topic Brown addressed concerns the teaching of Scripture within this setting presenting several examples of the «content» of a scripture course[113]. He again noted the importance for helping people make sound judgment. Many times Jesus is cited in the media as though he «foresaw the precise ethical concerns of twentieth century society and had issued directives for modern church structures and functioning»[114]. To counteract this students of the bible must realize that Jesus taught in a particular context and time and therefore requires a translation for our particular context and time. Brown then went on to show how the age of Jesus moved into the age of the early church guided by the Spirit. The formation of the church was not by a fixed plan but occurred under the movement of the Spirit (Acts 1–15). Brown saw the arguments of both ultraconservatives and ultraliberals rooted in a failure to recognize that the

---

[111] R.E. BROWN, «Communicating», 4. M. VIDAL, «The Relationship», 34, while speaking from a French context noted that Bible reading is not isolated to the Church. «More recently another locus of reading has emerged, that of society: bookstores, religious esoteric corners where different editions of the Bible are on display». His comments illustrate the need for a balanced approach to biblical interpretation that allows readers such as these to be addressed. The possibilities for evangelization in such situations are great.

[112] R.E. BROWN, «Communicating», 4.

[113] Brown gave examples from the OT and NT. The David narrative is used at the OT example. The academic level for this example ranges from students in high school or college to adults taking a course for general enrichment. Brown noted that «people still tend to have an ethereal view of religion and are easily scandalized in matters pertaining to Christianity and church when they encounter human weakness, sin, stupidity, or institutional arteriosclerosis». He demonstrated how David «is much closer to the kind of public religious person discussed in the media than is the transparently perfect saint about whom no evil can possibly be suspected». The religious institutions of Israel were an interplay of the divine and human which is clearly visible from the biblical accounts. Brown continued: «I need not insult your intelligence by drawing detailed parallels to the modern Christian situation, but I hope you see the possibility of this nonthreatening OT pattern to enable students to understand the interplay of the divine and the human in the church and to avoid the facile sarcasm about church institution that appears so often in the media».

[114] R.E. BROWN, «Communicating», 6.

NT period did not end with the public lifetime of Jesus but continued under the guidance of the Spirit. In this period decisions were made regarding the church itself, ministry in the church and the sacraments. These decisions are just as determinative as those made in the public ministry[115].

The third topic that Brown addressed is the appropriate use of the Bible in education today. Because of the state of education in the United States today, educators on higher levels cannot presume that the material covered in an earlier stage was retained. Thus a teacher or professor has to be aware that general information may be a necessary requirement of their course. For example in college level courses it may be general knowledge that students need, not specialized information. He went on to suggest that teaching the students how to intelligently work through a biblical passage may be the most effective way of teaching — the «exercise of helping students to think through a biblical text is almost the opposite of employing texts to persuade students to embrace one side or the other of a disputed issue».

Brown concluded the paper: «If we can in some way implant the message that people need to think through cited Scripture passages because both divine and human are present in every passage, we can contribute to their maturity as Christians facing complex issues. And thus we can contribute to the maturity of the church itself»[116].

Summary. The confusions raised through the use of critical exegesis in Catholic education was another factor that contributed to the crisis in biblical interpretation. Konstant described fundamentalism and the disregard for the sacramentality of the Bible as two problems that face biblical educators. Greater recognition that God speaks through the text would help solve these problems. He saw the identification of literary forms as an important element of the solution. Brown's speech noted the need to emphasize both the divine and human aspects of the bible in Catholic education. He encouraged the careful presentation of critical study that recognizes the various educational levels of the students. Several elements that contributed to the crisis in biblical interpretation and mentioned in Brown's article but are not considered in this presentation are: fundamentalism, tele-evangelism, the use of biblical citations by the secular press , and uncritical reflection as well as presentations on non-representative biblical scholarship.

---

[115] R.E. BROWN, «Communicating», 7.
[116] R.E. BROWN, «Communicating», 9.

7. Ecclesial Concern With Critical Exegesis

The seventh topic considered in this chapter is the acknowledged of the «crisis» in biblical interpretation by Catholic ecclesial institutions. The Synod of Bishops and the International Theological Commission (ITC)[117] both issued documents that mention the debate regarding biblical criticism as well as calling for a reform in the practice of biblical interpretation.

The 1985 Synod of Bishops, while discussing the implementation of the teachings of Vatican II, noted three criticisms of biblical scholarship. First, *Dei Verbum* has been overly neglected along with the Apostolic Exhortation *Evangelii Nuntiandi*. Second, *Dei Verbum* has been read in a fragmented and selective way. Third, in the search for the original meaning of the Sacred Scriptures, there was a lack of taking into proper account the living tradition of the church, as well as the official teaching of the Magisterium[118].

The three criticisms raised by the Synod were evaluated by K. Romaniuk in his article «Post-Vatican Biblical Criticism». The first observation of the Synod was that *Dei Verbum* has been neglected in biblical studies. Romaniuk noted two areas to which this criticism applies: biblical conferences and publications regarding biblical studies[119]. The second observation of the Synod was that *Dei Verbum* has been read in a fragmented or selective way. Romaniuk noted that although the Constitution encouraged critical studies, «it has come to pass that the analyses drawn upon the rules of literary criticism have been stretched to such limits in the post-conciliar era that they have begun to weary even those who had been enthusiastically pursuing such analyses themselves until now»[120]. Ro-

---

[117] Sister organization to the PBC.

[118] For English version see: Origins 15.27, 441-450. For the opposite view, that is that the magisterial authorities have not incorporated the results of critical exegesis into their statements see: C.E. GUDORF, «The Magisterium and the Bible».

[119] K. ROMANIUK, «Post-Vatican Biblical Criticism», 7, noted that at biblical conferences and congresses especially ecumenical or inter-faith meetings *Dei Verbum* has not been incorporated into discussions. Regarding biblical publications, he lamented that in commentaries, introductions, theologies and biblical catechesis there is little appropriation of the Constitution. He said: «thus, for example there did not appear any specifically new introductions to biblical studies, worked out on the principles enunciated in *Dei Verbum*. Nor do we have to date any distinctively new theory on divine inspiration and the canon of Holy Scripture».

[120] K. ROMANIUK, «Post-Vatican Biblical Criticism», 9. He saw the fragmentary approach to *Dei Verbum* as the source of this problem. Scholars who take and appropriate only several paragraphs of the document in their work are bound to this extreme. He specifically noted the absence of any full length treatment on the «the fifth point of the Constitution which treats of the need of obedience in faith in these matters». Fur-

maniuk saw the third observation of the Synod as a criticism that biblical exegesis neglects the living tradition of the church[121]. He evaluated this observation from two aspects: the relationship of biblical scholarship and patristic exegesis and the official statements of the magisterium. Regarding the relationship of contemporary biblical studies with patristic exegesis Romaniuk stated that modern scripture scholars do not consult the patristic exegesis in their studies[122]. Greater consultation of the Fathers could help modern exegetes see the inter-relationship between the testaments. Regarding the relationship between biblical scholars and the magisterium; he observed that biblical scholars have spent too much time lamenting the period when biblical scholarship was restricted by the magisterium so he suggested viewing the magisterial decisions and statements in their entirety. He particularly recalled the freedom that was given to scholars between 1941-1948. Romaniuk concluded the article praising the accomplishments of biblical scholarship over the past twenty years, and calling for greater fidelity to the principles of *Dei Verbum*[123].

The 1989 ITC document «On the Interpretation of Dogmas» referred to the crisis that exists between modern exegesis and dogmatic theology.

---

thermore he lamented that the sixth chapter which speaks of scriptures in the life of the church has been neglected.

[121] K. ROMANIUK, «Post-Vatican Biblical Criticism», 6. While I agree that there are three criticisms of the current implementation of *Dei Verbum*, I think the second and third critiques mentioned by Romaniuk are actually one. The third one to be added regards the pastoral dimension. The document states that «the false opposition between doctrinal and pastoral responsibilities must be avoided and overcome. In fact, the true intent of pastoral work consists in actualizing and making concrete the truth of salvation, which is in itself valid for all times. As true pastors, the bishops must point out the right way to strengthen the faith of the flock, keep dangers away from it». English translation: Origins, 15:27, 447.

[122] K. ROMANIUK, «Post-Vatican Biblical Criticism», 11-13. He suggested the following reasons: a) generally the Fathers had an inadequate knowledge of the ancient languages and the almost complete absence of textual criticism (Origen excepted). «As a result, the object under analysis is, in the case of the patristic exegesis, a text quite different from that under critical study by contemporary biblicists»; b) the excessive allegorizing in their interpretations - «For many Fathers of the church, the *literal sense* of the Scriptures is of little import, and in their view, ought not to be the object of discovery in reading the Word of God»; c) deficiencies in Patristic exegesis in areas of biblical history, geography and archeology; and d) the homiletic character of Patristic exegesis. Romaniuk notes that «while this stance of the modern scholar has our understanding, it is regrettable, nevertheless, that current *biblical* theology does not avail itself of patristic sources to a greater degree»

[123] K. ROMANIUK, «Post-Vatican Biblical Criticism», 14.

The conflict between exegesis and dogmatics is a modern phenomenon. In the wake of the Enlightenment, the tools of historical criticism were developed not without the intention of using them to achieve emancipation from early dogmatic authority. This criticism became ever more comprehensive. Soon not only the Scriptures and dogma were in conflict, but criticism led to questioning what lay behind the biblical text itself and was directed toward the "dogmatic coatings" which cover the Scriptures themselves. The development of historical criticism in sociopolitical and psychological criticism examined the text for sociopolitical antagonisms and suppressed psychic data. These lines of criticism have this in common: The dogma of the church as well as the Scriptures themselves are suspected of concealing an authentic or primordial reality, which may be uncovered only by means of critical inquiry.

Obviously the positive side and results of the Enlightenment's criticism of tradition should not be overlooked. The historical criticism of the Bible succeeded in making clear that Scripture itself is ecclesial and made its home in the paradosis of the early church. The establishment of the scriptural canon was a process involving decision on the part of the church. Thus exegesis led back to dogma and tradition[124].

The Commission concluded that the HCM and other methods (history of religion, structuralism, semiotics, social history, depth psychology) can contribute

to raising up the figure of Christ more meaningfully in our day. However, all these methods will be fruitful inasmuch as they are used with the obedience of faith and do not become autonomous. The communion of the church remains the locus in which the interpretation of Scripture is preserved from drifting with the changing currents of time[125].

8. The Crisis in Biblical Interpretation, 1988-1989

By the late 1980's many questions regarding biblical interpretation were being raised. In 1988, the Rockford Institute Center on Religion and Society sponsored an ecumenical conference that addressed the «crisis» in biblical interpretation. The conference involved twenty theologians of different denominations[126]. The conference was one of the preludes to the

---

124 ITC, *On the Interpretation of Dogmas*, 10.

125 ITC, *On the Interpretation of Dogmas*, 11.

126 Participants in the conference were: E. Achtemeier, K. Donfried, A. Dulles, T. Hopko, J. Komonchak, R. Malone, R.J. Neuhaus, T.C. Oden, C.J. Peter, C.H. Pinnock, J.H. Rodgers, J.F. Stafford, P.T. Stallsworth, M.Swalina, M. Waldstein, G. Weigel, D. Wells. In addition to the lecture given by Cardinal Ratzinger, lectures were given by R.E. Brown, W.H. Lazareth, and G. Lindbeck. R.J. NEUHAUS edited the pub-

1993 PBC document *Interpretation of the Bible in the Church*[127]. This section presents the views of the two catholic speakers at the event: Cardinal Ratzinger who delivered the keynote address, and R.E. Brown. Also considered in this section is an article by J.A. Fitzmyer that specifically addressed the Catholic use of the HCM[128], and a review of the Rockford Conference by J. Wicks.

J.A. Ratzinger: Biblical Interpretation in Crisis, 1988. Ratzinger began with a presentation on the current state of «crisis» in biblical studies and its roots in the practice of historical criticism. He opened his talk with imagery from Wladimir Solowjew's *History of the Antichrist* in which the antichrist portrays himself as an exegete who «earned his doctorate at Tübingen and had written an exegetical work which was recognized as pioneering in the field»[129].

Ratzinger noted the optimism with which historical criticism began its operation stating that «the polyphony of history could be heard again, rising from behind the monotone of traditional interpretations»[130]. With time, however, confusion became more and more a problem and the polyphony turned to noise. The text began to be more and more dissected and faith was divorced from the method[131]. Reactions to historical-critical exegesis added intensity to the «crisis». On the one hand there is funda-

---

lished collection of the four lectures, *Biblical Interpretation in Crisis*, along with an account of the conference proceedings.

127 R.J. NEUHAUS, *Biblical Interpretation in Crisis*, xii, remarked: «Cardinal Ratzinger has informed me subsequently that his paper and the questions engaged by the conference have been adopted for its next several years of work by the PBC. The commission will in due course, he says, want to pick up on the ecumenical examination of these issues so notably initiated in New York this January past. This volume, then carries the sign, "To Be Continued"».

128 The article seems to be prompted by the Rockford Conference.

129 J.A. RATZINGER, «Biblical Interpretation in Crisis», 1.

130 J.A. RATZINGER, «Biblical Interpretation in Crisis», 2.

131 J.A. RATZINGER, «Biblical Interpretation in Crisis», 2. He described the movement to confusion as follows: «But since God and divine action permeate the entire biblical account of history, one is obliged to begin with a complicated anatomy of the scriptural word. On one hand, there is the attempt to unravel the various threads (of the narrative) so that in the end one holds in one's hands what is the "really historical", which means the purely human element in events. On the other hand, one has to try to show how it happened that the idea of God became interwoven through it all. So it is that another "real" history is to be fashioned in place of the one given. Underneath the existing sources — that is to say, the biblical books themselves — we are supposed to find more original sources, which in turn become the criteria for interpretation. No one should be surprised that this procedure leads to the sprouting of ever more numerous hypotheses which finally turn into a jungle of contradictions».

mentalism that demands «literalness» and «realism». On the other hand there are materialist and feminist approaches that refuse to address the original intention of the text[132]. The question of hermeneutics further complicates the problem. Understanding the text in the world today is a question that is sometimes ignored. Ratzinger challenged this ignorance noting that just because someone has knowledge of the origin of the text does not mean that the person has an «understanding» of the text. Yet he also acknowledged that the question of hermeneutics is not so simple: «if "hermeneutics" is ever to become convincing, the inner harmony between historical analysis and hermeneutical synthesis must first be found»[133].

Following the introduction, Ratzinger concentrated on the role of historical criticism in the current crisis. The talk is divided into four sections: the central problem, a criticism of the HCM as taught by M. Dibelius and R. Bultmann, the philosophic roots of the method, and the basic elements of a new synthesis.

The Central Problem. Ratzinger described the central problem of the method as its claim of objectivity[134]. To avoid this problem, historical exegesis will have to read its conclusions «in a diachronic manner so that the appearance of a quasi-clinical-scientific certainty is avoided»[135]. He remarked that the appearance of certainty has caused the conclusions of historical-critical exegesis to be readily accepted. He suggested that if the model of natural science is going to be followed, perhaps the Heisenberg principle should be followed as well. «Heisenberg has shown that the outcome of a given experiment is heavily influenced by the point of view of the observer. So much is this the case that both the observer's question and observations continue to change themselves in the natural course of events»[136]. The recognition of an interaction between the exegete and the interpretation is an important critique of the method. «This insight should not lead us to skepticism about the method, but rather to an honest recognition of what its limits are, and perhaps how it might be purified»[137].

Criticism of the Method. Ratzinger continued his presentation with an examination of the HCM as used by Dibelius and Bultmann. He choose these two German Protestant scholars because of their influence on the

---

132 J.A. RATZINGER, «Biblical Interpretation in Crisis», 5.
133 J.A. RATZINGER, «Biblical Interpretation in Crisis», 4.
134 Ratzinger acknowledges that the method is not practiced everywhere with the same «starkness» with which he describes it.
135 J.A. RATZINGER, «Biblical Interpretation in Crisis», 6.
136 J.A. RATZINGER, «Biblical Interpretation in Crisis», 7. This is similar to de la Potterie's observations mentioned above, see page 177.
137 J.A. RATZINGER, «Biblical Interpretation in Crisis», 8.

development of the method. Ratzinger maintained they «have widely achieved an authority like unto dogma». In describing the genesis of their practice Ratzinger noted that both scholars developed their methods in reaction to «liberal theology» which sought to distinguish what was historical and what was unhistorical in the biblical accounts. Additionally they sought «to establish literary criteria which would reliably clarify the process by which the texts themselves were developed and would thus provide a true picture of the tradition»[138]. This goal to provide a true picture of the tradition was underlined by some misguided presuppositions such as: the priority of proclamation over event; the discontinuity between the phases of development; and the rule that the more complex must be later, the more simple earlier. He showed the deficiencies of these presuppositions noting that the principles of evolution should not be applied to spiritual realities: «Spiritual processes do not follow the rule of zoological genealogies»[139]. Ratzinger also argued that the idea of «pure form» is based on a «loaded idea of what is original». At the basis of this theory is the presupposition of word over event that originates with «Luther's fundamental distinction: the dialectic between the law and gospel»[140]. The result of such presuppositions is that the exegete builds a history of Jesus around what has been determined in advance. For example:

> Thus Jesus has to be conceived in strongly «Judaic» terms. Anything «Hellenistic» has to be removed from him. All apocalyptic, sacramental, mystical elements have to be pruned away. What remains is a strictly «eschatological» prophet, who really proclaims nothing of substance. He only cries out «eschatologically» in expectation of the «wholly other», of that transcendence which he powerfully presents before humanity in the form of the imminent end of the world[141].

The results for exegesis were two-fold. First, the exegete had to show how one moved from this view of Jesus to the view of the community that «were united in Jewish eschatology, stoic philosophy, and mystery religion in a wonderful syncretism». Second, the exegete had to find a way to connect the original message of Jesus to the Christian life of today. The second goal resulted in Bultmann's demythologization heavily influenced by the philosophy of Heidegger.

Philosophical Roots of the Method. Following his treatment of Bultmann and Dibelius's exegetical method, Ratzinger analyzed the philo-

---

138 J.A. RATZINGER, «Biblical Interpretation in Crisis», 9.
139 J.A. RATZINGER, «Biblical Interpretation in Crisis», 10.
140 J.A. RATZINGER, «Biblical Interpretation in Crisis», 12.
141 J.A. RATZINGER, «Biblical Interpretation in Crisis», 13.

sophical influences in their work. He saw the primary philosophical influence in the thought of Kant. He noted:

> According to him [Kant], the voice of being-in-itself cannot be heard by human beings. Man can hear it only indirectly in the postulates of practical reason, which have remained, as it were, the small opening through which he can make contact with the real, that is, his eternal destiny. For the rest, as far as the content of his intellectual life is concerned, he must limit himself to the realm of the categories. Thence comes the restriction to the positive, to the empirical, to the «exact» science, which by definition excludes the appearance of what is «wholly other», or the one who is wholly other, or a new initiative from another plane[142].

The theological result is that revelation recedes into the «pure formality of the eschatological stance, which corresponds to the Kantian split». With this as a basis, all that remains is explanation. «It is with this basic conviction that Bultmann, with the majority of modern exegetes, read the Bible»[143]. Thus, he saw the basic problem as philosophy not history. Ratzinger then raised the question «can one read the Bible in another way?»

A New Synthesis. In the final section of his talk, Ratzinger proposed a new synthesis. He saw the question as «how to join its [HCM] tools with a better philosophy which would entail fewer drawbacks foreign to the text, which would be less arbitrary, and which would offer greater possibilities for a true listening to the text itself»[144]. He made two suggestions to answer this question. First, he recommended a clarification in the relationship between methods in exegesis and methods in natural science. Exegetical science cannot make the claim to exactness and certitude that natural science makes. Exegesis should also become more aware of its proper object, God. Second, Ratzinger proposed a re-evaluation of the word-event relationship. Word and event need «to be considered equally original, if one wishes to remain true to the biblical perspective». Furthermore, a dualism between word and event cannot be tolerated because it «splits the biblical word off from creation and would substitute the principle of discontinuity for the organic continuity of meaning which exists between the OT and the NT»[145].

Ratzinger completed his presentation on the crisis in biblical interpretation with the following five points:

---

[142] J.A. RATZINGER, «Biblical Interpretation in Crisis», 15.
[143] J.A. RATZINGER, «Biblical Interpretation in Crisis», 16.
[144] J.A. RATZINGER, «Biblical Interpretation in Crisis», 17.
[145] J.A. RATZINGER, «Biblical Interpretation in Crisis», 20.

a) The time seems to have arrived for a new and thorough reflection on exegetical method.

b) Exegesis can no longer be studied in a unilinear, synchronic fashion, as is the case with scientific findings which do not depend upon their history but only upon the precision of their data.

c) Philological and scientific literary methods are and will remain critically important for a proper exegesis.

d) What we need now are not new hypotheses on the *Sitz im Leben*, on possible sources or on the subsequent process of handing down the material. What we do need is a critical look at the exegetical landscape we now have, so that we may return to the text and distinguish between those hypotheses which are helpful and those which are not.

e) The exegete must realize that he does not stand in some neutral area, above or outside history and the church. [146]

R.E. Brown, «The Contribution of Historical Criticism to Ecumenical Discussion», 1988. The focus of Brown's presentation was the contribution of historical biblical criticism to ecumenical discussion[147]. The talk was divided into three sections. In the first section, Brown discussed historical biblical criticism and its relationship to the *literal sense*[148]. He acknowledged that rationalist principles guided historical criticism in the eighteenth and nineteenth centuries but are no longer prevalent in exegetical studies. He found «that most theological apprehensions about historical criticism are focused on something past and are not relevant to the moderate and adapted form». The focus of current biblical criticism is demonstrating what «the biblical author conveyed to his readers in the text he wrote»[149].

---

[146] J.A. RATZINGER, «Biblical Interpretation in Crisis», 21-23.

[147] For more on the contributions of the HCM to ecumenical discussions see: R.E. BROWN, «Ecumenism and New Testament Research», «Episkope and Episcopate»; R.E. BROWN, ; R.E. BROWN – AL., *Mary in the New Testament*; J. REUMANN, «After Historical Criticism, What?».

[148] Brown does not specifically use the term *literal sense* in this presentation; however, his description is consistent with his use of the term in other presentations.

[149] R.E. BROWN, «Ecumenical Church Discussion», 24-29, clarifies this description. It is similar to the latter *NJBC* definition already discussed in this chapter.
The biblical author. Brown suggested that the term «author» should be understood in a much broader sense than the physical writer. He noted that authority does not come from the personal identity of the author. Historical criticism «shows that the evangelists were not merely literal reporters of the words of Jesus and at times went beyond him both in wording and meaning».

In the second section, Brown defined what he means by interchurch discussion. His presentation presumes a discussion among churches who have an ecclesiastical acceptance of inspiration and canonical authority («even if those terms are understood with slightly different nuances»); some appreciation of a liturgical use of the Bible; and a recognition that the Bible has a relevance to the life of the believing community. He furthermore noted complications due to the various degree that historical criticism and/or ecumenical discussions are accepted[150].

What the biblical author wrote. The determination of what an author meant in a passage is not always obvious. Though some scholars suggest analogies with other biblical texts, Brown noted that it is a dangerous simplification because of the variety in NT views. Ecumenical discussions «profit from being subject to the control of the written text rather than to speculations that go far beyond the text. Such a control can be very important in dealing with some sensitive issues of modern times». He provided examples regarding the role of women in the scriptures and presiders at liturgy.

Conveyed to his readers. Brown said that common sense will admit only a limited success in understanding what the human author intended. This is, because of the cultural, temporal and psychological context of the ages that separate the reader and the text. Biblical scholars should clarify their results as ranging from «certain, through probable and possible, to highly uncertain. Despite the difficulties involved, this meaning is fundamental to all interpretation and crucial to ecumenical discussion. Broader senses are possible, but «in ecumenical discussions one must be careful to recognize the limitations of these forms of broader interpretation/criticism for solving some of the historical and doctrinal issues that have divided the churches». Historical questions are not the only questions to investigate a text with but when historical questions are raised they should be answered with an historical approach. This is particularly helpful due to the different approaches the various denominations have toward the Scriptures.

«Some Christians can accept as authoritative doctrines articulated in the postbiblical era that are not critically detectable in the Bible — the authority of the later church is invoked as sufficient (whether or not those who invoke it recognize as clearly as they should that the doctrine goes beyond biblical understanding). Many Christians accept only what they can find clearly articulated by the biblical authors (even if they may be a bit naive about the limitations of the biblical evidence). It is very difficult for these two Christian positions to find a common ground. A study of the NT that not only respects the limitations of individual passages but also seeks lines of development within the early Christian picture lends support to an intermediary group of contemporary Christians who can accept church doctrine that goes beyond the biblical material provided that a connection or line of development can be found that would make the doctrine intelligible as a reflection of the revelation attested to in the Bible».

150 R.E. BROWN, «Ecumenical Church Discussion», 29-31, made three observations:
    1. «If one can judge from what is taught in their seminaries, most of the Christian churches of the West (Episcopalian, Lutheran, Methodist, Presbyterian, Roman Catholic, United Church of Christ) accept historical criticism as a valid tool (albeit a limited one) and so one does not have to defend the legitimacy of applying such criticism to

In the third section, Brown discussed the contribution of historical biblical criticism to ecumenical discussion. He acknowledged the limits of
historical criticism based on the exegete's goals. «Biblical critics are not
always impartial; and to establish views that they find sympathetic, they
sometimes produce analyses that do not do justice to ambiguities in the
biblical situation». He continued «to be helpful biblical criticism must be
adequate and representative — a desideratum that often cannot be
achieved without the interplay of opposing views»[151]. Yet in spite of this
historical criticism has proved helpful in theological discussion[152].

> Very often a representative biblical criticism will produce a picture of
> ambiguity. That may be a disappointment to those who oppose modern
> challenges and would like unquestionable biblical support. Too often
> biblical criticism is dismissed precisely as producing only ambiguities. In
> responding to that let me note three factors: a) Modern challenges to the
> church (not unlike past challenges) are often phrased in terms of certi-
> tude. A response that the situation was demonstrably ambiguous supplies
> a warning about the credibility that can be given to such bold affirma-
> tions about what should be done. b) The desire to find the Bible totally
> clear often has the implication that one's opponents are therefore either
> fools or knaves and destroys the possibility of dialogue. c) The recogni-
> tion that on many crucial questions the Bible is ambiguous is, in my
> judgment, the only approach that makes it possible for us who respect
> our ancestors in the divided churches to move beyond their disagree-
> ments[153].

Brown argued that the use of critical methodologies is «a major element
in forcing church theology (not some individual theologians) to come to
grips with factors that should bring greater nuance and maturity. The re-

---

biblical texts». Yet those involved in ecumenical discussion must be aware of an ultraconservative literalist approach that is very critical of ecumenical agreements.

2. «Some of the large churches of the East have not yet experimented with historical biblical criticism in a significant way. Some churches in the west reject the method
seeing it undermines the literal inerrancy of the Scriptures». Brown saw in this group a
slow process in seminary formation of gradual assimilation by through slow acceptance of the method. «A detectable process is that such professors will be purged from
the seminary faculties, usually in a recurring cyclic process every decade or so, until
the church or denomination moves closer to the mainstream of other Christians on this
matter».

3. «At the other extreme of the Christian spectrum, there are those whose allegiance
to their churches is marginal. For them ecumenism may consist of an acceptance of
Christians of similar mind, who ignore traditional doctrinal differences as irrelevant».

[151] R.E. BROWN, «Ecumenical Church Discussion», 31.
[152] R.E. BROWN, «Ecumenical Church Discussion», 33.
[153] R.E. BROWN, «Ecumenical Church Discussion», 33.

sults of biblical criticism shows that the churches have gone beyond the NT churches with their inchoate diversities»[154]. The recognition of this fact calls for a study of the «line of development» from the time of Jesus and the early church to the present. The lines may be diverse and so

> biblical criticism should force the church to examine why it has chosen one line of development rather than another. This may lead to a recognition that another church has followed a different biblical line of development and thus preserved another biblical value. That is not an affirmation of relativism but an encouragement to the churches to face ecumenism as an essential enrichment rather than a grudging concession[155].

Evaluation of these lines can then become important for determining a «hierarchy of doctrines». Brown argued that «without that step the churches will never come to a union that tolerates diversity on issues that rank lower in the hierarchy»[156]. The divisions in Christianity need to be healed both laterally (present) and vertically (past). «The first reaction of the churches will often be a refutation of the new approaches by citing familiar biblical passages that seem to bear on the issue, but representative biblical criticism may challenge whether those passages are really relevant or may find other passages that point in a different direction»[157]. The article concluded with positive comments on ecumenical discussions based on biblical scholarship in the USA[158].

Brown added an addenda to the published account of his lecture. This addenda contains his response to Cardinal Ratzinger's views on historical-critical exegesis. He began by noting three convergences between his

---

154 R.E. BROWN, «Ecumenical Church Discussion», 34.

155 R.E. BROWN, «Ecumenical Church Discussion», 35. For a similar view from an evangelical perspective see E.E. Johnson, «Dual Authorship and the Single Intended Meaning of Scripture».

156 R.E. BROWN, «Ecumenical Church Discussion», 35.

157 R.E. BROWN, «Ecumenical Church Discussion», 35.

158 R.E. BROWN, «Ecumenical Church Discussion», 36-37. He made final remarks about ecumenism in the USA. Prior to *Divino Afflante Spiritu* and *Dei Verbum* «neither clergy nor laity was interested in the Bible, so that reading or studying the Bible was regarded as a Protestant characteristic». Now «Scripture studies became the most attractive part of the curriculum in many seminaries; summer study sessions were organized to instruct priest who had finished their studies; there was a major movement to introduce a strong biblical element into religious education; and thousands of teachers of religion flocked to training sessions that would enable them to communicate biblical knowledge». The change has opened the lines of communication between Catholics and Protestants in the USA «even to the point of shared Bible classes and readings».

and Ratzinger's views on historical-critical exegesis. First, the wrong kind of exegesis is one which sees the Scriptures as only human. Second, historical criticism has made an enduring contribution to our understanding of the Bible. Cardinal Ratzinger wished to see the limitations overcome, «he advocates not "skepticism about the method" but an "honest recognition of its limits"». Third, both advocate a nonarbitrary way of going beyond the limitations of historical criticism that avoids fundamentalism and positivistic ecclesiasticism[159].

Brown then discussed three diverging points between Ratzinger's views and his own. First, Brown contrasted the general outlook of the two presentations. Brown saw his presentation as more optimistic concerning the state of exegesis. Part of the reason is accidental, each talk had a different focus. While Brown focused on the ecumenical aspects, Ratzinger gave a «general presentation and with a somewhat greater focus on the European scene as he experienced it both pastorally and academically»[160]. Brown stated that his own position is based in experience in the American exegesis. In Europe especially Germany the influence of Dibelius and Bultmann may be lingering but in America exegetes usually see them within a much wider scene. Brown then elaborated on his concerns regarding exegesis and education in America[161].

---

[159] R.E. BROWN, «Ecumenical Church Discussion», 37-40.

[160] R.E. BROWN, «Ecumenical Church Discussion», 40.

[161] R.E. BROWN, «Ecumenical Church Discussion», 42-43. He treated the topic on three education levels: a) university, b) college, and c) secondary and primary.

a. University-level academia. Browns biggest concern regarding the Scripture study on the university level is the disintegration of the Canon. Two specific points are made: «First, some were treating noncanonical works (e.g. gnostic gospels) as of equal value to the canonical works, not only for the reconstruction of earliest Christianity but for what the church of today should be (usually in the direction of less structure and less hierarchical authority). Second, some were claiming that nonextant, reconstructed, precanonical works and situations were the earliest form of Christianity, corrupted by the more institutional writers of the canonical works».

b. College-level Catholic religious education. Brown identified two concerns. First, many faculty have been trained in secular institutions without first having a background in Catholic theology. Second, «there is often a tendency to offer specialized Scripture courses exposing college students to the latest trends in scholarship with the contention that these students received basic religious and biblical knowledge in grammar and high schools». He continued: «A more realistic judgment would be that most Catholic college students know nothing about the Bible and should be instructed, not in the latest ideas but in elementary ways that would enable them intelligently to appreciate the Scriptures that they hear on Sunday and to read the Bible for their own spiritual development». Brown also saw the need to include the elementary elements of

Second, Brown discussed the divergent views regarding philosophy and methodology. He disagreed with Ratzinger's view that a philosophic system underlies the entire methodology. Brown noted that in his training he was never instructed about a philosophic system with which the method should be used. Nor did he see the method as separating word from event. After giving several examples from his own training as an exegete he said:

> all of this causes me to suggest that more frequently we should speak of the philosophy of the practitioners of the method rather than of the philosophy of the method itself. I realize that what the Cardinal has described has been the philosophy of many practitioners of the method, but the tact that I could learn the method entirely differently calls into question whether the flaws are in the method itself[162].

Brown's philosophical concerns were on a different epistemological and hermeneutical level. He critiqued hermeneutical philosophies that deny the ability to know something of the original meaning. «I reject that approach, even if I think it is important what the text says to me now. What the biblical text said to its first readers should be related to what the text says to me, because I am a Christian heir to the people of Israel and the people of the early church, and not independent of them»[163].

Third, Brown explained their different outlooks regarding the future of Catholic exegesis. While he shared Ratzinger's hopes for the future, he did not see it necessary to search for an ideal form of biblical criticism. Rather he was «more interested in a context in which various methods and backgrounds can be brought into play in a complementary way to give us as holistic a view of the Scripture as possible»[164]. In this regard Brown registered a concern with narrative criticism. He said it was fruitful but

---

biblical criticism on this level. Furthermore he criticized the Catholic universities that «play down their religious identity in order to gain governmental subsidies».

c. Secondary and Primary-level Catholic Religious Education. Brown noted that this level is much different than that of Germany. «Many who teach religion in Catholic high schools and grammar schools have had no formal modern training in Bible; they teach religion on the basis of what they learned in their own schooling many years ago, and sometimes on a volunteer level». He found this lack of education disturbing and warned that if there is not greater success by the end of the century, «a large number of American Catholics will succumb not to an exegesis inspired by rationalism and skepticism but to a fundamentalism heard on radio and television».

[162] R.E. BROWN, «Ecumenical Church Discussion», 46.
[163] R.E. BROWN, «Ecumenical Church Discussion», 46.
[164] R.E. BROWN, «Ecumenical Church Discussion», 47.

wondered if people will start to question the historicity of the event since it is not treated by the method[165].

Brown's final comments regarded some criticism raised at the conference regarding the Bible and ethical issues. He noted that one participant complained that the «careful nuances of biblical criticism prevented the Scripture from being used to meet some of the ethical challenges of today»[166]. He responded:

> That is true, but the problem lies not simply in a defect of biblical criticism. In biblical times many of the ethical issues that we encounter were not the focus of reflection, and therefore the biblical responses will not always give clear answers to our ethical issues. Both the teaching church and theological reflection, even if they are (and should be) heavily informed by the Bible, do go beyond the Bible. The Spirit continues to work and that work is not solely in and through biblical interpretation. I agree that the Bible, in a more-than-literal exegesis, can be of enormous help in facing modern issues. Realistically, however, we cannot avoid the question of church teaching that goes beyond the Bible[167].

J.A. Fitzmyer: Historical Criticism and Church Life, 1989. Fitzmyer placed his discussion on the relationship between the HCM and the church in the context of the current debate or «crisis» regarding biblical interpretation[168]. Following an historical presentation on the origins of the method, Fitzmyer described the method[169]. First, he gave a brief description of the method and the rationale for its use.

---

[165] Brown again stressed the importance of the *literal sense* — noting some changes in his upcoming *NJBC* article «Hermeneutics».

[166] R.E. BROWN, «Ecumenical Church Discussion», 49.

[167] R.E. BROWN, «Ecumenical Church Discussion», 49.

[168] J.A. FITZMYER, «Historical Criticism», 244-245. He began the discussion by identifying four groups who criticize the methodology. The first group includes integrists in the Catholic Church who label the method «modernists or neo-modernist», because they see it as emphasizing the human elements in the Bible and not paying sufficient attention to the Bible as the «Word of God». The second group includes liberal Catholics who claim that practitioners of the HCM comprise a «liberal consensus» that is «bringing the church to what can be called the end of Catholicism». The third group is not labeled. Fitzmyer identifies this group through their critique of the method. For this group, the HCM is «overly preoccupied with the prehistory of the text and consequently neglects its final form, its literary features, its canonical setting, and especially the theological meaning of the sacred text». The fourth group are the fundamentalists who insist on a literalist reading of the text refusing «to analyze the text or confront the problems that the text itself present. Problems are not admitted; harmonization of the text is pursued».

[169] Fitzmyer began his presentation with a brief summary on the development of the method. He mentions the use of some critical methods by Origen, Jerome, and

The method is called «historical-critical» because it borrows techniques of interpreting the Bible from historical and literary criticism. It recognizes that the Bible, through containing the Word of God, is an ancient record, composed indeed by a multiplicity of authors over a long period of time in antiquity. Being such an ancient composition, it has to be studied and analyzed like other ancient records. Since much of it presents a narrative account of events that affected the lives of ancient Jews and early Christians, the various accounts have to be analyzed against their proper human and historical backgrounds, in their contemporary contexts, and in their original languages. In effect, this method applies to the Bible all the critical techniques of classical philology, and in doing so it refuses a priori to exclude any critical analysis in its quest for the meaning of the text[170].

Second, he briefly outlined the steps or stages of the HCM. Two steps are borrowed from classical philology: the *introduction* and textual criticism. The *introduction* studies the authenticity of the writing, the integrity or unity of the writing, the date and place of composition, the occasion and purpose of the writing and its historical background. Textual criticism studies the various manuscripts in an attempt to find the best reading of a text. The introduction and textual criticism are followed by literary criticism which is concerned with the literary and stylistic character of the text as well as its content; source criticism which seeks to determine the prehistory of the biblical text; form criticism which seeks to determine the literary form or subform of a particular text; and redaction criticism which «seeks to determine how certain biblical writers using traditional materials, have modified, edited or redacted the sources or whatever they might have inherited from writers or communities before them in the interest of their own literary goal or purpose»[171].

Third, he described the goals of the method as used in NT studies. The goal of the method is to determine the human author's intention when he composed the work. «Since the truth that he has enshrined in his text is analogous to the form used, historical criticism teaches us that we cannot read an ancient text without the sophistication that the form calls for». Regarding NT studies, Fitzmyer added that the method has helped identify the three stages in the transmission of the gospel: what Jesus did and said; what the disciples preached about him, his words, and his deeds; and what

Augustine noting that their exegesis was mostly allegorical or «spiritual». He then described the development of critical method through the twentieth century.

[170] J.A. FITZMYER, «Historical Criticism», 249.
[171] J.A. FITZMYER, «Historical Criticism», 251.

the evangelists wrote about him[172]. Furthermore, «the relationship of stage three to stages one and two is *the* problem for twentieth century readers of these Gospels, and herein lies the crucial need of the HCM of gospel interpretation[173].

After describing the method, Fitzmyer discussed the presuppositions with which the method has been utilized. Although the method is neutral, an exegete's presuppositions will greatly affect the outcome. He stated that the method falls under suspicion today because «it was tainted at an important stage in its development with presuppositions that are not necessarily part of it»[174]. He gave two examples of such presuppositions in the history of exegesis: one is rationalist and antidogmatic, the other demythologizing and existentialist.

Fitzmyer used the life of Jesus research as an example of how a rationalist and antidogmatic presupposition has tainted the use of critical methodology. The presupposition was first pointed out by Schweitzer in his *Quest for the Historical Jesus*. He demonstrated that the work of Reimarus and Strauss, earlier practitioners of the method were «written with hate» — «not so much hate of the person of Jesus as of the supernatural nimbus with which it was so easy to surround him». The rationalist attacks on traditional Christianity, «especially in its supernatural aspects, were linked to an otherwise neutral method and tainted it unduly. What was at fault was the presuppositions with which the method was used, and not the method itself»[175].

Fitzmyer said the work of Schmidt, Dibelius and Bultmann provide an example of a demythologizing existentialist presupposition. Bultmann was the most influential. «He linked historical criticism with a form of kerygamtic theology that depended heavily on Luther's justification by faith alone, D.F. Strauss's mythical interpretation of the Gospels, and M. Heidegger's existentialism». The effect of this was that Bultmann effectively broke down the relationship between the ministry of Jesus and the work of the evangelists in the transmission of the gospel[176].

Fitzmyer then proceeded to explain the Catholic application of the HCM. He began by describing the goals of exegesis. Exegesis is that exercise in which meaning is «drawn out» from the text whether in the words, the phrases or as a whole. The meaning «drawn out» from the text

---

[172] He made reference here to the PBC document *Sancta Mater Ecclesia*.
[173] J.A. FITZMYER, «Historical Criticism», 252.
[174] J.A. FITZMYER, «Historical Criticism», 252.
[175] J.A. FITZMYER, «Historical Criticism», 252.
[176] J.A. FITZMYER, «Historical Criticism», 254.

is that meaning which was intended by the human author. This includes «not only the textual meaning (the sense of its words and phrases — what the medieval meant by the *literal sense*) but also its contextual meaning (their sense in a given paragraph or episode) and its relational meaning (their sense in relation to the book or the corpus of works as a whole)»[177]. The level of relational meaning is the locus for biblical theology. Here the exegete seeks to make an interpretation according to «the synthesis of ideas of the biblical writer. The combination of the textual, contextual, and relational meaning of a passage leads to the discovery of its religious and theological meaning — to its meaning as the Word of God couched in ancient human language[178].

After discussing the goals of Catholic exegesis, he described the pre-suppositions of Catholic exegetes. The exegete approaches the text acknowledging that it

> contains God's Word set forth in human words of long ago; that it has been composed under the guidance of the Spirit and has authority for the people of the Jewish-Christian heritage; that it is part of a restricted collection of sacred, authoritative writings (part of a canon); that it has been given by God to His people for their edification and salvation; and that it is properly expounded only in relation to the Tradition that has grown out of it within the communal faith-life of that people[179].

Fitzmyer concluded this section noting again that the method itself is neutral. The pre-suppositions with which it is used determine its orientation. Because the method is neutral further refinements are possible.

> New modes of biblical interpretation are proposed from time to time — some of them claiming to be of even a «post-critical» nature — and some of them serve to correct or refine the basic critical method....What is valid in the modes can be used to refine the basic method, but none of them is a substitute for that fundamental approach — nor can they be allowed to replace it[180].

The final topic in this article is the interpretation of the Bible and the life of the church. Fitzmyer highlighted the principles of critical exegesis recommended by the church. The basis of such research was the search for the *literal sense*. He noted that «Pius XII realized that the *spiritual sense* of Scripture, clearly intended by God, could not be something other than "the literal meaning of the words, intended and expressed by the sacred

---

177 J.A. FITZMYER, «Historical Criticism», 254.
178 J.A. FITZMYER, «Historical Criticism», 254.
179 J.A. FITZMYER, «Historical Criticism», 255.
180 J.A. FITZMYER, «Historical Criticism», 255.

writer"», and that the interpreter is bound to «disclose and expound this spiritual significance, intended and ordained by God»[181]. He then discussed the 1964 PBC document *On the Historical Truth of the Gospel* the substance of which was taken up by the Second Vatican Council in *Dei Verbum*. The section concluded with a consideration of the 1984 PBC document *Bible et christologie*. The document does not deal directly with the question of biblical methodology however it does refer to «the demands of biblical criticism which it clearly distinguishes from "critical hypotheses ... always subject to revision"»[182]. The basis for the critical approach is the belief that «God's revelation in Christ took place in the past, and the ancient record of that self-manifestation of God in him is disclosed to the church above all in the Bible, in the Word of God couched in ancient human wording»[183]. Fitzmyer saw this as the fundamental reason for the necessity and importance of the HCM for the church. «This, of course, is not to deny the guidance and assistance of the Spirit in church life. Yet that Spirit is never conceived of as a revealer. The Spirit guides the church through the centuries into a fuller and deeper understanding of the historical revelation once given in Christ Jesus»[184]. Fitzmyer acknowledged that a meaning beyond the historical biblical author is possible,

> but such a «meaning» that goes «beyond» that of the historical biblical author can never be understood as losing all homogeneity with the meaning of the original author. However, such a meaning that goes «beyond» the original biblical meaning may become part of the Spirit-guided post written status of the text, viz. that which results in genuine dogmatic Tradition.

---

[181] J.A. FITZMYER, «Historical Criticism», 256.

[182] The document noted the complexity of such questions. Fitzmyer quoted the document: «Indeed, many problems still remain obscure about the composition process of the sacred writings that finally emerged from their inspired authors. As a result, those who would dispense with the study of problems of this sort would be approaching Scripture only in a superficial way; wrongly judging that their way of reading Scripture is «theological», they would be setting off on a deceptive route. Solutions that are too easy can in no way provide the solid basis needed for studies in biblical theology, even when engaged in with full faith. (1.3.3)».

[183] J.A. FITZMYER, «Historical Criticism», 257.

[184] J.A. FITZMYER, «Historical Criticism», 258.

Fitzmyer concluded the article addressing the burdens placed on readers by the method[185]. The final article considered in this section is J. Wicks' review of the 1988 Rockford Conference.

J. Wicks: Biblical Criticism Criticized, 1991. Wicks reviewed the published lectures of the 1988 Rockford Conference and noted two significant items that were absent from the discussions: a discussion on the relationship between faith and the mediating word, and the place of Scriptures in day-to-day Christian activities.

Wicks suggested that exegesis can be and is practiced without the «deleterious assumptions about history and human understanding which Cardinal Ratzinger targeted in his speech»[186]. Exegetical study, however, is limited even when it reaches a close approximation to the original meaning because the ultimate value «in Christian life is faith's graced dynamic of movement into union with God. Faith is such that it transcends both biblical and ecclesial mediations, as it is brought into communion of life with Father, Son and Spirit»[187]. The biblical text and message is an intermediate point along the course of faith's movement into the reconciling and life-giving presence of the triune God.

An especially apposite sign of the point we are making is the fact that no reference to writing, even to inspired writing, nor to Scripture as written text, occurs in Chapter I of Vatican II's Constitution of Divine Revelation (*DV* 2-6). Revelation and faith certainly have a relation to Scripture, and the following chapters of the Constitution spell this out with all desirable clarity. But revelation and faith transcend Scripture. This consideration could well be raised in the debate over exegesis and interpretation, in order to promote a proper sense of proportion, based on a theological discernment between ultimate values and intermediate or penultimate concerns[188].

Wicks saw the interpretations resulting from exegetical studies as essential for two day-to-day activities widely practiced in the church: systematic theology and preaching. These activities «are properly, even inevitably, constrained to deal with particular questions or topics. The theologian must treat specific doctrines and the homilist must work from

---

185 The final two comments Fitzmyer made regarding scripture and the life of the church are: a call to recognize the difficulties regarding interpretation and the need to consult exegetical studies — cf. 2 Peter 3:15-17 and Acts 8; and praise for the role of the HCM in ecumenical discussions.

186 J. WICKS, «Biblical Criticism Criticized», 125.

187 J. WICKS, «Biblical Criticism Criticized», 126.

188 J. WICKS, «Biblical Criticism Criticized», 127.

individual texts chosen for liturgical reading»[189]. Wicks noted the need for the theologian to consult at least the best commentaries on the relevant issues. He wrote: «if exegesis has not played some role along the way, and if the final results are not homogeneous with what the texts originally meant, then the theologian must be faulted for not working at the level of seriousness required by his or her discipline and evocation»[190]. The preacher benefits also from consulting critical exegesis. The lectionary gives an essential orientation to preaching, an orientation is directed toward quite particular passages and not toward a global vision of revelation. The Sunday cycle and even more practically the weekday cycle call for attention to critical exegesis. Although the preacher cannot simply offer his community the results of critical exegesis such exegesis can be an incredible aid in homily preparation.

> Immediate reflections on words and sentences of a modern translation runs its own risk of passage via a short-circuit to an actualization for contemporary faith and life. Here the scholarly commentary can well play a protective role, and can perhaps be an appositive stimulant and guide to the preacher, at least at one point along the road traversed from the text to the homily. If the homilist has a sequence of texts to transmit and actualize over a given period of time, as in the daily liturgical preaching, the help of competent scholarship would seem even more relevant, especially in guarding against the facile moralizing on biblical passages that especially afflicts Catholic communities of worship[191].

Summary. Ratzinger recognized that the method's claim to objectivity has often times given the appearance of certitude to exegetical results, a certitude that is unreal. The claim of objectivity also fails to give proper attention to the interaction between the interpretation and the exegete. In his critique of the method as practiced by Bultmann and Dibelius he identified the flawed presuppositions that have radically affected the results of their exegesis. He further warned that practitioners today have been greatly influenced by these two exegetes and should address this influence in a «self-criticism» of the methodology. The «self-criticism» will not do away with critical exegesis but will call for a new synthesis of the method. He suggested that in the new synthesis exegetical methods cannot make claims to certitude on the basis of methodology; reconsideration should also be given to the event-word relationship; and the event represented by the word must be considered and respected.

---

189 J. WICKS, «Biblical Criticism Criticized», 127.
190 J. WICKS, «Biblical Criticism Criticized», 127.
191 J. WICKS, «Biblical Criticism Criticized», 128.

Brown, in his discussion of critical exegesis and ecumenism, acknowledged the philosophic presuppositions of eighteenth and nineteenth century exegesis but says that those presuppositions are not used by centrist exegetes of the present. He suggested that the benefit of using the Scriptures for ecumenical discussions is that the text provides a control for those discussions, a focal point, so to speak. Similar to Ratzinger he affirmed that critical exegesis is limited in its nature. The method cannot exhaust the meaning of the text. Broader interpretation, sometimes called a *spiritual sense*, is necessary yet this too has its limitations. He recommended that other methodologies might be used in interpretation but when historical questions are raised they should be considered using an historical approach. Regarding the question of doctrine and its relationship to biblical views, Brown proposed following a line of development to see how certain expressions were accepted and incorporated into dogmatic formula and how others were rejected. He also proposed the use of critical exegetical studies in ecumenical discussion that adequately represent differing views. Such details can provide a means of clarification, nuance and understanding.

Brown continued the discussion in his Addenda commenting on the convergences and divergences with Ratzinger's presentation. The convergences were viewing Scripture as divine and human; historical criticism has made an enduring contribution to biblical scholarship; honest recognition of the limits of the method is needed; and an honest nonarbitrary way of going beyond the limits is necessary. He saw the divergences due to the different academic settings from which he and Ratzinger came. Bultmann and Dibelius may have had a great influence on Catholic educators in Germany but not in America. Brown noted several other problems regarding critical exegesis and religious education in the United States. The divergences also regard philosophical issues. While Ratzinger criticized the philosophical underpinnings of the method, Brown saw the presuppositions as tied to the exegete not the method. He also raised some concerns about hermeneutical systems that deny the relevance of the human author's intention. Regarding the future of biblical studies Ratzinger proposed looking for an ideal form of biblical criticism while Brown sought a more «holistic» approach, the results of complementary methods.

Fitzmyer's contribution to the discussion is that he clarified the questions regarding the place of the HCM within Catholic exegesis[192]. In his

---

[192] F. RAURELL, «Lettera plurale del testo», also gave a presentation on the HCM as well as describing the structuralist approach. He saw as complementary a diachronic

article he gave definition to the terms in the discussion: the HCM, its techniques and goals; the goals of the Catholic use of HCM; and the presuppositions with which a Catholic exegete approaches the text[193]. He also gave a concise yet detailed analysis of what he means by «historical-critical method». A description of the «historical» and «critical» aspects of the method were also given. The list of the technical procedures and their purposes are indicated. The goal of the method, that is, identifying the author's intention, was clarified. Following the description he demonstrated both the neutrality of the method and the effect of the exegete's presuppositions on exegetical work. Catholic presuppositions were identified. The goal of Catholic exegesis using the HCM is to draw out the meaning of the text: textual, contextual, and relational. The relational included the meaning within the entire corpus. Biblical theology develops at this level. The presuppositions with which the exegete approaches the text are: the Scriptures are God's word in human words; the Scriptures are inspired and authoritative; the Scriptures are contained in a restricted canon; the Scriptures are properly expounded only in relation to the tradition and are interpreted within the communal faith-life of the church. Fitzmyer's article was a major contribution to the discussion especially regarding the clarification of terms and the Catholic understanding of the HCM. Particularly important was the movement toward a distinction between historical criticism and the HCM, for the discussion and debates up to this point rarely noted a distinction between the two approaches. Fitzmyer's presentation has numerous parallels with the first part *Interpretation of the Bible in the Church*.

J. Wicks suggested placing the debate within the broader context of faith. He notes the importance of the journey of faith that rises above exegesis and theological reflection. He proposed that this be included in the discussions. On a more practical level he considered the necessity of critical exegesis in systematic theology and preaching. These two disciplines usually address particular issues or passages. Critical exegesis is necessary because it also addresses particular biblical texts prior to addressing

---

and synchronic method. Fitzmyer, however, approaches the topic from a specifically Catholic understanding of the method and the context in which it is used. For this reason the article was more apt for this presentation.

[193] Prior to Fitzmyer's description, the defense of Catholic exegesis using HCM confined itself to an explanation of its results in coordination with magisterial directives especially regarding the *literal sense*. His description provides a clearer understanding of how a Catholic exegete defines and uses the method within the Catholic framework.

generalities. If theology and homiletics are to retain credibility they need to consider the results of exegesis.

9. Conclusion

The ten years that preceded the PBC's 1993 document *Interpretation of the Bible in the Church* were filled with discussions and debates on many different levels regarding biblical interpretation in the Church. This chapter has examined eight aspects of the pastoral and scholarly situation of this period that provides the background for the 1993 document. The period has been described as a crisis in biblical interpretation. The term crisis is an apt description of the period due to the convergence of the debate in several areas of church life as well as in several different although related fields of theological discipline. Concerns were raised in this period from different sectors of church life. Pastoral concerns had been raised regarding the gap between exegetical study and faithful reading of the Scriptures. Schneiders, Vanni, Brown, Konstant, all alluded to the problem during this period. Magisterial concerns were reflected in the 1985 Synod of Bishops and the 1989 ITC document. The Synod noted several aspects of *Dei Verbum* that modern exegesis has failed to implement[194]. In 1989 the ITC presents the relationship between critical exegesis and theology in terms of a conflict. In the academic world, the debates concerning critical method and biblical interpretation involved the individual disciplines of biblical studies, philosophical hermeneutics and fundamental theology. The place of the HCM in Catholic exegesis was the center of the debate. Ratzinger, in his description of the crisis, noted that this method has led to confusion and reaction. Part of the reaction was an increase in fundamentalism on hand and materialistic and feminist approaches on the other hand[195]. Another factor that contributed to the crisis was the lack of clarification regarding two particular areas: the description of the method and the practice of the method by Catholic exegetes. Because of this the discussion was in a sense scrambled and lacked a clear focus. *Interpretation of the Bible in the Church* helped clarify some of these issues. The conclusion now summarizes some of the primary concerns regarding the HCM raised in this debate.

---

[194] Specifically the directives dealing with pneumatic exegesis and pastoral application. The pneumatic aspect was also noted by de la Potterie, the pastoral application by Vanni.

[195] Konstant notes two problems of the day are fundamentalism and the failure to consider the sacramentality of the Scriptures; however, he does not relate these to the HCM.

The need for carefully nuanced discussion. Clarification of the debate was one of the problems that intensified the crisis. Early in the period the reaction over *The Birth of the Messiah* led to discussion on the method however the chief concerns and criticisms raised against the work did not deal with the method but the results of the study. Added to this even more important for the point was the lack of precision in the criticisms being raised against modern Catholic exegetical work. As mentioned above, these have been clearly identified by Brown in «Liberals, Conservatives». In later articles he continued to urge carefully nuanced discussions. He also encouraged discussions be based on method as practiced today, not as it has been practiced in the past[196]. Fitzmyer provided much clarification to the debate in his description not only of the method but the principles with which Catholic exegetes use the method as distinguished from the presuppositions of the past[197].

Problems with the Method. The main problems with the method that were identified in the debate are summarized here. First, critical exegesis as it has been practiced in the past, claimed an ability to make definitive conclusions regarding interpretation. Ratzinger and D'Ambrosio have noted the problems with this claim[198]. Modern hermeneutical studies would concur[199]. Second, critical exegesis does not seriously consider the spiritual or pneumatic aspect of the Scriptures. As mentioned above, the 1985 Synod of Bishops raised this concern[200]. De la Potterie lamented the split between the letter and the spirit in critical exegesis has not been mended in exegetical practices today[201]. Third, historical criticism is concerned with facts rather than truth; this leads to an over particularized

---

[196] R.E. BROWN, «Ecumenical Church Discussion», 31.

[197] J.A. FITZMYER, «Historical Criticism», 255.

[198] J.A. RATZINGER, *Biblical Interpretation in Crisis*, 6ff. M. D'AMBROSIO, «Henri de Lubac», 377ff.

[199] P. GRECH, «Hermeneutics», 418-421 for a summary of the thought of Schliermacher, Dilthey, and Gadamer in this regard. For a more detailed study see R.E. PALMER, *Hermeneutics*.
R.E. BROWN, «Ecumenical Church Discussion», 31, however, acknowledges a certain ambiguity in the results of scholarship. But at the same time there are ambiguities in the text that need to be considered. He does not see this as a negative criticism of the method, for the ambiguity can lead to discussion on the various trajectories. See summary above.

[200] For English version see: Origins 15.27, 441-450.

[201] I. DE LA POTTERIE, «Reading the Holy Scripture», 322-323. See Farkasfalvy and D'Ambrosio for similar concerns.

study of texts[202]. Fourth, the HCM is too isolated from other theological studies[203]. Fifth, the critical approach has not taken the canon seriously[204]. Sixth, Ratzinger argued that the method is corrupted by the radical division of form-content and kerygma-event[205]. Seventh, he also offered two criticisms of the method as practiced in the past: the method has disintegrated the text and faith has been divorced from the method[206]. Eighth, the method is inadequate to address the pastoral needs of the faithful. Vanni addressed this from the perspective of *Dei Verbum*'s directives concerning exegesis and actualization. Schneiders alluded to this in her article concerning the academy and the church.

Presuppositions and the method. The presuppositions with which the method developed has also raised some concerns. Several different views have been expressed in this chapter. D'Ambrosio noted the need to identify these pre-suppositions in the method because they interfere with the proper function of the method and in-effect lead to a new dogmatism[207]. Ratzinger developed a similar theme in his discussion[208]. Brown responded with the emphasis that the method is not tainted by presuppositions but rather the exegetes who use the method are influenced by presuppositions[209]. He also noted that centrist biblical scholars do not approach the text with the rationalistic presuppositions that were present in the development of the method. Fitzmyer concurred calling the method neutral, but warning about faulty presuppositions that have influenced exegetes in the past[210]. At the same time he described the presuppositions with which Catholic exegetes should approach the text.

Meaning Beyond the Literal Sense. It is an undisputed point that the quest for the author's intention or the *literal sense* is the goal of the

---

202 M. D'AMBROSIO, «Henri de Lubac», 377. De Lubac refers to this as «hyper-criticism».

203 This is reflected in the breakdown of the patristic and medieval synthesis that resulted in the critical studies. See the treatment of de la Potterie and D'Ambrosio above. D. FARKASFALVY, «In Search of a "Post-Critical" Method», 300, sees this also reflected in the breakdown in theological renewal (patristic, liturgical, and biblical) in the post-war era.

204 D. FARKASFALVY, «In Search of a "Post-Critical" Method», 303.

205 J.A. RATZINGER, *Biblical Interpretation in Crisis*, 9-12.

206 J.A. RATZINGER, *Biblical Interpretation in Crisis*, 2.

207 M. D'AMBROSIO, «Henri de Lubac and the Critique of Scientific Exegesis», 378.

208 J.A. RATZINGER, *Biblical Interpretation in Crisis*, 7.

209 R.E. BROWN, «Ecumenical Church Discussion», 45-46. He also acknowledges, 31, that exegetes have used the method in an impartial way.

210 J.A. FITZMYER, «Historical Criticism», 252.

HCM[211]. The discussions on meaning during this debate included the question of multiple and dynamic meaning, in other words, meaning beyond the literal. This was discussed above while considering the *spiritual sense* and pneumatic exegesis. It was also considered in the context of pastoral theology and hermeneutics. The pastoral questions were raised in Schneiders' article. She noted the validity and value of different approaches. Grech discussed the question in light of practice in the early church, indeed in the Bible itself, as well as from the perspective of modern hermeneutics. He observed that in the early church Origin saw the need for seeing the spiritual meaning within the literal meaning. The two were not isolated senses, distinct perhaps, but certainly related. Furthermore, meaning was discerned in the context of the canon, the rule of faith, and the magisterium. Meaning beyond the *literal sense* in the Bible was noted when considering re-readings and re-interpretations of earlier events in the light of latter situations in salvation history[212]. The *literal sense* also needs to be considered within the larger spectrum of the interpreter and the text. At the same time Grech insisted that the link with the *mens auctoris* cannot be broken[213]. Brown and Fitzmyer acknowledged that meaning may go beyond the *literal sense*[214] but this meaning must have a homogenous relationship with the *literal sense*.

Benefits of the Method. The benefits of the method were also discussed during this period. The basic defense of the method is its ability to determine the *literal sense*. The historical separation between the text and the present reader require an historical or diachronic approach. These arguments have been presented earlier in the paper, and mentioned several times above so they will not be reiterated. Other benefits of the method were also referred to in the discussions of this period. Brown, in his discussion on the Catholic education in the United States, held that critical exegesis can help prepare the faithful for educated evaluation of arguments based on the Bible raised by the fundamentalist approach, teleevangelists, and the mass media[215]. He also described the benefits of the HCM for ecumenical discussions[216]. The critical approach helps in understanding the different strands of thought emerging in the early church. Studying the ways in which these trajectories have developed can aid in

---

[211] See above or R.E. BROWN – S.M. SCHNEIDERS, «Hermeneutics», 1148-1149.
[212] P. GRECH, «Hermeneutics», 418.
[213] P. GRECH, «Hermeneutics», 423.
[214] R.E. BROWN – S.M. SCHNEIDERS, «Hermeneutics», 1153 and J.A. FITZMYER, «Historical Criticism», 254, 258.
[215] R.E. BROWN, «Communicating», 6-9.
[216] R.E. BROWN, «Ecumenical Church Discussion», 33-37.

ecumenical discussion. Fitzmyer specifically defended the role of historical criticism in analyzing the relationship between stage III and stage I of
the gospel transmission (terms from *Sancta Mater Ecclesia*). Revelation
is historically grounded and conditioned, the witness of such revelation in
the Bible requires some elements of historical study[217]. Wicks saw the
additional benefit of critical exegesis is beneficial for systematic theology
and preaching in its consideration of specific passages and texts[218].

The Future of the HCM in Catholic Biblical Studies. The debates also
contained suggestions for the future of Catholic biblical studies[219]. The
suggestions that are related to the HCM are summarized here. Farkasfalvy
saw a new «post-critical» method that will reflect the integrated exegesis
of the period just after *Divino Afflante Spiritu*[220]. D'Ambrosio sought to
move beyond the segmented approach to a synthetic exegesis that sees the
HCM in its proper place[221]. Ratzinger's views suggested a new synthesis
that differentiates itself from the principles used in natural science and
holds together the form and content. He also remarked that exegesis
needs to be done in the Church, its results be considered within the history of exegesis. At the same time he appreciated the indispensable contributions of philological and scientific literary criticisms[222]. Fitzmyer acknowledged that the newer methods can supplement the HCM but cannot
replace it[223]. The ITC document maintained that the HCM and the newer
approaches to be fruitful cannot become autonomous disciplines but must
be practiced within the faith life of the Church[224]. Brown admitted that the
HCM alone is insufficient to exhaust the meaning from the text so sup-
plemental methods are needed to determine the more-than-*literal senses*
of a text[225]. He noted that all exegesis must consider both the human and
the divine aspects of the text. He was optimistic about the future of
Catholic exegesis seeing the development of complementary methods and
their integration with the HCM: «I am more interested in a context in

---

[217] J.A. FITZMYER, «Historical Criticism», 252.

[218] J. WICKS, «Biblical Criticism Criticized», 128-129.

[219] For similar suggestions from the earlier period see: L. SWAIN, «The Interpretation of the Bible» (*HCTIS*, 116-118); T. PETERS, «The Use of Analogy» (*HCTIS*,
120-123); F. DREYFUS, «Exégèse en Sorbonne» (*HCTIS*, 177-182); R. PESCH,
«Exegese als Wissenschaft» (*HCTIS*, 192-194).

[220] D. FARKASFALVY, «In Search of a "Post-Critical" Method».

[221] M. D'AMBROSIO, «Henri de Lubac», 387.

[222] J.A. RATZINGER, *Biblical Interpretation in Crisis*, 21-23.

[223] J.A. FITZMYER, «Historical Criticism», 255.

[224] ITC, *On the Interpretation of Dogmas*, 11.

[225] R.E. BROWN – S.M. SCHNEIDERS, «Hermeneutics», 1153.

which various methods and backgrounds can be brought into play in a complementary way to give us as holistic a view of the Scripture as possible»[226].

---

[226] R.E. BROWN, «Ecumenical Church Discussion», 47.

CHAPTER VI

The Interpretation of the Bible in the Church

The third period of Catholic critical scholarship is represented by the PBC's *Interpretation of the Bible in the Church*. The previous chapter described the pastoral and scholarly context that led to the document. By the early—to mid—1980's discussions regarding biblical interpretation in the church had turned into a debate. This debate was eventually referred to as a «crisis» involving three arenas — the academic, pastoral and magisterial. The PBC document was the official church's response to this crisis. Work on the document began in 1989 under the direction of the Secretary of the PBC, H. Cazelles and continued in 1990 under the direction of his successor A. Vanhoye. The Commission completed the work in December of 1992[1].

---

[1] A. VANHOYE, «L'interpretazione», 5-11, described the development of the document. H. Cazelles solicited monographs on particular themes from the members of the PBC. In the plenary session of 1989, they were presented and discussed. Three subcommissions were then formed to work on a schema for a synthetic document. The first outline for the proposed document was divided into three chapters: a) the description and value of diverse methods of interpretation; b) indications of other dimensions of Catholic interpretation; and c) reflection on the relationship between exegesis and other theological disciplines and with the pastoral ministry. The PBC discussed this schema at the plenary session of 1991. In this session all the parts of the schema were discussed. After the meetings, the observations were collated and translated into French. In January 1992, all the members were asked to submit observations and criticisms. This became the subject matter for the plenary session in April. This session concluded with a vote on the major or controversial issues. After this session, the work was revised again. Final emendations were made before the text was finalized in the December session of 1992.

The members of the PBC from 1989-1992 included: a) those completing terms in 1989 — H. Cazelles, P.L. Monsegwo, J.E. Terra, J.-D. Dominique, J. Dupont, J. Gnilka, A. Jankowski, J.F. McHugh, and J. Pathrapankal; b) those on the commis-

The immediate occasion for its publication was commemoration of the one-hundredth anniversary of Leo XIII's *Providentissimus Deus* and the fiftieth anniversary of Pius XII's *Divino Afflante Spiritu*. Cardinal Ratzinger, Prefect of the Congregation for the Doctrine of the Faith and the President of the PBC, presented *Interpretation of the Bible in the Church* to Pope John Paul II on April 23, 1993.

This chapter studies the document in a manner consistent with the earlier presentations on ecclesial documents. The chapter contains three sections. The first section briefly describes the introductory documents to *Interpretation of the Bible in the Church*. These documents are Pope John Paul II's «Address» and Cardinal Ratzinger's «Preface». The second section presents a summary of the contents of *Interpretation of the Bible in the Church* along with a discussion of the HCM as exposed in the document. The third concludes the chapter with an evaluation of the place of the HCM in Catholic exegesis according to the PBC document[2].

1. Introductory Documents

1.1 *John Paul II's Address on* Interpretation of the Bible in the Church

After receiving *Interpretation of the Bible in the Church* from Cardinal Ratzinger, John Paul II gave an address praising the document. The Pope began his remarks by thanking Cardinal Ratzinger for taking the initiative to confront the question of biblical interpretation. He referred to this question as «a vital problem». After noting the anniversaries of *Providentissimus Deus* and *Divino Afflante Spiritu*, he considered the following: the development and changing attitudes toward biblical studies in the years between the two encyclicals[3], the harmony between Catholic exegesis and the mystery of the incarnation, and the new PBC document[4]. The

---

sion for the duration of the project — M. Dumais, J. Fitzmyer, J. Lambrecht, J. Loza Vera, D. León Muñoz, G. Ravasi, L. Ruppert, G. Segalla, A. Vanhoye, J.-L. Vesco; c) those who began there term in 1990 — J. Briend, B.N. Burtubla, B. Byrne, A. Fuchs, A.J. Levoratti, J.R. Raja, H. Ritt, A. Schenker, L.R. Stachowiak; d) A. Mouhanna began his term in 1991. (Source: *Annuario Pontificio*, 1989, 1990, 1991, 1992)

[2] The English translations and references are taken from the Libreria Editrice Vaticana edition of *Interpretation of the Bible in the Church*.

[3] JOHN PAUL II, *Address*, §5. *EB* §1244, English trans., 11. In this section John Paul recalls how each document preserved the incarnational aspect of the Scriptures while facing different difficulties. (see Chapter III, page 42).

[4] JOHN PAUL II, *Address*, §12-15. *EB* §1253-1257. English trans., 17-20. He specifically praises the following three characteristics of the document: the spirit of open-

theological import of this address is the pontiff's evaluation of the incarnational aspects of Catholic exegetical principles.

John Paul presented the complexities of interpreting the inspired text using incarnational imagery. He noted that the parallelism between the Scriptures (in their composition and collection) and the incarnation provides a basis for understanding their complex nature. The written Word of God was part of the preparation for the incarnation of the Word of God. These written words became «an abiding means of communication and communion between the chosen people and their one Lord» and because of their prophetic aspect «it was possible to recognize the fulfillment of God's plan». The writings of the new covenant attest to the Word's presence among us in an abiding way. «Joined to the writings of the first covenant ... [they] are a verifiable means of communication and communion between the believing people and God, the Father, Son and Holy Spirit»[5].

The realism of the incarnation causes the church to place great importance on the historical-critical study of the Bible that includes the identification and study of literary forms. John Paul noted that some Christians take the opposite approach seeing the words of the text as having an absolute value independent of the conditions of human language. The fundamental error involved in this approach is a false idea of God.

> The God of the Bible is not an absolute Being who, crushing everything he touches, would suppress all differences and all nuances. On the contrary, he is God the Creator, who created the astonishing variety of beings «each according to its kind», as the Genesis account says repeatedly. Far from destroying differences, God respects them and makes use of them. Although he expresses himself in human language, he does not give each expression a uniform value, but uses its possible nuances with extreme flexibility and likewise accepts its limitations. That is what makes the task of exegetes so complex, so necessary and so fascinating! None of the human aspects of language can be neglected[6].

The complexity of the text requires diligent study of all the new methods.

At the same time the divine aspect of the scriptures cannot be neglected. «First and foremost, it [Catholic exegesis] must help the Christian people more clearly perceive the word of God in those texts so that they can bet-

---

ness to various approaches to the text, the synthesis of balance and moderation, and its stress on the fact that «the biblical Word is at work speaking universally, in time and space, to all humanity».

5 JOHN PAUL II, *Address*, §6. *EB*, §1245. English trans., 12.
6 JOHN PAUL II, *Address*, §8. *EB*, §1247. English trans., 14.

ter accept them in order to live in full communion with God». In this regard four qualities are necessary for exegetes. First, they should have a «vigorous spiritual life» that sustains the intellectual work[7]. Second, they should manifest a fidelity to the church that recognizes true exegesis as communitarian not individualistic[8]. Third, exegetes need to place their studies within the framework of the Tradition and the Magisterium[9]. Fourth, they must remain close to the preaching of God's word «by devoting part of their time to this ministry and by maintaining relations with those who exercise it and helping them with publications of pastoral exegesis»[10].

1.2 Cardinal Ratzinger's «Preface»

In the beginning of his «Preface», Cardinal Ratzinger noted that the study of the Bible, the soul of theology, is a never-ending endeavor. The emergence of the HCM opened a new era in the history of exegesis. The method has contributed to a deeper understanding of the text. Yet the method also has hidden dangers such as the over-emphasis of the past «so that it [biblical text] is no longer taken in its actuality», and the over-emphasis on the human dimension of the text at the expense of its divine aspect[11]. Ratzinger points out that anything which aids in understanding the truth is worthwhile for theology: «It is in this sense that we must seek how to use this method in theological research. Everything that shrinks our horizon and hinders us from seeing and hearing beyond that which is merely human must be opened up». The emergence of the HCM set in motion a discussion (that continues today) of its scope and proper configuration[12], including questions surrounding the «methodological spectrum» of current exegetical work. The debates prompted the PBC to consider the task of interpretation of the bible. This resulted in the

---

[7] JOHN PAUL II, Address, §8. EB, §1248. English trans., 15.

[8] JOHN PAUL II, Address, §8. EB, §1249. English trans., 15.

[9] JOHN PAUL II, Address, §8. EB, §1251. English trans., 16.

[10] JOHN PAUL II, Address, §11. EB, §1252. English trans., 17. He continues «Thus they will avoid becoming lost in the complexities of abstract scientific research which distances them from the true meaning of the Scriptures. Indeed, this meaning is inseparable from their goal, which is to put believers in to a personal relationship with God».

[11] J.A. RATZINGER, «Preface». EB, §1259. English trans., 25.

[12] J.A. RATZINGER, «Preface». EB, §1260. English trans., 25. The Cardinal also notes that the document is not seen as an end of the discussion but rather a contribution to it.

Interpretation of the Bible in the Church[13]. Cardinal Ratzinger saw the significance of the document as containing

> a well-grounded overview of the panorama of present-day methods and in this way offers to the inquirer an orientation to the possibilities and limits of these approaches. Accordingly, the text of the document inquires into how the meaning of scripture might become known — this meaning in which the human word and God's word work together in the singularity of historical events and the eternity of the everlasting Word that is contemporary in every age. The biblical word comes from a real past. It comes not only from the past however, but at the same time from the eternity of God and leads us into God's eternity, but again along the way through time, to which the past, the present and the future belong[14].

2. *The Interpretation of the Bible in the Church*

The evaluation of *Interpretation of the Bible in the Church* that follows is similar to the treatment of the other ecclesial documents discussed in the Chapters Three and Four. The first section summarizes the contents of the document[15]. The second section presents the HCM as exposed in the document.

2.1 *The Contents of the Document*

Interpretation of the Bible in the Church begins with an introduction that sets forth the state of the question today. The introduction describes the current state of confusion in the church regarding biblical interpretation and, in particular, the use of the HCM in Catholic exegesis[16]. The

---

13 J.A. RATZINGER, «Preface». *EB*, §1262. English trans., 26. Cardinal Ratzinger also notes the new role of the PBC after Vatican II. It is no longer an organ of the teaching office, «but rather a commission of scholars who, in their scientific and ecclesial responsibility as believing exegetes, take positions on important problems of scriptural interpretation». In this way they «enjoy the confidence of the teaching office».

14 J.A. RATZINGER, «Preface». *EB*, §1262. English trans., 27.

15 Additional bibliography for the individual sections and topics addressed in the document can be found in J.A. FITZMYER, «The Interpretation of the Bible in the Church» and G. GHIBERTI – F. MOSETTO, *L'Interpretazione della Bibbia nella Chiesa*.

16 The document notes that through out the history of the church the question of interpretation has «continually been raised». The current state of confusion was discussed in Chapter V. The document also acknowledges the major contributions the HCM has made in biblical studies. These include the advancement of scholarly research in the academic world, the opening of avenues to ecumenical discussion, a renewal in theology that resulted from more attention to the Bible and an increased interest in the Bible

method is brought into question by scholars and faithful alike. On the one hand, scholars have witnessed a multiplication of methods used in biblical studies. Some see this as a sign of richness; others as a sign of confusion. On the other hand, the faithful see the HCM as deficient from the standpoint of faith[17]. The «state of confusion» has caused some critics of the HCM to suggest the substitution of the method with simpler approaches. These approaches include the following: some form of synchronic reading; a «spiritual» reading guided by personal inspiration; a reading that seeks the Christ of «their own personal vision»; a reading that simply addresses the problems of life today — immediate answers to all kinds of questions; and a sectarian approach that proposes «as the only way of interpretation one that has been revealed to them alone». The goal of the document is

> to attend to the criticism and the complaints, and also to the hopes and aspirations which are being expressed in this matter, to asses the possibilities opened up by the new methods and approaches and finally, to try to determine more precisely the direction which best corresponds to the mission of exegesis in the Catholic church[18].

The document addresses the question of biblical interpretation in four parts. The study begins with the various exegetical methodologies whose validity is the immediate concern of current debate. The document then takes a step beyond exegesis to the philosophical-theological understanding of hermeneutics. Methods and approaches must fit into the broader category of how the act of understanding written texts takes place (regarding written texts in general and the biblical texts in particular).

---

among Catholics. For more detailed information on this last point see the following: J.A. CRAMPSEY, «Scripture and the Church»; D. KONSTANT, «The Use of the Bible»; R. MAHONY, «The Bible»; G. O'COLLINS, «*Dei Verbum* and Biblical Scholarship»; M. VIDAL, «The Relationship». Notably absent from the document's presentation is the polemic that was present in the earlier period.

[17] See S.M. SCHNEIDERS, «Church and Biblical Scholarship in Dialogue». T. CURTIN, *HCTIS*, 134, summarizes J. AUDINET, «The Banquet of Scripture». He notes that the insufficiency is recognized by the faithful: «The historical approach to the text is a necessary preliminary for a genuine encounter with the text, and essential if one is to avoid an anecdotal or magical view of the Bible, but on its own it leads to a dead end. This has been the bitter discovery of many catechists who have tried this approach on children and adolescents». He goes on to state that «adult groups at least have the advantage that they soon realize that they are looking for something else, and that they want something from Scripture beyond *what happened*, even when it has been expertly explained on the basis of the results of the latest scholarship».

[18] The Commission notes that it will not address all questions relating to the Bible (e.g. inspiration), only those questions on methodology and interpretation.

Following this discussion the document situates the exegetical-hermeneutical endeavor in the context of the Catholic faith. The final section presents the work of interpreting God's word, which speaks in time and place, to the living church today. The organization of the discussion moves from a narrow focus to a broad vision or framework of interpretation. The four parts of the document are summarized below (see figure nine on page 236).

Part One: Methods and Approaches. The initial part of the document presents and evaluates the various methodologies and approaches used today in biblical interpretation[19]. Each method or approach is governed by distinctive sets of rules used to aid interpretation. They are essentially limited in their function. For this reason «Catholic exegesis does not claim any particular scientific method as its own»[20].

The methodologies and approaches are divided into two groups: diachronic and synchronic. Diachronic methodology is presented first. The HCM is the subject of this presentation (see below, page 245). The synchronic approaches are presented in the following categories: new literary methods (rhetorical, narrative, and semiotic analyses); approaches based on tradition (canonical approach, recourse to Jewish traditions of interpretation and *Wirkungsgeschichte*); approaches based on human sciences (sociological, cultural-anthropological, and psychological-psychoanalytical) and contextual approaches (liberationist and feminist). The commission briefly describes and evaluates each method. The descriptions outline the rules or principle procedures of the method. The evaluations identify the benefits and limits of each method. The section concludes with a criticism of the fundamentalist approach to interpretation[21].

Part Two: Hermeneutical Questions. The second part of the document places the question of methodology within the broader context of hermeneutical understanding. The PBC addresses the question of understanding the Bible in two ways. First, using modern hermeneutics the Bible is considered as a written text. Second, using the *senses of Scripture* the Bible is discussed as an inspired text.

---

[19] *EB*, §1274. English trans., 33. In a footnote the terminology is explained: «By an exegetical "method" we understand a group of scientific procedures employed in order to explain texts. We speak of an "approach" when it is a question of an inquiry proceeding from a particular point of view».

[20] *EB*, §1423. English trans., 85.

[21] J.A. RATZINGER, *Biblical Interpretation in Crisis*, 5, used the contextual and the fundamentalist approaches to describe two fringe reactions to historical-critical exegesis. He notes their limits in reference to the rejection of historical-critical exegesis.

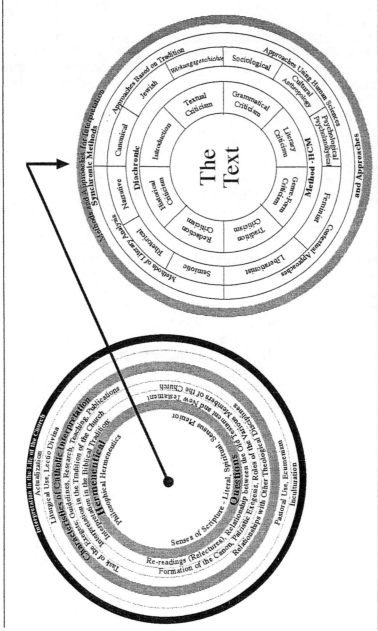

The Framework for Catholic Biblical Interpretation
As presented in the 1993 PBC Document *Interpretation of the Bible in the Church*

Figure 9: The Framework for Catholic Biblical Interpretation

The first section notes the contribution of modern philosophical hermeneutics with regard to the act of understanding the written text. Particular attention is given to the approaches formulated by Bultmann, Gadamer, and Ricoeur. Modern hermeneutics is significant for biblical interpretation because it demands the «incorporation of the methods of literary and historical criticism within a broader model of interpretation»[22], and so continue the interpretive task of bringing the Word of God to all ages. The characteristics of biblical hermeneutics stem from its object:

> The events of salvation and their accomplishment in the person of Jesus Christ give meaning to all human history. New interpretation in the course of time can only be the unveiling or unfolding of this wealth of meaning. Reason alone cannot fully comprehend the account of these events given in the Bible. Particular presuppositions, such as the faith lived in ecclesial community and the light of the Spirit, control its interpretation. As the reader matures in the life of the Spirit, so there grows also his or her capacity to understand the realities of which the Bible speaks[23].

The second section describes the hermeneutical implications arising from the inspired nature of the Bible. The document addresses the plurality of meaning in biblical texts. Modern theories of language and hermeneutics affirm that written texts are open to a plurality of meaning. Describing this plurality in the Bible is particularly complex due to the presence of numerous literary forms. The inspired character of the Scriptures (in their composition and collection) allows meaning to be described in terms of the senses of scripture: the *literal sense*, the *spiritual sense*, and the *sensus plenior*[24].

The *literal sense*, according to the PBC, is «that which has been expressed by the inspired human authors»[25]. Usually a text has one *literal*

---

[22] *EB*, §1396. English trans., 75.

[23] *EB*, §1401. English trans., 77.

[24] The concept of multiple senses is consistent with earlier ecclesial documents as well as exegetical practice (see Chapters II–IV). The insistence of singular meaning by historical-critical exegetes was a reaction to movements that placed an external meaning on the text detached completely from the *literal sense*. The theory of singular meaning has never fully withstood its critics. The proponents of multiple meaning point to the limitations imposed by the *literal sense* and its failure to convincingly treat re-readings and meaning exposed through the unity of the canon.

[25] *EB*, §1407. English trans., 79. See also: *Divino Afflante Spiritu, EB,* 550. *OCT,* 740; *Dei Verbum* §12. *EB*, §689. *OCT,* §971. The description of the *literal sense* has developed in this document. The earlier descriptions in *Divino Afflante Spiritu* and *Dei Verbum* associated the sense with the author's intention. This description has come under attack in recent times. *Interpretation of the Bible in the Church*

sense; it can, however, have several for the following reasons: «a human author can intend to refer at one and the same time to more than one level of reality»; and «even when a human utterance appears to have only one meaning, divine inspiration can guide the expression in such way as to create more than one meaning»[26]. Thus the text has a dynamic aspect in which a fuller understanding of the meaning can come at a latter time. Here exegesis «should seek rather to determine the direction of thought expressed by the text; this direction, far from working towards a limitation of meaning, will on the contrary dispose the exegete to perceive extensions of it that are more or less foreseeable in advance»[27]. Re-readings in particular have shown how a text can gain new meaning when placed into a new context.

The *spiritual sense* is a meaning beyond the *literal sense*. «The paschal event, the death and resurrection of Jesus, has established a radically new historical context, which sheds fresh light upon the ancient texts and causes them to undergo a change in meaning»[28]. In light of the paschal mystery a *spiritual sense* may emerge from the text. Thus «we can define the *spiritual sense*, as understood by Christian faith, as the meaning expressed by the biblical texts when read, under the influence of the Holy Spirit, in the context of the paschal mystery of Christ and of the new life which flows from it»[29]. The document clarifies two points regarding the

---

uses a new definition or description of the *literal sense*. The new definition does not mention the author's intention rather confines the literal meaning to the «words expressed by the human author». The reformulation allows for a broader understanding of the text all the while respecting the historical condition and value of the original meaning. The new description continues to require the use of the HCM for the *literal sense* is «ascertained by a careful analysis of the text, within its literary and historical context, according to its ancient literary genre and according to the literary convention of its time of composition». J.A. FITZMYER, *The Biblical Commission's Document*, 120 notes the significance of the change. (The question of the *literal sense* will be discussed again below and in Chapter VII).

[26] The document notes the tendency of exegetes using the HCM to seek a single meaning in the *literal sense*. In the earlier debate J.L. MCKENZIE, «Interpretation» and R.E. BROWN, «Hermeneutics» argued for a singular meaning.

[27] *EB*, §1409. English trans., 80. For a similar explanation see R.E. BROWN – S.M. SCHNEIDERS, «Hermeneutics», 1157.

[28] *EB*, §1412. English trans., 81.

[29] *EB*, §1413. English trans., 81. *Interpretation of the Bible in the Church* describes the *spiritual sense* more precisely than previous ecclesial statements. *Providentissimus Deus* states that the *literal sense* should not be departed from «except only where reason makes it untenable or necessity requires» (*EB*, §112; *OCT*, §322). Yet «there is sometimes in such passages a fullness and a hidden depth of meaning which the letter hardly expresses and which the laws of interpretation hardly warrant. Moreover, the

relationship between the two senses. First, there is not necessarily a distinction between the two senses. A text already has a *spiritual sense* in the *literal sense* if the text refers to the paschal mystery or the new life resulting from it. Second, when there is a distinction between the two, the *spiritual sense* can never be stripped of its connection with the *literal sense*; if this happens one could no longer speak of a «fulfillment» of the Scriptures. Thus, spiritual interpretation is only possible when three levels of reality are held together: the biblical text, the paschal mystery and the present circumstances of life in the Spirit[30].

The *sensus plenior* is that meaning intended by God but not clearly expressed by the human author. The document notes that at times rereadings as well as internal developments in revelation can indicate a *fuller sense* (e.g. Matt 1:23). The document suggests that the *fuller sense* is actually a *spiritual sense* in instances where the *spiritual sense* is distinct from the *literal sense*. The *fuller sense* is guaranteed by the Holy Spirit who «can guide human authors in the choice of expressions in such a way that the latter will express a truth the fullest depths of which will be more fully revealed in the course of time — on the one hand, through further

---

literal sense frequently admits other senses, adapted to illustrate dogma or to confirm morality» (*EB* §108, *OCT* §316). *Divino Afflante Spiritu* allows for a *spiritual sense* «provided it be clearly intended by God» (*EB*, §552; *OCT*, §743). Pius specifically uses the relationship of the OT and NT in this regard. *Dei Verbum* likewise notes a *spiritual sense* in relation to the canonical nature of the Scriptures but stresses the spiritual in the literal by way of the human author, since he is inspired, his intention is reflective of the divine intention (*DV* §12-13. *EB*, §688-691. *OCT*, §970-973). *Interpretation of the Bible in the Church* associates the *spiritual sense* with a christological understanding particularly related to the OT while allowing a typological aspect when tied to the way a biblical text describes an ancient reality.

The term *spiritual sense* or «spiritual exegesis» has also been used in the recent debate. Part of the concern raised by exegetes has been the lack of clarity for the expression. For example, D. FARKASFALVY, «In Search of a "Post-Critical" Method», 305, saw the *spiritual sense* as a «an exegesis that sees the exegete and his word also as part of the unified and universal salvation history and thus about an exegesis that is capable of discovering valid analogies between the salvific meaning of the ancient text and the actual saving deeds of the same God through the same Christ». De la Potterie called for a pneumatic exegesis which regarded the *spiritual sense* in a very general terms as God's abiding presence in the church. The clarification of the term *spiritual sense* in *Interpretation of the Bible in the Church* may alleviate some of the reservations exegetes had regarding the ambiguity of the expression (R.E. BROWN – S.M. SCHNEIDERS, «Hermeneutics», 1157 and J.A. FITZMYER, «Historical Criticism», 244).

[30] *EB*, §1417. English trans., 82.

divine interventions which clarify the meaning of texts and, on the other, through the insertion of texts into the canon of Scripture»[31].

Part Three: Characteristics of Catholic Interpretation. The third part of the document places the exegetical-hermeneutical discussion within a particularly Catholic understanding of biblical interpretation. The document notes that Catholic exegesis «deliberately places itself within the living tradition of the church, whose first concern is fidelity to the revelation attested by the Bible»[32]. Exegetes must approach the text in the same living tradition in order to understand the text. In this way they will have an affinity with the text and the proper pre-understanding necessary for understanding the text. The exegete, aided with this pre-understanding, can examine the historical character of the text while giving due attention to the Word of God. The primary characteristics of such exegesis are summarized as: christological, canonical and ecclesial (see below, page 256).

Part Three is divided into four sections. The Commission describes the practice of Catholic interpretation from the historical perspective, beginning with biblical interpretation in the text itself then in the living tradition of the church. Following this succinct overview, the role of the Catholic exegete is presented in activities as diverse as exegesis, research, teaching and publications[33]. The final section presents the place of exegesis within

---

[31] *EB*, §1422. English trans., 84. The *fuller sense* or *sensus plenior* has not been mentioned in an ecclesial document prior to *Interpretation of the Bible in the Church.* The term here is carefully presented and warning is given to avoid subjective interpretation. It is included to help explain the meaning of texts that have been continually understood to mean something in light of the whole content of revelation that seems to be distinct from the original intention. The *fuller sense* is another way of speaking of the meaning of a text in the light of the entire canon and revelation. For further reading see bibliographic references in Chapter IV, footnote 7.

[32] *EB*, §1224. English trans., 85.

[33] It is important to recognize educational levels of the reading audience when presenting the results of critical exegesis (e.g. seminaries, religious houses of study, universities). Attention should be given to the literary, historical, social, and theological values of the texts. A balance should be struck between a «synthetic exposition» and «in-depth treatments» (Similar to the instructions for seminary training in *Providentissimus Deus* (*EB* §108-117; *OCT* §316-328). R.E. Brown addresses the use of the HCM in catechetical/educational setting in the following articles: «Ecumenical Church Discussion», 36-46; «Hermeneutics», NJBC, 1164-1165; «Communicating». Printed publications as well as other means of communication (radio, television, etc.) should complement teaching. Again it should be recognized that regardless of the academic backgrounds of audiences targeted, it is important for Catholic exegetes to participate at all levels (highly academic to popular).

the broader spectrum of Catholic theology, specifically its relationship to systematic and moral theology.

Catholic exegetes approach the text with a pre-understanding that holds together both «the modern scientific culture and the religious tradition emanating from Israel and the early Christian community». The result is an awareness of the dynamic progression of understanding[34]. This dynamic understanding has been part of biblical interpretation from the earliest times. It is particularly exemplified by re-readings and the interrelatedness of the testaments[35]. The document also reminds exegetes and theologians that one of the primary characteristics of the Bible is the absence of systematization: «The Bible is a repository of many ways of interpreting the same events and reflecting upon the same problems. In itself it urges us to avoid excessive simplification and narrowness of spirit»[36].

Dynamic understanding of the text continues to develop in the tradition of the church. The document points out the role of the Holy Spirit in the development of a deeper understanding and «progressive clarification» of the received revelation[37]. The formation of the canon and patristic exegesis

---

[34] U. VANNI, «Exegesis and Actualization», 350, sees this dynamism suggested in *Dei Verbum* — a dynamism that suggests «a continuous, almost infinite development in which there is always some element to be discerned with regard both to the understanding of the meaning of the text and its explanation».

[35] *EB*, §1434. English trans., 88. The relationship is not one of «simple correspondence» but rather one of «mutual illumination» and «a progress that is dialectic».

The Commission notes the following consequences for biblical interpretation today based on the inter-biblical interpretation: a) Since the Scriptures have come into existence on the basis of a consensus of a believing community, a similar consensus on essential matters is required by the living community of faith; b) The interpretation of the Bible should involve some aspect of creativity; new questions should be asked and responded to «out of the Bible»; c) Interpretation must show a certain pluralism. «No single interpretation can exhaust the meaning of the whole which is a symphony of many voices»; d) Interpretation takes place in the heart of the church: in its plurality and its unity, and within its tradition of faith; e) Interpretation requires full participation on the part of the exegete in the life and faith of the believing community of their time; f) Interpretation of the Scripture involves the work of sifting and setting aside; it stands in continuity with earlier exegetical traditions, many elements of which it preserves and makes its own. In other matters, however, it will go its own way, seeking to make further progress.

[36] *EB*, §1349. English trans., 90.

[37] I. DE LA POTTERIE, «Reading Holy Scripture "In the Spirit"», 323-324, saw the HCM as deficient in this regard. He notes the Father's ability to incorporate a study of the *literal sense* into the much broader *spiritual sense*. Though his definition of *spiritual sense* may be too broad he recognizes a dynamic aspect to understanding in the meaning of a text that has to be addressed. He suggests the developing a type of *Wirkungsgeschichte* as a remedy.

hold an important place in this clarification. With the formation of the canon the «texts ceased to be merely the expression of a particular author's inspiration; they became the common property of the whole people of God»[38]. The Fathers of the church who had a particular role in the formation of the canon also had «a foundational role in relation to the living tradition which unceasingly accompanies and guides the church's reading and interpretation of Scripture»[39]. This particular contribution is «to have drawn out from the totality of Scripture the basic orientations which shaped the doctrinal tradition of the church, and to have provided a rich theological teaching for the instruction and spiritual sustenance of the faithful»[40]. The living tradition continues to the present guaranteeing the

---

R.E. BROWN, «Ecumenical Church Discussion», 29, also sees an importance in mapping out the connection between the text's original meaning and its later understanding. He describes this as a «line of development» moving from the *literal sense* to the *more-than-literal senses*. He sees the identification of the strands of interpretation that the various churches have followed as helpful for ecumenical discussions.

J.A. FITZMYER, «Historical Criticism», 258, acknowledges that meaning may go beyond the historical biblical authors' intention «in the Spirit guided post-written status of the text that results in genuine dogmatic tradition». Fitzmyer believes the study of such meaning is beyond the scope of the biblicist and is more properly within the realm of the dogmatic theologian. This limitation may be too restrictive especially regarding re-readings and canonical interpretation. See John Paul II, *Address*,§5, *EB*, §1244. English trans., 11, «Determining the *spiritual sense*, then belongs itself to the realm of exegetical science».

[38] *EB*, §1449. English trans., 93.

[39] *EB*, §1454. English trans., 95.

[40] *EB*, §1454. English trans., 95. The importance of the Fathers for biblical studies today is clarified in this document more than in previous documents. *Providentissimus Deus* suggested the Fathers as authoritative guides especially regarding interpretations on faith and morals (*EB*, §110; *OCT*, §321). *Divino Afflante Spiritu* acknowledged that patristic exegesis was «distinguished by a certain subtle insight into heavenly things and by a marvelous keenness of intellect, that enables them to penetrate to the very innermost meaning of the divine word and bring to light all that can help elucidate the teaching of Christ and promote holiness of life» (*EB*, §554; *OCT*, §745). *Dei Verbum* mentioned the importance of patristic studies for better understanding of the Scriptures, but does not give particular guidelines for their use. The PBC document is more specific in addressing the value of patristic exegesis. It gives two reasons explaining why patristic exegesis must be taken seriously. First, the Fathers' had an intimate role in the formation of the canon, providing, in a sense, the «human element» in the process of canonization. Second, the Fathers' appreciation of the christological, canonical and ecclesial aspects of biblical interpretation make them valuable examples of Catholic exegesis. The Fathers are not so much examples for biblical methodology but for a proper implementation of exegesis within a broader context. The document was less keen in praising the continuation of the Fathers' allegorical style. The document states «whatever its pastoral usefulness might have been in the

members of the church a role in interpretation. All the faithful have a role in the interpretation of the Scriptures: the bishops, priests and deacons, presiders at the eucharistic community, educators in the faith, individual Christians, and exegetes. Yet the responsibility for *authentic* interpretation belongs to the Magisterium alone. Thus, exegesis is not an isolated exercise but takes place within a living tradition.

Part Four: Interpretation of the Bible in the Church. The fourth part of the document deals with interpretation in the life of the church and covers three specific areas: actualization, inculturation, and the use of the scriptures in the liturgy. Actualization is reading the biblical text in the contemporary situation. In other words, it seeks to hear the biblical message for the present day. The extra-historical value is possible because the Word of God is addressed to all people and in all times. The aim of actualization is to respect the circumstances of the past while hermeneutically addressing it to the present[41]. The document encourages a careful practice of actualization so that a purely subjective reading is avoided[42]. Inculturation arises from reading the text within a specific geographical context (as dif-

---

past, modern exegesis cannot ascribe true interpretive value to this kind of procedure» (see *Divino Afflante Spiritu, EB*, §553).

R.E. BROWN – S.M. SCHNEIDERS, «Hermeneutics», 1164. Brown sees the role of the Fathers pertaining more to dogmatic theology than to biblical studies due to their heavily *more-than-literal* approach. However, he does acknowledge the need to «emulate the success of the fathers in having the Bible nourish the faith, life, teaching, and preaching of the Christian community». See also C. KANNENGIESSER, «The Bible».

41 *EB*, §1511-1520. English trans., 115-116. The living tradition of the community aids in the process. The methods vary. The following are the three steps are involved in actualization: «a) to hear the Word from within one's own concrete situation; b) to identify aspects of the present situation highlighted or put in question by the biblical text; c) to draw from the fullness of meaning contained in the biblical text those elements capable of advancing the present situation in a way that is productive and consonant with the saving will of God in Christ» As mentioned in the previous chapter, U. VANNI, «Exegesis and Actualization», 356, sees actualization as a possible means of verifying the results of exegetical endeavors. He sees a reciprocal relationship as providing a deeper understanding of the text involved. X. LÉON-DUFOUR, «Qu'attendre d'un exégète?» (*HCTIS*, 147) sees the need for the exegete to recognize the theological truth in the scriptures as they have been recognized through time — this is the place where actualization takes place. For the views of B. Maggioni and F. Dreyfus regarding actualization see *HCTIS*, 280-294.

42 False readings are specifically mentioned including the following: tendentious interpretations that use the text for a personal agenda; fundamental theoretical principles at variance with the general orientation of the bible (rationalism, atheistic materialism); and readings contrary to evangelical charity (racial segregation, anti-Semitism, sexism).

ferentiated from actualization which regards a temporal separation). It involves two steps. First, translations of the Scriptures into modern languages. Second, an interpretation is given «which would set the biblical message in more explicit relationship with the ways of feeling, thinking, living, and self-expression which are proper to the local culture»[43]. The final section of part four deals with the use of the bible in the church. Four particular areas are mentioned: the liturgy[44], *lectio divino*[45], pastoral ministry[46] and in ecumenical discussions[47].

---

[43] *EB*, §1525. English trans., 118. Additionally a process of «mutual enrichment» occurs: «On the one hand, the treasures contained in diverse cultures allow the Word of God to produce new fruits and, on the other hand, the light of the Word allows for a certain selectivity with respect to what cultures have to offer: harmful elements can be left aside and the development of valuable ones encouraged». This is similar to Vanni's views on actualization, see footnote 42.

[44] *EB*, §1528-1534. English trans., 119-120. In the liturgy «the written text becomes the living word», through which Christ speaks to his church. The renewal following the Vatican II added a new emphasis to the Bible: in the emphasis on the homily, the re-organization of the lectionary, the Liturgy of the Word element in the celebrations of the Sacraments, and in the Liturgy of the Hours. For more on the interaction between exegesis and the liturgy see D. KONSTANT, «The Use of the Bible within the Church» and J. WICKS, «Biblical Criticism Criticized», 127-128.

[45] *EB*, §1535-1538 . English trans., 121. *Lectio Divino* is a reading on the group or individual level of the biblical texts which, prompted by the Holy Spirit, leads to «meditation, prayer and contemplation». Widely practiced in the early church and especially successful in the «golden age of monasticism» it is once again being utilized in church life.

[46] Pastoral ministry also includes the use of the Scriptures. Three areas are identified: catechesis, preaching and the biblical apostolate. Catechesis, the explanation of the Word of God, has sacred Scripture as its first source. «Catechesis should proceed from the historical context of divine revelation so as to present persons and events of the OT and NT in the light of God's overall plan». Various kinds of hermeneutic will be employed leading to various types of commentary. The document warns against a superficial presentation (chronological presentation of names, events, dates, etc.).

Preaching entails drawing spiritual sustenance from the ancient texts, adapted to the present needs of the Christian community. «The explanation of the biblical texts given in the course of the homily cannot enter into great detail. It is, accordingly, fitting to explain the central contribution of texts, that which is most enlightening for faith and most stimulating for the progress of Christ life, both on the community and individual level».

The biblical apostolate has numerous means for promoting the Bible as the word of God and the source of life. Methods include: translation of the bible into modern languages, formation of study groups, conferences on the Bible, publication of journals, and propagating the Bible through mass media.

[47] The ecumenical movement seeks to restore the unity of God's people. «Most of the issues which the ecumenical dialogue has to confront are related in some way to the interpretation of biblical texts». The issues discussed in the movement are various:

Conclusions of the Document. The document identifies two specific conclusions to its presentation on biblical interpretation. The first is that «biblical exegesis fulfills, in the church and in the world, an indispensable task»[48]. The second is that «the very nature of biblical texts means that interpreting them will require continued use of the HCM at least in its principal procedures»[49]. The primary caution is to recognize its limitations. The conclusions will be discussed in the next section.

2.2 *The HCM as Exposed in the Document*

The debate over the HCM and its place in Catholic exegesis prompted the PBC to write *The Interpretation of the Bible in the Church*. The document adds to the discussion by providing a comprehensive treatment on the topic of interpretation. The previous section gave a survey of the document's contents. This section examines the HCM as presented in the document. The PBC treats the method primarily in «Part One: Methodologies and Approaches». Other references to the method will be considered in the next section of this chapter.

The first part of the *Interpretation of the Bible in the Church* deals with the methods and approaches for interpretation. The HCM is the first method treated in this section. The presentation is divided into four sections: the history of the method, the principles of the method, description of the method and an evaluation[50].

History of the Method. The presentation begins by stating that the HCM is «the indispensable method for the scientific study of the meaning of ancient texts»[51]. The document then describes its historical development. It roots the method in the patristic period, particularly in the works of Origen, Jerome and Augustine (see Chapter II of this thesis). The development expanded greatly in the Renaissance with the *recursus ad fontes*. Textual criticism developed first, followed by literary criticism, form criticism and redaction criticism. The document mentions several signifi-

---

theological issues (eschatology, admission of women to the ministerial priesthood), canonical and juridical issues (administration of the universal and local churches), and strictly biblical issues (canon, hermeneutical questions). Exegesis has greatly helped in ecumenical discussions.

48 *EB*, §1555. English trans., 128.

49 *EB*, §1557. English trans., 129.

50 The presentation has numerous similarities with Fitzmyer's presentation in «Historical Criticism: Its Role in Biblical Interpretation and Church Life» especially in the description of the method. Refer to Chapter I for a more in-depth description of the method and additional bibliography.

51 *EB*, §1275. English trans., 34.

cant theories proposed by the HCM[52]. The section concludes «all this has made it possible to understand far more accurately the intention of the authors and editors of the Bible, as well as the message that they addressed to their first readers. The achievement of these results has lent the HCM an importance of the highest order»[53].

Principles of the Method. The «principles» section defines the method as «historical», «critical», and «analytical». The method is «historical» because it studies the Bible from an historical point-of-view, «...and above all because it seeks to shed light upon the historical processes which gave rise to biblical texts, diachronic processes that were often complex and involved a long period of time»[54]. As a «critical» method «it operates with the help of scientific criteria that seek to be as objective as possible»[55]. As an «analytical» method it studies the text as any other ancient writing; redaction criticism allows «the exegete to gain a better grasp of the content of divine revelation»[56].

Description of the Method. The «description» section briefly presents the method's component disciplines: textual, linguistic (morphology and syntax) and semantic analysis, literary criticism, genre criticism, tradition criticism, redaction criticism and (if applicable) historical criticism[57]. After redaction criticism the interpretation is given in two ways. First, the text is «explained as it stands on the basis of the mutual relationships between its diverse elements, and with an eye to its character as a message communicated by the author to his contemporaries» Second, the demands of the text are considered from the perspective of action and life.

Evaluation of the Method. The «evaluation» section makes an assessment of the method as practiced today. First it states that the method, «when used in an objective manner, implies of itself no *a priori*»[58]. The document notes that the early practice of scientific exegesis was marred at times by a conscious separation from faith[59]. However, in the present

---

[52] *EB*, §1276. English trans., 35. Specifically mentioned are the Documentary Hypothesis and the Two Source Theory. The mention of practitioners is limited to R. Simon, H. Gunkel, M. Dibelius, and R. Bultmann.

[53] *EB*, §1278. English trans., 37.

[54] *EB*, §1279. English trans., 37. The commission

[55] *EB*, §1280. English trans., 37. See below for a discussion on the limits of objectivity (page 256).

[56] *EB*, §1280. English trans., 37. Perhaps this evaluation is oversimplified.

[57] For an in-depth description of the method see Chapter I of this dissertation.

[58] *EB*, §1285. English trans., 39. For more on the presuppositions of the exegete and its influence on interpretation see below, page 254.

[59] *EB*, §1286. English trans., 39. The «classical» use of the method shows its limits in two ways. First, it has no concern for «other possibilities of meaning which

form this is no longer the norm; in fact, the method has led to «a more precise understanding of the truth of sacred Scripture». Additionally the method's identification of literary forms is necessary for determining the *literal sense* as called for by *Divino Afflante Spiritu.* The use of the newer synchronic methods is legitimate but cannot replace a diachronic approach[60]. The section concludes by recalling the goal of the ḤCM — «to determine, particularly in a diachronic manner, the meaning expressed by the biblical authors and editors», and by encouraging the use of the HCM in conjunction with other methods and approaches.

3. **The Place of the HCM in Catholic Exegesis**

The debate over the HCM that prompted writing of the *Interpretation of the Bible in the Church* (see Chapter Five) addressed variously related issues concerning the proper place of the HCM in Catholic exegesis. Several authors suggested a broader vision of the interpretive endeavor. This was never realized because the authors tended to focus on particular issues[61]. The current PBC document presents the overall framework for Catholic biblical interpretation and in doing so identifies the place of the HCM in Catholic exegesis as necessary but limited. This section of the chapter identifies and discusses the necessity, limits and possibilities for overcoming the limits of the HCM in Catholic exegesis as presented in *Interpretation of the Bible in the Church.*

---

have been revealed at later stages of the biblical revelation and history of the Church» (*EB*, §1287. English trans., 40). Second, it emphasizes form over content. The document notes that this limitation has been corrected through a more diversified semantics and the evaluation of the text from the point-of-view of action and life. See the previous chapter for Ratzinger's critique of the form-content separation. For an in-depth study of the early practice see R.A. HARRISVILLE – W. SUNDBERG, *The Bible in the Modern Culture.*

[60] *EB*, §1289. English trans., 40. «We must take care not to replace the historicizing tendency, for which the older historical-critical exegesis is open to criticism, with the opposite excess, that of neglecting history in favor of an exegesis which would be exclusively synchronic». The document is clear regarding the value of the HCM for Catholic exegesis. However the document is just as clear that the HCM is not sufficient in itself for interpretation because «no scientific method for the study of the Bible is fully adequate to comprehend the biblical texts in all their richness». The additional methods suggested in Part One of *IBC* are also limited in the interpretation they give to a text. The shortcomings of these methods lie primarily in the fact that they are synchronic methods. When speaking of the limitations the document suggests the supplementation of the diachronic (ḤCM) approach as a corrective. Perhaps it would be better to suggest that the HCM ought to be the foundational approach with other methods providing a broader perspective. See below, 252 and 260.

[61] See the conclusions at the end of Chapter V.

3.1 Why is the HCM necessary?

The PBC document *Interpretation of the Bible in the Church* defended the use of the HCM in Catholic exegesis as a necessary component of Catholic biblical interpretation. The second point of the conclusion calls for its continued use: «...the very nature of the biblical texts means that interpreting them will require continued use of the *historical-critical method*, at least in its principal procedures»[62]. The following list gives the principal reasons identified or implied in the document for using the HCM in Catholic exegesis.

The Bible is historically conditioned and therefore requires the HCM for understanding the texts. The need for historical-critical exegesis is due to the fact that the Bible is a compilation of various ancient texts composed in different places, by different people, over a long period of time[63]. In other words, the Scriptures are an historically conditioned collection of writings. Since the process of composition of the sacred texts happened through time (diachronic), the method used to study the text requires a diachronic *element* for a proper understanding[64].

Another aspect of historical conditioning that the document acknowledges is the *historical character* of biblical revelation which must be taken seriously «for the two testaments express in human words bearing the stamp of their time the historical revelation communicated by God in various ways, concerning himself and his plan of salvation. Consequently,

---

[62] *EB,* §1557. English trans., 129.

[63] EB, §1275. English trans., 34. The opening statement on biblical methodologies states: «the HCM is the indispensable method for the scientific study of the meaning of ancient texts. Holy Scripture, inasmuch as it is the "Word of God in human language", has been composed by human authors in all its various parts and in all the sources that lie behind them. Because of this, its proper understanding not only admits the use of the method but actually requires it».

[64] *EB,* §1279. English trans., 37. This does not exclude viewing the text as a «classic» that can have a life of its own. The method does not exhaust the meaning of a text but enables the reader to gain insight to it on another level. An easy example is phraseology and idiom. If certain words or phrases have a peculiar nuance or usage then the average reader approaching the text may only have a limited access to the meaning, subtle differences will not be comprehended. Another example concerns historical references in Psalm 137. The allusion to Babylon may or may not be understood by the reader. If the reader understands the historical reference to the exile then the imagery in the rest of the psalm will be richer in significance. In these cases the HCM provides access to an aspect of meaning that may not be addressed otherwise. The concept of the Bible as a «classic» with a life of its own after the author's composition was discussed above (see below, footnote 101).

exegetes have to make use of the HCM»[65]. The document points out the benefits of this type of study:

> Exegesis creates, in particular, a more lively and precise awareness of the historical character of biblical inspiration. It shows that the process of inspiration is historical, not only because it took place over the course of the history of Israel and of the early church, but also because it came about through the agency of human beings, all of them conditioned by their time and all, under the guidance of the Spirit, playing an active role in the life of the people of God[66].

The importance of the HCM as linked to the historical conditioning of the biblical texts is noted several times in the document. This union must be kept in mind by exegetes[67] in their exegetical publications[68], and in seminary and catechetical instruction[69].

---

[65] *EB*, §1474. English trans., 102. See also *EB*, §1556. English trans., 128. «The eternal Word became incarnate at a precise period of history, within a clearly defined cultural and social environment. Anyone who desires to understand the Word of God should humbly seek it out there where it has made itself visible and accept to this end the necessary help of human knowledge». The document does not discuss the question of biblical inspiration. Perhaps a discussion on inspiration in light of modern hermeneutic theory would have been helpful. See P. GRECH, «Language of Scripture», 166-174.

[66] *EB*, §1490. English trans., 109. At the same time the text has a value that is absolute, in the sense that it is beyond the historical. This value is «open both to interpretation and to being brought up-to-date which means being detached, to some extent, from its historical conditioning in the past and being transplanted into the historical conditioning of the present».

[67] *EB*, §1499. English trans., 111. «The primary task of exegete is to determine as accurately as possible the meaning of the biblical texts in their own proper context, that is, first of all, in their particular literary and historical context and then in the context of the wider canon of Scripture» This statement is made in the context of the discussion of the relationship between systematic theology and exegesis. The goal described here of studying the text from a literary and historical perspective necessitates the HCM. The second part of this goal will require a supplementation or modification of the HCM for exegesis (see below under limits of HCM).

[68] *EB*, §1486. English trans., 106. «This requires that exegetes take into consideration the reasonable demands of educated and cultured persons of our time, clearly distinguishing for their benefit what in the Bible is to be regarded as secondary detail conditioned by a particular age, what must be interpreted as the language of myth and what is to be regarded as the true historical and inspired meaning. The biblical writings were not composed in modern language nor in the style of the twentieth century. The forms of expression and literary genres employed in the Hebrew, Aramaic, or Greek text must be made meaningful to men and women of today, who otherwise would be tempted to lose all interest in the Bible or else to interpret it in a simplistic way that is literalist or simply fanciful».

[69] See above footnote 33.

The identification of the literal sense requires the HCM[70]. The PBC, echoing *Divino Afflante Spiritu*, affirmed that the *literal sense* as one of the primary goals of exegesis. «According to *Divino Afflante Spiritu*, the search for the *literal sense* of Scripture is an essential task of exegesis and, in order to fulfill this task, it is necessary to determine the literary genre of texts, something which the HCM helps to achieve»[71]. Later in the document the PBC clarifies the definition of *literal sense* used in *Divino Afflante Spiritu* as that «which has been expressed directly by the inspired human author»[72]. The new definition, while giving more possibility for broader interpretation, still requires the use of HCM:

> One arrives at this sense (*literal sense*) by means of a careful analysis of the text, within its literary and historical context. The principal task of exegesis is to carry out this analysis, making use of all the resources of literary and historical research, with a view to defining the *literal sense* of the biblical texts with the greatest possible accuracy. To this end, the study of ancient literary genres is particularly necessary[73].

Actualization and inculturation require the use of the HCM. Actualization and inculturation are two processes by which the ancient biblical text is understood a setting differentiated by time and space. The change of setting brings with it a new context for understanding; for that understanding to be true to its historical expression, some connection to the original meaning is necessary. At least some elements of the HCM are required for these processes to be properly grounded and avoid a purely subjective interpretation.

The HCM is needed for the process of actualization for it begins with a correct exegesis that includes «determination of its *literal sense*. Persons engaged in the work of actualization who do not themselves have training

---

[70] For a fuller discussion on the literal see below: 255 under the heading — The HCM tends toward a narrow interpretation of the biblical text.

[71] *EB*, §1286. English trans., 39. See also 36-37, following the brief history of the method the document states: «All this has made it possible to understand far more accurately the intention of the authors and editors of the Bible, as well as the message that they addressed to their first readers. The achievement of these results has lent the historical-critical method an importance of the highest order».

[72] *EB*, §1407. English trans., 79. «how it [study of Sacred Scripture] deserves the kind of attentive and objective study that will allow a better appreciation of its literary, historical, social and theological value. They [exegetes] cannot reset content simply with the conveying of a series of facts to be passively absorbed but should give a genuine introduction to exegetical method, explaining the principle steps, so that students will be in a position to exercise their own personal judgment»

[73] *EB*, §1407. English trans., 79.

in exegetical procedures should have recourse to good introductions to Scripture; this will ensure that their interpretation proceeds in the right direction»[74].

Inculturation includes translating the text into modern languages[75]. The document states:

> The first stage of inculturation consists in *translating* the inspired Scripture into another language. ... A translation, of course, is always more than a simple transcription of the original text. The passage from one language to another necessarily involves a change of cultural context: concepts are not identical and symbols have a different meaning, for they come up against other traditions of thought and other ways of life[76].

Translation requires attention to the historical conditioning of language thus requires at least some elements of the HCM[77].

The HCM is necessary for understanding the ancient techniques of exegesis which in turn are necessary for understanding «re-readings» and the NT's use of the OT. Catholic exegesis requires an appreciation of the unity of the Scriptures based primarily on a christological understanding of history. The Christ-event makes it necessary to read the OT in the fullness of its significance. The document presents this theme in several sections including the discussion of the *spiritual sense*, «rereadings», and canonical interpretation. The presence of inter-biblical interpretation requires not only an appreciation of the divine action recognized through the *spiritual sense* and canonical interpretation, but also from the human perspective of ancient techniques of exegesis. The HCM can aid in the identification of these techniques. This in turn leads to a better understanding of the texts involved. Exegetes must however take care not to place the exegetical requirements of today on the biblical authors. They should rather «acquire a knowledge of ancient techniques

---

74 *EB*, §1514. English trans., 115.

75 Following *Dei Verbum*.

76 *EB*, §1523. English trans., 118. The document, 124, lauds the work of the *biblical apostolate* that has worked diligently in providing biblical translations in every language so that the Bible may be made known as the Word of God and the source of life. See R.E. BROWN – S.M. SCHNEIDERS, «Hermeneutics», NJBC, 1147.

77 Also involved here is the translating into a level most appropriate for the audience who is hearing the word. The different English translations many times characterized by dynamic equivalent and formal correspondence are valuable in that they can serve different educational and maturity levels (i.e. children, adolescents, adults).

of exegesis, so as to be able to interpret correctly the way in which a scriptural author has used them»[78].

The HCM is required to supplement synchronic methodologies and approaches to the bible. The document notes numerous types of synchronic methodologies and approaches that are being used today in exegetical studies. Synchronic studies focus their attention on the text in its final form. The document points out the benefits of such studies but also suggests that they be supplemented by diachronic studies (HCM) as well. Specific references are made to the following approaches: rhetorical criticism[79], narrative analysis[80], semiotic analysis[81], canonical criticism[82], and *Wirkungsgeschichte*[83]. The general principle regarding the relationship between diachronic and synchronic methodologies is recalled below:

---

[78] *EB*, §1438. English trans., 90. While the HCM can provide the preliminary ground work for this endeavor it is necessary to move beyond how an individual author used a particular text to see the heremeneutical principles involved. Cf. P. GRECH, «The "Testimonia" and Modern Hermeneutics»; ID., «Interprophetic Reinterpretation and Old Testament Eschatology».

[79] *EB*, §1304. English trans., 44. The document states that the limits of rhetorical criticism are based in its synchronic approach. Questions are raised concerning the imposition of current ideas on the author of the ancient text. The document states: «Its [rhetorical criticism] application to biblical texts raises several question. Did the authors of these texts belong to the more educated levels of society? To what extent did they follow the rules of rhetoric in their work of composition? What kind of rhetoric is relevant for the analysis of any given text: Greco-Roman or Semitic? Is there sometimes the risk of attributing to certain biblical texts a rhetorical structure that is really too sophisticated?». A diachronic method, or at least some elements of the method, are needed to answer these questions.

[80] *EB*, §1311-1312. English trans., 46-47. The document suggests the distinction made in narrative criticism between the «real author» and the «implied author» can perhaps make interpretation more complex. The commission suggests caution against imposing pre-established models onto a biblical text, and recommends that the method be supplemented by the diachronic.

[81] *EB*, §1321. English trans., 49. The limits of the semiotic or structuralist approach center around «the refusal to accept individual personal identity within the text and extra-textual reference beyond it». The Word of God is spoken in history and speaks to us through the human authors. The semiotic approach risks «remaining at the level of formal study of the content of texts, failing to draw out the message». The criticism is similar to the one raised against form criticism. A diachronic supplement is necessary to give due consideration to the historical aspect of the text and the human author.

[82] *EB*, §1326. English trans., 51. The document specifically states that canonical criticism does not hope to supplant the HCM but to complete it providing a method of placing the study of individual texts within the whole of the biblical tradition.

[83] *EB*, §1342. English trans., 56. The document notes that *Wirkungsgeschichte* is limited for it sometimes results in interpretations that are «tendentious and false, bane-

It follows that the biblical writings cannot be correctly understood without an examination of the historical circumstances that shaped them. «Diachronic» research will always be indispensable for exegesis. Whatever be their own interest and value, «synchronic» approaches cannot replace it. To function in a way that will be faithful, synchronic approaches should accept the conclusions of the diachronic, at least according to their main lines[84].

The HCM is helpful for ecumenical discussion. The final point in this section is the role of the HCM in aiding ecumenical discussions. The ecclesial dimension of biblical interpretation requires an openness to ecumenism[85]. The PBC document notes that the HCM has helped provide a basis for ecumenical understanding of the biblical texts[86]. Such understanding does not necessitate the method; rather it highlights its benefits, for this reason it is included in this list[87].

3.2 *Why is the HCM limited?*

The PBC document noted the reasons that necessitate historical-critical exegesis for Catholic interpretation but it also recognizes the limits of the

---

ful in their effect — such as, for example, those that have promoted anti-Semitism or other forms of racial discrimination or, yet again, various kinds of millenarian delusions». The discipline cannot be autonomous. Though the document does not specifically mention it, the HCM can provide a basis for which the continued understanding of the text can be judged, that is the *literal sense*.

[84] *EB*, §1558. English trans., 129.

[85] *EB*, §1478. English trans., 103. As mentioned in the previous chapter R.E. BROWN, «Ecumenical Church Discussion», 27, sees the concentration on the literal-historical meaning as important for ecumenical discussions and as a starting point for future discussion on the lines-of-trajectory that different churches have followed with regard to interpretation.

[86] *EB*, §1552. English trans., 126. «Most of the issues which ecumenical dialogue has to confront are related in some way to the interpretation of biblical texts ... Although it cannot claim to resolve all these issues by itself, biblical exegesis is called upon to make an important contribution in the ecumenical area. A remarkable degree of progress has already been achieved. Through the adoption of the same methods and analogous hermeneutical points of view, exegetes of various Christian confessions have arrived at a remarkable level of agreement in the interpretation of Scripture, as is shown by the text and notes of a number of ecumenical translations of the Bible, as well as by other publications». See R.E. BROWN, «Ecumenical Church Discussion», 29-36.

[87] The distinction is important because the Catholic use of the HCM requires a specific framework for its use that may not be the case in individual Protestant denominations (as was pointed out by R.E. BROWN, «Ecumenical Church Discussion»). Since the framework is different the value and limits of the method will be different.

method. It states that «no scientific method for the study of the Bible is *fully adequate* to comprehend the biblical texts in all their richness. For all its overall validity, the HCM cannot claim to be totally sufficient in this respect. It necessarily has to leave aside many aspects of the writings it studies»[88]. The point is raised again in the conclusion: Exegetes cannot «accord to it [HCM] a sole validity. All methods pertaining to the interpretation of texts are entitled to make their contribution to the exegesis of the Bible»[89]. The limits of the method become apparent when the method is placed within the whole framework of Catholic biblical interpretation. The limits identified or inferred by the document are categorized below.

The HCM has shown limits in its classical practice. As mentioned in the Introduction above, the HCM reached its present formulation chiefly in the late nineteenth century to the mid-twentieth century. The PBC document briefly describes this development. The commission notes how reaction to insufficiencies in the individual criticisms led to the further development of the method through the incorporation of newer disciplines. The general term used to describe the faults of the classical practice is «hyper-criticism». Included in this criticism are two points. First, there was a restrictive attention to the historical meaning with no room for further understanding — «It [classical use of HCM] restricts itself to a search for the meaning of the biblical text within the historical circumstances that gave rise to it and is not concerned with other possibilities of meaning which have been revealed at later stages of the biblical revelation and in the history of the church»[90]. Second, there was an overemphasis on particular aspects of the method — for example, the document describes the extremes of literary criticism that «restricted itself to the task of dissecting and dismantling the text in order to identify the various sources. It did not pay sufficient attention to the final form of the biblical text and to the message which it conveyed in the state in which it actually exists»[91].

The HCM is limited by the presuppositions of the exegete. The classical use of the method has come under heavy criticism as being tainted by philosophical systems that underlie its use. In this context the document

---

[88] *EB*, §1291. English trans., 41.
[89] *EB*, §1474. English trans., 102.
[90] *EB*, §1287. English trans., 40.
[91] *EB*, §1277. English trans., 35. J.A. RATZINGER, *Biblical Interpretation in Crisis*, 2, is perhaps more clear: «Underneath the existing sources — that is to say, the biblical books themselves — we are supposed to find more original sources, which in turn become the criteria for interpretation. No one should be surprised that this procedure leads to the sprouting of ever more numerous hypotheses which finally turn into a jungle of contradictions».

distinguishes the method from the exegete. The method itself has no *a priori* philosophical system attached but the way in which it is utilized is certainly affected by the presuppositions of the exegete[92]. A proper pre-understanding is necessary for an effective use of the HCM for «access to a proper understanding of biblical texts is only granted to the person who has an affinity with what the text is saying on the basis of life experience»[93]. A faulty or inadequate pre-understanding can limit the effectiveness of any method[94].

The HCM tends toward a narrow interpretation of the biblical text. The HCM, in its quest to determine *the literal sense*, tends to identify the meaning of particular passages[95]. It also studies the relationship of such passages to its context within the whole book and/or corpus (usually based on a common author). The method, however, does not provide a means to move beyond this level. Additionally, the classical practice held that normally only one meaning could properly represent the *literal sense*[96]. As mentioned above, *Interpretation of the Bible in the Church*

---

[92] *EB*, §1285-1288. English trans., 39-40. See also *EB*, §1398. English trans., 76. The document states «all exegesis of the accounts of these events necessarily involves the exegete's own subjectivity». J.A. RATZINGER, *Biblical Interpretation in Crisis*, 6-8, notes that this interaction of the exegete and the interpretation prohibits a claim to «pure objectivity» which in turn prohibits any claim to «certainty» in the conclusions of historical-critical exegesis. Cf. J.A. FITZMYER, «Historical Criticism», 252-255; D. FARKASFALVY, «In Search of a "Post-Critical" Method», 295-296; M. D'AMBROSIO, «Henre de Lubac», 376-378. For more on the distinction between the exegete and the method see J.A. FITZMYER, «Historical Criticism», 252; R.E. BROWN, «Ecumenical Church Discussion», 46.

[93] *EB*, §1398. English trans., 76.

[94] *EB*, §1278. English trans., 36.

[95] *EB*, §1411. English trans., 80.

[96] *EB*, §1403. English trans., 78. «All the effort of historical-critical exegesis goes into defining "the" precise sense of this or that biblical text seen within the circumstances in which it was produced». T. CURTIN, *HCTIS*, 129, notes that this «narrowness» as one of the characteristics of English speaking exegetes between 1965-1975. He states: «The first (perspective) was a clear distinction between an exegetical and any other interpretation of Scripture. Exegesis, now concerned for the *literal sense* and the study of the origins of the biblical text as a guide to its meaning, has its own scientific criteria that must be observed. These criteria are not to be confused with any theological norms which have their own field of operation». As the discussion continued it became more apparent that this concept was not a valid approach. The theological basis of exegesis was being replaced by the scientific. The present document raises a warning about this in its general conclusions: «....Catholic exegesis should avoid as much as possible this kind of professional bias and maintain its identity as a *theological discipline*, the principle aim of which is the deepening of *faith*"» (see *EB*, §1549.

notes that due to advancements in the theories of language and philosophical hermeneutics, a plurality of meaning for texts must be admitted, a
meaning that the HCM has difficulty ascertaining[97]. As a consequence the
interpretation offered by historical-critical exegesis can be narrow or limited.

The HCM is limited in its identification of the spiritual sense. HCM's
fourth limitation involves its identification of the *spiritual sense.* As mentioned above the *spiritual sense* is «the meaning expressed by the biblical
texts when read, under the influence of the Holy Spirit, in the context of the
paschal mystery of Christ and of the new life which flows from it»[98]. The
HCM readily seeks the *spiritual sense* in those passages where the *literal
sense* is the *spiritual sense.* However, in the cases where the two senses are
distinct (especially in the OT) the method does not provide a methodological step that seeks to identify this sense. In these cases the method is seriously deficient in ascertaining the meaning of the text[99]. The same is true
for the HCM's identification of the *sensus plenior.*

*The HCM as a method does not properly seek to identify the chris-
tological, canonical and ecclesial aspects of the text.* The characteristics of
Catholic exegesis require three elements of the text to be identified and expounded: the christological, the canonical and the ecclesial. These characteristics are considered basic to Catholic exegesis; however the HCM does
not methodologically seek to identifying these elements.

Christological Aspect. The christological aspect is rooted in the belief
that the definitive revelation of God comes in Jesus. The Christ-event becomes the center of all history. Any Christian understanding of history
must take this into consideration and the meaning of all scriptures must be
seen in this light. The HCM proposes no methodological step to highlight
the christological aspect. Historical-critical exegesis of the NT naturally
lends itself to such interpretation. OT texts, on the other hand, lack this dimension and need to be supplemented.

Canonical Aspect. The document notes the inter-relatedness of the two
testaments. The forming of a collection brings about a new understanding
of the text in its relationship with other texts. At times this understanding is
christological when the OT is understood in light of the NT. Other

---

English trans., 130). For more discussion on the *literal sense* see footnote 25.

[97] See above pages 235-240.

[98] *EB*, §1413. English trans., 81. See above, page 238.

[99] The deficiencies regarding the *spiritual sense* are similar to the weaknesses noted in
the next paragraph regarding the characteristics of Catholic exegesis: christological, canonical and ecclesial.

times the NT can be better understood in light of the OT. Additionally the presence of re-readings within the OT require attention be given to the canonical aspect. Although this meaning is occasionally uncovered through literary criticism, the HCM does not specifically aim to include the canonical aspect in its interpretation.

Ecclesial Aspect. The writing, editing, and collection of the texts all reflect a communitarian aspect. All Scripture was rooted in the communities of ancient Israel and subsequently in the early church[100]. A proper affinity between the exegete and the text will be lacking without the ecclesial aspect, as a result the exegesis will be limited and narrow[101]. Since the HCM contains no *a priori* presuppositions, the method itself does not take into consideration this necessary component of interpretation. Rather it is up to the exegete to make this ecclesial connection. Therefore the method has to be supplemented with the proper disposition of the exegete.

The HCM used by itself provides no evaluation of the interplay between the reader and the text that is necessary for understanding. The document noted that according to Ricoeur, the proper meaning of the text

---

[100] *EB,* §1478. English trans., 103. Cf. *EB,* §1449. English trans., 93. «The communities of the Old Covenant (ranging from particular groups, such as those connected with prophetic circles or to the priesthood, to the people as a whole) recognized in a certain number of texts the Word of God capable of arousing their faith and providing guidance for daily life; they received these texts as a patrimony to be preserved and handed on. In this way these texts ceased to be merely the expression of a particular author's inspiration; they become the common property of the whole people of God».

[101] P. GRECH, «Language of Scripture», 174, sees the ecclesial aspect from the perspective of canonization. He points out the limits of the method in his description of the Bible as a «classic»: «Through the living tradition of the church and the activity of the Spirit in them, believers recognized certain writings as "classical" because they saw in them either the cause of their faith or the completeness of its expression. They created the canon as much as they themselves were created, as faithful, by the canon. A reciprocal mirroring and dialogue ensued. Christians were born into the language of the sacred writings but the writings were recognized as sacred because they corresponded to the scattered fragments of communitary experiential language alive in the church. Not only so, but just as the later prophets in the OT re-read the older prophets from the view-point of their own days, and NT writers used a completely new pre-understanding of the older texts, so also the church re-read the scriptures from the standpoint and with the pre-understanding of her actual history, thus becoming not merely reader, but, in a sense, also author of new intuitions which sparked forth from the texts, intuitions which may not enter into the categories of philological exegesis but which are perfectly legitimate, if we remember that the word of God is living and ever active».

T. CURTIN, *HCTIS,* has evaluated the ecclesial/communal discussion in the debate after *Dei Verbum.* For the views of G. Montague and E. Schüssler-Fiorenza see 271-280. For G. Montague and E. Schüssler-Fiorenza see 271-280. For J. SUDBRACK see 196. For R. Schnackenburg, see 218.

«can be fully grasped only as it is actualized in the lives of the readers who appropriate it»[102]. The point that resounds is «the question of overcoming the distance between the time of the authors and first addressees of the biblical texts and our own contemporary age, and of doing so in a way that permits a correct actualization of the scriptural message so that the Christian life of faith may find nourishment»[103]. The classical practice of the HCM had no methodological step to address this relationship. The document does note that following the critical procedures the text is explained «... with an eye to the demands of the text from the point of view of action and life»[104]. The presentation, however, seems to indicate a gap between the method and explanation.

The HCM as a neutral method could fail to recognize the Bible as the Word of God. The HCM is a neutral method with no *a priori* presuppositions attached to it. This was previously discussed from the perspective of the exegete's presuppositions. A related issue raised by this neutrality is the possibility to disregard of the Bible as the Word of God that speaks to all peoples of all ages. The HCM is a method that can be used with any ancient text. Therefore the method in itself does not lend itself to recognize the uniqueness of the biblical text. The method in itself is limited since the recognition of the Bible as a sacred text is left to the exegete. The document points out that the need for a hermeneutical approach to overcome this deficiency[105].

The HCM fails to consider the dynamic development beyond the text. The HCM so concentrates its efforts on the historical meaning of the text

---

[102] *EB*, §1395. English trans., 75.

[103] *EB*, §1396. English trans., 75. X. LÉON-DUFOUR, *Étude d'Evangile*, (*HCTIS*, 136), sees this tied to the faith of the exegete, «If the exegete has faith, then his research will above all be inspired by the desire to bring to his readers, in their own situation, not just information on the life of Jesus, but a lesson of life which, having once enlightened a particular situation of the early church, can today be applied to their present condition. Indeed, what is the goal of exegesis if not to examine with all the resources of science the unfathomable Word, in order to actualize for our times the past event which continues to dominate the centuries?»

[104] *EB*, §1283. English trans., 38.

[105] *EB*, §1475. English trans., 102, «In their work of interpretation, Catholic exegetes must never forget that they are interpreting is the *Word of God*. Their common task is not finished when they have simply determined sources, defined forms or explained literary procedures. They arrive at the true goal of their work only when they have explained the meaning of the biblical text as God's word for today. To this end, they must take into consideration the various hermeneutical perspectives which help towards grasping the contemporary meaning of the biblical message and which make it responsive to the needs of those who read Scripture today».

that no element of the procedure evaluates the text from the standpoint of the living tradition of the church. Thus the dynamic element of the text is not addressed. The lack of addressing this elements of understanding was discussed previously from the vantage point of the formation of the text[106]. The document also considers the understanding of the text in the history of the church. The method of itself does not exclude this meaning but it has no way to methodologically consider it: «Concerned above all to establish the meaning of texts by situating them in their original historical context, this method has at times shown itself insufficiently attentive to the dynamic aspect of meaning and to the possibility that meaning can continue to develop»[107].

The limits of the HCM in association with sociological approaches. The document pointed out the close relationship between historical-critical exegesis and the sociological approach to the scriptures[108]. The approach has been incorporated on various levels into the HCM, especially regarding form-criticism and historical-criticism. One major limitation regarding these studies is the fact that the biblical and extra-biblical texts available do not provide the type of documentation that is adequate for a comprehensive picture of ancient society.

---

[106] The failure to address the dynamic element of the text was also discussed under the following limitations: the HCM tends toward a narrow interpretation of the biblical text, the HCM is limited in its identification of the *spiritual sense*, and the HCM as a method does not properly seek to identify the christological, canonical, and ecclesial aspects of the text.

[107] *EB*, §1538. English trans., 129. See also *EB*, §1409. English trans., 80. Thus, the HCM has «too often tended to limit the meaning of texts by tying in too rigidly to precise historical circumstances. It should seek rather to determine the direction of thought expressed by the text; this direction, far from working towards a limitation of meaning, will on the contrary dispose the exegete to perceive extensions of it that are more or less foreseeable in advance». At the same time «one must reject as inauthentic every interpretation alien to the meaning expressed by the human authors in their written text».

[108] *EB*, §1348. English trans., 59. The document notes the benefits of the sociological for exegesis. «Knowledge of sociological data which help us understand the economic, cultural and religious functioning of the biblical world is indispensable for historical criticism. The task incumbent upon the exegete, to gain a better understanding of the early church's witness to faith, cannot be achieved in a fully rigorous way without the scientific research which studies the strict relationship that exists between the texts of the NT and the life as actually lived by the early church».

3.3 *What are the ways in which the limitations of the method are rectified?*

The limits of the HCM were identified by *Interpretation of the Bible in the Church* as they became evident in the larger framework of the Catholic understanding of biblical interpretation. At the same time, the document insists on the continued use of the method and gives suggestions on how the its limitations might be overcome. The following are the suggestions either stated by or implied in the document.

Exegetical inter-disciplinary cooperation is needed. Individual scholars working alone will never be able to successfully conduct the exegetical enterprise. The task is too large. The document suggests a division of labor «especially in *research*, which demands specialists in different fields»[109]. Cooperation and collaboration among the different concentrations will help overcome the limits imposed by the specialization.

The HCM must be used in conjunction with other methodologies to be effective for Catholic exegesis. The Commission notes that no one exegetical method is the exclusive method for Catholic exegesis. The HCM, though necessary for Catholic exegesis is not the exclusive method. Rather it *needs* to be supplemented to move beyond its limited approach. The various method and approaches listed in Part One of the document give guidelines for moving beyond the limited scope of the HCM. Particularly important are those methods that treat the text in a broader context. Especially helpful are the approaches based on tradition: canonical criticism, approach through recourse to Jewish traditions of interpretation and *Wirkungsgeschichte*[110].

The HCM must be used in conjunction with or coordinated with other branches of theology — each must know the limits of its competency while seeking to inform and learn from the others. Interdisciplinary cooperation is needed to move beyond the limits imposed on Catholic exegesis by the HCM[111]. Systematic theology and moral theology interact and overlap with exegetical studies. The relationship should be close and

---

[109] *EB,* §1480. English trans., 103.

[110] The call for the development of a catholic *Wirkungsgeschichte* occurred several times during the discussions of the earlier period. For example: I. DE LA POTTERIE, «Reading Holy Scripture»; J. GNILKA, «Methodik und Hermeneutik» (*HCTIS,* 226-228); P. GRELOT, «La pratique» (*HCTIS,* 261-264; J. SUDBRACK, «Modern Schriftauslegung» (*HCTIS,* 195-197).

[111] John Paul II, *Address,* §16. *EB,* §1258. English trans., 20. John Paul notes in his concluding remarks that this «interdisciplinary cooperation» as the next step in the discussion. «The increasing complexity of the task requires everyone's effort and a broad interdisciplinary cooperation».

complex: «On the one hand, systematic theology has an influence upon the presuppositions with which exegetes approach biblical texts. On the other hand, exegesis provides the other theological disciplines with data fundamental for their operation»[112]. The interrelated but distinct roles of the exegete and theologian are described below:

> The primary task of the exegete is to determine as accurately as possible the meaning of biblical texts in their own proper context, that is, first of all, in their particular literary and historical context and then in the context of the wider canon of Scripture. In the course of carrying out this task, the exegete expounds the theological meaning of texts when such a meaning is present This paves the way for a relationship of continuity between exegesis and further theological reflection. But the point-of-view is not the same, for the work of the exegete is fundamentally historical and descriptive and restricts itself to the interpretation of the Bible.

> Theologians as such have a role that is more speculative and more systematic in nature. For this reason, they are really interested only in certain texts and aspects of the Bible and deal, besides with much other data which is not biblical — patristic writings, conciliar definitions, other documents of the magisterium, the liturgy — as well as systems of philosophy and the cultural, social and political situation of the contemporary world. Their task is not simply to interpret the Bible; their aim is to present an understanding of the Christian faith that bears the mark of a

---

[112] *EB*, §1488. English trans., 107. See also *EB*, §1494. English trans., 109. The presuppositions with which a Catholic exegete approaches the text include recognizing the Bible as an inspired text «entrusted to the church for the nurturing of faith and guidance of the Christian life». The certainties of faith come to the theologian as developed in an ecclesial community. Exegesis needs systematic theology and likewise systematic theology needs the work of exegesis. Exegesis can help systematic theologians avoid two extremes: a dualism which would separate doctrinal truth from its linguistic expression and fundamentalism. Making distinctions while avoiding a separation will help maintain a proper tension.

Exegesis and moral theology is complicated by the fact that «often the biblical texts are not concerned to distinguish universal and moral principles from particular prescriptions of ritual purity and legal ordinances. All are mixed together. On the other hand, the Bible reflects a considerable moral development which finds its completion in the NT» (*EB*, §1496. English trans., 109). Despite the complexities moral theologians «have a right to put to exegetes many question which will stimulate exegetical research. In many cases the response may be that no biblical text explicitly addresses the problem proposed. But even when such is the case, the witness of the Bible taken within the framework of the forceful dynamic that governs it as a whole, will certainly indicated a fruitful direction to follow» (*EB*, §1497. English trans., 110).

full reflection upon all its aspects and especially that of its crucial relationship to human existence[113].

Attention to the dynamic aspect of the scriptures, possibly an added step. The document suggests that the HCM should pay more attention to the dynamic aspect of meaning particularly in reference to re-readings and the further understanding of the texts unfolded in history[114]. Complementing the method with other methodologies (e.g. canonical criticism or *Wirkungsgeschichte*) will provide a means for addressing the dynamic aspect of meaning. However the document might also suggest an additional step to be added to the HCM beyond redaction criticism that methodologically considers specific christological-canonical-ecclesial aspects of the reading.

4. Summary

Scientific exegesis has been encouraged, at least cautiously, in the church since the promulgation of *Providentissimus Deus*. While questions and answers proposed by historical-critical studies have initially caused discussion and debate in the Church, they have led to a better understanding of the text. The delicate balance between the human and divine aspects require our understanding of that relationship be continually challenged and examined. The PBC's *Interpretation of the Bible in the Church* undertakes such an evaluation, prompted by the debate on interpretation that followed *Dei Verbum*. The debate involved exegetes, theologians, pastors and the faithful. At the center of this discussion was the question «what, if any, is the role of the HCM in Catholic exegesis?».

Theological speculation preceding this document addressed the topic from various vantage points. Chapter V presented representative views of various exegetes and theologians. Many times a scholar addressed the topic from a very limited perspective — primarily from the areas in which they were experts. The difficulty for discussion became the fact that not everyone is speaking on the same issues. Granted that there were so many

---

[113] *EB*, §1500. English trans., 111. For a more detailed discussion on the relationship of exegesis to systematic theology see *HCTIS*, 202-204, 247-260.

[114] *EB*, §1409. English trans., 80. «Historical-critical exegesis has too often tended to limit the meaning of texts by tying it too rigidly to precise historical circumstances. It should seek rather to determine the direction of thought expressed by the text; this direction, far from working towards a limitation of meaning, will on the contrary dispose the exegete to perceive extensions of it that are more or less foreseeable in advance».

issues involved in the topic of biblical interpretation it seems difficult for any one theologian or exegete to address or include all.

That the HCM was a limited method was agreed by most theologians and exegetes. Defining its limits, and ways to overcome them, were the subject of discussions and debates. These were complicated by different understandings of what HCM or historical-critical exegesis, means; the need to distinguish between the catholic use of the method and the «classical»; and the lack of a clear framework for the discussion. Furthermore the call to go beyond the HCM to a broader vision of interpretation was confused by the numerous aspects under consideration: pneumatic interpretation, the divine-human interaction of the texts, patristic exegesis, philosophical presuppositions, the *senses of scripture*, philosophical hermeneutics, newer methodologies, actualization, pastoral relevance, and liturgical concerns.

Interpretation of the Bible in the Church attempted to address the topic, seeking to describe the relationships of the various concerns. The result is a concise framework of the Catholic interpretive endeavor. The primary focus of the document is how to interpret the Scriptures in the church. Related issues such as inspiration and revelation were not addressed as in previous documents since the Commission preferred to stay exclusively within the topic of interpretation.

The document places the debate concerning the HCM and its relationship with other areas of Catholic interpretation in a comprehensive framework that respects the need for historical-critical exegesis while recognizing its limits. The limits on the method imposed by specialization needed to be supplemented by inter-disciplinary cooperation and involvement if the limits are to be overcome.

The discussion is not over as Cardinal Ratzinger mentioned in the «Preface». Due to the incarnational nature of the Scriptures the discussion will continue indefinitely — always seeking better ways to describe and appreciate the divine and human interaction of «the Word of God in the words of men». For the present discussion the document clarifies some of the complications mentioned above so that a more focused discussion may continue.

The next chapter will discuss the reception of the document among theologians and exegetes and will evaluate the theological exchange between them that continued after the publication of this document. The significance of the document in relationship to other ecclesial documents on biblical interpretation will be included in the final chapter of the dissertation.

CHAPTER VII

The Discussion Following *Interpretation of the Bible in the Church*

The discussion among theologians and exegetes prior to the 1993 document has continued following its publication. The document's presentation on the framework and vision of Catholic biblical interpretation has demonstrated the value and limits of the HCM for Catholic exegesis. The document was received very positively by the scholarly community as witnessed in the numerous reviews, articles and commentaries published after its release[1].

---

[1] Reviews included: «Die Auslegung der Bibel in der Kirche»; E. ARENS, «Roma y la interpretación de la Biblia»; B. BYRNE, «New Vatican Document on the Bible»; E. COTHENET, «Commission Biblique Pontificale»; J. DORÉ, «*L'Interprétation de la Bible dans l'Église*»; J.A. FITZMYER, «The Interpretation of the Bible in the Church Today»; C. FOCANT, «*L'interprétation de la Bible dans l'Église*»; H. HAAG, «Bilanz eines Jahrhunderts»; K. KERTELGE, «*Die Interpretation der Bibel in der Kirche*»; J. KREMER, «*Die Interpretation der Bibel in der Kirche*»; J.L. VESCO, *L'Interprétation de la Bible dans l'Église*; A. VANHOYE, «Il nuovo documento»; R.D. WINTHERUP, «A new Magna Carta?».

More in-depth articles on various aspects of the document included: J. BEGLEY, «Modern Theories of Interpretation»; S. CIPRIANI, «*L'interpretazione della Bibbia nella chiesa*»; J. DORÉ, «Méthode exégètique»; A. DULLES, «*The Interpretion of the Bible in the Church*»; J.A. FITZMYER, «Problems»; P. GRECH, «L'ermeneutica biblica nel xx secolo»; L.D. MUNOZ, «Los sentidos de la escrítura»; R.E. MURPHY, «Reflections on "Actualization" of the Bible»; J.P. SCULLION, «Experience Encounters the Sacred Text»; M. SEVIN, «L'approche des textes bibliques»; M.A. TÁBET, «L'interpretazione»; A. VANHOYE, «L'interpretazione della Bibbia nella chiesa»; P. WILLIAMSON, «Actualization», ID., «Catholicism and the Bible».

Commentaries on the document included: J.A. FITZMYER, *The Biblical Commission's Document;* G. GHIBERTI – F. MOSETTO, *L'Interpretazione della Bibbia nella Chiesa* (including articles by: G. Ghiberti, A. Pitta, F. Mosetto, M. Pesce, G. Segalla, R. Fabris, R. Vignolo, F. Lambiasi, and M. Làconi); J. Loza Vera, «*La Interpretación de la Biblia en la Iglesia*».

Cardinal Ratzinger hoped in his «Preface» to *Interpretation of the Bible in the Church* that the discussion regarding biblical interpretation would be ongoing once the document was issued. The dialogue has continued albeit not with the same volume of the period preceding the publication of the document. This chapter considers the reception of the document's treatment of the HCM among scholars and theologians[2]. The chapter contains two sections: the first deals with biblical hermeneutics; the second examines the place of the HCM in Catholic exegesis.

1. Continued Discussion on Biblical Hermeneutics

Interpretation of the Bible in the Church identified the benefits of modern hermeneutics for biblical studies[3]. One such advantage is the theoretical support for multiple meanings of a text[4]. Scullion describes the differ-

---

For non-Catholic reviews of the document see: J.L. HOULDEN, *Interpretation of the Bible in the Church* a collection that contains articles by P.M. Blowers, J.D. Levenson, R.P. Carrol, J.L. Holman, J.L. Houlden, J. Muddiman, and K. Stevenson. This work also includes two articles by Catholic scholars — R.L. Wilken and P. Hebblethwaite. See also I.H. MARSHALL, «Review Article».

[2] The presentation will be brief. Due to the relatively short period of time since the publication of the document, no attempt will be made to evaluate its impact on exegetical studies in the Church. More time is needed to make such an evaluation.

[3] For a more detailed explanation of the hermeneutical systems refereed to in *Interpretation of the bible in the Church* see: P. GRECH, «L'ermeneutica biblica nel xx secolo». J. BEGLEY, «Modern Theories of Interpretation», 91, summarizes the current state of philosophical hermeneutics thus:

«Hermeneutics is in a far more developed state than it was in the time of Schleiermacher — there is a vast amount of material available for diligent readers to make their own and work out their own approach. True, there is no general theory that does full justice to author, text, and reader, but at least the complexity of the task of producing one is better realized. Texts are of different kinds so one needs also particular theories which will take account of their differences. The interpretation of a poem is not on the same level as the interpretation of a book of science. Moreover, the theories so far have concerned themselves with written texts, putting to one side the interpretation of speech, non-verbal communication, pictures, etc. The application of the present theories to these other fields will have to be done with due caution. As far as their application to the interpretation of the sacred scriptures is concerned, the document of the Biblical Commission referred to at the beginning to this article seems to me to provide useful guidelines. The Bible is a sacred, not a secular book. Philosophical hermeneutics is applicable only up to a point. As the Commission remarks: "the faith lived in ecclesial community and the light of the Spirit, control its application". But the modern theories of interpretation have done at least a good demolition job on Positivism and Rationalism, our enemies in the past».

[4] R. VIGNOLO, «Questioni di Ermeneutica», 280, sees the development of biblical hermeneutics in three periods. The ancient and medieval periods are represented by the

ence in this understanding as a characteristic distinction between modern and post-modern interpretation.

In the modern world the hard sciences served as the paradigm of critical thought: one could arrive at the content of meaning through dispassionate critical investigation. Applied to Scripture this meant that one who approached the text without presuppositions and critically would arrive at *the* correct meaning of the text.

Yet in a postmodern world both the possibility of dispassionate critical investigation as well as univocal meaning has been questioned. Some of the newer methods of biblical criticism resonate with these postmodern themes. As the contextual approaches to Scripture correctly point out, everyone approaches the text with presuppositions or an agenda, whether these are explicitly acknowledged or not. Moreover, literary critics have made us more aware that narratives can have a multiplicity of meanings. The notion of polyvency is not totally new to biblical studies. The Church has consistently talked about different levels of meanings, for example, the *literal sense* and the *spiritual* or *fuller sense*[5].

Ongoing insights in modern hermeneutical theory have spurred the development of newer methodologies that seek to determine more than one meaning in the text[6]. The question continually raised is: «What is the re-

---

spiritual and *literal senses*. The era of historical-critical exegesis insisted on one sense, the *literal sense*. The present period sees a plurality of meaning once again prompted by modern philosophical hermeneutics.

[5] J.P. SCULLION, «Experience Encounters the Sacred Text», 26. The influence of scientific understanding, particularly regarding the absolutizing of results, was addressed by J.A. Ratzinger in the debate prior to *Interpretation of the Bible in the Church*; it, however, has not been explicitly treated in the document.

[6] D. BERGANT, «Fundamentalism and the Biblical Commission», 219, discusses the issue of plurality of meaning from the perspective of actualization and canonical interpretation. She sees the interaction between the reader and the text requiring the following four principles of interpretation: recognition of the «ambiguity of reality»; the reading of a text as a «mirror» that bids the readers to discover their identity; theologizing by seeking to identify the action of God in the text, and deciding how to morally respond to God's action in the text. She gives the following example of how a plurality of meaning may emerge from a single text read in a different context:

«The Bible depicts the action of God in two fundamental modes: support or challenge...Consider the beatitude, "Blessed are you poor" (Luke 6:20). Within a context of ill-fortune, this is an encouraging message that might elicit sentiments of hope. On the other hand, those who enjoy plenty might wonder whether the blessing of others will be accomplished at their expense. This might cause them to reflect on the appropriateness of their own good fortune in the face of other's dire needs. This is an example of what is meant by the "ambiguity of reality". It is clear that the meaning of the text is the same in each situation, but its rhetorical function differs. Holding the pas-

lationship between original meaning and latter understanding?». Burkhard notes a certain point of ambiguity in the document regarding the plurality of meaning and a dynamic understanding. He notes that in Part IV the document speaks of a later discovery of a meaning latent in the text. Part III, however, speaks of re-readings where a more dynamic aspect is emphasized: «These more recent writings allude to older ones,, create "re-reading" (relecutres) which develop new aspects of meaning, sometimes quite different from the original sense». He concludes that although the invitation to a more dynamic understanding of actualization is present in the document, «the full impact of hermeneutical thinking and its effect on biblical interpretation has yet to emerge clearly and forcefully»[7].

Modern hermeneutical philosophy demands that a text can have a new understanding in different contexts. The validity of such interpretation lies in its connection to the meaning that emerged in the original context. In this case the newer understanding is not another meaning attached to the text but rather a nuanced meaning. On the other hand a meaning of the text that is contrary or contradictory to the original context would be considered invalid. If a meaning that later emerges does not contradict the

---

sage up as a "mirror", interpreters must be clear about what they see reflected there. Are they the poor referred to in the passage? If not, just what is their situation in relation to the poor? This is not the time for adapting the meaning of "poor" so that everyone is somehow included in the category and can be comforted by the promise of the message. It is the time for honest self-identification, which is necessary so that everyone hears the right message. The next step is the search for God's action recounted in or implied by the passage. Here, God promises blessing for the poor. Finally, the biblical message calls for a fitting response. But what makes a response fitting? At this point, the acknowledgment of one's situation plays a pivotal role».

Using Bergant's interpretive criteria might be more problematic on different literary forms (for example historical texts of the OT, or narrative texts in general).

[7] J.J. BURKHARD, «The Use of Scripture», 38. Burkhard then comments on the implications for preaching:

«How then might the preacher read and proclaim a biblical text? There must be a movement from the text to speech, from letter to life-giving spirit. In the process the interpreter admits his or her role of service to the text and its emerging meaning. The primacy of authority resides *with* (not *in*) the text. But the authority of the text must be educed and allowed to become productive of life. Here lies the concomitant activity of the spoken word brought into existence out of the experience of the preacher and the assembly. There is an interplay between the text's meaning and the interpreter's and the assembly's experience. No single factor produces meaning. Effectively, then, this means an active disponsiblility of the text, as evidenced in study of the text by employing several exegetic-hermeneutical methods, by prayerful surrender to the text as God's word, and by careful attention to the assembly and its contemporary experience. All three are essential to correct interpretation and effective proclamation: method, biblical authority, and experience of the community».

original one then it is valid; when the meaning of the original is contra-
dicted it is invalid[8]. Modern hermeneutics discusses multiple meaning
from the perspective of texts in general. The *senses of Scripture* have been
used, as mentioned above, to describe the different levels of meaning in
the Bible.

1.1 *The Senses of Scripture*

The discussion on the *senses* has continued since the publication *Interpretation of the Bible in the Church*. The insufficiency of the terms has
become more and more apparent. The *senses of Scripture* are terms required because of inspiration[9]. The possibility of multiple meaning in a

---

[8] Although the principle of non-contradiction is an adequate marker for individual
texts and latter meaning, it is insufficient for the cases where intra-biblial texts manifest a plurality of meaning. The multiplicity of meaning within the biblical cannon
cannot be explained by this principle. Fitzmyer and Brown seem content to leave this
inability as a note — that contradictory positions or at least conflicting texts exist in
the Bible. They propose that it is the task of the systematic theologian is to work
these out. Their proposal to delegate the task of resolving contradictions to systematic
theologians does not work in light of this new document. Exegetes have to recognize
the broader significance of a biblical passage in their work (i.e. to move beyond the
particular passages to broader biblical themes) and attempt to address the implications
of biblical meaning. (As an aside, it is important so that the reader is not abandoned to
over specialization). In this way both aspects of the inspired text, the writing/editing
and the collecting, are recognized and its canonical integrity is preserved.

[9] The *senses of Scripture* question rests on the doctrine of inspiration. The *senses*
are terms or concepts used to describe (not analyze) the way in which meaning is present in this uniquely divine and human text. This relationship is described as incarnational in *Divino Afflante Spiritu* and *Dei Verbum*. J.A. FITZMYER, *The Soul of Theology*, 58, notes that the failure to recognize this incarnational aspect is one of the
major faults of fundamentalist interpretation.

«The basic problem of the fundamentalist reading of the Bible is its failure to
reckon with the truth of the Incarnation itself, its flight from the interplay of the divine and the human in approaching God. It has difficulty in admitting that God's Word
has been couched in *human* language and has been produced under divine inspiration by
human authors with varied abilities and resources, gifted and limited, or otherwise. It
tends to treat the biblical text as though it were dictated *verbatim* by the Spirit and
fails to recognize that God's Word has been formulated in time-conditioned human
language and phraseology. It neglects the literary genres and modes of human thought
in which texts have been formulated over long periods of time in diverse historical
situations. It also insists unduly on the inerrancy of details, especially those dealing
with historical or would-be scientific matters, and tends to regard as historical everything narrated in the past tense without regard for what might have been intended only
as symbolic or figurative. It can also be very narrow in its outlook, seeing reality in
an antiquated biblical world-view that inhibits dialogue with a wider view of culture
and belief. It often uses an uncritical reading of some biblical texts to derive from them

text flows, in part, from its inspired character. The plurality of meaning in the Bible can be described in two ways. First, an individual passage may have multiple meanings. Second, texts read within the biblical corpus may manifest a multiplicity of meaning[10]. Divine inspiration provides the unity of this collection and the means for avoiding arbitrary interpretation. As mentioned previously in Chapter VII, the meanings labeled by, these terms are the source of much debate and discussion. The PBC document has definitely not concluded the discussion on meaning in the scriptures nor on the *senses of Scripture*. This section presents aspects of the ongoing discussion. The bulk of attention is given to the *literal sense* because of its relationship to the HCM.

The *literal sense*. The *literal sense* is important because of its relationship to the inspired nature of the text. There is a line of thought that argues for a strict reading of *literal sense*. God inspires the human authors, according to *Dei Verbum* §12, to use their talents and abilities to put down the inspired text. In this way one can say that the authors meaning is the inspired meaning. Thus when the *literal sense* is identified, the divine meaning is identified. In this way each *literal sense* is an inspired sense.

Interpretation of the Bible in the Church defines the *literal sense* as that meaning «which has been expressed directly by the inspired human authors»[11]. This definition can be read narrowly or broadly. A narrow interpretation sees a strict connection between the *intention* of the author

---

political conceptions and social attitudes that are prejudiced, racist, and simply contrary to the Christian gospel itself. Finally, in its dependence on the principle of *sola Scriptura*, fundamentalism servers the interpretation of the Bible from the Spirit-guided tradition that genuinely grew out of it within the Christian faith-community. It is thus often anti-church, neglecting creeds, dogmas, and liturgical practices that are part of the ecclesiastical tradition».

Fitzmyer continues to explain how even in the Catholic church some of these attitudes have been manifested «in covert ways» in the call to return to a «pre-critical» way of approaching the Bible.

[10] Plurality of meaning can also be described from the perspective of the reader. Interpretations developed from the first time a book or passage was received and read. This continued as that text was distributed to other communities and as it was handed on through time to new generations. The process of reading and re-reading continues to the present day. As this occurred different understandings of the text emerged and were incorporated into the lived faith expression of persons and communities. The study of this development, *Wirkungsgeschichte*, has been proposed as a way of studying the dynamic of understanding. Cf. P. GRECH, «L'ermeneutica biblica nel xx secolo», 411. The field is open for further research. Examples of this type of study can be found in the following: U. LUZ, *Matthew 1-7: A Continental Commentary*; *Matthew in History*.

[11] *EB*, §1407. English trans., 79. See Chapter VI, pages 7-8 especially footnote 21.

and the words expressed. This affirms the older definition of authorial intention[12]. A broader interpretation does not have such a great insistence on the author's intention but rather treats the words the human author chose to express a particular concept or reality. The words carry the meaning and the meaning lies in these words. This does not eliminate the author's intention but allows for a meaning beyond the intentions but based on the words.

Fitzmyer is perhaps the most prolific writer on the topic of the *senses of Scripture* since 1993[13]. He follows a narrow reading of the document that falls very closely (if not explicitly) within the authorial intention definition of the *literal sense*[14]. Similarly, R.E. Brown insists on a high level of authority for the author's intention. The authorial intention definition of the *literal sense*, however, continues to be scrutinized. Four questions can be used to identify the main themes of this discussion[15].

Who are the authors? A problem with basing the meaning of the text on the author's intention is identifying the author. Historical-critical studies have concluded that several authors and/or redactors were involved in the composition and editing of many biblical texts[16]. The process of editing can even extend beyond the period of canonization. R.E. Brown addresses this problem by noting that the author is somewhat equivalent to *authority* in the ancient usage[17]. Appeal to this *authority*, however, does

---

[12] This reading agrees with the description of the *literal sense* in *Divino Afflante Spiritu* (cf. *EB*, §550; *OCT*, §740).

[13] For his writings in the period under discussion see: J.A. FITZMYER, *The Biblical Commission's Document;* «The Interpretation of the Bible in the Church Today»; «Problems of Literal and Spiritual Senses of Scripture»; *The Soul of Theology*; and «The Senses of Scripture Today».

[14] Although he notes the significance of the change in his commentary, Fitzmyer's other articles (see footnote 13) stress the author's *intention*.

[15] Some of these questions have been raised in the earlier debate. The presentation is included to demonstrate that the question of *senses* is unresolved.

[16] L. ALONSO SCHÖKEL, «Tres notas de hermenéutica», 74, acknowledges the problem of multiple authors and editors. He defends the use of the HCM but agrees with Ska and the *Interpretation of the Bible in the Church* that it need be complemented.

[17] R.E. BROWN – S.M. SCHNEIDERS, «Hermeneutics», 1148-1149. See also R.E. BROWN, *An Introduction to the New Testament*, 35-40. The NJBC article notes : «The ancient understanding of author was wider than the popular modern conception of writer. In reference to the biblical books, for instance, the designation "author" covers at least five different relationships between the person whose name is attached to a book and the work attributed to the person. By modern standards most of the biblical books are anonymous or pseudonymous, with many of them the product of complex growth and collective contribution.... Despite all these complications, the reference to the author's intention in the definition affirms that those who produced the biblical

not convincingly argue for an interpretation based on the authorial intention. The fact that numerous authors and editors could have worked on the
texts does not undermine the authority of the text but begs the question
«whose intention is to be followed?». The question cannot be answered
simply «the final redactor» because in certain cases the final redaction was
done in a much later period (for example, the Johannine comma[18], the
ending of the Gospel of Mark) where a gap occurs between the completion of the basic text and its acceptance by the Church in its final form[19].

Can «intention» be identified? Another problem raised by authorial intention is: how does one identify an intention in the writing? Brown remarks that the intention normally can be identified by a somewhat common sense approach as the meaning conveyed by the words of the text.
He described the *literal sense* as that which the human author intended
and communicated by his words[20]. The reason for the distinction is so
that the exegete does not get overly speculative about what the human
author intended (i.e. saying the author intended something that is not conveyed by the words he used)[21]. Vignolo observes some difficulties involved with this definition. He says that making an evaluation of the psychology or intellect of a particular author is not easy. He sees the new
formula (*Interpretation of the Bible in the Church*) as wisely reformulated
to purposely avoid this problem. The reformulation frees the *literal sense*
from the author's intellect or psychology and instead reintegrates it with
the text as an objective communication[22].

---

books had in their times a message to convey to their readers and that it is very important for us to have this message in mind when we read the texts and ask what they now
mean for us». In the later work, 40, Brown clarifies further clarifies the term «author»
as «the final or substantial author of the (NT) book».

[18] For an explanation see B.M. METZGER, *A Textual Commentary*, 187-189.

[19] R.E. BROWN – S.M. SCHNEIDERS, «Hermeneutics», 1149, notes the problem
and says that «In instances like this (referring to examples from Isaiah and Amos), the
quest for the *literal sense* includes both the sense that the parts originally had before
editing and the sense of the book after editing». Brown directs the reader to the section
on redaction criticism for more information. Although redaction criticism is a valid and
necessary way of studying these cases it does not eliminate the problem of the *literal
sense* defined as authorial intention. R.E. BROWN, *An Introduction to the New Testament*, 40, further clarifies that it is the final canonical form which has authority. The
clarifications Brown raises are all good points to be considered when studying the biblical texts but regarding the definition of the *literal sense* they lose force.

[20] R.E. BROWN, *An Introduction to the New Testament*, 40.

[21] R.E. BROWN, *An Introduction to the New Testament*, 41.

[22] R. VIGNOLO, «Questioni di Ermeneutica», 283-284, specifically notes the
change in the definition of the *literal sense*. The formula, he believes, was selected
with utmost care. The combination of the adverb with the participle suggests an in-

What is the relationship between inspiration and the literal sense? The inspiration of the texts applies to the authors and editors of the work until it has been canonized and fixed. In this sense the *literal sense* would not refer to the author's intention but the meaning within the historical context in which the text reached its basic or substantial form[23]. In this way the inspired authors' and editors' intentions are respected but not canonized. An analogous example can be found in the covenant between God and His People. The earlier covenant was provisional, authoritative for a time until the fullness of revelation came about the established the new covenant in the paschal mystery. The new covenant does not eliminate the value of the old but transforms or fulfills it. A similar dynamic takes place in the composition of the sacred writings. The earlier editions of the text, in their numerous redactions are seen as inspired and provisionally authoritative until they were placed in the canon. They become permanently authoritative at that time. Their inspired nature continues throughout the whole process, but the degree of their authority must be differentiated. The *literal sense*, in this instance, refers to the historically rooted meaning of the inspired text. It respects the inspired author/editors of the text because to understand the historically rooted meaning one must attempt some identification of the author's intention in the composition (especially with the synoptics) but does not have to be confined by this intention. Furthermore it underscores the dynamic nature of both the composition and understanding of the text.

What is the relationship between authorial intention and re-readings? The problems raised by re-readings are serious for a definition of the *literal sense* based on the author's intention. If God inspires a human author to write a text, then later another inspired author uses that text in a different way than originally intended by the initial author, the text will have a new meaning. How should one refer to this new meaning? It is not the «literal-authorial sense», because the second meaning does not necessarily find its root in the original inspired author. In this case the canonical aspect comes into play again with relation to inspiration. The character of inspiration reaches the fullest expression in the final form when the

---

trinsic unity of form and content that reflects a similar correlation between the subjective and objective, between the act and product of the inspired writings. The sense directly expressed naturally implies intentionally tied to expression that makes it manifest. When speaking of the *literal sense* from the point-of-view of the human author the document speaks of the sense *expressed*; when speaking of the *literal sense* from the point-of-view of the divine author the document speaks of *intention*. Thus the *literal sense* is not limited to what the author intended but what they stated.

23 This does not mean that the later additions are not inspired.

texts is placed in the canon. In the aforementioned case both meanings are accepted as canonical and inspired but to call the second meaning an added *literal sense* is problematic because a different human author is involved writing from another historical context. A better way to refer to this meaning is its *spiritual sense* (as used by *Interpretation of the Bible in the Church*).

The four questions identified point out the benefit of a broad reading of the PBC's new formulation of the *literal sense*. The meaning of the text is tied to the inspired human author's words but not strictly to his intention. The document does not completely solve this problem, but the change in formulation acknowledges it and begins seeking a solution.

The spiritual sense. The term *spiritual sense* is not easy to define. Fitzmyer calls the *spiritual sense* a «weasel word»[24]. The term has been used to validate or justify a conjectured meaning that is more a reflection of the exegete's imagination than an interpretation of the text as it stands. The term is frequently equated with *inspired sense*. *Interpretation of the Bible in the Church* clarifies the meaning of the term in two ways. First it acknowledged that the *literal sense* is also an inspired sense. Second, when a christological understanding can be detected beyond the *literal sense* it is called a *spiritual sense*. With this clarification the term *spiritual sense* should not be equated with inspiration even though inspiration guarantees it. Inspiration is taken as a base for all the senses. The text itself is inspired. New meaning may emerge beyond the inspired *literal sense* particularly for OT passages read in the light of further revelation. The provisional status of the first covenant does not remove its value but places its authority under the more perfect second one. Thus one must read a biblical work in the light of the paschal mystery in which case a

---

[24] J.A. FITZMYER, *The Soul of Theology*, 63; ID., «Problems of Literal and Spiritual Senses of Scripture», 169; T.H. STAHEL – J.A. FITZMYER, «An Interview with J.A. Fitzmyer», 10. Fitzmyer continues to raise concerns about the *spiritual sense*. He explains: «That impression of the method has sometimes been given in the past, a kind of halfway use of the method that has led dogmatic theologians to be skeptical: and they call for a "mixture". For example, Avery Dulles, in one of his books calls for use of the HCM, joined with a *spiritual sense*. The difficulty I have with that second part is that I don't know what such people mean by the *spiritual sense* of Scripture. "Spiritual" in this usage can be a weasel-word at times. People employ it in all sorts of ways. Sometimes it even includes the "accommodated" sense, a sheerly arbitrary use of a text to illustrate or support some idea». He continues to note that the *spiritual sense* is tied to a Christological sense as described by Pius XII. He suggests that the *Interpretation of the Bible in the Church* extends this meaning to seeing the OT as anticipatory of the NT but continues to root the *spiritual sense* in the Paschal Mystery».

spiritual sense can emerge[25]. The confusion caused by the terminology will be discussed below.

Although a *spiritual sense* has been recognized in the biblical texts in the past, modern hermeneutical philosophy has bolstered more of a scientific foundation by demonstrating that a text can have multiple meanings. *Interpretation of the Bible in the Church* however does warn that care must be taken in identifying multiple meaning. Fitzmyer reiterates the need to *carefully* identify a *spiritual sense* so to avoid attributing human ingenuity to divine inspiration. The question could be raised «doesn't "reading in the Spirit" guarantee an interpretation? Yes, from the point-of-view of the Spirit. No, from the point-of-view of the individual. The individual can read the Scriptures in the Spirit but an evaluation of this reading and interpretation must move beyond the individual if its authenticity is to be validated. The guidelines given in *Interpretation of the Bible in the Church* may be helpful in this validation. Care must be taken neither to lightly dismiss the *spiritual sense* nor to give free reign to the imagination and allegorical interpretations. The roots of the *spiritual sense* remain the words expressed by the inspired human author and the meaning that emerges in light of the entire canon.

The Sensus Plenior. Sensus plenior is a relatively new term, used in an official document for the first time in *Interpretation of the Bible in the Church*. Brown noted in his article on hermeneutics in the NJBC that the discussion among scholars regarding the *sensus plenior* had for all practical purposes ended. Not only was the concept rarely discussed but the formula was not even occasionally referred to in exegetical commentary. Many scholars argue the vagueness of the description leaves the door wide open for arbitrary interpretation.

Additional confusion was raised regarding the example of the *sensus plenior* cited in *Interpretation of the Bible in the Church*. The reference is the interpretation of Isaiah 7:14. The document stated: «For example, the context of Matt 1:23 gives a fuller sense to the prophecy of Isa 7:14 in regard to the *almah* who will conceive, by using the translation of the Septuagint (*parthenos*): "The virgin will conceive"»[26]. The confussion does not involve the interpretation, but the reference to the *sensus plenior*. This could be refered to as a *spiritual sense* (using the definition of the *Interpretation of the Bible in the Church*. The question is asked, what function does the *sensus plenior* represent. The answer provided by *In-*

---

25 J.A. FITZMYER, *The Soul of Theology*, 65, speaks of the *spiritual sense* as an «added» sense.
26 *EB*, §1421. English trans., 84.

terpretation of the Bible in the Church is that the term represents those times when the *spiritual sense* is separated from the *literal sense*. Perhaps the description of the *sensus plenior* may need to be re-defined because as it stands it only adds to the confusion.[27] (See Chapter VIII for more discussion on the *senses of Scripture*).

1.2 Problems with Terminology

The terminology used to describe the *senses* of inspired scriptures have shown flexibility in the history of their use. They have changed meaning or definition through clarification and re-formulation. The present use of the terms have been expressed in *Interpretation of the Bible in the Church*. The formulations have caused much confusion. Suggestions are still made regarding better terminology. For example, Grech speaks of the *literal sense* as historical-contextual meaning rather than a reflection of the author's intention[28]. Fitzmyer distinguishes between the *literal sense* and the *canonical sense*[29]. Brown, in his *Introduction to the New Testament*, treats the topic as the *more-than-literal senses*. Brown describes

---

[27] S. CIPRIANI, «L'interpretazione della Bibbia nella chiesa», 11. J.P. SCULLION, «Experience Encounters the Sacred Text», 26, in his discussion of the three senses as presented in the document refers to the example of Isaiah 7:14. In his reference he collapses the *sensus plenior* into the *spiritual sense*. This is mentioned as an example of the confusion over the term *sensus plenior*.

[28] P. GRECH, «L'ermeneutica biblica nel xx secolo», 104.

[29] J.A. FITZMYER, *The Soul of Theology*, 62, gives several examples of how the *canonical sense* develops beyond the *literal sense* but does not invalidate the *literal sense*. Henotes: «For instance, the Canticle of Canticles, so expressive of mutual human love between man and woman, was quickly understood in Judaism as an expression of the relationship of Israel and God. Indeed, this was the reason why it found its way into the Jewish canon, both Palestinian and Alexandrian. Yet when the Christian canon adopted that part of the Hebrew Scriptures, Canticles took on still another canonical sense, which led in time to multiple allegorical interpretations of it as expressive of the relationship between the Church and Christ as the loved ones. To take yet another example, the meaning of the Woman of Revelation 12, clothed with the sun, with the moon under her feet, and crowned with stars. The primary meaning of the woman is usually understood to be Israel giving birth to the Messiah and to other offspring, the Christian people of God, the Church. So one would have to understand chapter. 12, when the Book of Revelation is considered in and for itself. When that book is considered as part of the Christian canon, however, along with other New Testament writings, especially with the Gospels according to Luke and John, the various images of the Virgin, the woman at the foot of the cross, and the woman who gave birth to him who is for Christians "the Messiah", all conspire to yield what may be a canonical sense, which was further allegorized in the mariological interpretation of this chapter that came to the fore in the forth century». See also R.E. BROWN – AL., *Mary in the New Testament*, 219-239».

two *more-than-literal senses*: the *canonical sense* and the *sense as un-derstood by the Church in later periods*[30].

A technical term is good only to the extent that it enables one to differ-entiate — in this case to distinguish between different aspects of the in-spired biblical text. The terms which have been used in the past may have out-run their usefulness because of the confusion that they have gener-ated. Perhaps new terms or definitions for special hermeneutics would be beneficial. Three terms are suggested here: the *historical-literary sense*, the *canonical sense*, and the *sensus plenior*.

The historical-literary sense is that basic meaning of the text determined through historical-critical or diachronic methods aiming to determine the basic meaning of the words expressed by the inspired human author. Here the definition is basically the same as PBC's definition of the *literal sense*. This term is eliminated because of its heavy association with *authorial intention*.

The *canonical sense* is that sense which emerges from the text in light of the paschal mystery and the new life in the church. The definition here is basically the same as the PBC's definition for the *spiritual sense*. The term is changed because of the inspired nature of all the sense and the confusion between the *spiritual sense* and the *sensus plenior* as described in the document. The term would be similar to Brown and Fitzmyer's with the stipulation that the identification of the canonical sense also falls within the realm of exegesis (not to exclude the systematic theologian).

The *sensus plenior* is that sense which represents the meaning of the text as it has been re-read in different contexts through-out the history of the Church[31]. In this case the term used by the PBC is retained but the meaning extended to include its *Wirkungsgeschichte*[32].

---

30 R.E. BROWN, *An Introduction to the New Testament*, 20-47. Brown sees these two as important but does not elaborate on their importance in relationship with the *literal sense*. Brown's chapter on hermeneutics is divided into four parts: methodology, inspiration/revelation, the *literal sense*, and the wider meaning beyond the literal. Comparing the chapter to the earlier R.E. BROWN – S.M. SCHNEIDERS, «Hermeneutics», we notice a reworking of the treatment of hermeneutics. The basis of the earlier article was the division of the methodologies according to the senses. Here the methodologies are treated as a separate category (as in the *Interpretation of the Bible in the Church*).

31 V. FUSCO, «Un secolo di metodo storico nell'esegesi», 82-83. Fusco thinks it is important to go back to the historical-literary context to understand the text but when it comes to interpretation the current situation must be taken into account so to see the power of the text

32 P. GRECH, «L'ermeneutica biblica nel xx secolo», 104, notes that the hermeneu-tics suggested in *Interpretation of the Bible in the Church* admits an «historical sense»

The first two senses: *historical-literary* and *canonical* enjoy a special status because of their immediate relationship to the text. The *sensus plenior* must in some demonstrable way be connected to the first two meanings if one is to say that his understanding is *based* on the biblical text[33].

The inspired nature of the Scriptures requires terminology ,for describing the multifaceted nature of the text. The terms and/or definitions used today cause much confusion. *Interpretation of the Bible in the Church* has attempted to ease the confusion but in some ways has added to it. The discussion on the *senses of Scripture* will continue in the future.

2. Continued Discussion Regarding the Place of the HCM in Catholic Exegesis

The present section considers continuing discussion on the HCM by scholars and theologians. Recent scholarship has moved in the direction of how the document treats the method. This section considers the discussion under the following topics: the description of the HCM; the need to distinguish between HCM and historical criticism; individual criticisms and peripheral sciences; the separation of diachronic and synchronic methodologies; the relationship between the method and the exegete; the utilization of multiple methods; and finally, the relationship between exegesis and theology[34].

The description of the HCM. The document gives a description of the HCM as a diachronic method consisting of several technical procedures (i.e. textual criticism to redaction criticism) employed to understand the

---

which the author transmitted to his contemporaries. An additional element of *Wirkungsgeschichte* is needed so that the diverse situations may find parallel with the original situation, as well as times when the passage has been used in the history of the Church both pastorally and theologically so that a contemporary application may be made. All the while acknowledging that in the ultimate analysis it will be the Holy Spirit who initially inspired the text, will reveal its significance for the present.

[33] R.E. BROWN, *An Introduction to the New Testament*, 41-46, suggests a «later-development» sense. As previously mentioned, he eliminates the use of *sensus plenior* because of its ineffectual use. Here however the term is used for Browns «later-development» or Grech's suggestion of a *Wirkungsgeschicte*.

[34] The document admittedly did not treat every topic dealing with the scriptures (e.g. inspiration). J. ASURMENDI, «Cien años de exegesis católica», 82, notes the absence of a discussion on the relationship between the genesis and progression of revelation and the biblical text. He also specifically notes the absence of mention on inspired texts and how they fit into the problem of interpretation (Vulgate, LXX, MT, etc.). Another topic not specifically discussed was the relationship between Scripture and tradition.

meaning of a particular text. The question that arises is «does the HCM exist as it is described in the document?»[35]. Three points need to be made before considering the question.

First, the document expounds a general description of the method verging on being a step-by-step procedure. As noted in Chapter I, the HCM is not a strict step-by-step method but rather a collection of different disciplines most of which are diachronic in emphasis. The method developed historically as a collection of critical methods that, as the document points out, sometimes developed in reaction to the overemphasis of another procedure.

Second, different texts require different procedures due to the variety of biblical texts[36]. Component techniques of the method cannot be equivalently applied to every biblical text. For example, all texts do not need an extensive examination for sources; in fact, it would be erroneous to suppose a source when there is no evidence or indication to support one. How far does one go in breaking down a text in looking for sources? When does over-particularization take place? Not every biblical text, pericope or passage is disposed for an examination using the entire HCM, the exegete has to make judicious decisions as to what particular disciplines apply.

Third, several techniques have developed into independent specialized disciplines. The fruits of such specialization, if taken out of the context of the broader field of scholarship, may seem too narrow or restricted (as in the earlier practice when form criticism developed in reaction to source, and redaction in reaction to form). This is not to deny that there are legitimate cases where specialization is a benefit to biblical studies. Two particular examples are textual criticism and philology[37]. Textual criticism, although used in exegetical commentary, is often a specialized area of research. For certain publications textual criticism is the only discipline

---

35 Several commentators note or allude to this question. G. GHIBERTI, «Il metodo storico-critico», 138 particularly notes that the document itself acknowledges the method has gone through many changes. The method has been adapted to the situation in which it is utilized. J.L. VERA, «*La Interpretación de la Biblia en la Iglesia*», 84 asks the question is it a method or methods? He notes that the document speaks singularly of the method when in actuality it is a composite of many complementary but diverse disciplines.

36 The challenge presented by different literary forms and genres is considered by the document in the section on hermeneutical understanding, but it does not specifically related to a methodological study (cf. *EB*, §1403-1404. English trans., 78).

37 Historical criticism is another example. Refer to Chapter I for examples of how this has developed into a specialized field.

used to study particular texts. The method is obviously needed for the original texts do not exist. Although exegetes are trained in textual criticism it is an area for specialists — especially regarding the production of composite editions. Expertise is also needed for philological studies given the particularities of Greek, Hebrew, and other ANE languages and the nature of comparative language work. Exegetes have facility in these languages but are also informed by the results of this highly specialized field.

Returning to the question: «does the HCM exist as it is described in the document?». The answer is «yes» in a general sense and «no» in a particular sense. Generally speaking the method consists of the different critical procedures that have all been incorporated into the method over the last several hundred years. However, in the particular application of the method a constant re-configuration is required to meet the demands of the biblical text being studied. Thus, the presentation on the HCM in *Interpretation of the Bible in the Church* is a synthetic rather than an analytic treatment[38].

The Need to Distinguish between the HCM and Historical Criticism. The debate over the value and limits of the HCM in the years prior to the publication of *Interpretation of the Bible in the Church* rarely made a distinction between the HCM and historical criticism. *Interpretation of the Bible in the Church* addresses this issue when it states: «When the texts studied belong to a historical literary genre or are related to events of history, historical criticism completes literary criticism, so as to determine the historical significance of the text, in the modern sense of this expression»[39]. The document indicates that historical criticism is an element or a discipline within the method but that it is only used in cases where the text is specifically tied to a historical event or a historical literary genre. Thus historical criticism is not used for every text. It to some extent is presented as an added feature to be used only carefully.

The distinction between the method as a whole and the individual disciplines that comprise it is important for future discussions. The failure to distinguish between the two can cause confusion and hinder future development of biblical methodology. The HCM cannot be invalidated due to the deficiencies of one its component disciplines. For example, L.T. Johnson, in evaluating the method of the *Jesus Seminar*, rightly points out the gross weaknesses of its approach in researching the historical Jesus. However he makes no distinction between the HCM and historical criti-

---

[38] See G. GHIBERTI, «Il metodo storico-critico», 109.
[39] *EB*, 1284. English trans., 38.

cism[40]; instead he describes the method of the *Jesus Seminar* as the historical-critical method. As a result his judgment of the method employed by the *Jesus Seminar* can be confused as a judgment against the HCM. However, the method he critiques is not the HCM but a particular type of «historical criticism». Although the two are inter-related at times, their distinctiveness must be kept in mind. Clearer terminology may be needed so that a more accurate evaluation may emerge from the discussion[41].

The Question of Individual Criticisms and Peripheral Sciences. As mentioned above, the PBC presents the individual disciplines of the HCM in a synthetic treatment. Consequently the disciplines are not evaluated in much detail. Any future discussions may wish to consider more closely these individual criticisms as well as peripheral sciences. Standing alone critical procedures have their own particular goals that are governed by a specific set of rules[42]. The value and validity of these rules may be addressed in future discussions to determine the strengths and limits of the particular component disciplines of the HCM. Furthermore, the document largely ignores peripheral sciences like archaeology, ANE historical studies, cultural and sociological studies of the ANE/Greco-Roman world, etc. Although such studies are not explicit components of the HCM, they are important for understanding the original historical context[43]. Questions regarding the value of extra-biblical studies and the extent to which they

---

40 See L.T. JOHNSON, *The Real Jesus*. Johnson does not take the PBC document into consideration while giving his analysis of the *Jesus Seminar* and historical criticism in general. Instead, in his conclusions, he proposes a new model for understanding the interpretive process especially regarding historical aspects. He states, 171: «What is often lacking is reflection on the fundamental models or paradigms within which methods function. These are often what is "taken for granted" or "assumed". They are also what are most often in need of criticism». The model of which he speaks is an «imaginative construal of the subject being studied, as well as a structured picture of both process and product: a model is a paradigm within which the data pertinent to a discipline makes sense». He proposes an «experience/interpretation model» that has four dimensions: anthropological, historical, literary, and religious. His model is helpful but limited in scope. A more complete «model» is present in *Interpretation of the Bible in the Church*.

41 The confusion that results from terminology is similar to the confusion which accompanied the earlier debate over *higher* and *lower criticisms*. See Chapter I, footnote 2.

42 J.L. VERA, «*La Interpretación de la Bibia en la Iglesia*», 86.

43 G. GHIBERTI, «Il metodo storico-critico», 123. See also: *Divino Afflante Spiritu*, *EB*, §561. English trans., 757.

should influence exegetical studies need to be addressed in future discussions[44].

The Separation between Diachronic and Synchronic Methodologies. *Interpretation of the Bible in the Church* speaks of the interaction and complementarity of diachronic and synchronic methodologies. The document calls for the HCM to be used in conjunction with, or more properly as a base for, the synchronic methods and approaches[45]. In many cases the techniques of the HCM are already included in the procedures for synchronic interpretation[46]. For example an exegete using narrative criticism will usually incorporate textual criticism, philological studies and literary criticism (in the broad sense) to a certain degree. On the level of academic research these first three criticisms are usually the starting point for any exegetical study. These three elements are necessary to understand the text at a most basic level, in other words, these studies are necessary to comprehend the text[47].

The Utilization of Multiplicity of Methods. The PBC acknowledged the difficulties arising from the use of multiple methods. This was one of the reasons that prompted the 1993 document. The Commission accepts a plurality of methods because each allows a different aspect of the text to be examined. It explicitly states that there is no one method of Catholic

---

[44] The need for language additional language studies is an undisputed; however, when the discussion moves to the contributions of archeology and historical criticism the question becomes much more complex. Even within the field of archeology debates concerning the study of «biblical archeology», «Palestinian archeology» etc. can by contentious and divisive.

[45] M. SEVIN, «L'approche des textes bibliques» gives an example of how the different methodologies and approaches can be used in conjunction to gain a better understanding of the text. He takes Luke 7:11-17 and briefly describes the results of historical-critical, rhetorical critical, narratology, semiotics, canonical implications, Jewish interpretation, and *Wirkungsgeschichte* and how each contributes differently in understanding the text. The approach is good for illustration, but a more in-depth version may reveal conflicts that need to be addressed.

[46] See J.L. SKA, «Le Pentateuque». Some commentaries use synchronic approaches but base these studies on diachronic method. This is by no means saying that there will not be problems, tensions or outright contradictions between the different approaches which will require resolution.

[47] E. ARENS, «Roma y la interpretación de la Biblia», 67-68, distinguishes between comprehension and interpretation. In order to render an interpretation the reader must be able to comprehend the text. Comprehension — not interpretation — is actually the first stage in understanding. In other words before readers can determine the theological significance of a text they must first know what it says. The HCM, or at least certain components of it such as literary criticism, genre criticism and translation, is needed for such understanding.

exegesis. Even though the use of multiple methods run the risk of arbitrary interpretation, the same can be said when comparing the results of a single method. The point of multiple methods is that no one method can exhaust the depth of meaning in the text[48].

Fusco sees the hermeneutical framework underlying the application of a method providing the structure for exegesis since a monolithic uniformed methodology does not exist. The integration of the results of various methods will prevent arbitrariness. The diversity reflects the richness of exegesis, in the manner of approach characteristic of the different exegetes, schools and traditions. Exegesis is never purely a science it is also an art[49]. Vera concurs noting that methods are beneficial, but if they become absolutes they will hinder rather than help understanding. Instead of engaging the reader in an experience of salvation they could become a barrier defeating the purpose for which they exist[50].

Fitzmyer notes the importance of having the results of synchronic methods coordinated with the results of the HCM. He agrees that the multiple methods can be an aid to interpretation. However, warns that the newer literary methods of studying the text run the risk of absolutizing the literary character of the text. He quotes T.S. Eliot:

> While I acknowledge the legitimacy of this enjoyment, I am more acutely aware of its abuse. The persons who enjoy these writings *solely* because of their literary merit are essentially parasites; and we know that parasites,

---

48 J.P. SCULLION, «Experience Encounters the Sacred Text», 26ff, uses the example of the Good Samaritan to show how multiple methods can aid in determining the meaning of a text. He illustrate this by presenting the results of a historical-critical study coupled with the results of narrative criticism. He concludes: «This extreme emphasis on the Samaritan forces us to acknowledge something we did not expect and really cannot accept, namely, that a Samaritan could be called "good". The story does not have a moral; it is more an experience, an experience of seeing our religious and ethnic worldview turned upside down and even shattered. The original hearers of this story underwent a transforming experience. The literary approach enables us not just to understand the meaning of the text but to undergo a similar experience. Since we are the co-creators of the story, we are already engaged and involved in the experience of the text». The difficulty with his example is not the interpretation, but limiting its significance to something experiential. When Scullion states that there is no moral, it seems to close off the possibility of multiple meaning. Placed in the immediate context Jesus asks the lawyer: «Who then was the neighbor?» The lawyer responds: «the one who treated him with mercy», to which Jesus says «Go and do the same». The context provides an explicit moral imperative to the story. This does not contradict the experiential meaning that Scullian detects but indicates the possibility of a plurality meaning, the very point Scullion makes in the rest of his article.

49 V. FUSCO, «Un secolo», 91-92.

50 J.L. VERA, «*La Interpretación de la Biblia en la Iglesia*», 117.

when they become too numerous, are pests. I could fulminate against the men of letters who have gone into ecstasies of 'the Bible as literature,' the Bible as 'the noblest monument of English prose.' Those who talk of the Bible as a monument of English prose' are merely admitting it as a monument over the grave of Christianity. I must try to avoid the by-paths of my discourse: it is enough to suggest that just as the work of Clarendon, or Gibbon, or Buffon, or Bradley would be of inferior literary value if it were insignificant as history, science and philosophy respectively, so that the Bible has had a *literary* influence upon English literature *not* because it has been considered as literature, but because it has been considered as the report of the Word of God. And the fact that men of letters now discuss it as literature probably indicates the *end* of its 'literary' influence[51].

Interpretation of the Bible in the Church is wise to encourage more interaction among exegetes who employ different critical methods so that individual results can contribute to a greater understanding of the biblical texts. More time is needed to evaluate the problems and possibilities of this recommendations.

The Relationship between Method and the Exegete. The document makes a distinction between the method and the exegete when it states that no *a priori* philosophical presuppositions are attached to the method[52]. In

---

[51] J.A. FITZMYER, *The Soul of Theology*, 41-42, quoting T.S. ELIOT, *Selected Essays: New Edition*, 344-345. The example reflects a certain progression of thought among literary critics who treat the Bible simply as literature. In a way the interpretation that guides this movement is an application of philosophical hermeneutics without the necessary inclusion of special hermeneutics.

The document also cautions against a purely literary approach to the biblical texts. Fitzmyer is particularly helpful in an American university context where the bible is treated from a purely literary perspective. One notable evaluation is Harold Bloom's work *The Western Canon*, where the Bible (King James English Version) is included as part of the larger literary canon of western civilization. Bloom is a noted literary scholar. The danger of equating the Bible with other Western literature is failing to recognize the uniqueness of the work. This will render any interpretation very limited. While speaking on the literary character of the Yahwist source as a literary work Bloom states, 5-6: «The ultimate shock implicit in this canon-making originality comes when we realize that the Western worship of God — by Jews, Christians, and Moslems — is the worship of a literary character, J's Yahweh, however adulterated by pious revisionists. The only comparable shocks I know come when we realize that the Jesus loved by Christians is a literary character largely invented by the author of the Gospel of Mark...».

[52] C. MARUCCI, «*L'interpretatione della Bibbia nella Chiesa*», 591, makes the case that it is unreasonable to say that the method has no *a priori* presuppositions since the determination of which type of method is to be used (either in the general sense or

theory this is true. However, the method never exists outside its use by a human interpreter. There is no way to place all these formula into a computer and generate an independent unbiased interpretation. The art of exegesis is a living exercise of both mind (reason) and heart (faith). Method and commentator are drawn together in unity. This is by no means a weakness of exegesis but rather adds to the diversity of insight to the meaning of the biblical text. When the PBC document distinguishes between the exegete and his method it notes that the exegete must have a proper pre-understanding or pre-comprehension to understand the text. This provides the proper affinity between the reader/listener and the object that is being read. The pre-comprehension necessary for interpreting the Bible is faith[53].

That faith is the proper disposition is expressed in *Dei Verbum* when it states that the Bible should be interpreted in the same Spirit with which it was written[54]. The focus on the diverse elements of a text such as philological, literary, historical, psychological and sociological may be interesting, but without faith they cannot get to the essence of the text. Vanhoye compares the emphasis on these aspects of the text with gnawing at the bark but not penetrating to the substance[55]. In such cases, the study would be very limited theologically and would in fact contradict *Dei Verbum*'s description of Scripture as the soul of theology[56].

Vanhoye continues his discussion on pre-comprehension by pointing out the need to distinguish between faith and tradition. He says that exegetes should never suspend the faith for the sake of study but they should make a distinction between faith and tradition. The distinction is necessary because dogmatic formulations should flow out of the Scriptures not vice

---

particularly regarding components of the HCM) implies a choice based on predetermined factors.

[53] An example from another field may be helpful. A person who picks up a medical text book needs to have a certain understanding of medicine in general to comprehend the text. Even if they are able to read the words they will make no sense without the proper disposition to uncover what the text is trying to communicate. This is also true for a person reading the biblical text. Faith is necessary to understand the message contained therein.

[54] A. VANHOYE, «Dopo la *Divino Afflante Spiritu*», 46, continues seeing a similar pattern in I Cor 2:14 «Now the natural person (*psychikos*) does not accept what pertains to the Spirit of God, for to him it is foolishness, and he cannot understand it, because it is judged spiritually (*pneumatikôs*)».

[55] Referring to a comment by Leo XIII in *Providentissimus Deus*, EB, §112. OCT, §322.

[56] See also A. VANHOYE, «Esegesi e teologia».

versa[57]. Thus, exegetes must be prepared to abandon certain opinions which are the fruit of human evolution and not from the abundance of the Word of God. The Bible never contradicts the Great Tradition of faith from which it was born, but it may in fact contradict particular traditions within the Great Tradition. Vanhoye states that discerning these propositions may be difficult and painful sometimes but constitutes ,a necessary condition for the authentic progress of theology. It is not a stretch nor a suspension of the proper faith, but a preparation for a purification of the faith that renders it more authentic and pure[58].

Most of the discussion up to this point regarding the exegete and the method has dealt with the initial stages of exegesis. Yet the means by which an exegete communicates the results of his work is also important[59]. The two principal ways an exegete communicates the results of his/her work are teaching and publications. The precise way results are taught or publicized can be varied and diverse. The diversity can be classified according to three different categories: purpose, audience and context.

Purpose. The purpose of an exegetical publication or classroom/lecture activity can vary between spiritual (e.g. personal conversion of heart), pastoral (e.g. communal conversion aided by leaders in the community) and/or academic (e.g. a scholarly examination of a text). Depending on the subject matter, the three will often overlap but in general an exegetical publication exclusively emphasizes one of the three.

Audience. The audience is another consideration in communicating the results of exegesis. Who is reading or hearing the results? Different levels

---

[57] A. VANHOYE, «Dopo la *Divino Afflante Spiritu*», 47. A pre-exilic OT text is not attributed a significance that depends on the post-exilic tradition. A phrase in the NT is not to be given the precise christological definitions of the councils, only arrived at after long centuries of theological reflection.

[58] A. VANHOYE, «Dopo la *Divino Afflante Spiritu*», 47.

[59] J. DORÉ, «Méthode exégètique», 34-35, notes that some tasks in exegesis are especially geared to the technical while others are geared to the pastoral application. Furthermore the document itself admits of experts having specialized papers or publications in different areas. J.A. FITZMYER, *The Soul of Theology*, 63-64, states: «the exposition of Scripture that seeks to set forth the meaning of the Word of God in this way would reduce to silence those who claim that "they scarcely ever find anything in biblical commentaries to raise their hearts to God, to nourish their souls or promote interior life". This complaint about sterile commentaries comes from Pius XII himself in his encyclical as he may well have been referring to the writings of some commentators who have used the historical-critical method. Yet the real question is, how have such commentators used the method? Do they allow presuppositions of faith to enhance and enrich its own proper effects? Do they seek to elucidate this *literal, spiritual sense?*».

of education and maturity should affect the way an exegete presents his/her work. The differences have to be acknowledged by the commentator and the results of his investigations must be communicated in a manner that is understandable to his/her audience. Factors to be considered when speaking to an audience include its: age, maturity level, level of formal education, level of religious education, and religious affinity/practice. No single work will be able to cover the vast spectrum of possibilities. An exegete naturally makes particular choices when writing or teaching.

Context. Another consideration is the context to which the commentary/writing is communicated. One setting could be the strictly academic, another could be pastors preparing homilies, another context may be teachers/catechists who instruct children or adults. The different contexts require different styles and emphases in the writings depending on the audience. The highly scientific commentary using original languages and the full ranges of critical techniques will not be fitting for the average reader (even with a high level of education) due to its specialized material. At the same time a commentary written for homily preparation might not necessarily be the best for a university setting[60].

The criticism raised in earlier debates that the HCM inadequately addresses pastoral concerns frequently fails to mention the different purposes, audiences, and contexts that affect the way exegetical results are communicated. A book written on a highly academic level will emphasize the scientific content may seem to overwhelm the average reader. This may be necessary if the book is designed as a reference work to provide information or to stimulate scholarly debate. Other books can provide a pastoral application or interpretation. *Interpretation of the Bible in the Church* acknowledges these differences and sees them as a benefit to the Church[61].

The Relationship between Exegesis and Theology. The relationship between the exegesis and theology was the subject of much debate prior to the document. The discussions continue. The document serves as an

---

[60] Several biblical publications in the English speaking world can serve as an example. Commentary series like *The Anchor Bible* , *Word Biblical Commentary, Sacra Pagina,* and the *New Jerome Biblical Commentary* are more suitable for an academic context. *The New Testament Message, The Old Testament Message,* and *The Collegeville Bible Commentary,* are useful in pastoral or spiritual contexts. The same principle is true for periodicals based on biblical studies. The *Catholic Biblical Association of America* publishes the *Catholic Biblical Quarterly* for highly educated readers and *The Bible Today* for a wider audience.

[61] *EB*, 1482-1487. English trans., 104-106.

aid in distinguishing the competencies of each discipline and the areas
where they overlap. At the same time the PBC desired more cooperation
between the two disciplines since, the subject matter and the goals they
treat are ultimately the same. The document sufficiently delimits the areas
for each field. The relationship can be conceptualized in the form of three
concentric circles. The inner circle represents the base meaning of a text,
in its historical-literary context. The middle circle represents the meaning
of the text in the larger canonical tradition (or as the *Interpretation of the
Bible in the Church* states — the christological, canonical, and ecclesial
aspects), and the outer circle represents the theological systematization of
the biblical material including material from the great Tradition. The exegete works in the inner two circles, the theologian in the outer two. Thus
the bridge is in the second circle. This is the area where interdisciplinary
cooperation can have its greatest effect[62].

---

[62] For consideration of the relationship between exegesis and systematic theology
see: J.A. FITZMYER, *The Soul of Theology*, 54-92; K. BERGER, «Exegesis and Systematic Theology»; J.J. BURKHARD, «The Use of Scripture»; R.P. CARROLL, «The
Bible in the Church»; J.T. FORESTELL, «The Church and the Bible»; F. LAMBIASI,
«Dimensioni Caratteristiche».

J.A. FITZMYER, *The Soul of Theology*, 80, limits exegesis to determining the *literal sense*. Anything beyond this, such as the «line of development» falls into the
realm of systematic theology. In one sense his understanding agrees with *Interpretation
of the Bible in the Church* especially when it distinguishes between the role of the
exegete and systematic theologian (*EB*, 1499. English trans., 111.). On the other hand
a determination of the *spiritual sense* is also in the province of the exegete (cf. JOHN
PAUL II, *Introduction, EB*, 1244. English trans., 11.). Furthermore the line of development of which Fitzmyer speaks begins in the biblical period and moves through the
canonization period and thus falls into the province of the exegete. It would be better
not to think in terms of clear lines of demarcation as though one should not cross.
Rather there is clearly a *via media* that has room for both theological disciplines.

G. O'COLLINS – D. KENDALL, *The Bible for Theology*, draw ten principles for using the Bible in systematic theological studies: a) the principle of faithful hearing; b)
the principle of active hearing; c) the principle of the community and its creeds; d) the
principle of biblical convergence; e) the principle of exegetical consensus; f) the prin-
ciple of metathemes and metanarratives; g) the principle of continuity within discontinuity; h) the principle of eschatological provisionality; i) the principle of philosophical assistance; and j) the principle of inculturation. The explanations and examples for
each principle demonstrate how the Bible can be used in systematic theology while
respecting the findings of exegetical studies. This is especially true of the principle of
exegetical consensus. Although the work describes how to use these findings in systematic theology many of the principles are reflective of the guidelines suggested by
Interpretation of the Bible in the Church and could also be applied to exegetical studies.

The relationship between exegesis and systematic theology is an important topic
but beyond the scope of this presentation. *Interpretation of the Bible in the Church*

Discussions since the issuance of *Interpretation of the Bible in the Church* rehashed the earlier debates. If the call for more inter-disciplinary cooperation and coordination is heeded the relationship will be fruitful; however, it will take time for the interdisciplinary work to develop. If it truly is to make a contribution to the development of theology, these co-operative inquiries cannot merely be on the level of conferences and professional associations. Meaningful and creative demonstrations of scholarly collaboration, expressed in joint publications, inter-departmental theological courses, and academic research are imperative.

3 Conclusion

Interpretation of the Bible in the Church was well received after its publication. The document made a valuable contribution to the discussions regarding biblical interpretation. Chapter VII has evaluated its specific contribution concerning biblical hermeneutics and the HCM. The impact of the document on Catholic exegetical studies cannot be evaluated in-depth presently due to its relatively recent date of issue. Discussion on the place of the HCM in Catholic exegesis will undoubtedly continue; as Cardinal Ratzinger pointed out, the document is not the end of the discussion but a contribution to it.

---

provides a general description of the dynamic relationship between the two disciplines. The possibilities lying therein will only be discovered in the actual attempts of inter-cooperative work.

CHAPTER VIII

Summary and Conclusions

The HCM is a compilation of several individual critical disciplines that seeks to determine the *literal sense* of the passages it studies. This *literal sense* has been described in different ways, from the obvious sense, to the author's intention, to the meaning expressed in the words of the inspired author. The basis of this sense is an historical-literary meaning. The HCM seeks to determine this meaning through its diachronic and synchronic techniques.

The diachronic aspect of the study recognizes the historical aspect of the writing. The meaning that the words and images convey are all historically conditioned, the HCM aims to discover this meaning and to describe it in the words and images of the present. Textual criticism aims to reach the original wording of the inspired text because the original manuscripts are no longer in existence. Philological analysis enables the reader to understand concepts and images that are no longer used today. Literary criticism examines the literary composition of the work demonstrating the unifying style and structure of the work, and when sources have been used they are identified. Genre criticism identifies the genres used in the work, the social setting for which they were created, and the influence this has on the written form. Tradition criticism isolates elements of the tradition from the text and seeks to gain an insight to how the tradition developed prior to its final form. Historical criticism may complete the diachronic study if the text deals with or claims historical reliability. Following this phase of HCM, the exegete is prepared to study the text in its final form. The synchronic study of redaction criticism completes the process. The exegete utilizes the knowledge of the text from previous studies. He examines how the final author used the sources, forms, and traditions. Moreover, he studies how the author adapted the older material or composed new material to give indication to his theological message.

The method is not a rigid set of procedures but a set of general guidelines for approaching the text. Exegetes modify the process and application of these procedures as required by the particular texts being studied. The results of such studies are communicated to audiences of various educational levels with distinct concerns.

The HCM has been the source of much debate in the history of Catholic exegesis. The debates have varied in intensity and concerns. The debates in the early church regarding the *literal* and *spiritual senses* reflect the later debates concerning the methodology itself. The goal of this dissertation, as mentioned in the Introduction, has been to describe the place of the HCM in Catholic exegesis by identifying its necessity and limits. To this end a historical approach was taken. Following an introduction to the method and its procedures the dissertation considered the method's acceptance in four different periods.

1. The Elements of the HCM in Patristic and Medieval Literature

The first period considered was that of the early Church. Although the HCM did not develop until following the Renaissance numerous elements of the individual criticisms can be found in the exegesis of the early Church. For this reason this dissertation began its historical investigation with this period. The approach taken in this section of the dissertation followed three steps. First the development of thought concerning the *literal sense* was outlined. Second elements of the HCM were identified in the literature of the period. Third these elements were analyzed regarding their necessities and limits.

The *literal sense*, as described in this period, has three aspects: the verbal, the historical, and the authorial intention. Regardless of the description, determining *literal sense* necessitated the use of critical techniques and tools. This was especially true regarding problematic texts. Elements from each component discipline of the HCM, save redaction criticism, were identified in the literature of this period.

The limitations of the critical techniques were based on the fact that the *literal sense* itself is limited. Inspiration and the formation of the canon witnessed a meaning in the text beyond the *literal*. This meaning was described in different ways whether it be through Origen's tri-fold senses, the *theoria* of the Antiochenes or the four senses of the Middle Ages. In this context, the limits of the critical elements were obvious. However, the limitations did not eliminate the need for using these procedures. Rather the limitations required that the procedures be utilized within a broader framework or understanding of Christian exegesis.

2. The HCM in Ecclesial Documents:
Providentissimus Deus to *Divino Afflante Spiritu*

Although numerous elements of the HCM can be found in the exegesis of the early Church, it was not until the fifteenth century that the method began to be developed in a more systematic manner. Catholic involvement was sparse in the development of the method until the late nineteenth century. From that time to the present, the use of the HCM in Catholic exegesis has been debated. The Church's response to these debates are reflected in a series of documents.

The second period considered in this historical study examines the official Catholic response to critical methodology in the years 1893-1943. The documents representing this period included the following: *Providentissimus Deus*, the 1905-1915 PBC Decisions, *Spiritus Paraclitus*, and *Divino Afflante Spiritu*.

Providentissimus Deus and *Divino Afflante Spiritu* represented two bookends for this period. Both documents developed out of very different historical contexts. *Providentissimus Deus* primarily addressed the rationalist attacks on the divine character of the Scriptures. *Divino Afflante Spiritu* responded to fundamentalist attacks on the human character of the Scriptures. Despite the different historical situations each document affirmed, albeit to a different degree, the need for Catholic exegetes to use the HCM. John Paul II pointed this out as an important characteristic of each document. The documents did not react to abuses in the method by dismissing it; rather they highlighted its valid elements. The period also saw a reaction against critical scholarship in the PBC Decisions. These decisions, however, are seen today as provisional and temporary. The restraints placed on critical exegesis were due to pastoral rather than scholarly ones.

Providentissimus Deus noted the need to study the original language texts as well as original languages. Recent discoveries of these manuscripts and the questions raised regarding authenticity encouraged a cautious adaptation of the critical method. Elements of the HCM that need to be included in the study are the *Introduction*, textual criticism, original language studies and philology and literary criticism. While *Providentissimus Deus* addressed the topic from the perspective of the divine author, *Divino Afflante Spiritu* addressed it from the perspective of the human author. Pius XII noted that the new discoveries in the Holy Land needed to be considered when studying the scriptures. He affirms and encourages the use of the HCM especially philology and textual criticism, the study of the original texts, as well as literary criticism and the auxiliary sciences.

The encouragement for using the HCM was based, in both cases, on the importance of the *literal sense* for understanding the texts. The *literal sense* was described in different ways in these documents. *Providentissimus Deus* described it as the obvious sense in other words the verbal or historical meaning. *Spiritus Paraclitus* followed along these lines almost equating the *literal sense* with the historical meaning of the text. *Divino Afflante Spiritu* also emphasized the importance of the *literal sense*. Pius XII described this as the meaning intended by the author. The three descriptions in these documents (verbal, historical, author's intention) reflected those of the patristic and medieval period.

Despite the varied definitions, the *literal sense* necessitated the use of the HCM. The degree to which the method was approved depended in large part, on the historical circumstances surrounding its development and included the presuppositions with which it was used. The limitations of the method were also noted. The documents also indicate that due to inspiration, meaning in the text can go beyond the *literal sense*. In this regard, Pius XII specifically noted the canonical relationship of the two testaments. Allowance has to be made for a deeper meaning in the text; however, no guidelines are given for determining it. The criteria for judging this meaning are the Fathers, the Magisterium and the analogy of faith.

3. The HCM in Ecclesial Documents:
Sancta Mater Ecclesia to *Dei Verbum*

The third period considered in the dissertation covered the years between 1943 and 1965. Toward the middle of the 1950's the debate concerning the use of the HCM in Catholic exegesis began anew and was particularly visible in the preparations for the Second Vatican Council. The outcome of this debate was another affirmation of the necessity of the HCM for Catholic exegesis based on the historical condition of the Sacred Texts. The primary ecclesial documents studied in this section were *Sancta Mater Ecclesia* and *Dei Verbum*.

Sancta Mater Ecclesia dealt with the historical transmission of the Gospel through three consecutive periods: the age of Jesus, the age of the apostles and the age of the evangelists. In each stage the gospel message was historically conditioned so that it might be understood by those receiving it. *Dei Verbum* incorporated this theme within its fifth chapter[1].

The Dogmatic Constitution also gave guidelines for biblical interpretation based on the divine-human cooperation in the composition of the texts. It emphasized that the human author worked in freedom under the influence of the Spirit. This needs to be considered when doing exegetical work. However, attention must also be given to the divine character of the text specifically reflected in the canonical collection. Thus, the HCM is required but must be used within a broader context, that of the canon and the Spirit.

Furthermore, *Dei Verbum* recognizes an ongoing aspect of revelation in which God speaks through the Scriptures to people of different times and cultures. Although the HCM aids in determining the historical sense, and can help make the Scriptures accessible to people of the different times through translations and notes; it cannot exhaust meaning in the Scriptures. Due to this limitation, the results of biblical studies must be evaluated within the larger context of the Tradition and Magisterium.

4. The HCM in *Interpretation of the Bible in the Church*

The final period considered in the dissertation was the period between 1978 and the present. After the publication of Raymond Brown's *Birth of the Messiah* in 1978, a new debate began regarding the place of the HCM in Catholic exegesis. This debate was eventually referred to as a «crisis» in biblical interpretation. In many ways this debate was a continuation of the discussions of the earlier period. The dissatisfaction with the HCM was demonstrated from three perspectives: the pastoral, the scholarly, and the magisterial.

The primary pastoral concern was that historical-critical exegesis created a gap between scholarship and the faithful; between the academy and the Church. The faithful had limited access to exegetical studies due to its technical nature. The perception was that only those who were educated as specialists could have access to the material. Another critique leveled from a pastoral perspective was that the concentration on the historical meaning neglected the present reality.

Scholarly concerns were varied, these included the following: the philosophical underpinnings of the method, the presuppositions of exegetes using the method; and the relationships between critical exegesis and actualization, hermeneutics, and the numerous newer synchronic methods.

---

[1] *DV*, §18-19. *EB*, §696-698; *OCT*, §978-980.

The Place of the HCM in Catholic Exegesis: Necessary but Limited

	The Necessity of the HCM	The Limits of the HCM
Elements of the HCM in Patristic and Medieval Literature	Problems in the text require critical evaluation. Understanding the original text requires critical procedures. Determining the literal sense requires critical methodology.	Critical procedures have a narrow focus. The literal sense can not always be determined. Critical procedures are not very helpful in identifying senses other than the literal. Critical practices tend toward the technical and not towards the pastoral.
Providentissimus Deus to Divino Afflante Spiritu	The HCM is needed to help determine the literal sense. The HCM is needed for the study of the original language texts. Discovery of ancient texts and manuscripts necessitate textual criticism. Archeological discoveries require historical critical methodology. The historical condition of the text requires literary criticism to understand the language.	The critical methodology has been tainted with rationalist philosophy. The literal sense is limited. Art of true criticism receives validity within larger framework. Absence of spiritual meaning in the exegesis of the day (PD).
Sancta Mater Ecclesia and Dei Verbum	The Gospel message is historically conditioned therefore it must be understood from a historical perspective. Determining the literal sense requires the use of the HCM. Modern translations of the Bible require the HCM.	Certain philosophical and theological principles taint form-criticism. The HCM does not of itself take into consideration the canonical collection, the tradition of the church and the analogy of faith.
Interpretation of the Bible in the Church	The Bible is historically conditioned and therefore requires the HCM for understanding the texts. The identification of the literal sense requires the use of the HCM. Actualization and inculturation require the use of the HCM. The HCM is necessary for understanding the ancient techniques of exegesis which in turn are necessary for understanding «re-readings» and the NT's use of the OT. The HCM is required to supplement synchronic methodologies and approaches to the bible. The HCM is helpful for ecumenical discussion.	The HCM has shown limits in its classical practice. The HCM is limited by the presuppositions of the exegete. The HCM tends toward a narrow interpretation of the biblical text. The HCM is limited in its identification of the spiritual sense. The HCM as a method does not properly seek to identify the christological, canonical and ecclesial aspects of the text. The HCM used by itself provides no evaluation of the interplay between reader & text which is necessary for understanding. The HCM as a neutral method could fail to recognize the Bible as the Word of God. The HCM fails to consider the dynamic development beyond the text. The limits of the HCM in association with sociological approaches.

Overcoming the Limitations of the HCM

Exegetical inter-disciplinary cooperation is needed.
The HCM must be used in conjunction with other methodologies to be effective for Catholic exegesis.
The HCM must be used in conjunction with or coordinated with other branches of theology — each must know the limits of its competency while seeking to inform and learn from the others.
Attention to the dynamic aspect of the scriptures, possibly an added step.

Figure 10: Summary of the Necessities and Limits of the HCM

Magisterial concerns included questions concerning the proper implementation of *Dei Verbum* and the relationship between exegesis and theology. Those criticizing the method, however, did not call for its total dismissal but for a re-evaluation of its proper formulation or configuration for use in Catholic exegesis.

The defenders of the method emphasized the historical condition of the texts which requires an historical approach to understand their meaning. The defense also included an appeal to earlier ecclesial statements on the topic, specifically regarding the *literal sense*. The defenders also demonstrated the benefits derived from the use of historical-critical exegesis for ecumenical discussions, for use in Catholic education in an American setting, for homily preparation, and for use in systematic theology. The questions raised regarding the philosophical underpinnings of the method were answered by suggesting that the critique of philosophical biases should not be attributed so much to the method but rather to the exegete who uses the method.

During the debate, concerns regarding the *literal sense* were also raised. The primary issue was the limitations it placed on the role of the Holy Spirit in the act of interpretation. It was argued that the Scriptures are not a dead document of the past but a living word to the present. This was reinforced by modern hermeneutical studies which noted that texts could speak outside their original historical setting. Those writing about the limits of the *literal sense* demanded that it be supplemented by other senses.

The debate during these years lacked a clear direction. The earlier years of the debate had to deal with a lack of clearly nuanced thought. Brown and others insisted on an honest appraisal of their work and exegesis. The debate also witnessed a lack of clearly defined terms for the debate. The method was often the focal point of the discussion but a Catholic understanding of the method was not presented until Joseph Fitzmyer's 1989 article "Historical Criticism. Its Role in Biblical Interpretation and Church Life." Furthermore, arguments for a re-formulation or re-configuration of the method frequently offered only vague suggestions for the methodological process.

Interpretation of the Bible in the Church represents the official Church's response to this crisis. The PBC document is a comprehensive statement on biblical interpretation. The document replies to the various concerns and questions raised in the earlier debate, especially regarding the place of the HCM in Catholic exegetical studies and biblical interpretation. The organization of the document helps identify this place. The document presents a comprehensive and synthetic vision of biblical interpretation.

Methodologies are presented first, beginning with the HCM followed by various synchronic approaches. Since, no method can exhaust the meaning of the text, the HCM is used to ascertain the historical meaning of the texts while other methods are used to evaluate meaning beyond this. The methodologies and approaches however are not used in a vacuum. Part Two of the document places these methodologies within the framework of hermeneutics. Philosophical hermeneutics demonstrate that meaning can exist beyond the historical. Biblical hermeneutics dem-onstrate the complexities of interpretation due to the inspired nature of the Scriptures. Part Three places this methodological-hermeneutical framework within the context of the Catholic faith. Part Four presents the interpretive endeavor within the context of the living church today. The document concludes that the HCM will continue to be required for Catholic exegesis, at least in its principle procedures.

The presentation of the HCM in this context helped to identify its necessities and limits. As in previous ecclesial documents, the hermeneutical basis of the HCM is the *literal sense. Interpretation of the Bible in the Church* reformulates its definition calling it «that which has been expressed by the inspired human authors». The reformulation recognizes a meaning beyond the authors intention without negating nor neglecting it. Thus, the authors intention is still important but it is not the locus of meaning, the inspired text is. The meaning of the text is historically conditioned but not limited to this meaning. While HCM is required to ascertain this meaning other methods help to identify meaning beyond it.

Discussion regarding the HCM and biblical interpretation continued after the publication of *Interpretation of the Bible in the Church*. The discussions on biblical hermeneutics continue to focus on theories of multiple meaning. The relationship among these meanings and the original is still debated. The clear presentation of the HCM in *Interpretation of the Bible in the Church* provided an avenue for a more focused discussion regarding the HCM. The method, it was noted, is employed with a large amount of flexibility. It is not used as an absolute. The manner in which the method is employed will vary with different texts as well as the manner by which exegetes employ it. Attempting to form an ideal step by step methodology that could be applied to every text would lead to the same criticisms raised about the HCM in its earlier development; that is, the claim to objectivity and certainty. Perhaps the next stage in discussion will aim at the individual critical disciplines of the HCM, the value and limits of these procedures and the rules that govern them. Further consideration should also be given to the relationship between biblical studies and the peripheral sciences such as archeology and comparative literature. Other points made in the discussion include: the distinction between the HCM and historical criticism, the dependent relationship of synchronic methodologies on the HCM (or at least elements of the method), and the varied purposes in exegetical studies.

5. The Place of the HCM in Catholic Exegesis

The question posed in the beginning of the dissertation was "What is the place of the HCM in Catholic exegesis?" The question was addressed to four different periods in Catholic exegesis beginning with the early church and ending with the current situation. The conclusions to each of these studies answered the question by identifying and evaluating the necessities and limits of the HCM as understood in each period. The compiled list of reasons that necessitate and limit the use of the method for Catholic biblical interpretation is provided on page 296. The general conclusion identifies the necessities and limits of the HCM for Catholic exegesis today.

5.1 *Why is the HCM necessary?*

Why is the HCM necessary? The reasons that necessitate the use of the HCM in Catholic exegesis are summarized in six points.

1. *The HCM is needed to determine the literal sense.* In each of the four periods discussed earlier ascertaining the *literal sense* has been an essential part of exegetical studies. In the patristic period the *literal sense* was described in three different ways: the verbal, the historical, and the authorial intention. Toward the end of the patristic period and through to the modern period the *literal sense* was defined as the author's intention. The advent of modern philosophical hermeneutics has raised questions concerning the ability to know this intention. However the studies still insist on a link with the historically written and conditioned text. *Interpretation of the Bible in the Church* describes the *literal sense* as «that directly expressed by the human author» although this definition allows room for broader interpretations based on the text, it does not eliminate their ties with the original meaning. Thus regardless of the its definition, identifying the *literal sense* necessitates the use of the HCM in Catholic exegesis.

2. *The HCM is needed so that the original texts may be read, studied and translated.* The value of the original language texts was appreciated in the patristic period. Figures such as Origen and Jerome realized the importance of using these texts as the basis of biblical studies. Although the *Vulgate* became the standard text for a time, the original language texts are

still required for serious biblical study. The study and translation of these texts continue to necessitate the HCM especially grammatical-criticism, literary criticism, and genre criticism.

3. *The HCM is needed to determine the original reading from the numerous textual witnesses.* This need was recognized in the patristic period by Origen, Jerome and Eusebius. In the fifteenth and sixteenth centuries, following the first printed editions, the need for textual criticism became more obvious. In the mid-nineteenth to mid-twentieth centuries the discovery of numerous biblical manuscripts caused a certain urgency for textual criticism. Although the urgency is no longer present, the need still for textual studies still exists. In NT studies, the text of the GNT[4] and the Nestle-Aland[27] has become the standard text. However, it does not solve all the problems of textual criticism. Theories on the textual transmission still continue to be discussed. In OT studies, work continues on producing a standard edition with a much more developed *apparatus criticus* than that of the *Biblia Hebraica*. Studies also continue on the Dead Sea Scrolls.

4. *The HCM is needed to address problems due to the historical condition of the text.* Problems of historicity in the text continue to require the HCM. As mentioned earlier, historical criticism must be distinguished from the HCM as a whole, however this discipline is still needed. Although most scholars today agree that the Bible was not written as a history in the modern sense, the Bible still remains a witness to the history of salvation. Historical questions concerning events in the Bible raised either inside or outside the church need to be taken seriously. These questions often require a historical-critical study of the Bible. For example, archeological excavations continue in the Holy Land with much information gleaned from their analysis. At times the finds cause a conflict with the biblical accounts. These studies cannot be ignored but their results should be engaged and evaluated along with historical-critical biblical studies.

5. *The HCM is needed to address problems raised by the biblical text.* The biblical text itself proposes questions regarding interpretation. Questions relating to problems such as historical conflicts, questions based on manuscript differences, and questions concerning form and content which are prompted by the text require a critical approach. At different times in the history of exegesis these problems were addressed. The critical approach gives insight to possible solutions for these difficulties. The rise in the fundamentalist approach today, especially in the United States, increases the need for a sound critical approach to explain some of the complexities of the biblical text.

6. *The HCM helps facilitate ecumenical discussion.* The original or historical meaning of a text or passage has been a common ground starting point for many ecumenical discussions. Brown and others have noted the contributions that historical-critical exegesis has made to the ecumenical movement. As *Interpretation of the Bible in the Church* has pointed out these discussions need to continue, and the HCM remains a valuable asset for these discussions.

5.2 Why is the HCM limited?

The reasons that limit the use of the HCM in Catholic exegesis are summarized in five points:

1. The HCM is limited by its hermeneutical foundation, the *literal sense*. The *literal sense*, as discussed above, is an inspired sense; however, it is not the only sense to the text for the Holy Spirit through inspiration can allow the words to take on a deeper meaning in later understanding. The additional senses whether they are termed *spiritual sense* and *sensus plenior* or *canonical sense* and *more-than-literal senses* are valid and valuable meanings. These meanings are not easily detected using the HCM. The use of other methods, the recourse to the tradition of the Church and to magisterial statements may make this meaning more apparent. Furthermore, due to the limitations of the *literal sense* the HCM does not properly seek to identify the christological, canonical and ecclesial aspects of the text. Integration of the results of synchronic exegesis may help to remove these limitations.

2. The HCM is limited by the presuppositions of exegetes. Although the method in itself is neutral, the presuppositions with which exegetes approaches the text can assert a large influence on the results of their exegesis. Therefore if the exegesis is to be valid the exegete will have to approach the text with the correct presuppositions. In the history of the method various philosophical systems have influenced exegetes and sometimes have tainted the results of their studies. *Interpretation of the Bible in the Church* has identified the presuppositions that Catholic exegetes need for correct exegesis. The presuppositions include the recognition of the Word of God in the Scriptures, the inspired nature that appreciates both the human and the divine in the Scriptures, the movement of the Holy Spirit in the collecting of the works into the canon, the role of the magisterium in interpreting the text, and the recognition that tradition is also a witness to Revelation.

3. Exegesis can be fruitful only within the larger framework of the Church. Proper affinity with the text is needed for valid interpretation. The

Bible is a book of the Church: it developed in the Church and was collected into a canon within the church. So to properly understand the meaning of this text exegesis must be done in the faith-life of the Church. The neutrality of the HCM does not take this into consideration, therefore exegetes have to incorporate this understanding into their presuppositions.

4. The HCM tends toward narrow interpretations. The HCM is limited because it's focus is too narrow. The quest for the original historical-literary meaning limits the method to a meaning in the past. The search for the historical-literary meaning also tends to focus on particular passages and isolated texts without moving to the broader implications of meaning within the canon. The HCM can also tend to emphasize the technical aspects of exegesis to the neglect of the spiritual and pastoral dimensions of the text. Since these are the reasons the text exist in the first place, such failure to treat these items would be a gross neglect. Integration of specialized studies with the results of other methods may provide a solution.

5. The HCM used by itself provides no evaluation of the interplay between the reader and the text. The interaction between the reader and the text can provide insight into the meaning of the text. The results of this interaction in actualization or inculturation today or the study of the text's history of effects (*Wirkungsgeschichte*) can lend insight into how the text was understood through history. These interpretations can be valid developments of the original meaning and may have practical application today, but the HCM provides no way to investigate them.

The study of the HCM in this dissertation has focused on its place in Catholic exegesis. It concludes that the HCM has had an important role in Catholic exegetical studies and suggests that despite its limitations it is still necessary for exegetical work today.

ABBREVIATIONS

AB	Anchor Bible
ABD	*Anchor Bible Dictionary*, ed. D.N. Freedman, Garden City 1992.
ACQR	*American Catholic Quarterly Review*
ACR	*Australian Catholic Record*
AEcR	*American Ecclesiastical Review*
ANCL	Anti-Nicene Christian Library
ANE	Ancient Near East
ANFa	Anti-Nicene Fathers, ed. A. Roberts – J. Donaldson, Edinburgh 1867.
Anton.	*Antonianum*
Asp.	*Asprenas*
AThR	*Anglican Theological Review*
Bib.	*Biblica*
BiKi	*Bibel und Kirche*
BiRe	*Bible Review*
BiTod	*Bible Today*
BJRL	*Bulletin of the John Ryland's Library*
BSTR	*Biblioteca di studi religiosi*
BTB	*Biblical Theology Bulletin*
CathAct	*Catholic Action*
CBQ	*Catholic Biblical Quarterly*
CCR	*Canadian Catholic Review*
CDios	*Ciudad de Dios*
Ch.	Chapter
CHB	*Cambridge History of the Bible*, I, ed. P. R. Ackroyd – C.F. Evans, Cambridge 1970; II, ed. G.W.H. Lampe, 1969; III, ed. S.L. Greenslade, 1963.
ChiSt	*Chicago Studies*
CivCatt	*Civiltà Cattolica*
CleR	*Clergy Review*
Conc.	*Concilium*

ConJ	*Concordia Journal*
cont.	continued
CoTh	*Collectanea theologica.* Warszawa
Cross Cur	*Cross Currents*
CUB	*Catholic University Bulletin*
CurrTheolMiss	*Currents in Theology and Mission*
CW	*Catholic World*
DFT	*Dictionary of Fundamental Theology*, ed. R. Latourelle – R. Fisichella, New York 1994.
Div.	*Divinitas*
DR	*Downside Review*
DT	*Divus Thomas*
DublR	*Dublin Review*
EB	*Enchiridion Biblicum: Documenti della Chiesa sulla Sacra Scrittura*, Bologna 1994[2]
EcR	*Ecclesiastical Review*
EEC	*Encyclopedia of Early Christianity*, ed. A. di Berardino, trans. A. Walford, Cambridge 1992.
EpRe	*Epworth Review*
EspVie	*Espirit et vie*
EstBib	*Estudios bíblicos*
ET	*Expository Times*
EThL	*Ephemerides theologicae Louvanienses*
EvQ	*Evangelical Quarterly*
FOC	Fathers of the Church Series
GNT[4]	*Greek New Testament*, ed. K.A. Aland – M. Black – C.M. Martini – B.M. Metzger – A. Wikgren, Stuttgart 1993[4]
Gr.	*Gregorianum*
HCM	historical-critical method
HCTIS	T. CURTIN, *Historical Criticism and the Theological Interpretation of Scripture. Discussion of a Biblical Hermeneutic 1958-1963*, Roma 1987.
HE	EUSEBIUS' *Historia Ecclesiastica*, trans. K. Lake – J.E.L. Oulton, Cambridge 1994[2].
Her.	*Hermathena*
HeyJ	*Heythrop Journal*
HPR	*Homiletic and Pastoral Review*
HThR	*Harvard Theological Review*
IBC	*The Interpretation of the Bible in the Church*
IBSt	*Irish Biblical Studies*
IDB	*Interpreter's Dictionary of the Bible*, ed. G.A. Buttrick, Nashville TN, 1962.
IER	*Irish Ecclesiastical Review*
IJT	*Indian Journal of Theology*

Interp.	*Interpretation*
ITC	International Theological Commission
ITQ	*Irish Theological Quaterly*
JBC	*Jerome Biblical Commentary*, ed. R.E. Brown – J.A. Fitzmyer – R.E. Murphy, Englewood Cliffs, NJ 1968.
JBL	*Journal of Biblical Literature*
JES	*Journal of Ecumenical Studies*
JETS	*Journal of the Evangelical Theological Society*
JSSt	*Journal of Semitic Studies*
JThS	*Journal of Theological Studies*
Laur.	*Laurentianum*
LCL	Loeb Classical Library
LiLi	*Living Light*
LouvSt	*Louvain Studies*
LumVit	*Lumen vitae*
Mar.	*Marianum*
MSSNTS	Monograph Series. Society for New Testament Studies
N-A^{27}	Nestle-Aland, *Novum Testamentum Graece*, ed. B. Aland – K. Aland – M. Black – C.M. Martini – B. Metzger – A. Wikgren, Stuttgart 1993^{27}.
NCR	*National Catholic Reporter*
NJBC	*New Jerome Biblical Commentary*, ed. R.E. Brown – J.A. Fitzmyer – R.E. Murphy, Englewood Cliffs, NJ 1990.
NPNF	Nicene and Post-Nicene Fathers, Series I, ed. P. Schaff, Edinburgh 1886; Series II, ed. P. Schaff – H. Wace, Edinburgh 1890.
NRTh	*Nouvelle revue théologique*
NT	New Testament
NTOA	Novum Testamentum et Orbis Antiquus
NTS	*New Testament Studies*
OCT	*Official Catholic Teaching, Biblical Interpretation*, ed. J.J. Megivern, Wilmington NC, 1978
OR	*Osservatore Romano*
OT	Old Testament
PG	Patrologiae cursus completus. Accurante Jacques-Paul Migne. Series Graeca
P.I.B.	Pontificio Istituto Biblico — Roma
PL	Patrologiae cursus completus. Accurante Jacques-Paul Migne. Series Latina
PSB	*Princeton Seminary Bulletin*
RB	*Revue biblique*
RdT	*Rassegna di teologia*
REAug	*Revue des études augustiennes*
RevSr	*Revue des sciences religieuses*

RF	*Razón y fé*
RICP	*Revue de l'Institut Catholique de Paris*
RThom	*Revue thomiste*
RUO	*Revue de l'Univérsité d'Ottawa*
SacDoc	*Sacra dottrina*
Salm.	*Salamanticensis*
SalTer	*Sal Terrae*
SBET	*Scottish Bulletin of Evangelical Theology*
SBL	*Society of Biblical Literature*
SBL.DS	*Society of Biblical Literature. Dissertation Series*
ScC	*Scuola cattolica*
ScEs	*Science et esprit*
ScrB	*Scripture Bulletin*
ScrTh	*Scripta theologica*
ser.	Series
SJT	*Scottish Journal of Theology*
SME	*Sancta Mater Ecclesia*
StPat	*Studia Patavina*
StPatr	*Studia patristca*
StZ	*Stimmen der Zeit*
SubBi	*Subsidia biblica*
ThD	*Theology Digest*
ThTo	*Theology Today*
trans.	translation
TS	*Theological Studies*
UnSa	*Unam sanctam*
UTS	*Untersuchungen zur Theologie der Seelsorge*
VD	*Verbum Domini*
vol.	volume

BIBLIOGRAPHY

ABBOTT, W.M., «Pius XII's Encyclical on Bible Study», *BiTod* 7 (1963) 439-443.

Acta et Documenta Concilio Oecumenico Vaticano II, Series I, Vatican City 1960-1961; Series II, Vatican City 1965-1985.

AHERN, B., «Textual Directives of the Encyclical *Divino Afflante Spiritu*», *CBQ* 7 (1945) 340-347.

————, «Gathering the Fragments of Fear and Scholarship», *Worship* 35 (1961) 160-165.

————, «*On Divine Revelation*», *HPR* 66 (1966) 557-565.

————, «Scriptural Aspects of *Dei Verbum*», in *Vatican II: An Interfaith Appraisal*, ed. J.H. Miller, Notre Dame – London 1966, 54-67.

ALAND, K., *The Text of the New Testament*, Grand Rapids 1987.

ALBERIGO, G., «The Announcement of the Council. From the Security of the Fortress to the Lure of the Quest», in *History of Vatican II* I, ed. G. Alberigo – J.A. Komonchak, Maryknoll 1995, 1-54.

ALBERIGO, G. – KOMONCHAK, J.A., *History of Vatican II*, I, Maryknoll 1995; II, Maryknoll 1997.

ALEMANY, J.J., «Must There Be Tension Between Exegesis and Dogmatic Theology?», *Conc.* 6 (1994) 93-100.

ALONSO SCHÖKEL, L., «Dove va l'esegesi cattolica?», *CivCatt* 26 (1960) 449-460.

————, «El processo de la inspiración. Hablar y escribir», *Bib.* 46 (1965) 269-286.

————, «Es dificil leer la Biblia?», *RF* 209 (1984) 200-210.

————, *The Inspired Word. Scripture in the Light of Language and Literature*, New York 1965.

————, «Is Exegesis Necessary?», *Conc.* 7 (1971) 30-38.

ALONSO SCHÖKEL, L., «La constitución *Dei Verbum* en el momento actual», *RF* 178 (1968) 237-244.

——, «La Palabra de Dios según la constitución conciliar», *SalTer* 54 (1966), 1-7.

——, «Of Methods and Models», *UTS* 36 (1985) 3-13.

——, «Trends. Plurality of Methods, Priority of Issues», *UTS* 40 (1988) 285-297.

——, «Tre notas de hermenéutica», *EstBib* 55 (1997), 73-87.

——, «Toward a New Synthesis?», *ChiSt* 3 (1964) 185-199.

——, «Unità e composizione della costituzione *Dei Verbum*», in *Il dinamismo della tradizione* Brescia 1970, 7-15.

ALONSO SCHÖKEL, L. – ARTOLA, A.M., ed., *La Palabra de Dios en la historia de los hombres. Comentario temático a la constitución "Dei Verbum" del Vaticano II sobre la divina revelación*, Bilbao 1991.

ANGRISANI SNFILLIPPO, M.L., «Cassiodorus», *EEC* 149-150.

ANTONIUTTI, I., «Célébration du cinquantième anniversaire de l'encyclique *Providentissimus Deus*, November 18, 1943», *Revue de l'Université de Ottawa* 14 (1944) 102-132.

AP-THOMAS, D.R., *A Primer of Old Testament Criticism*, Philadelphia 1971.

ARENS, E., «Roma y la interpretación de la Biblia», *Páginas* 128 (1994) 64-77.

ARMDERING, C.E., *The Old Testament and Criticism*, New York 1983.

ARNS, E.P., *La technique du livre d'après S. Jérôme*, Paris 1953.

ASURMENDI, J., «Cien años de exégesis católica», *Salmanticensis* 41 (1994) 67-82.

AUDINET, J., «The Banquet of Scripture. The Bible and Adult Catechesis», *Conc.* 7.10 (1971) 129-140.

AUNE, D.E., *The New Testament in Its Literary Environment*, Philadelphia 1987.

BAILEY, J.L., «Genre Analysis», in *Hearing the New Testament: Strategies for Interpretation*, ed. J.B. Green, Grand Rapids 1995, 197-221.

BAILEY, J.L. – BROEK, L. V., *Literary Forms in the New Testament. A Handbook*, Louisivlle 1992.

VON BALTHASAR, H.U., «God is His Own Exegete», *Communio* 13 (1986) 280-287.

BARNES, T.D., «The Composition of Eusebius' Onomasticon», *JThS* 26 (1975) 412-415.

BARR, J., «St. Jerome and the Sound of Hebrew», *JSSt* 12 (1967) 1-36.

BARR, J., «St. Jerome's Appreciation of Hebrew», *BJRL* 49 (1966) 280-302.

BARRINGER, R., «What is New and What is Old. Patristic Exegesis», *CCR* 11 (1993) 7-15.

BARTHELEMY, D., *Critique textuelle de l'Ancien Testament*, OBO 50, Fribourg and Gottingen 1982.

BARTON, J., «Form Criticism. OT», *ABD* II, 838-841.

————, *Reading the Old Testament. Method in Biblical Study*, London 1996.

————, «Redaction Criticism. OT», *ABD* V, 645-647.

BAUM, G., «Vatican II's Constitution on Revelation. History and Interpretation», *TS* 28 (1967) 51-75.

BEA, A., «*Divino Afflante Spiritu*», *Bib.* 24 (1943) 313-322.

————, «Il modernismo biblico secondo l'enciclica *Pascendi*», *Div.* 2 (1958) 9-24.

————, «L'enciclica *Divino Afflante Spiritu*», *CivCatt* 94 (1943) 212-224.

————, *San Pio X. Promotore degli studi biblici. Fondatore del Pontificio Istituto Biblico*, Roma 1955.

BEARDSLEE, W., *Literary Criticism of the New Testament*, Philadelphia 1970.

BEAUCHAMP, P., «État et méthod de l'exégèse», *Esprit* 41 (1973) 843-858.

BEGLEY, J., «Modern Theories of Interpretation», *ACR* 73 (1996) 81-91.

BELLET, M., *Crise du biblisme, chance de la bible*, Paris 1973.

BENSON, J., «The History of the HCM in the Church. A Survey», *Dialog* 12 (1973) 94-103.

————, *The Secrets of Mt. Sinai. The Story of the World's Oldest Bible - Codex Sinaticus*, Garden City, New York 1986.

BEOZZO, J.O., «The External Climate», in *History of Vatican II* I, ed. G. Alberigo – J.A. Komonchak, Maryknoll 1995, 357-404.

BERGANT, D., «Fundamentalism and the Biblical Commission», *ChiSt* 34 (1995) 209-221.

BERGER, K., «Exegesis and Systematic Theology — The Exegete's Perspective», *Conc.* 6 (1994) 83-92.

BERNARD, J.H., «The Greek MSS used by St. Jerome», *Her.* XI (1901) 335-342.

BEST, E., «The Literal Meaning of Scripture. The Historical Critical Method and the Interpretation of Scripture», *Proceedings of the Irish Biblical Association* 5 (1981) 14-35.

BIRDSALL, J.N., «The New Testament Text», in *CHB* I, 308-377.

BLACK, D.A. – DOCKERY, D.S., ed., *New Testament Criticism and Interpretation*, Grand Rapids 1991.

BLACK, E., «Historicity of the Bible, Pt. 1», *HPR* 81 (1981) 13-23.

BLOWERS, P.M. – LEVENSON, J.D. – WILKEN, R.L., «Interpreting the Bible. Three Views», *First Things* 45 (1994) 40-46.

———, «Three Views from the USA», in *The Interpretation of the Bible in the Church*, ed. J.L. Houlden, London 1995, 112-128.

BODINE, W.R., «Linguistics and Biblical Study», *ABD* IV, 327-332.

BOER, W.D., «Hermeneutic Problems in Early Christian Literature», *Vigiliae Christianae* 1 (1947) 150-167.

BOISMARD, M.E., «Two-Source Hypothesis», *ABD* VI, 671-682.

BOTHA, J.E., «Style in the New Testament. The Need for Serious Reconsideration», in *New Testament Text and Language* 44, ed. C.A. Evans – S.E. Porter, Sheffield 1997, 114-129.

BOURKE, M.M., «Review of R.E. Brown's *Birth of the Messiah*», *CBQ* 40 (1978) 122-124.

BOYLE, J.F., «Faith Seeking Understanding. Medieval Exegesis», *CCR* 11 (1993) 9-13.

BRANDI, S.M., *La questione biblica e l'enciclica «Providentissimus Deus» di S.S. Leone XIII*, Roma 1894.

BRAUN, F.M., *The Work of Père Lagrange*, Milwaukee 1963.

BROCK, S.F. – FRITSCH, C.T. – JELLICOE, S., ed., *Studies in the Septuagint. Origins, Recensions, and Interpetations. Selected with a Prolegomenon*, Leiden 1974.

BROCK, S.P., «Origen's Aims as a Textual Critic of the Old Testament», *StPatr* 10 (1970) 215-218.

BROOKE, A.E. – MCLEAN, N. – THACKERAY, H.S., *The Old Testament in Greek*, Cambridge 1906.

BROTZMAN, E., *Old Testament Textual Criticism. A Practical Introduction*, Grand Rapids 1994.

BROWN, D., «St. Jerome as a Biblical Exegete», *IBSt* 5 (1983) 138-155.

———, *Vir Trilinguis. A Study in the Biblical Exegesis of St. Jerome*, Kampen 1992.

BROWN, R.E., «"And the Lord Said"? Biblical Reflections on Scripture as the Word of God», *TS* 42 (1981) 3-19.

———, *Biblical Exegesis and Church Doctrine*, New York 1985.

———, *Biblical Reflections on Crises Facing the Church*, New York 1975.

———, *The Birth of the Messiah*, New York 1993[2].

BROWN, R.E., «Communicating the Divine and Human in Scripture», *Origins* 22 (1992) 1-9.

————, «The Contribution of Historical Biblical Criticism to Ecumenical Church Discussion», in *Biblical Interpretation in Crisis: The Ratzinger Conference on Bible and the Church*, ed. R.J. Neuhaus, Grand Rapids 1989, 24-49.

————, *The Critical Meaning of the Bible*, New York 1981.

————, «Ecumenism and New Testament Research», *JES* 1 (1964) 299-314.

————, *Episkope and Episcopate in Ecumenical Perspective*, 102, Geneva 1980.

————, «Historical-Critical Exegesis and Attempts at Revisionism», *BiTod* 23 (1985) 157-165.

————, «The Importance of How Doctrine is Understood», *Origins* 10 (1981) 737-743.

————, *An Introduction to the New Testament*, New York 1997.

————, «Liberals, Ultraconservatives, and the Misinterpretation of Catholic Biblical Exegesis», *CrossCur* 34 (1984) 311-328.

————, «The Meaning of the Bible», *ThD* 28 (1980) 305-319.

————, «The Problem of the *Sensus Plenior*», *EThL* 43 (1967) 460-469.

————, «Scripture and Dogma Today», *America* 157 (1987) 286-289.

————, «The *Sensus Plenior* in the Last Ten Years», *CBQ* 25 (1963) 262-285.

————, *The «Sensus Plenior» of Sacred Scripture*, Baltimore 1955.

BROWN, R.E. – COLLINS, T.A., «Church Pronouncements», *NJBC* 1166-1174.

BROWN, R.E. – DONFRIED, K.P. – FITZMYER, J.A. – REUMANN, J., *Mary in the New Testament*, New York 1978.

BROWN, R.E. – JOHNSON, D.W. – O'CONNELL, K.G., «Texts and Versions», *NJBC* 1083-1112.

BROWN, R.E. – SCHNEIDERS, S.M., «Hermeneutics», *NJBC*, 1146-1165.

BROWN, S., «New Directions in Biblical Interpretation», *BiTod* 27 (1989) 197-202.

BRYAN, C., «The Preachers and the Critics. Thoughts on Historical Criticism», *AThR* 74 (1992) 37-53.

BURGHARDT, W.J., «On Early Christian Exegesis», *TS* 11 (1950) 78-116.

BURKHARD, J.J., «The Use of Scripture in Theology and Preaching. Experience, Interpretation and Ecclesial Identity.», *NTRev* 8 (1995) 30-44.

BURNSTEIN, E., «La compétence de Jérôme en hébreu. Explication de certaines erreurs», *REAug* 21 (1975) 3-12.

BYRNE, B., «A New Vatican Document on the Bible», *ACR* 72 (1994) 325-329.

CABA, J., «Historicity of the Gospels (*Dei Verbum* 19). Genesis and Fruits of the Conciliar Text», in *Vatican II: Assessment and Perspectives*, I, ed. R. Latourelle, Mahwah – New York 1988, 220-266.

———, «Métodos exegéticos en el estudio actual del Nuevo Testamento», *Gr.* 73 (1992) 611-669.

CARLEN, M.C., *Guide to the Documents of Pius XII (1939-49)*, Westminster, MD 1951.

———, *A Guide to the Encyclicals of the Roman Pontiffs from Leo XIII to the Present Day (1878-1937)*, New York 1939.

CARROLL, R.P., «Cracks in the Soul of Theology», in *The Interpretation of the Bible in the Church*, ed. J.L. Houlden, London 1995, 142-155.

«The Catholic Church and Bible Interpretation», *Bible Review* 10.4 (1994) 32-35.

CHANTRAINE, G., «Exegesis and Contemplation in the Work of Hans Urs von Balthasar», *Communio* 16 (1989) 366-383.

CHARLESWORTH, J.H., «The Centenary of the École Biblique», *PSB* 12 (1991) 56-61.

CIPRIANI, S., «L'interpretazione della Bibbia nella chiesa», *Asp.* 42 (1995) 5-20.

———, «Presupposti dottrinali espliciti e impliciti della "Instructio" della Pontificia Commissione Biblica sui Vangeli», *DT* 68 (1965) 242-254.

CLEMENTS, R.E., *A Century of Old Testament Study*, Guildford, UK 1982.

COCONNIER, M.T., «L'encyclique *Providentissimus Deus* des études bibliques», *RThom* 1 (1893) 665-675.

COLLINS, J.J., «Biblical Scholarship and the Church», *ChiSt* 17 (1981) 121-135.

———, «*Providentissimus Deus*», *HPR* 44 (1943) 112-117.

COLLINS, R.F., «Augustine of Hippo Precursor of Modern Biblical Scholarship», *LouvSt* 12 (1987) 131-151.

COLLINS, R.F., «Hearing the Word. Methods of Biblical Interpretation», *LiLi* 31 (1994) 3-9.

———, *Introduction to the New Testament*, London 1983.

COLOMBO, G., «Bibbia e teologia. Dalla *Providentissimus Deus* alla *Dei Verbum*», *StPat* 41 (1994) 439-456.

CONZELMANN, H. – LINDEMANN, A., *Arbeitsbuch zum Neuen Testament*, Peabody 1988.

CORMICAN, P.J., «The Inerrancy of Scripture in Light of the Encyclical *Providentissimus Deus*», *CW* 61 (1895) 1-13.

COSTACURTA, B., «Esegesi e lettura credente della scrittura», *Gr.* 73 (1992) 739-745.

COTHENET, E., «Commission Biblique Pontificale. *L'interprétation de la Bible dans l'Église*», *EspVie* 104 (1994) 121-126.

COTTER, A.C., «The Antecedents of the Encyclical *Providentissimus Deus*», *CBQ* 5 (1943) 117-124.

COUVE DE MURVILLE, M., «The Catholic Church and the Critical Study of the Bible», *EpRe* 13 (1986) 76-86.

CRAMPSEY, J.A., «Scripture and the Church», *Month* 247 (1985) 419-422.

CROSS, F. M. – TALMON, S., *Qumran and the History of the Biblical Texts*, Cambridge 1975.

CROUZEL, H., «Origen», *EEC* II, 621.

CULLEY, R.C., ed., *Oral Tradition and Old Testament Studies*, Missoula 1976.

CUMMINGS, J.T., «St. Jerome as Translator and Exegete», *StPatr* XII (1975) 279-282.

CUNNINGHAM, A., «Reading the Scriptures. A Patristic Perspective», *ChiSt* 19 (1980) 189-200.

CURTIN, T.R., *Historical Criticism and the Theological Interpretation of Scripture. The Catholic Discussion of a Biblical Hermeneutic. 1958-93*, Roma 1987.

D'AMBROSIO, M., «Henri de Lubac and the Critique of Scientific Exegesis», *Communio* 19 (1992) 365-388.

DAVIDSON, R. – LEANEY, A.R., *Biblical Criticism*, London 1970.

DEIST, F., *Towards the Text of the Old Testament*, Pretoria 1978.

———, *Witnesses to the Old Testament*, Pretoria 1988.

«Die Auslegung der Bibel in der Kirche», *BiKi* 49 (1994) 58-60.

«*Divino Afflante Spiritu*», *CathAct* 25 (1943) 3-4.

DOCKERY, D.S., *Biblical Interpretation. Then and Now*, Grand Rapids 1992.

DONAHUE, F., «Modern or Early Church Interpretation?», *BiTod* 26 (1988) 35-38.

DONAHUE, J.R., «The Changing Shape of Catholic Biblical Scholarship», in *Hermes and Athena: Biblical Exegesis and Philosophical Theology* 7, ed. E. Stump – T.P. Flint, Notre Dame 1993.

———, «A Journey Remembered. Catholic Biblical Scholarship Fifty Years After *Divino Afflante Spiritu*», *America* 169.7 (1993) 6-11.

DORÉ, J., «L'Interprétation de la Bible dans l'Église», *Etudes* 382 (1995) 227-232.

———, «Méthodes exégètique et enseignement de l'exégèse. Sur l'instruction de la commission biblique pontificale. L'interprétation de la bible dans l'Église», *RICP* 52 (1994) 33-40.

DREHER, B., «Exegesis and Proclamation», in *Theology, Exegesis and Proclamation* 64, ed. R. Murphy, New York 1971, 56-66.

DREYFUS, F., «Exégèse en Sorbonne, exégèse en Église», *RB* 82 (1975) 321-359.

DULLES, A., *The Craft of Theology*, New York 1995.

———, «*The Interpretation of the Bible in the Church*. A Theological Appraisal», in *Kirche sein: Nachkonziliare Theologie im Dienst der Kirchenreform*, Fs. J. Pottmeyer, Freiburg 1994,

———, «Scripture. Recent Protestant and Catholic Views», *ThTo* 37 (1980) 7-26.

DUNCKER, P.G., «Biblical Criticism. Instructions of the Church and Excesses of Form Criticism», *CBQ* 25 (1963) 22-33.

DUNGAN, D.L., «Two-Gospel Hypothesis», *ABD* VI, 671-679.

DUNN, J.P., «Review of R.E. Brown's *Birth of the Messiah*», *ScotJT* 33 (1980) 85-87.

DUPUY, B.D., *La révélation divine. Constitution dogmatique «Dei Verbum»*, *UnSa* 70a,b, Paris 1968.

EISSFELDT, O., *The Old Testament. An Introduction*, Oxford 1965.

ELLIOT, J.K., *A Bibliography of Greek New Testament Manuscripts*, MSSNTS 62, Cambridge 1989.

ELLIOT, K. – MOIR, I., *Manuscripts and the Text of the New Testament*, Edinburgh 1995.

EPP, E.J., «The Eclectic Method in New Testament Textual Criticisms. Solution or Symptom?», *HThR* 69 (1976) 211-257.

EPP, E.J., «Textual Criticism», in *The New Testament and Its Modern Interpretation* 3, ed. E.J. Epp – G.W. McRae, Philadelphia 1989, 75-126.

———, «Textual Criticism. New Testament», *ABD* VI, 412-435.

———, «Toward the Clarification of the Term "Textual Variant"», in *Studies in New Testament Language and Text*, Fs. G.D. Kilpatrick, Leiden 1976, 150-173.

EPP, E.J. – FEE, G.D., ed., *New Testament Textual Criticism. Its Significance for Exegesis*, London 1981.

———, *Studies in the Theory and Method of New Testament Textual Criticism*, Grand Rapids 1993.

FABRIS, R., «Bibbia e magisterio. Dalla *Providentissimus Deus* (1893) alla *Dei Verbum* (1965)», *StPat* 42 (1994) 315-340.

FARKASFALVY, D., «The Case for Spiritual Exegesis», *Communio* 10 (1983) 332-350.

———, «In Search of a "Post-critical" Method of Biblical Interpretation for Catholic Theology», *Communio* 13 (1986) 288-307.

FARRAR, F.W., *History of Interpretation*, Bampton Lectures 1885 Grand Rapids 1961.

FARRELL, T.J., «Kelber's Breakthrough», *Semeia* 39 (1987) 27-46.

FEE, G.D., *New Testament Exegesis. A Handbook for Students and Pastors*, Louisville 1993.

———, «The Textual Criticism of the New Testament», in *Biblical Criticism: Historical, Literary, and Textual*, ed. R.K. Harrison, Grand Rapids 1978.

FERGUSON, E., ed., *The Bible in the Early Church*, New York – London 1993.

FERGUSON, D.S., *Biblical Hermeneutics. An Introduction*, London 1986.

FEUILLET, A., «Réflexions d'actualité sur les recherches exégètiques», *RThom* 71 (1971) 246-279.

FIELD, F., *Origenis Hexapla*, 1-2, Oxford 1875.

FINAN, T. – TWOMEY, V., *Scriptural Interpretation in the Fathers*, Cambridge 1995.

FINEGAN, J., *Encountering New Testament Manuscripts. A Working Introduction to Textual Criticism*, London 1974.

FISHBANE, M., «The Teacher and the Hermeneutical Task. A Reinterpretation of Medieval Exegesis», in *The Garments of Torah: Essays on Biblical Hermeneutics*, Bloomington – Indianapolis 1988, 112-133.

FITZMYER, J.A., *The Biblical Commission's Document «The Interpretation of the Bible in the Church»*, SubBi 18, Roma 1995.

————, «Commentary on the Instruction on the Historical Truth of the Bible», *TS* 24 (1964) 386-408.

————, «Historical Criticism. Its Role in Biblical Interpretation and Church Life», *TS* 50 (1989) 244-259.

————, «The Interpretation of the Bible in the Church», *America* 169.17 (1993) 12-15.

————, «The Interpretation of the Bible in the Church Today», *ITQ* 62 (1997) 84-100.

————, *An Introductory Bibliography for the Study of Scripture*, SubBi 3, Roma 1990.

————, «Problems of Literal and Spiritual Senses of Scripture», *LouvSt* 20 (1995) 134-146.

————, «A Recent Roman Scriptural Controversy», *TS* 22 (1961) 426-444.

————, *Scripture, The Soul of Theology*, New York 1994.

————, «The Senses of Scripture Today», *ITQ* 62 (1997) 101-117.

FITZMYER, J.A. – BROWN, R.E., «Danger Also from the Left», *BiTod* 23 (1985) 105-110.

FLESSEMAN VAN LEER, E., *Tradition and Scripture in the Early Church*, Assen 1955.

FOCANT, C., «L'interprétation de la Bible dans l'Église», *RThL* 25 (1994) 348-354.

FOGARTY, G.P., *American Catholic Biblical Scholarship*, San Franscisco 1989.

FORESTELL, J.T., «The Church and the Bible», *CCR* 13 (1995) 11-21.

FOUILLOUX, É., «The Antepreparatory Phase. The Slow Emergence from Inertia (January, 1959 – October, 1962)», in *History of Vatican II* I, ed. G.K. Alberigo – J.A. Komonchak, Maryknoll 1995, 55-166.

FRANZMAN, M.H., «The Historical-Critical Method», *ConJ* 6 (1980) 101-102.

FREYER, N.S., «The Historical-Critical Method — Yes or No?», *Scriptura* 20 (1987) 41-70.

FRIEDMAN, R.E., «Torah», *ABD* VI, 609-622.

FROEHLICH, K., *Biblical Interpretation in the Early Church*, Philadelphia 1984.

FRUCHON, P., «Exégèse biblique et tradition», *Esprit* 35 (1967) 883-897.

FULLER, R.H., *Critical Introduction to the New Testament*, London 1966.

———, «Review of R.E. Brown's *Birth of the Messiah*», *CBQ* 40 (1978) 116-124.

FUSCO, V., «Un secolo di metodo storico nell'esegesi cattolica (1893-1993)», *StPat* 41 (1994) 341-398.

GALBIATI, E., «I generi letterari secondo il P. Lagrange e la *Divino Afflante Spiritu*», *ScC* 75 (1947) 117-186, 282-192.

GAMBLE, H.Y., «The Canon of the New Testament», in *The New Testament and Its Modern Interpreters*, ed. E.J. Epp – G.W. MacRae, Philadelphia – Atlanta 1989, 201-243.

———, *The New Testament Canon. Its Making and Meaning*, Guides to Biblical Scholarship: New Testament Series, Philadelphia 1985.

GERHARDSSON, B., *Memory and Manuscript*, Uppsala – Copenhagen 1961.

GHIBERTI, G., «Il metodo storico-critico», in *L'Interpretazione della Bibbia nella Chiesa*, ed. G. Ghiberti – F. Mosetto, Torino 1998.

GHIBERTI, G., – MOSETTO, F., *L'Interpretazione della Bibbia nella Chiesa*, Torino 1998.

GILBERT, M., «Cinquant'anni di magistero romano sull'ermeneutica biblica. Leone XIII (1893) — Pio XII (1943)», in *Chiesa e Sacra Scrittura: Un secolo di magistero ecclesiastico e studi biblici* 17, Roma 1994, 11-33.

———, «New Horizons and Present Needs. Exegesis Since Vatican II», in *Vatican II: Assessment and Perspectives* I, ed. R. Latourelle, Mahwah – New York 1988, 321-343.

GILBY, T., *St. Thomas Acquinas Summa Theologica. Latin Text, English Translation, Introduction, Notes, Appendices, and Glossary*, I, Cambridge 1964.

GNILKA, J., «Methodik und Hermeneutik. Gedanken zur Situation der Exegese», in *Neues Testament und Kirche*, ed. R. Schnackenburg, Freiburg 1974, 458-475.

GOELZER, H., *Étude lexicographique et grammaticale de la latine de saint Jérôme*, Paris 1884.

GOSHEN-GOTTSTEIN, M.H., «The Textual Criticism of the Old Testament. Rise, Decline, Rebirth», *JBL* 102 (1983) 365-399.

GRANNAN, C.P., «A program of biblical studies», *CUB* 1 (1895) 35-52.

GRANT, R. – TRACY, D., *A Short History of the Interpretation of the Bible*, Philadelphia 1984.

GRANT, R.M., *Heresy and Criticism in Early Christian Literature*, Louisville 1993.

GRANT, R.M., «Literary Criticism and the New Testament Canon», in *New Testament Interpretation and Methods* 45, ed. C.A. Evans, – S.E. Porter, Sheffield 1997, 82-101.

GRAYSON, A.K. – THOMPSON, T.L. – LATEINER, D., «Historiography», *ABD* III, 205-219.

GRECH, P., «L'ermeneutica biblica nel xx secolo», *StPat* 41 (1994) 399-411.

————, *Ermeneutica e Teologia biblica*, Roma 1986.

————, «Hermeneutics», DFT, 416-425.

————, «Interprophetic Re-interpretation and Old Testament Eschatology», *Augustinianum* 9 (1969) 235-265.

————, «The Language of Scripture and Its Interpretation: An Essay», *BTB* 6 (1976) 161-176

————, «The Old Testament as a Christological Source in the Apostolic Age», *BTB* 5 (1975) 127-144.

————, «The "Testimonia" and Modern Hermeneutics», *NTS* 19 (1976) 318-324.

GREENLEE, J.H., *Introduction to New Testament Textual Criticism*, Peabody 1995[2].

GREER, R.A., «The Christian Bible and Its Interpretation», in *Early Biblical Interpretation*, ed. J.L. Kugel – R.A. Greer, Philadelphia 1986, 109-203.

GRELOT, P., Exégèse biblique au carrefour», *NRTh* 98 (1976) 416-434, 481-511.

————, «La pratique de la méthod historique en exégèse biblique», *Quatre Fleuves* 7 (1977) 15-37.

GRIBOMONT, J., «Hexapla», *EEC* I, 390.

————, «The Translators», in *Patrology* III, ed. J. Quasten, Allen, TX 1977, 195-254.

GROLLENBERG, L., *Bible Study for the Twenty-first Century*, 1976.

GRUENTHANER, M.J., «Fiftieth Anniversary of the Encyclical *Providentissimus Deus*», *CBQ* 5 (1943) 115-116.

GUDORF, C.E., «The Magisterium and the Bible. North American Experience», *Conc.* (1991) 79-90.

HABEL, N.C., *Literary Criticism of the Old Testament*, Guides to Biblical Scholarship, Philadelphia 1971.

HAMILTON, G., «*Divino Afflante Spiritu*. Catholic Interpretation of Scripture», *CCR* (1988) 171-176.

HANSON, R.P.C., «Biblical Exegesis in the Early Church», in *CHB* I, 412-453.

HARRINGTON, D., *Interpreting the Old Testament*, Old Testament Message 1, Wilmington 1981.

HARRISVILLE, R.A. – SUNDBERG, W., *The Bible in the Modern Culture*, Grand Rapids 1995.

HARTDEGEN, S., «The Influence of the Encyclical *Providentissimus Deus* on Subsequent Scripture Study», *CBQ* 5 (1943) 141-159.

HARTMAN, L.F., «St. Jerome as an Exegete», in *A Monument to St. Jerome*, ed. F.X. Murphy, New York 1952, 37-81.

HAYES, J.H., *An Introduction to Old Testament Study*, Nashville 1979.

HAYES, J.H. – HOLLADAY, C.R., *Biblical Exegesis. A Beginner's Handbook*, Atlanta 1987.

HAYWARD, C.T., *Jerome's Hebrew Questions on Genesis*, Oxford 1995.

HEBBLETHWAITE, P., «The Bible in the Church», in *The Interpretation of the Bible in the Church*, ed. J.L. Houlden, London 1995, 101-106.

———, «The Bible in the Church», *Tablet* 248 (1994) 444-445.

———, «New Scripture Document "Thinking in Centuries"», *NCR* 30/21 (1994) 13-14.

HEDLEY, J.C., «Pope Leo XIII and the Bible», *Tablet* 83 (1894) 529-531.

HELLIN, G., *Concilii Vaticani II Synopsis in ordinem redigens schemata cum relationibus necnon Patrum orationes atque animadversiones. Constitutio Dogmatica De Divina Revelatione — Dei Verbum*, Citta del Vaticano 1962.

HEUSER, H.J., «The Encyclical *Providentissimus Deus*», *AEcR* 10 (1894) 107-117.

HILL, R.C., «St. John Chrysostom and the Incarnation of the Word in Scripture», *Compass* 14 (1980) 34-38.

HOLMAN, J.L., «A Dutch Catholic Perspective», in *The Interpretation of the Bible in the Church*, ed. J.L. Houlden, London 1995, 129-134.

HOULDEN, J.L., «An Anglican Reaction», in *The Interpretation of the Bible in the Church*, ed. J.L. Houlden, London 1995, 107-111.

HOWLETT, J.A., «The Higher Criticism and Archaeology», *DublR* 115 (1894) 70-95.

HULLEY, K.K., «Principles of Textual Criticism Known to St. Jerome», *Harvard Studies in Classical Philology* LV (1944) 87-109.

JAY, P., «Saint Jérôme et le triple sens de l'Écriture», *REAug* 26 (1980) 214-227.

JELLICOE, S., *The Septuagint and Modern Study*, Oxford 1968.

JOHNSON, E.E., «Dual Authorship and the Single Intended Meaning of Scripture», *BSTR* 143 (1986) 218-227.

JOHNSON, H.J., «Leo XIII, Cardinal Newman and the Inerrancy of Scripture», *DR* 69 (1951) 411-427.

JOHNSON, H.W., «The "Analogy of Faith" and Exegetical Methodology. A Preliminary Discussion on Relationships», *JETS* 31 (1988) 69-80.

JOHNSON, L.T., «The Crisis in Biblical Scholarship», *Commonweal* 60 (1993) 18-21.

———, «Review of R.E. Brown's *Birth of the Messiah*», *HeyJ* 19 (1978) 439-441.

———, *The Real Jesus. The Misguided Quest for the Historical Jesus and the Truth of the Traditional Gospels*, San Francisco 1996.

KAISER, O. – KÜMMEL, W.G., *Exegetical Method. A Student's Handbook*, New York 1981.

KAMESAR, A., *Jerome, Greek Scholarship, and the Hebrew Bible. A Study of the Quaestiones Hebraicae in Genesim*, Oxford 1993.

KANNENGIESSER, C., «The Bible as Read in the Early Church. Patristic Exegesis and Its Presuppositions», *Conc.* (1991) 29-36.

KEARNS, G.A., «The Instruction on the Historical Truth of the Gospels. Some First Impressions», *Angelicum* 41 (1964) 218-234.

KELLY, G.A., *The Church's Problem with Bible Scholars*, Chicago 1985.

———, *The New Biblical Theorists. Raymond E. Brown and Beyond*, Ann Arbor 1983.

KELLY, J.N.D., *Jerome. His Life, Writings, and Controversies*, London 1975.

KENNEDY, G.T., «The Holy Office Monitum on the Teaching of Scripture», *AEcR* 145 (1961) 145-151.

———, «A Reply to Fr. Moran», *AEcR* 146 (1962) 181-191.

KENYON, F., *Our Bible and the Ancient Manuscripts*, London 1939.

———, *The Text of the Greek Bible*, London 1937.

KERTELGE, K., «*Die Interpretation der Bibel in der Kirche*. Zum gleichnamigen Dokument der Päpstlichen Bibelkömmission vom 23 April 1993», *TThZ* 104 (1995) 1-11.

KLEIN, R.W., *Textual Criticism of the Old Testament. The Septuagint After Qumran*, Philadelphia 1974.

KLEINHANS, A., «De progressu doctrine et praxi ecclesiasticae per litteras encyclicas *Divino Afflante Spiritu*», *Anton.* 24 (1949) 3-18.

KNIGHT, D.A., *Rediscovering the Traditions of Israel*, SBL.DS 9, Missaula 1973.

KNIGHT, D.A., «Tradition History», *ABD* VI, 633-638.

KOCH, D.A., «Source Criticism (NT)», *ABD* VI, 165-171.

KOMONCHAK, J.A., «The Struggle for the Council During the Preparation of Vatican II», in *History of Vatican II* I, ed. G. Alberigo – J.A. Komonchak, Maryknoll 1995, 167-356.

KONSTANT, D., «The Use of the Bible Within the Church», *ScrB* 21 (1991) 8-14.

KREMER, J., «Die Interpretation der Bibel in der Kirche. Marginalien zum neuesten Dokument der Päpstlichen Bibelkömmission», *StZ* 212/3 (1994) 151-166.

KRENTZ, E., «Biblical Interpretation for a New Millennium», *CurrTheolMiss* 20 (1993) 345-359.

KUGELMAN, R., «No Freedom From Truth», *Sign* 23 (1943) 219-220.

KÜMMEL, W.G., *Introduction to the New Testament*, Nashville 1975.

LA BONNARDIÈRE, A.-M., «L'Épître aux Hébreux dans l'oeuvre de saint Augustin», *REAug* 3 (1957) 137-162.

LAGHI, P. – GILBERT, M. – VANHOYE, A., *Chiesa e Sacra Scrittura. Un secolo di magistero ecclesiastico e studi biblici*, SubBib 17, Roma 1994.

LAGRANGE, M.J., «Bulletin. Methode historique dans l'étude de l'Ancien Testament», *RB* 12 (1903) 134-139.

———, «Les sources du Pentateuque», *RB* 7 (1898) 10-32.

———, *Personal Reflections and Memories*, New York 1985.

———, «À propos de l'encyclique *Providentissimus Deus*», *RB* 4 (1895) 48-64.

LAISTNER, M.L., «Antiochene Exegesis in Western Europe during the Middle Ages», *HThR* 40 (1947) 19-31.

LAKE, K. – OULTON, J.E.L., *Eusebius. The Ecclesiastical History*, LCL 265, Cambridge 1932, 1994.

LAMBIASI, F., «Dimensioni caratteristiche dell'interpretazione cattolica», in *L'Interpretazione della Bibbia nella Chiesa*, ed. G. Ghiberti – F. Mosetto, Torino 1998.

LAMPE, G.W.H., «The Exposition and Exegesis of Scripture to Gregory the Great», in *CHB* II, 155-183.

LAPOINTE, R., «Hermeneutics Today», *BTB* 2 (1972) 107-154.

———, *Les trois dimensions de l'herméneutique*, Paris 1967.

LATOURELLE, R., *Vatican II. Assessment and Perspectives. Twenty-Five Years After (1962-87)*, New York – Mahwah 1988.

LAURENTIN, R., «Exégèses réductrices des Évangeles de l'enfance», *Mar.* 41 (1979) 76-100.

――――, *The Truth of Christmas Beyond the Myths*, Petersham 1985.

LECLERCQ, J., «The Exposition and Exegesis of Scripture. From Gregory the Great to St. Bernard», in *CHB* II, 183-196.

LEFEBURE, M., *Conflicting Ways of Interpreting the Bible*, Concilium 138, New York 1980.

LEGRAND, L., «The Authority of Scripture in the Modern Period. Roman Catholic Developments», *IJT* 23 (1974) 78-84.

LÉON-DUFOUR, X., *Études d'Evangile*, Paris 1965.

――――, «L'exégèse, trente ans après», *Etudes* 340 (1974) 279-295.

――――, «L'exégète et l'événement historique», *RevSR* 58 (1970) 551-560.

――――, «Qu'attendre d'un exégète?», *Etudes* 327 (1967) 316-330.

LEVENSON, J.D., «The Bible. Unexamined Comments of Criticism», *First Things* 30 (1979) 24-33.

LEVIE, J., «La crise de l'Ancien Testament. Soixante années d'études bibliques», *NRTh* 56 (1929) 818-839.

LILLY, J.L., «Fiftieth Anniversary of *Providentissimus Deus*», *EcR* 109 (1943) 437-443.

LINDSAY, W.M., *Isidori. Etymologiarum*, Oxford 1911.

LINNEMANN, E., *Historical Criticism of the Bible. Methodology or Ideology*, Grand Rapids 1990.

LLAMOS, J., «La encíclica *Divino Afflante Spiritu*. Reflexiones y comentarios», *CDios* 156 (1944) 363-381.

LOEWE, R., «The Medieval History of the Latin Vulgate», in *CHB* III, 102-154.

――――, «The "Plain" Meaning of Scripture in Early Jewish Exegesis», *Papers of the Institute of Jewish Studies London* 1 (1946) 140-185.

LOHFINK, G., *The Bible Now I Get It. A Form-Critical Handbook*, New York 1979.

LOHFINK, N., «Zur historisch-kritischen Methode», in *Bibelauslegung im Wandel. Ein Exeget ortet seine Wissenschaft*, Frankfurt 1967, 50-75.

LORETZ, O., «The Church and Biblical Exegesis», *Conc.* 7 (1971) 67-79.

LOUW, J.P., «Semantics», *ABD* V, 1077-1081.

LOZA VERA, J., «*La Interpretación de la Biblia en la Iglesia*», *AnaMnesis* 4 (1994) 77-117.

DE LUBAC, H., *Exégèse médiévale. Les quatre sens de l'Écriture*, I, Paris 1959.

LYONNET, S., ed., *La Bibbia nella Chiesa dopo la "Dei Verbum". Studi sulla costituzione conciliare*, Roma 1969.

————, «A Word on Chapters IV and VI of *Dei Verbum*. The Amazing Journey Involved in the Process of Drafting the Conciliar Text», in *Vatican II: Assessment and Perspectives* I, ed. R. Latourelle, Mahwah – New York 1988, 157-207.

MAAS, A.J., «A Negative View of the Encyclical *Providentissimus Deus*», *ACQR* 20 (1895) 162-175.

McCARTER, P.K., *Textual Criticism. Recovery of the Text of the Hebrew Bible*, Philadelphia 1986.

McCOOL, F.J., «The Preacher and the Historical Witness of the Gospels», *TS* 21 (1960) 517-543.

McELENEY, N.J., «Review of R.E. Brown's *Birth of the Messiah*», *TS* 39 (1978) 771-772.

McHUGH, J., «A New Approach to the Infancy Narratives», *Mar.* 40 (1978) 277-287.

McKENZIE, J.L., «Biblical Studies Since 1950», *CrossCur* 31 (1981-1982) 400-406.

————, «Interpretation», in *Dictionary of the Bible*, Hong Kong 1965,

————, «Problems of Hermeneutics in Roman Catholic Exegesis», *JBL* 77 (1958) 197-204.

McKENZIE, S.L. – HAYNES, S.R., *To Each Its Own Meaning. An Introduction to Biblical Criticisms and their Application*, London 1993.

McKNIGHT, E.V., *What is Form Criticism?*, Guides to Biblical Scholarship Philadelphia 1973.

McNALLY, R.E., *The Bible in the Early Middle Ages*, Atlanta 1986.

MAGUIRE, E., «Encyclical of Pope Leo XIII on the Study of Sacred Scriptures», *IER* 3/15 (1894) 55-64.

MAHONY, R., «The Bible in the Life of the Catholic Church», *BiTod* 22 (1984) 93-99.

MAIER, G., *The End of the Historical-Critical Method*, St. Louis 1977.

DE MARGERIE, B., *An Introduction to the History of Exegesis*, Petersham 1990.

MARLE, R., «Fede e interpretazione», *CivCatt* 120/2 (1969) 228-238.

MARSHALL, I.H., «Review Article. *The Interpretation of the Bible in the Church*», *SBET* 13 (1995) 72-75.

MARTINI, C.M., «Preface to the *NJBC*», *NJBC*, xv-xvi.

MARUCCI, C., «*L'interpretazione della Bibbia nella Chiesa*. Presentazione del recente documento dalla Pontifica Commissione Biblica», *RdT* 35 (1994) 587-594.

MEGIVERN, J.J., *Official Catholic Teachings. Biblical Interpretation*, Wilmington 1978.

METZGER, B.M., «Explicit References in the Works of Origen to Variant Readings in the New Testament Manuscripts», in *Biblical and Patristic Studies in Memory of Robert Pierce Casey*, ed. J.N. Birdsall – R.W. Thomson, Frieburg 1963, 78-95.

METZGER, B.M., «Lucian and the Lucianic Recession of the Greek Bible», *NTS* 8 (1962) 194-196.

————, «St. Jerome's Explicit References to Variant Readings in Manuscripts of the New Testament», in *Text and Interpretation: Studies in the New Testament Presented to Michael Black*, Fs. M. Black, Cambridge 1979, 179-190.

————, *The Text of the New Testament. Its Transmission, Corruption and Restoration*, Oxford 1968.

————, «Textual Criticism among the Church Fathers», *StPatr* XII (1975) 340-349.

MEYER, B.F., «The Challenges of Text and Reader to the Historical Critical Method», *Conc.* (1991) 3-12.

MIEROW, C.C., *The Letters of St. Jerome (1-22)*, ACW 33, Westminster, MD 1963.

MIGUENS, M., «Review of R.E. Brown's *Birth of the Messiah*», *Communio* 7 (1980) 24-54.

MOLINA PALMA, M.A., «La interpretación de la Escritura en el Espíritu. Estudio histórico y teológico de un principio herméneutico de la constitución "Dei Verbum", 12», *Burgos* 1987.

MOLONEY, F.J., «Catholic Biblical Scholarship», *ACR* 70 (1993) 275-288.

————, «Whither Catholic Biblical Studies?», *ACR* 66 (1989) 83-93.

————, «The Infancy Narratives», *CleR* 64 (1979) 161-166.

MORAN, W.L., «Father Kennedy's Exegesis of the Holy Office Monitum», *AEcR* 146 (1962) 174-180.

MOULTON, J.H., *The Vocabulary of the Greek Testament Illustrated from the Papyri and Other Non-Literary Sources*, London 1957.

MUDDIMAN, J., «Light on Biblical Authority. Anglican-Roman Catholic Dialogue», in *The Interpretation of the Bible in the Church*, ed. J.L. Houlden, London 1995, 135-141.

MUNOZ, L.D., «Los sentidos de la Escrítura. Perspectivas del documento de la Pontifica Comisión Bíblica (1993) sobre "La Interpretación de la Biblia en la Iglesía"», *ScrTh* 27 (1995) 99-122.

MURILLO, L., «Las letras apostólicas de S.S. León XIII sobre los estudios bíblicos y la exégesis contempóranea», *RF* 5 (1903) 417-430.

MURPHY, R.E., «The Role of the Bible in Roman Catholic Theology», *Interp.* 25 (1971) 78-94.

MURPHY, R.E., «Reflections on "Actualization" of the Bible», BTB 26 (1996) 19-31.

MURPHY, R.T., «The Teaching of the Encyclical *Providentissimus Deus*», *CBQ* 5 (1943) 125-140.

MURPHY-O'CONNOR, J., «Again Under Attack», *BiTod* 22 (1984) 107-110.

————, *The École Biblique and the New Testament. A Century of Scholarship (1890-1990)*, NTOA 13, Fribourg 1990.

MYNORS, R.A.B., *Institutiones*, Oxford 1937.

NASH, H., «The Exegesis of the School of Antioch», *JBL* 11 (1961) 22-37.

NASSIF, B., «The "Spiritual Exegesis" of Scripture. The School of Antioch Revisited», *AThR* 75 (1993) 437-470.

NATIONS, A.L., «Historical Criticism and the Current Methodological Crisis», *SJT* 36 (1987) 59-71.

NAZZARO, V., «Hadrian», *EEC* I, 369.

NEIL, W., «The Critical and Theological Use of the Bible», in *CHB* III, 238-293.

NEUHAUS, R.J., ed., *Biblical Interpretation in Crisis. The Ratzinger Conference on Bible and Church*, Grand Rapids 1989.

NEWTON, W.L., «*Providentissimus Deus*», *RUO* 14 (1944) 123-126.

NICHOLS, A., *The Shape of Catholic Theology*, Edinburgh 1991.

NIELSEN, E., *Oral Tradition*, Studies in Biblical Theology 11, London 1954.

NORTH, R. «A Review of R.E. Brown's *Birth of the Messiah*», *Cross Cur* (1978) 464-467.

O'COLLINS, G., «At the Origins of *Dei Verbum*», *HeyJ* 26 (1985) 5-13.

————, «*Dei Verbum* and Biblical Scholarship», *ScrB* 21 (1990) 2-7.

————, «Revelation Past and Present», in *Vatican II: Assessment and Perspectives* I, ed. R. Latourelle, Mahwah – New York 1988, 125-137.

————, «A Review of R.E. Brown's *Birth of the Messiah*», *Gr.* 59 (1978) 756-757.

O'COLLINGS, G. – KENDALL, D., *The Bible for Theology*, New York – Mahwah 1997.

O'DOHERTY, E., «The Conjectures of Jean Astruc», *CBQ* 15 (1953) 300-304.

O'FEARGHAIL, F., «Philo and the Fathers. The Letter and the Spirit», in *Scriptural Interpretation in the Fathers* 1, ed. T. Finan – V. Twomey, Cambridge 1995, 39-60.

O'FLYNN, J.A., «*Divino Afflante Spiritu*; The New Encyclical on the Scriptures», *Irish Ecclesiastical Record* 63 (1944) 289-300.

O'GRADY, J., «Biblical Methodologies», *ChiSt* 29 (1990) 87-100.

O'MALLEY, T.P., *Tertullian and the Bible*, Latinitas Christianorum Primaeva 21, Nijmegen 1967.

O'NEILL, J.C. – BAIRD, W., «Biblical Criticism», *ABD* 1, 258-262.

ORCHARD, B., «*Dei Verbum* and the Synoptic Gospels», *DR* 108 (1990) 199-213.

P.I.B., «Pontificium Institutum Biblicum et recens libellus R.mi.D.ni A. Romeo», *VD* 39 (1961) 3-17.

PARE, U.E., «The Church and the Bible. Leo XIII. *Providentissimus Deus*. Pius XII *Divino Afflante Spiritu*», *CCR* (1995) 7-15.

PATTERSON, P. – JAMES, R., «The Historical-Critical Study of the Bible. Dangerous or Helpful?», *Theological Educator* 37 (1988) 45-74.

PERRIN, N., *What is Redaction Criticism?*, Guides to Biblical Scholarship: New Testament Series, Philadelphia 1970.

PERROT, C., «Les pratiques de l'histoire critique dans l'exégèse du Nouveau Testament», *RICP* 24 (1987) 25-48.

PETERS, T., «The Use of Analogy in Historical Method», *CBQ* 35 (1973) 475-482.

PIROT, L., *L'oeuvre exégètique de Theodore de Mopsueste*, Rome 1913.

DE LA POTTERIE, I., «Interpretation of the Holy Scripture in the Spirit in Which It Was Written (*Dei Verbum* 12c)», in *Vatican II: Assessment and Perspectives* I, ed. R. Latourelle, Mahwah – New York 1988, 220-266.

————, «L'esegesi Biblica, scienza della fede», in *L'essegesi cristiana oggi*, ed. I. de la Potterie, Casale Monferrato 1991, 127-165.

————, «L'Istituto Biblico negli ottant'anni della sua storia», *CivCatt* 140 (1989) 166-172.

————, «La vérité de l'Écriture et l'herméneutique biblique», *RThL* 18 (1987) 171-186.

DE LA POTTERIE, I., «Preface», in *An Introduction to the History of Exegesis*, ed. B. de Margerie, Petersham 1993, vii-xii.

————, «Reading Holy Scripture "In the Spirit". Is the Patristic Way of Reading the Bible Still Possible Today?», *Communio* 13 (1986) 308-325.

PRETE, B., «L'enciclica *Providentissimus Deus* nel settantennio della sua promulgazione», *SacDot* 8 (1963) 337-354.

PREUS, J.E., *St. Jerome's Translation Terminology*, Minnesota 1951.

PRICKETT, S., ed., *Reading the Text. Biblical Criticism and Literary Theory*, Oxford 1991.

QUASTEN, J., *Patrology*, I–IV, Allen, TX 1950.

RALPH, M.N., «The Bible and the Adult Roman Catholic. A Missing Piece in Adult Parish Catechesis», *LiLi* 1993 (1993) 43-50.

RAST, W.E., *Tradition History and the Old Testament*, Guides to Biblical Scholarship, Philadelphia 1972.

RATZINGER, J. – GRILLMEIER, A. – RIGAUX, B., «Dogmatic Constitution on Divine Revelation», in *Commentary on the Documents of Vatican II* III, ed. H. Vorgrimler, New York 1969, 155-272.

————, «Biblical Interpretation in Crisis. On the Question of the Foundations and Approaches of Exegesis Today», in *Biblical Interpretation in Crisis: The Ratzinger Conference on Bible and Church* 3, ed. R.J. Neuhaus, Grand Rapids 1989, 1-24.

RAURELL, F., «Lettera plurale del testo. Metodi biblici», *Laur.* 29 (1988) 251-286.

REDFORD, J., «The Quest of the Historical Epipha» *CleR* 64 (1979) 5-11.

RENDTORFF, R., *Das Alte Testament. Einführung*, London 1985.

REUMANN, J., «After Historical Criticism, What? Trends in Biblical Interpretation and Ecumenical Interfaith Dialogues», *JES* 29 (1992) 55-86.

RICHARDSON, E.C., *Liber de viris illustribus*, Leipzig 1896.

RICHES, J. K., *A Century of New Testament Study*, Valley Forge 1993.

RIDDLE, M.B., «Introductory Essay to "The Harmony to the Gospels"», in *Nicean and Post-Nicean Fathers: First Series* VI, Grand Rapids 67-70.

RIGAUX, B., «Dogmatic Constitution on Divine Revelation. Chapter V — The New Testament», in *Commentary on the Documents of Vatican II*, III, ed. H. Vorgrimler, New York 1969, 252-261.

RIGGS, J.R., «The "Fuller Meaning" of Scripture. A Hermeneutical Question for Evangelicals», *Grace Theological Journal* 7 (1986) 213-227.

ROBERTS, B.J., *The Old Testament Text and Versions. The Hebrew Text in Transmission and the History of the Ancient Versions*, Cardiff 1951.

ROBERTS, C.H., «Books Until the Greco-Roman World and in the New Testament», in *CHB* I, 48-66.

ROBERTSON, D.W., *On Christian Doctrine*, New York 1958.

ROBINSON, R.B., *Roman Catholic Exegesis Since Divino Afflante Spiritu. Hermeneutical Implications*, SBL.DS 111, Atlanta 1982.

RODD, C.S., «A Review of R.E. Brown's *Birth of the Messiah*», ET 90 (1979) 65.

ROGERSON, J. – ROWLAND, C. – LINDARS, B., *The Study and Use of the Bible*, The History of Christian Theology 2, Grand Rapids 1988.

ROGERSON, J.W. – JEANROND, W.G., «Interpretation, History of», *ABD* III, 424-443.

ROMANIUK, K., «Post-Vatican Biblical Criticism and the Living Tradition and the Magisterium of the Church», *CoTh* 57 (1987) 5-15.

ROMEO, A., «L'enciclica *Divino Afflante Spiritu* e le opiniones novae», *Div* 4 (1960) 387-346.

RUFFINI, C.E., «The Bible and its Genuine Historical and Objective Truth», *AEcR* 146 (1962) 361-368.

————, «Literary Genres and Working Hypotheses in Recent Biblical Studies», *AEcR* 145 (1961) 362-365.

RUPPERT, L. – KLAUCK, H.-J., «*Die Interpretation der Bibel in der Kirche. Das Dokument der Päpstlichen Bibelkommission*», SBS 161, Stuttgart 1995.

RYNNE, X., *Letters from Vatican City*, New York 1963.

————, *Vatican II*, New York 1968.

SADOWSKI, F., *The Church Fathers on the Bible*, New York 1987.

SANCHEZ, M.G., «Inspiración e interpretación de la Escritura a la luz de la *Dei Verbum* del Concilio Vaticano II», *Escrit Vedat* 21 (1991), 7-49.

SANDERS, J.A., «Scripture as Canon for Post-modern Times», *BTB* 25.2 (1995) 56-63.

SCALISE, C.J., «The *Sensus Literalis*. A Hermeneutical Key to Biblical Exegesis», *SJT* 42 (1989) 45-65.

SCHMIDT, S., *Augustine Bea. The Cardinal of Unity*, New Rochelle, NY 1992.

SCHNEIDERS, S.M., «Church and Biblical Scholarship in Dialogue», *ThTo* 42 (1985) 353-358.

——, «Faith, Hermeneutics, and the Literal Sense of Scripture», *TS* 39 (1978) 719-736.

——, «From Exegesis to Hermeneutics. The Problem of the Contemporary Meaning of Scripture», *Horizons* 89 (1981) 23-29.

——, «God's Word for God's People», *BiTod* 22 (1984) 100-106.

SCHOLDER, K., *The Birth of Modern Critical Theology*, London 1990.

SCHUMACHER, M., «Tolle, Lege», *CBQ* 6 (1944) 53-60.

SCHÜSSLER-FIORENZA, E., «The Ethics of Biblical Interpretation. Decentering Biblical Scholarship», *JBL* 107 (1988) 3-17.

SCULLION, J.P., «Experience Encounters the Sacred Text. *The Interpretation of the Bible in the Church*», *NTRev* 8 (1995) 18-29.

SEMPLE, W.H., «St. Jerome as Biblical Translator», *BJRL* 48 (1965-6) 227-243.

SEVIN, M., «L'approche des textes bibliques», *LumVit* 50 (1995) 253-260.

SHANKS, H., «The Catholic Church and Bible Interpretation», *BiRe* 10 (1994) 32-35.

SHEA, J., «Using Scripture in Pastoral Settings», *ChiSt* 23 (1984) 131-139.

SHEEHAN, T., *Revolution in the Church*, New York Review of Books, New York June 14, 1984.

SIEGMAN, E.F., «The Decrees of the Pontifical Biblical Commission. A Recent Clarification», *CBQ* 18 (1956) 23-29.

——, «Influence of the encyclical *Providentissimus Deus* on subsequent Scripture study; reply», *CBQ* 5 (1943) 474-475.

SIMONETTI, M., *Biblical Interpretation in the Early Church. An Historical Introduction to Patristic Exegesis*, Edinburgh 1994.

——, *Lettera e/o Allegoria. Un contributo alla storia dell'esegesi patristica*, Studia Ephemerides 23, Roma 1985.

SKA, J., «Le Pentateuque: état de la recherche à partir de quelques récentes Introductiones», *Bib.* 77 (1996) 245-265.

SLOYAN, G.S., «Conceived by the Holy Ghost, Born of the Virgin Mary», *Interp.* 33 (1979) 81-84.

SMALLEY, B., «The Exposition and Exegesis of Scripture. The Bible in the Medieval Schools», in *CHB* II, 197-219.

——, *The Study of the Bible in the Middle Ages*, Oxford 1952.

SOGGIN, J.A., *Introduction to the Old Testament*, Philadelphia 1980.

SOULEN, R.N., *Handbook of Biblical Criticism*, Atlanta 1981.

SPADAFORA, F., *Leone XIII e gli studi biblici*, Rovigo 1976.

STAHEL, T.H. – FITZMYER, J. A., «Scripture, the Soul of Theology. An Interview with Joseph A. Fitzmyer», *America* 172 (1995) 8-12.

STANLEY, D., «Towards a Biblical Theology of the New Testament. Modern Trends in Catholic Scriptural Scholarship», in *The McCauley Lectures 1958* West Hartford 1959, 267-281.

STEIN, R.H., «Redaction Criticism. NT», *ABD* V, 647-650.

STEINMETZ, C., *The Bible in the Sixteenth Century*, Durham 1990.

STENDAHL, K., «Biblical Theology, Contemporary», *IDB*, 418-432.

STEVENSON, K., «A Liturgist's Response», in *The Interpretation of the Bible in the Church*, ed. J.L. Houlden, London 1995, 156-163.

STICKLER, A., «Pontifical Universitas Romana», *Semarium* 14 (1962) 651-670.

STRECKER, G., *History of New Testament Literature*, Harrisburg 1992.

STUHLMACHER, P., *Historical Criticism and Theological Interpretation of Scripture. Toward a Hermeneutics of Consent*, Philadelphia 1977.

SUELZER, A., «Modern Old Testament Criticism», *NJBC*, 1113-1129.

SUTCLIFFE, E.F., «*Divino Afflante Spiritu* and a quotation», *CleR* 24 (1944) 541-544.

————, «Golden jubilee of *Providentissimus Deus*», *CleR* 23 (1943) 356-366.

————, «Pope Pius XII on the Study of the Bible», *CleR* 24 (1944) 305-313.

SWAIN, L., «The Interpretation of the Bible», in *A New Catholic Commentary on Holy Scripture*, ed. R.C. Fuller, Camden 1969, 46a-52b.

SWETE, H.B., *Theodori episcopi Mossuesteni in Epistolas B. Pauli Commentarii*, Cambridge 1880,1882.

————, *An Introduction to the Old Testament in Greek*, Cambridge 1902.

TÁBET, M.A., «L'interpretation della Bibbia nella Chiesa in documento della PCB», *Annales Theologici* 8 (1994) 23-68.

TATE, W.R., *Biblical Interpretation. An Integrated Approach*, Peabody 1991.

TAYLOR, V., *The Text of the New Testament. A Short Introduction*, London 1961.

THEOBALD, C., «L'exégèse catholique au moment de la crise moderniste», *Le monde contemporain et la Bible*, BBT 8, ed. C. Savart – J.-N. Aletti, Paris 1985, 387-439.

TORJESEN, K.J., *Hermeneutical Proceedure and Theological Method in Origen's Exegesis*, New York 1986.

TOV, E., *The Text-Critical Use of the Septuagint in Biblical Research*, Jerusalem 1981.

——, *Textual Criticism of the Hebrew Bible*, Minneapolis 1992.

——, «Textual Criticism. Old Testament», *ABD* VI, 393-412.

TUCKER, G.M., *Form Criticism of the Old Testament*, Guides to Biblical Scholarship, Philadelphia 1971.

TUCKETT, C.M., «Synoptic Problem», *ABD* VI, 263-270.

VACCARI, A., «La theoria antiochena nella scuola esegetica di Antiochia», *Bib.* 1 (1920) 3-36.

——, «Pio X e gli studi biblici», in *Pio Decimo novello beato* Rovigo 1951, 563-570.

VAGANAY, L., *Initiation à la critique textuelle du Nouveau Testament*, Paris 1986.

VALLAURI, E., «Il metodo storico-critico alla sbarra», *Laur.* 30 (1989) 174-223.

VAN BEEK, G.W., «Archeology», *IDB* I, 195-207.

VANHOYE, A., «Esegesi e teologia. A cinquant'anni dalla *Divino Afflante Spiritu*», *SacDoc* 39 (1994) 7-30.

——, «Esegesi biblico et theologia. La question de methode», *Seminarium* 31 (1991) 267-278.

——, «Il nuovo documento della Commissione Biblica», *OR*, November 27 1993.

——, «L'interpretazione della Bibbia nella chiesa. Riflessione circa un documento della Commissione Biblica», *CivCatt* 145 (1994) 3-15.

——, «Passé et présent de la Commission Biblique», *Gr.* 74 (1993) 261-275.

VANNI, U., «Exegesis and Actualization in the Light of *Dei Verbum*», in *Vatican II: Assessment and Perspectives* I, ed. R. Latourelle, Mahwah – New York 1988, 344-363.

VANUTELLI, P., «Dopo l'enciclica *Divino Afflante Spiritu*. Meditare», *OR* 83 (1943) 2.

VAWTER, B., «The Fuller Sense. Some Considerations», *CBQ* 26 (1964) 1964.

VAWTER, B., «History and the Word», *CBQ* 29 (1967) 512-523.

«Venticinque anni dopo l'enciclica *Providentissimus*», *CivCatt* 4, 361-74; 5, 356-66 (1918)

VESCO, J.L., *L'Interpretation de la Bible dans l'Église. Allocution du Sa Saintée le Pape Jean-Paul II et document de la Commission Biblique Pontificale*, Paris 1994.

VIDAL, M., «The Relationship between Scripture and Church», *ScrB* (1992) 33-38.

VIGNOLO, R., «Questione di ermeneutica», in *L'Interpretazione della Bibbia nella Chiesa*, ed. G. Ghiberti – F. Mosetto, Torino 1998, 261-198.

VOGELS, W., «Biblical Exegesis and the Homily. Two Decades in Retrospect and Prospect», *ScEs* 34 (1982) 289-314.

WANSBROUGH, H., «A Review of R.E. Brown's *Birth of the Messiah*», *Tablet* 232 (1978) 304.

WATSON, G., «Origen and the Literal Interpretation of Scripture», in *Scriptural Interpretation in the Fathers*, ed. T. Finan – V. Twomey, Cambridge 1995, 75-84.

WCELA, E.A., «Vatican II. On Revelation», *BiTod* 21 (1983) 12-19.

WEINGREEN, J., *Introduction to the Critical Study of the Text of the Hebrew Bible*, London 1982.

WENHAM, G.J., «The Place of Biblical Criticism in Theological Study», *Themelios* 14 (1989) 84-89.

WICKS, J., «Biblical Criticism Criticized», *Gr.* 72 (1991) 117-128.

WILES, M.F., «Theodore of Mopsuestia as Representative of the Antiochene School», in *CHB* I, 489-510.

WILKINSON, J., «L'Apport de saint Jérôme a la topographie», *RB* 81 (1974) 245-257.

WILLIAMSON, P., «Actualization. A New Emphasis in Catholic Scripture Study», *America* 172 (1995) 17-19.

WINK, W., *The Bible in Human Transformation. Toward a New Paradigm for Bible Study*, Philadelphia 1973.

WINTHERUP, R.D., «A New Magna Carta for Catholic Biblical Scholarship?», *BiTod* 32 (1994) 336-341.

WITTSTADT, K., «On the Eve of the Second Vatican Council (July 1 – October 10, 1962)», in *History of Vatican II* I, ed. G.-K. Alberigo – J.A. Komonchak, Maryknoll 1995, 405-500.

WONG, D.W.F., «The Loss of the Christian Mind in Biblical Scholarship», *EvQ* 64 (1992) 23-36.

WONNEBERGER, R., *Understanding the BHS. A Manual for the Users of Biblia Hebraica Stuttgartensia*, Rome 1984.

YODER, P., *From Word to Life. A Guide to the Art of Bible Study*, Kitchener, Ontario 1982.

ZAHAROPOULOS, D.Z., *Theodore of Mopsuestia on the Bible*, Theological Inquiries, New York 1989.

ZERWICK, M., «De S. Scrittura in Constitutione dogmatica *Dei Verbum*», *VD* 44 (1966) 17-42.

ZIESLER, J., «Historical Criticism and a Rational Faith», *ET* 105 (1994) 270-274.

INDEX OF NAMES

INDEX OF SUBJECTS AND TERMS

GENERAL INDEX

TESI GREGORIANA

Since 1995, the series «Tesi Gregoriana» has made available to the general public some of the best doctoral theses done at the Pontifical Gregorian University. The typesetting is done by the authors themselves following norms established and controlled by the University.

Published Volumes [Series: Theology]

1. NELLO FIGA, Antonio, *Teorema de la opción fundamental. Bases para su adecuada utilización en teología moral*, 1995, pp. 380.

2. BENTOGLIO, Gabriele, *Apertura e disponibilità. L'accoglienza nell'epistolario paolino*, 1995, pp. 376.

3. PISO, Alfeu, *Igreja e sacramentos. Renovação da Teologia Sacramentária na América Latina*, 1995, pp. 260.

4. PALAKEEL, Joseph, *The Use of Analogy in Theological Discourse. An Investigation in Ecumenical Perspective*, 1995, pp. 392.

5. KIZHAKKEPARAMPIL, Isaac, *The Invocation of the Holy Spirit as Constitutive of the Sacraments according to Cardinal Yves Congar*, 1995, pp. 200.

6. MROSO, Agapit J., *The Church in Africa and the New Evangelisation. A Theologico-Pastoral Study of the Orientations of John Paul II*, 1995, pp. 456.

7. NANGELIMALIL, Jacob, *The Relationship between the Eucharistic Liturgy, the Interior Life and the Social Witness of the Church according to Joseph Cardinal Parecattil*, 1996, pp. 224.

8. GIBBS, Philip, *The Word in the Third World. Divine Revelation in the Theology of Jen-Marc Éla, Aloysius Pieris and Gustavo Gutiérrez*, 1996, pp. 448.

9. DELL'ORO, Roberto, *Esperienza morale e persona. Per una reinterpretazione dell'etica fenomenologica di Dietrich von Hildebrand*, 1996, pp. 240.

10. BELLANDI, Andrea, *Fede cristiana come «stare e comprendere». La giustificazione dei fondamenti della fede in Joseph Ratzinger*, 1996, pp. 416.

11. BEDRIÑAN, Claudio, *La dimensión socio-política del mensaje teológico del Apocalipsis*, 1996, pp. 364.

12. GWYNNE, Paul, *Special Divine Action. Key Issues in the Contemporary Debate (1965-1995)*, 1996, pp. 376.

13. NIÑO, Francisco, *La Iglesia en la ciudad. El fenómeno de las grandes ciudades en América Latina, como problema teológico y como desafío pastoral*, 1996, pp. 492.

14. BRODEUR, Scott, *The Holy Spirit's Agency in the Resurrection of the Dead. An Exegetico-Theological Study of 1 Corinthians 15,44b-49 and Romans 8,9-13*, 1996, pp. 300.

15. ZAMBON, Gaudenzio, *Laicato e tipologie ecclesiali. Ricerca storica sulla «Teologia del laicato» in Italia alla luce del Concilio Vaticano II (1950-1980)*, 1996, pp. 548.

16. ALVES DE MELO, Antonio, *A Evangelização no Brasil. Dimensões teológicas e desafios pastorais. O debate teológico e eclesial (1952-1995)*, 1996, pp. 428.

17. APARICIO VALLS, María del Carmen, *La plenitud del ser humano en Cristo. La Revelación en la «Gaudium et Spes»*, 1997, pp. 308.

18. MARTIN, Seán Charles, *«Pauli Testamentum». 2 Timothy and the Last Words of Moses*, 1997, pp. 312.

19. RUSH, Ormond, *The Reception of Doctrine. An Appropriation of Hans Robert Jauss' Reception Aesthetics and Literary Hermeneutics*, 1997, pp. 424.

20. MIMEAULT, Jules, *La sotériologie de François-Xavier Durrwell. Exposé et réflexions critiques*, 1997, pp. 476.

21. CAPIZZI, Nunzio, *L'uso di Fil 2,6-11 nella cristologia contemporanea (1965-1993)*, 1997, pp. 528.

22. NANDKISORE, Robert, *Hoffnung auf Erlösung. Die Eschatologie im Werk Hans Urs von Balthasars*, 1997, pp. 304.

23. PERKOVIĆ, Marinko, *«Il cammino a Dio» e «La direzione alla vita»: L'ordine morale nelle opere di Jordan Kuničić, O.P. (1908-1974)*, 1997, pp. 336.

24. DOMERGUE, Benoît, *La réincarnation et la divinisation de l'homme dans les religions. Approche phénoménologique et théologique*, 1997, pp. 300.

25. FARKAŠ, Pavol, *La «donna» di Apocalisse 12. Storia, bilancio, nuove prospettive*, 1997, pp. 276.

26. OLIVER, Robert W., *The Vocation of the Laity to Evangelization. An Ecclesiological Inquiry into the Synod on the Laity (1987)*, Christifideles laici *(1989) and Documents of the NCCB (1987-1996)*, 1997, pp. 364.

27. SPATAFORA, Andrea, *From the «Temple of God» to God as the Temple. A Biblical Theological Study of the Temple in the Book of Revelation*, 1997, pp. 340.

28. IACOBONE, Pasquale, *Mysterium Trinitatis. Dogma e Iconografia nell'Italia medievale*, 1997, pp. 512.

29. CASTAÑO FONSECA, Adolfo M., *Δικαιοσύνη en Mateo. Una interpretación teológica a partir de 3,15 y 21,32*, 1997, pp. 344.

30. CABRIA ORTEGA, José Luis, *Relación teología-filosofía en el pensamiento de Xavier Zubiri*, 1997, pp. 580.

31. SCHERRER, Thierry, *La gloire de Dieu dans l'oeuvre de saint Irénée*, 1997, pp. 328.

32. PASCUZZI, Maria, *Ethics, Ecclesiology and Church Discipline. A Rhetorical Analysis of 1Cor 5,1-13*, 1997, pp. 240.

33. LOPES GONÇALVES, Paulo Sérgio, *Liberationis mysterium. O projeto sistemático da teologia da libertação. Um estudo teológico na perspectiva da regula fidei*, 1997, pp. 464.

34. KOLACINSKI, Mariusz, *Dio fonte del diritto naturale*, 1997, pp. 296.

35. LIMA CORRÊA, Maria de Lourdes, *Salvação entre juízo, conversão e graça. A perspectiva escatológica de Os 14,2-9*, 1998, pp. 360.

36. MEIATTINI, Giulio, *«Sentire cum Christo». La teologia dell'esperienza cristiana nell'opera di H.U. von Balthasar*, 1998, pp. 432.

37. KESSLER, Thomas W., *Peter as the First Witness of the Risen Lord. An Historical and Theological Investigation*, 1998, pp. 240.

38. BIORD CASTILLO Raúl, *La Resurrección de Cristo como Revelación. Análisis del tema en la teología fundamental a partir de la* Dei Verbum, 1998, pp. 308.

39. LÓPEZ, Javier, *La figura de la bestia entre historia y profecía. Investigación teológico-bíblica de Apocalipsis 13,1-8,* 1998, pp. 308.

40. SCARAFONI, Paolo, *Amore salvifico. Una lettura del mistero della salvezza. Uno studio comparativo di alcune soteriologie cattoliche postconciliari,* 1998, pp. 240.

41. BARRIOS PRIETO, Manuel Enrique, *Antropologia teologica. Temi principali di antropologia teologica usando un metodo di «correlazione» a partire dalle opere di John Macquarrie,* 1998, pp. 416.

42. LEWIS, Scott M., *«So That God May Be All in All». The Apocalyptic Message of 1 Corinthians 15,12-34,* 1998, pp. 252.

43. ROSSETTI, Carlo Lorenzo, *«Sei diventato Tempio di Dio». Il mistero del Tempio e dell'abitazione divina negli scritti di Origene,* 1998, pp. 232.

44. CERVERA BARRANCO, Pablo, *La incorporación en la Iglesia mediante el bautismo y la profesión de la fe según el Concilio Vaticano II,* 1998, pp. 372.

45. NETO, Laudelino, *Fé cristã e cultura latino-americana. Uma análise a partir das Conferências de Puebla e Santo Domingo,* 1998, pp. 340.

46. BRITO GUIMARÃES, Pedro, *Os sacramentos como atos eclesiais e proféticos. Um contributo ao conceito dogmático de sacramento à luz da exegese contemporânea,* 1998, pp. 448.

47. CALABRETTA, Rose B., *Baptism and Confirmation. The Vocation and Mission of the Laity in the Writings of Virgil Michel, O.S.B.,* 1998, pp. 320.

48. OTERO LÁZARO, Tomás, *Col 1,15-20 en el contexto de la carta,* 1999, pp.312.

49. KOWALCZYK, Dariusz, *La personalità in Dio. Dal metodo trascendentale di Karl Rahner verso un orientamento dialogico in Heinrich Ott,* 1999, pp. 484.

50. PRIOR, Joseph G., *The Historical-Critical Method in Catholic Exegesis,* 1999, pp. 350.